Collecting Foreign-Made

TOY
SOLDIERS

Identification and value guide

Richard O'Brien

Published by

krause publications

700 E. State Street • Iola, WI 54990-0001
Telephone: 715/445-2214

Please call or write for our free catalog. Our toll-free number to
place an order or obtain a free catalog is 800-258-0929 or please use our regular business telephone
715-445-2214 for editorial comment and further information.

ISBN: 0-89689-122-4
Printed in the United States of America

This book is dedicated to the publications *Old Toy Soldier, Toy Soldier Review, Plastic Figure & Playset Collector, The Worlds of Plastic Figures, Plastic Warrior* and *Toy Soldier & Model Figure,* for all they have done for the hobby.

Contents

Introduction and Acknowledgments

Anyone who looks over this edition will soon begin to wonder why I, not K. Warren Mitchell, am the nominal author. All those bylines, all those photo credits...The truth is, he's even more responsible for this book than it appears.

After I had completed *Collecting American-Made Toy Soldiers,* Edition No. 3, which is devoted almost wholly to U.S. makes, Mitch asked me, "But what about foreign-made soldiers?" I answered that I supposed I'd go back to including them in the succeeding edition (as I had in the first two), assuming the third edition of *Soldiers* sold enough to justify a new one. But, of course, it would take at least a couple of years before we'd know that. He sounded less than happy with my reply.

Once off the phone, I found myself continuing to think about Mitch and his obvious unease with the situation. He's not only is a major dealer in toy soldiers, he seems to love them. For many years, he has constantly contributed much information to collectors, just for the sake of getting out the news. Since I'm a collector, too, his misery, in a sense, was my misery. Then it occurred to me. Why not ask Books Americana publisher Dan Alexander if he'd like to do an all-foreign volume, as well? Not likely, but...so I called. Somewhat to my amazement, Dan said yes. Immediately, I called Mitch. Just as quickly, he said he'd get right to work. Not only with his own contributions, but also by enlisting contributors. Jumping aboard at Mitch's behest and fulsome thanks to all, were toy-soldier experts Joseph F. Saine, Will Beierwaltes, Lenoir Josey, Lou Sandbote, Vadis Godbey, William Doyle Galleries, Steve Balkin, Guernsey's, Tom Fiegal and Gus and Renee Hansen.

Also enthusiastically pitching in (I did a little recruiting myself) were Jack Matthews, Jim Theobald, Bob Hornung, Arnold Rolak, Tim Oei, Ray Haradin, Robert D. Worthen, Bill O'Brien, Norman Joplin and Jim Hillestad. Plastics expert Paul Stadinger of Stad's not only made his own contributions, he put me in touch with those amiable Plastic Warriors, Brian Carrick and Paul Morehead, who generously provided much information, as well as photos. Gramercy to all you folks, too.

And, oh yes. Thanks, Mitch.

RICHARD O'BRIEN
January 1997

Photo courtesy Joseph F. Saine.

6

Condition Guide

The price of a toy soldier depends not only on its desirability, but on its condition.

Mint: It means just that; the condition in which it was originally issued--perfect, regardless of age, not the slightest blemish. Needless to say, this is a fairly rare state of affairs, but enough soldiers exist in mint condition to make it an employable term. Many people, hoping to dispose of toys, are tempted to call them Mint when they are really Near Mint, Very Good or sometimes even just Good. Inevitably, this can result in unhappiness all around and, not infrequently, in a canceled sale.

Excellent: Close to Mint, with only a minute amount of paint missing and very fresh-looking.

Very Good: Indicates a soldier that has obviously seen use; with signs of wear and aging, but with most of its paint remaining and, in general, having a freshness to its appearance that makes it seem attractive and collectible to all but the most discriminating.

Good: Signals a soldier that has seen considerable wear, but has at least one-half to one-third of its original paint and is basically sound. A collector will collect it, but will often not be wholly satisfied with it as an example of his collection and thus prices are well below that which the same item in mint can command.

Condition below Good results in another drastic drop in price, and figures with missing parts, although otherwise in excellent condition, will usually fall into this lower-priced category. Near-Mint, Fine, Very Fine and similar terms often found in sellers' descriptions, denote conditions between Mint and Very Good and are priced accordingly.

Plastic soldiers rarely have their condition described on dealers' lists. It's hard to damage plastic and thus it's almost always acceptable-looking. Scuffed or broken plastic toy soldiers are almost worthless. The small minority that are painted will usually be described by the percentage of paint still on the figure and priced accordingly.

The key to grading is to avoid wishful thinking. Grading can sometimes be a problem for the uninitiated, but common sense will usually prevail; when possible, a consultation with an expert in the field can often clear up lingering doubts. A toy in its original box is worth up to 10% to 20% more if the box is in mint condition, with the price dropping as condition lessens. *Prices given here are in U.S. dollars.*

Finally, it should be pointed out that this book is merely a *guide* to prices and not the absolute last word on

An unusual and striking hollowcast metal 54mm range Indian with rifle concealing himself behind a horse, as seen from both sides. The maker is unknown but thought to be English, and circa 1950. The tail is repaired and may be incorrect. No price found. Steven White Collection. Photo by Orville C. Britton.

the price of a soldier. Prices may inflate or deflate in the months it takes to publish a book. Even on the same day, a soldier can vary in price, depending on the dealer, the buyer, the geographical area in which it's being sold and whether it's being offered in the first, expectant rush of a show or in its last, draggy minutes, when the dealer finds himself confronted with having to pack up all that stuff again. Employed by itself, *Collecting Foreign-Made Toy Soldiers* should at least prevent serious mistakes being made. Used with the assistance of a few current prices found in ads, lists or on dealer tables, it can get the prospective buyer or seller much nearer to the current (always fuzzily defined) market price.

Because of space problems this book, with just a few exceptions for spice, confines itself to soldiers that were made and painted by the factory and normally sold in U.S. toy stores, hobby shops, variety stores and department stores.

England

England
Plastic
54mm (approx. 2-1/4")
HO (approx. 1")

⚔ **Airfix** ⚔

Airfix produced some of the world's most beautifully designed toy soldiers; they were vigorous, attractive, highly realistic and superbly detailed. Perhaps the greatest of its figures are the Space Warriors and Medieval Foot Soldiers. Located in London, Airfix seems to have begun plastic production about 1962, in both sizes. The firm is still in business and has begun reissuing some of its sets, after a discontinuation of the line for some years.

According to *Plastic Warrior*'s separate publication, *The Plastic Warrior Guide to U.K. Makers of Plastic Toy Figures*, John Niblett, who died in 1980, designed the firm's early 54mm figures. Ron Cameron, who sculpted many ranges for Britains, "including the bulk of their Deetail range," is said to have designed the later part of the Airfix output. But according to the publication, some of the figures have also been attributed to Charles Stadden, or "more probably members of his design studio team."

L to R: AC1, AC2, AC3, AC4, AC5. Airfix cowboys. Value $2.00 each if in cream color. Courtesy Paul Stadinger - Stad's.

Top, L to R: ABA1, ABA2, ABA3, ABA4, ABA5, ABA6, ABA7. Airfix WWII British 8th Army. Officer $2.00, others $1.00 each. Bottom, L to R: AMF1, AMF2, AMF3, AMF4, AMF5, AMF6. Airfix Medieval Foot Soldiers, value $2.50 each. Not shown is the climber for the ladder.

Top, L to R: AGI1, AGI2, AGI3, AGI4, AGI5, AGI6, AGI7, AGI8. Airfix German Infantry. Value officer $2.00, others $1.00. Bottom, L to R: ASW1, ASW2, ASW3, ASW4, ASW5, ASW6, ASW7. Airfix Space Warriors. Value $1.50 each.

Top, L to R: ANA1, ANA2, ANA3, ANA4, ANA5, ANA6, ANA7. Airfix NATO Infantry, value $1.00 each. Bottom, L to R: AMB1, AMB2, AMB3, AMB4, AMB5, AMB6. Airfix Modern British, value $1.00 each.

Top, L to R: AGH1, AGH2, AGH3, AGH4, AGH5, AGH6, AGH7. Bottom, L to R: AGH8, AGH9, AGH10, AGH11, AGH12, AGH13. Airfix Ghurkas. Officer $4.00, others $2.00 each.

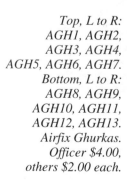

L to R: AUSP1, AUSP2, AUSP3, AUSP4. Airfix U.S. Paratroopers, value $1.50 each. Courtesy Paul Stadinger - Stad's.

L to R: AUSP5, AUSP6, AUSP7, AUSP8, AUSP9. Airfix U.S. Paratroopers, value $1.50 each. Courtesy Paul Stadinger - Stad's.

L to R: AGP1, AGP2, AGP3, AGP4. Airfix German Paratroopers, value $2.00 each. Courtesy Paul Stadinger - Stad's.

⚔ **Benbros Ltd** ⚔

by K. Warren Mitchell

Formed about 1951 by Nathan and Jack Benninson. Well-sculpted and painted for the classic toy-figure look, these are similar in style to Timpo. Best known for its Robin Hood series, cowboys and Indians. Ceased production around 1967.

Marked under the base as "BENBROS" or "BENSON." ("XB" numbers are the author's, for coding purposes.) *Prices are for very good condition.* Photos by K. Warren Mitchell.

		VG
XB-1	Robin Hood firing bow	$20.00
XB-2	Little John with staff	20.00

L to R: XB-2, XB-3, XB-9, XB-5, XB-1.

XB-3	Will Scarlet with sword	20.00
XB-4	Mutch the Miller's son	15.00

L to R: XB-4, XB-6, XB-7, XB-8.

XB-5	Friar Tuck with staff	20.00
XB-6	Maid Marian	20.00

		VG
XB-7	Sheriff of Nottingham	20.00
XB-8	Man at Arms with axe	15.00
XB-9	Bishop of Hereford	20.00
XB-10	Stag	10.00
XB-11	R.C.M.P. mounted, detachable	12.00
XB-12	R.C.M.P., dismounted, hands on hips	7.00
XB-13	Farm girl seated on shire horse, waving, detachable	25.00

XB-11.

XB-13.

XB-14	Hussar officer on rearing horse	13.00
XB-15	Queen Elizabeth, mounted	25.00
XB-16	Buffalo Bill, mounted with lasso	35.00
XB-17	Cowboy tied to tree	25.00
XB-18	Cowboy with lasso	10.00
XB-19	Bandit with mask	8.00

XB-14.

L to R: XB-19, XB-21.

		VG
XB-20	Cowboy surrendering	8.00
XB-21	Crouching bandit with mail bag	8.00
XB-22	Cowboy with pistol	8.00
XB-23	Sheriff standing with pistol	8.00
XB-24	Cowboy clubbing with rifle	9.00
XB-25	Cowboy wounded by arrow	10.00
XB-26	Howitzer	20.00

L to R: XB-22, XB-23, XB-25.

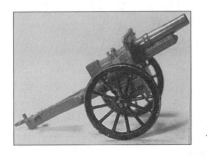

XB-26.

England
Metal, Hollowcast
54mm (2-1/8") most
common size found

✕ **Britains** ✕

Britains have long been the most collected of all toy soldiers, and it seems likely they will be for some time to come. There are a number of reasons for this. Perhaps the foremost is that, due to the superior quality of their painting and their general design, they are almost always pleasing to the eye. In addition, there is the long continuity of the line, its breadth and depth. Britains soldiers represent virtually every modern army of the past nine decades, and the line of British soldiers alone offers a staggering variety of regiments.

Their initial price has been a help, too, in making them attractive to collectors. Many people collect because they remember having owned a company's products during their childhood; Britains' soldiers have always been reasonably priced; therefore, they were accessible to a large number of children. This is a company that is still in business; therefore, it presumably continues to attract children who will, in time, become collectors. Finally, it's even possible that the momentum of Britains' explosion onto the scene is still carrying the company along.

Put simply, it was Britains that revolutionized the toy soldier business. In 1893, it is believed, William Britain Jr. conceived the idea of developing a hollowcast lead soldier. Prior to this, all lead soldiers had been solid, and most had come from Germany. But by the simple expedient of pouring lead alloy into a mold and then immediately pouring out all but that which adhered to the sides of the mold, Britain came up with a soldier that saved money in lead and shipping.

Britains had been founded around 1850 by William Britain Sr., who, from the first, designed and manufactured toys. These were mechanical and appear to have been successful, but on a small scale. However, this was the age of the Industrial Revolution and the introduction of mass marketing. Toy trains were already in vogue, and it was decided to match the figures to the then-popular No. 1 Gauge trains. This worked out to a 54mm-high toy soldier. (A simple stroke, but it had its brilliance. Many toy soldier makers have failed, or not been as successful as they might have been, because their figures were manufactured without an eye to fitting any sort of scale.)

Britains' early soldiers were a bit awkward-looking, and may have been designed by an outside hand. However, within a few years, William Britain Jr. had mastered the art of sculpting; until the 1920s, his stamp was on all of Britains' soldiers. From that time on, other members of the family and factory also had a hand in the design.

The sale of soldiers got off to a slow start, until the Britains convinced Gamages to present them as a sales promotion in their store. From that point on, the company was established and continued almost without hesitation through World War I, the 1920s and the Depression, until World War II forced a temporary halt. Production resumed in 1946 (or possibly late 1945) and has continued to this day.

The firm was located until 1959 at 28 Lambton Road in Hornsey Rise, on the outskirts of London. During that time, it became the largest manufacturer of toy soldiers in the world, with 500 employees in 1937. Although it is said Britains paid well, and that there was tremendous loyalty to the company by its workers, at least one outside observer saw it another way. Robert H. Greenwell observed in the January 1938 *Toys and Bicycles* that "an inspection of the factory discloses the fact that most of the work is done by emaciated looking children fourteen years of age and over," which sounds very much like the working conditions of the U.S.'s Barclay. Greenwell also described the work and contributed a few figures: "The boys sit at long benches and mold with hand molds and place the silvery looking, yet hot, toys in large containers to be carried upstairs where girls of the same age and older spray or paint by hand the gay synthetic regalia that makes them so vivid and lifelike. This unique factory (carries) 'in stock' at all times 2,000 types of lead soldiers and novelties."

William Britain

Notes on Britains

by K. Warren Mitchell

Pricing

For most W. Britains collectors, paint condition is everything. Mismatched sets, damaged pieces, restored or repainted pieces reduce the prices shown--in most cases, substantially.

All set prices are based on the set being in the proper box, and the box being in comparable condition to the soldiers themselves. A set without a box is generally valued at 10% to 20% less.

Grading

The grading of W. Britains figures is generally more restrictive. There is no *Mint* price shown, since such a small percentage of sets are found in that condition. Naturally, a truly *Mint* set would command a premium over the price shown (*Mint* being absolutely in the condition it was when it left the factory). Normal accepted grading is as follows: *Excellent*--a minor chip or two on a figure; *Very Good*--some gloss and at least 95% of the paint remaining; *Good*--played with, dullish paint, but still at least 80% of paint remains. Unless extremely rare, a figure or set below *Good* loses a great deal of its desirability/collectibility to most collectors.

Set Numbers and Contents

W. Britains generally used the same set number for a given set since its beginning in 1893. Boxes changed, labels changed, contents changed in number, poses and painting changed, but #1 remained the Life Guards through 73 years. In 1960, most standard eight-piece "foot" sets were reduced by one piece. Standard five-piece mounted sets were reduced to four pieces.

In 1961, new cellophane window boxes were used. In 1962, the new numbering system of 9000 series began. NOTE: Out of consideration for space and simplicity, the new 9000 number appears next to the original number of the set, if it was continued after 1962. Newly formed sets after 1962 are listed at the end of the regular numbers. Keep in mind that in the case of sets carrying 9000 series number, the value shown for the regular numbered set will normally have to be adjusted to take into consideration a change in contents, where applicable. Set numbers are in order. Where the sequence skips a number, it indicates that the missing number was a FARM, ZOO or other nonmilitary item, which, in turn, can be found under its own special title. Refer to "Order of Appearance."

Order of Appearance

To simplify finding and identifying pieces and sets, this section has been set up in the following order: Standard military sets, half boxes, picture packs, farm, railway, hunt, zoo, circus, garden, 2nd quality paint, misc., and plastic.

Identifying

The following is a very basic guide for determining what you have. One of the reasons for W. Britains popularity through the years was its dedication to basic uniform accuracy, compared to its contemporaries. Generally, a headgear and "facings" (collar and cuff colors) actually denoted a given regiment. Another reason was the moveable arm existing on the majority of figures made shortly after 1900. In fact, the company advertised this feature on many early set labels.

After 1900, the underside of the bases and horse bellies were marked with a variety of embossed words: "W. BRITAINS LTD.," "PROPERTIES," "COPYRIGHT," "MADE IN ENGLAND," and often all of these. NOTE: The simple word "England" or abbreviation "COPYRT." appearing on a figure, means it is not a W. BRITAINS figure, but rather any one of many competitors. A date under the base or horse belly appeared on many prewar Britains' figures, but it is not really indicative of when the figure was made, but only when the mold was made (and then used until worn out or pose changed). This is also true of those carrying the French word "DEPOSE" (which means EXPORT). W. Britains' had a Paris branch until 1923, when it was closed, and all the molds returned to England. The molds generally continued to be used, and "DEPOSE" has even showed up on a few postwar pieces.

"Dating" of W. Britains

Determining the age of a Britains' figure is difficult, unless you know what "version" it is, and can compare paint style. There are some simple rules-of-thumb to follow that can aid even the most casual collector.

First, if it's boxed, and the box label reads "Regiments of All Nations," it's postwar production of 1949-60. Not all postwar sets carried the "R.O.A.N." label. Some very popular sets continued to carry a prewar label (i.e.: #24, 32, 1711, etc.).

Sets carrying stock # of 1920 or higher were only issued postwar (after 1945).

Mustaches appeared on most British regiments until the British Army passed a regulation against "facial hair" in about 1936. W. Britains properly deleted mustaches in painting in late 1936-37.

The earliest versions of artillery pieces and horse-drawn wagons were unpainted (gun-metal grey).

The swords of earliest mounted figures were very thick from 1893 to about 1920. First bases were round or blunt oval for foot figures, with the transition to rectangular bases starting around 1907. A few sets continued "round" bases throughout the prewar period, such as the Officers of the Royal Army Medical Corps (in #137), Japanese charging of set #134, Serbians charging of set #173.

The mid- to late 1930s contained many khaki sets of British and U.S. Army in action. The poses and khaki were the same. When outside their boxes, the only way to tell them apart is that during that period the British had black shoes and boots, green gaiters and packs, while the U.S. had brown shoes and boots, and brown gaiters and packs. U.S. always had grey helmets, while the British varied with grey or khaki.

Motor vehicles started with smooth white rubber tires, then ribbed white tires, then black ribbed tires from late prewar to postwar, until the introduction of plastic tires about 1958. Grey metal tires appear for a short period in the late 1930s.

The following charts were designed to aid in identifying only the standard sets in which a regiment was featured exclusively, or if it appeared differently attired or posed in mixed display set. Also, only those sets are shown which are in the most popular scale of W. BRITAINS in North America--the 54mm or 2-1/8" model.

Infantry of the Line

Red tunic, dark blue trousers, dark blue spike helmet (except where noted).

	Facings	In Set
The Buffs (East Kent Regt.)	Tan	#16 Standing on guard, plus a number of display sets
East Yorkshire	White	113 At attention
Green Howards	Green	255 Marching
Loyal North Lancashire	White	1564 At slope, and 2125 standing and kneeling on guard
Middlesex	Yellow	76 At slope, plus many display sets
Royal Irish	Blue	156 Firing in standing, kneeling and prone positions
Royal Lancaster	Blue (white helmet)	148 Running at trail
Royal Norfolk	Yellow	73 Marching
Royal West Surrey	Blue	29 (Large display) marching and on-guard, plus many other mixed regt. display sets. Also 2086 in 3 positions firing.
Royal Warwickshire	Blue	206 At present arms
Royal Sussex	Blue (1st version in white helmet then blue)	36 At slope
Somerset Light Inf.	Blue (Dark green helmet)	17 Standing and kneeling on guard, plus 40
York & Lancaster	White	96 Running at trail

NOTE:
(1) The above regiments, and many others, appear marching in scarce "Parade" series (sets 1556-1602), but are hard to verify without a box present.
(2) Officers sometimes were given gold collar and cuffs.

Foot Guard

Regiments can be identified by the color of plume (or lack of) on their bearskin hats. All had red tunics and dark blue trousers.

W. BRITAINS' standard-size foot figure is about 54mm (or 2-1/8" tall), and was made with several grades of paint. Most 1st quality figures have moveable arm and detailed painting; as shown in photo-figure "A." 2nd quality figures generally limited the number of colors painted, little detail and "fixed" arm, as in photo-figure "B."

W. BRITAINS' terms for standard military poses, often noted on box label, are generally used by other makers, even today. The term simply refers to the position of the rifle. The following are the most commonly used.

A (left), B(right).

L to R: #1, #2, #3, #4.

L to R: #5, #6, #7.

#8

#1: at slope, marching
#2: on guard
#3: slung rifle
#4: at trail

#5: at attention (after 1925)
#6: at attention (pre-1925)
#7: at ease
#8: at present

Foot Guard

	Plume	In Set
Coldstream Guards	Red on right	#37 Band, #90, 3 positions firing, 93 display, assorted poses, 120 kneeling firing, 1327 3 positions firing (prewar only) and several mixed display sets.
Grenadier Guards	White on left side	34 Standing firing, 111 at attention, 312 marching in winter dress, 329 sentry and box (prewar only) 438 marching, 460 1st version color party, 1283 3 positions firing, 1327 3 positions firing (postwar only), 2113 band, 2121 3 positions firing, and many mixed display sets.
Irish Guards	Light blue on right	107 Marching, 124 lying firing, 1078 at present arms, 2096 pipe band, 2123 marching and several mixed displays.
Scots Guards	No plume	69 Pipers, 70 running at trail, 75 marching, 82 pioneers with axes, 130 display, assorted poses, 329 sentry with box (postwar only), 431 marching, 446 marching, 460 color party with flags, 1722 drum and pipe band, 2084 color party, 2122 marching with flag, and many mixed display sets.
Welsh Guards	White plume with green horizontal line, on left	253 Marching, 2083 at ease, 2108 drum and fife band

NOTES:
(1) Figures with red plume on left are from set 1634 or 1637, and are Governor General's Foot Guards of Canada.
(2) Many of the Irish Guard and Scots Guard sets in marching pose, also included appropriate Piper.
(3) All "facings" are dark blue.
(4) Guards are sometimes confused with Fusiliers of sets #7 and #74 because of large headgear. Fusilier headgear is narrower, and red tunic has white cross straps.

Highlanders

Can be identified by color of hatching on kilts and type of headgear. Usually red tunics.

	Tartan	In Set
Argyll & Sutherland	Grass green on dark green background	#15 Feather bonnet, charging #2063 sun helmet, firing
Black Watch	Dark green, no hatching	#11 Feather bonnet, charging #122 Sun helmet, standing firing #449 Feather bonnet, marching #480 Feather bonnet, marching #2109 Pipe band, feather bonnet #2111 Color party, feather bonnet #2126 Charging party, feather bonnet #2179 Small pipe band, and several mixed display sets
Cameron	Red and yellow on dark blue background	#89 Sun helmets, various firing positions #114 Sun helmets (khaki tunic) marching #2025 Sun helmet, various firing positions
Gordon	Yellow on dark green background	#77 Feather bonnets, marching #118 Sun helmets, lying firing #157 Sun helmets, various firing positions #437 Officers on foot and mounted, feather bonnets #441 Feather bonnets, marching #482 Feather bonnets, marching #1325 Sun helmets, various firing positions and various mixed display sets
Seaforth	Red and white on dark green background	#88 Feather bonnet, charging #112 Feather bonnet, marching #2062 Feather bonnet, charging

HIGHLANDERS and LOWLANDER IN TREWS (PLAID TROUSERS):

Highland Light Infantry	Red and white hatching on dark green	#213, Shako hat, marching
Royal Scots	Red and yellow hatching on dark green	#212, Kilmornock bonnet, marching
King's Own Scottish Borderers	Red and white hatching on dark green (or blue)	#1395, Kilmornock bonnet, marching
Cameronians (Scottish Rifles)	White hatching only on dark green	#1913, Shako hat, marching

NOTES:

(1) Sometimes confused with set 114, is similar set 1901, the Cape Town Highlanders, who also had khaki tunics, and sun helmets. Set 1901 has Gordon tartan on kilts and khaki sun helmets.

(2) Pipers that accompanied some of the above sets would have proper tartan to match.

Heavy Cavalry

Best identified by the headgear.

HOUSEHOLD CAVALRY:

	Headgear	In Set
1st Life Guards	Silver helmet with white plume, silver breast-plate, red sleeves (with swords)	#1 Trotting horse, #4 painted gold gilt, #5 painted gold gilt, #72 large black plume, #400 gray winter cloaks #101 Band (in jockey caps, with gold and maroon striped tunic), #430 summer and winter dress, #2029 mounted at halt and dismounted, #2085 carrying lances, #2118 mounted and dismounted, and many mixed display sets
2nd Life Guard	Silver helmet with white plume, silver breast-plate, red sleeves, carrying carbines	#43 At gallop, in display, #129 carrying lances, plus many mixed display sets
Royal Horse Guards	Silver helmet with red plume, silver breast-plate, blue sleeves, with swords	#2 Trotting horse, #103 band (jockey caps with blue and gold stripe tunic), #1343 in grey winter cloaks, #2085 carrying lances, and many mixed display sets

DRAGOON GUARDS:

1st Dragoon Guards	Brass helmet with red plume, red carrying swords	In set #129 trotting horses, #2074 on trotting horses, cantering and walking horses
2nd Dragoon Guards "Queens Bays"	Brass helmet with black plume, red tunic, carry lances	#44 galloping horses, plus 2 mixed display sets
5th Dragoon Guards	Brass helmet with red and white plume, red tunic, carry swords	#3 Trotting horses
6th Dragoon Guards	Brass helmet with white plume, blue tunic, carry carbines	#106 At gallop
7th Dragoon Guards	Brass helmet with black and white plume, red tunic, lance slung behind arm	#127 Trotting horses

Light Cavalry

Best identified by headgear.

DRAGOONS:

1st Royal Dragoons	Silver helmet with black plume, red tunic, carry swords	#31 Trotting horses
2nd Dragoons (Royal Scot Greys)	Black bearskin as foot guards, red tunic, grey horses, carry swords	#32 Walking horses, #59 walking horses, #1720 band (kettle drummer has white bearskin hat), #1721 larger band, #2119 mounted and dismounted, and many display sets

HUSSARS: Best identified by plume and busby bag (color swatch down the right side of cap)

3rd Hussars	Light blue bag, white plume, carry carbines	#13 Cantering horses
4th Hussars	Yellow busby bag, red plume, carry swords	#8 Galloping horses, plus two mixed display sets
7th Hussars	Red busby bag, white plume, carry swords	#2075 Trotting and cantering horses
10th Hussars	Red busby bag, white over black plume, empty handed	#315 Horse at halt
11th Hussars	Red busby bag, white over red plume, bright red breeches	#12 Cantering horses, with carbines, #182 dismounted with horses, empty handed. #270 mounted and dismounted, all empty handed plus many mixed display sets
13th Hussars	Tan or white busby bag, white plume with swords	#99 Cantering horses

LANCERS: Best identified by plume and plastron (contrasting panel on chest of tunic), all with lances

5th Royal Irish Lancers	Red plastron, green plume	#23 At halt, plus 2 mixed display sets
9th Queen's Royal Lancers	Red plastron, black and white plume	#24 At halt, plus 2 mixed display sets
12th Royal Lancers	Red plastron, red plume	#128 Lance slung behind arm, trotting horses, #129 large display, with lances also at carry as well as slung, #2076 trotting horses, lances at carry, plus mixed display set
16th Lancers	Black plastron, black plume, red tunic	#33 At halt, lance at carry, plus mixed display sets
17th Lancers	White plastron, white sun helmet	#81 Trotting and cantering horses, lances at carry, included in set 73 with normal lancer cap and white plume, also in display set #131
21st Lancers	Light blue plastron, white plume on lancer cap	#100 On cantering horses, lance at carry, #94 in khaki uniform with sun helmet, and later in steel helmets, appeared in #1407 mixed display also in sun helmet, then steel helmet, on galloping horses

NOTE: Following the combining of the 5th and 16th Lancers in the British Army, W. Britains deleted set #23 and started in the early 1930s to call set #33 the 16th/5th Lancers, continuing as such postwar, in normal dress of the 16th.

Regiments of the Indian Army

These have always been of great interest to the average Britains' collectors. With the similarity of poses, uniforms and colors, and the frequent changing of the set titles, these same sets have always been a bit confusing. The following should help identify the various regiments.

NOTES: A "turban" is made up of the KULLAH, which is a cone shaped cap, the WRAP turban fabric wound

around the cone, and the FLASHES or SLASHES of color appearing on the wrap.

Mounted sets generally came as four Troopers plus a Trumpeter, but in some cases may appear with native officer instead of Trumpeter. Always on galloping horses.

CAVALRY:

Set #	Title	Pcs	Carry	Tunic	Turban Wrap/Kullah/Flash
45	3d Madras renamed in 1937 "7th LIGHT CAVALRY OF INDIA" (Also appear in #61 as 15 pc. set	5	Swords	Pale Blue	Dark Blue/Yellow/White
46	10th BENGAL LANCERS renamed in 1927 "HODSON'S HORSES, 4th DUKE OF CAMBRIDGE'S OWN." (Also appear in #63 as 10 pc. set)	5	Lances	Dark Blue Red Plastron	(KULLAH became Red) Dark Blue/Red/White
47	1st BENGAL NATIVE CAVALRY renamed "SKINNER'S HORSE" about 1935, SEE #271 for change. (Also appear in #62 as 10 pc. set)	5	Swords	Khaki with Black Plastron Yellow (after 1934)	Red/Blue/Yellow
60	1st BOMBAY LANCERS	15	Lances	lt. green until 1920, then bright green	Black/Red/White
64	2nd MADRAS LANCERS (combined with infantry) renamed "16th LIGHT CAVALRY" in 1938	13	Lances	lt. Blue	Turban wrap is 1/2 dark blue and 1/2 white, with light blue flashes on white portion
66	1st BOMBAY LANCERS renamed "13th DUKE OF CONNAUGHTS' OWN"	5	Lances	lt. green in early sets, dark green until about 1950, then dark blue	Dark Blue/Red/White
271	SKINNER'S HORSE, "1st DUKE OF YORK'S OWN" (NOTE: Britains duplicated regiments in #47. Short lived from 1928-35, then #271 dropped, and #47 given yellow tunics and lances.	5	Lances	Yellow	Black/Red/Yellow
2013	INDIAN ARMY MOUNTED	12	Sword	Olive Drab	All Khaki

INFANTRY:

Set #	Title	Pose	Tunic/Facings	Turban Wrap/Kullah/Flash
64	7th BENGAL INFANTRY (part set with 2nd MADRAS LANCERS) replaced by 3/7th RAJPUT REGT. at slope of #1342 around 1935	Early at trail, then slope	Red/Yellow Red/Yellow	Blue/Red/White
67	1st MADRAS NATIVE INF. by 1930 renamed "Corps of Madras Pioneers"	At trail then slope At slope	Red/White Red/White	Blue/Red/White Rare White also appears
68	2nd BOMBAY NATIVE INF. included pioneer with axe prior to 1920. Renamed in 1935 "4th Bombay Grenadiers"	At trail, then slope At slope	Blue/Red Blue/Red	Blue/Red/White White/Red
252	1st MADRAS NATIVE INF. (Part set with 3rd MADRAS CAVALRY)	(as in #67)		
1342	3/7th RAJPUT REGT.	At slope	Red/Yellow	Blue/Red/White
1641	3/12th (SIKH) FRONTIER FORCE	At slope	Khaki/Dark Blue	Khaki/Black
1892	INDIAN INFANTRY (with British Officer)	At trail	Olive drab	Pale green
1893	INDIAN ARMY SERVICE CORP. (with British officer and mule)	At trail	Olive drab	Pale green

(Special thanks to the late Lee Schaffer and Bill Miele for their help, as well as Christie's East, Phillips of New York, Joanne and Ron Ruddell, the late Hank Anton for some helpful photos and Will Beierwaltes for drawing of headgear).

End Notes by K. Warren Mitchell

1st Quality Military

	G	VG	EXC
1. (9206) The Life Guards, 5 pieces, 1st version	$110.00	$165.00	$220.00
Second version (tin wire sword)	85.00	115.00	150.00
Postwar version	70.00	105.00	140.00
Postwar officer	15.00	22.50	30.00
Postwar Trooper	12.00	17.50	25.00

	G	VG	EXC
2. (9209) Horse Guards, mounted, 5 pieces, 2nd Version (tin wire sword), 1897	90.00	135.00	170.00
Postwar version	86.00	120.00	160.00
Postwar officer	15.00	22.50	30.00
Postwar Trooper	12.00	17.50	25.00

#1 1st version tin sword.

#1 Last version.

#2 1st version officer tin sword.

#2 2nd version trooper tin sword.

#2 3rd version thick sword.

#2 4th version trooper & officer.

#3 1st version trooper & officer.

	G	VG	EXC
3. Fifth Dragoon Guards, 5 pieces, produced from 1893-1941 (Officer on rearing horse, Troopers on trotting horses after 1901), 1st version 1893-96	150.00	225.00	300.00
2nd version, 1897-1902 (tin wire sword, "1902" on horse belly)	90.00	150.00	210.00
Prewar v. officer	20.00	30.00	40.00
Prewar v. Trooper	15.00	22.50	30.00
4. Gilt Household Cavalry (single)	20.00	30.00	45.00
5. Gilt Household Cavalry (single)	20.00	30.00	45.00
6. Boer Cavalry, set 5 pieces (black hats)	400.00	650.00	950.00
Officer, fixed arm, 1st version	50.00	100.00	150.00
Trooper, fixed arm, 1st version	40.00	80.00	120.00

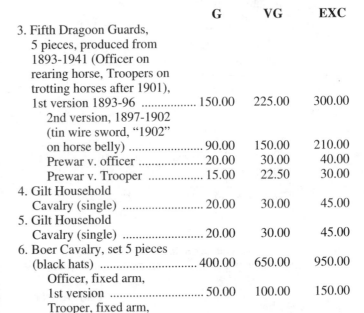

#6 1st version trooper & officer (fixed arm).

#3 3rd version.

#6 3rd version (moveable arm).

#7 1st version.

#7 2nd & 3rd versions (note back-pack).

#7 4th version.

	G	VG	EXC
7. Royal Fusiliers, slope arms,			
8 pieces, 1st version 125.00	187.50	250.00
Late 1930s 80.00	105.00	135.00
Late 1930s v. officer 10.50	15.00	20.00
Late 1930s v. Troop 8.00	12.00	15.00
8. The Fourth Hussars			
(Queens's Own) on			
galloping horses, Trumpeter			
earlier on galloping horse,			
later on trotting horse,			
5 pieces, "1901" 125.00	165.00	220.00
Postwar 85.00	115.50	150.00
Postwar v. Trumpeter 12.50	18.75	25.00
Postwar v. Trooper 11.00	16.50	22.00
9. Rifle Brigade at the Slope,			
eight pieces 1897-1918 .... 200.00	300.00	400.00

#10 Later tin flag version.

#8 Postwar trooper.

	G	VG	EXC
10. Officer, Band and Colours			
of the Salvation Army,			
eight pieces (all male);			
standard bearer, 2 cornet			
players, 5 Officers, early			
flag is cast, later is tin 800.00	1800.00	2800.00
Standard bearer, tin flag 75.00	210.00	250.00
Officer 35.00	52.50	170.00
11. (9135) Black Watch			
1st version, running			
at trail, plugged-in hand			
(1893-1903) 7 pieces 150.00	235.00	350.00

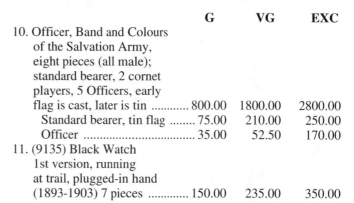

#9 L to R: 1st, 2nd, 4th, 3rd (note rifle & base change).

*#11   Postwar,
1st version.*

#11 Royal Highlanders.

	G	VG	EXC
(Royal Highlanders) charging, eight pieces, postwar includes Piper,			
early versions	55.00	82.50	110.00
Postwar version, 8 pieces	50.00	75.00	100.00
Postwar version, 6 pieces	40.00	60.00	80.00
Early Piper	11.00	16.50	22.00
Early Troop	5.00	7.50	10.00
Postwar Piper	8.00	12.00	16.00
Postwar Troop	4.00	6.00	8.00

12. Prince Albert's own 11th Hussars, 5 pieces, includes

	G	VG	EXC
officer, 1st version	150.00	225.00	300.00
1930s version	115.00	172.50	230.00
1930s v. officer	20.00	30.00	40.00
1930s v. Trooper	17.50	26.25	35.00

#12 1st version trooper, 2nd version officer (moveable arm, rectangular base).

#12 1st version trooper.

#12 3rd version officer.

#12 3rd version trooper.

13. 3rd Hussars, 5 pieces, officer, "1903"

	G	VG	EXC
(on horse belly)	110.00	185.00	250.00
Officer, "1903"	20.00	45.00	65.00
Trooper, "1903"	15.00	30.00	40.00

#13 3rd version short carbine.

#13 1st version officer - horse with throat plume and tin sword.

	G	VG	EXC
14. Women Officers, Timbrel Band and the War Cry (Salvation Army), eight pieces, all women, four empty-handed, two with tambourines, one with collection plate, one with Society's publication			
The War Cry, 1906	800.00	1500.00	2000.00
Empty-Handed Woman	80.00	140.00	200.00
15. Argyll & Sutherland Highlanders, running, eight pieces, (round base)			
early version	110.00	140.00	200.00
1930s	85.00	120.00	170.00
1930s officer	8.00	12.00	16.00
1930s Troop	6.00	9.00	12.00
16. East Kent Regiment, on guard, with Bugler, drummer, officer, 9 pieces			
early, 8 pieces later	100.00	185.00	275.00
Officer	10.00	15.00	20.00
Troop	9.00	13.50	18.00
17. (9143) Somerset Light Infantry, standing and kneeling on guard,			
eight pieces, Prewar	75.00	125.00	175.00

#14 Late short skirt version.

#16 1st version, on guard & bugler.

#17 1st version.

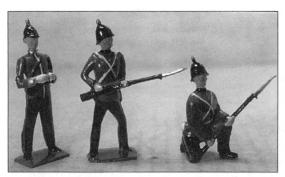

#17 last version.

#19 1st version.

#19 2nd version.

#24 1st version fixed arm, rear horse legs crossed.

#24 2nd version moveable arm.

#24 Postwar lance slung behind arm.

#24 Postwar officer.

#25

	G	VG	EXC
Postwar	50.00	85.00	120.00
Troop, each	5.00	9.00	13.00

18. Worcestershire Infantry,
    standing and kneeling on
    guard, eight pieces
    (round base), officer,

	G	VG	EXC
drummer added 1910	120.00	200.00	300.00
Officer	15.00	22.00	28.00
Troop	11.00	16.00	22.00

#18 3rd version, rectangular base.

19. First West India Regiment,
    early sets have marching fixed
    arm officer, 9 pieces, 8 pieces

	G	VG	EXC
later, 1st version (1897)	200.00	400.00	600.00
2nd version, 1910, with mtd. officer	150.00	350.00	550.00
Prewar	120.00	205.00	380.00
Prewar officer	12.50	18.50	25.00
Prewar Troop	10.00	15.00	20.00

20. Display Box, Russian
    and Japanese infantry

	G	VG	EXC
and cavalry, 26 pieces	1000.00	1800.00	2600.00

21. Display Box, 1st Life Guards,
    11th Hussars, West India
    Regiment, East Kent

	G	VG	EXC
Regiment, 27 pieces	900.00	1700.00	2500.00

22. Display Box, 5th Lancers,
    Horse Guards Black Watch,
    Worcestershire Regiment,
    produced through 1937,
    27 pieces .... No Price Found

23. 5th Royal Irish Lancers,
    mounted at halt 1894-1932,
    cross-legged horse

	G	VG	EXC
pre-1903, 5 pieces	160.00	240.00	320.00

#23 Early officer.

	G	VG	EXC
24. (9216) 9th Lancers, mounted at halt, 1894-1941, lances slung on right arm,			
5 pieces, Prewar	130.00	185.00	240.00
Postwar	75.00	125.00	175.00
Postwar officer	16.00	25.00	35.00
Postwar Trooper	12.00	18.00	25.00

25. Soldiers to shoot, 4 pieces,
    kneeling line infantry, red
    tunic, spiked helmet, hollow
    tube rifle, shoots pin via

	G	VG	EXC
snapping strip of metal	400.00	550.00	750.00
(price for one piece)	75.00	130.00	175.00

26. Boer Infantry,

	G	VG	EXC
c1899, 8 pieces	800.00	1200.00	1800.00
Boer Troop, each	90.00	135.00	180.00

#26 1st version.

#26 3rd version.

	G	VG	EXC
27. Band of the Line, 12 pieces,			
Pre and Postwar pieces	135.00	225.00	350.00
Each	10.00	14.00	18.00
Pre and Postwar drummer	11.00	16.50	22.00
28. (9420) Mountain Gun of the Royal Artillery, 14 pieces, Mounted officer, 4 mules, 6 marching gunners, 3 pieces of small gun			
that fit together, Prewar	225.00	337.50	450.00
Postwar	155.00	225.00	325.00
Officer, 1930s Mounted	14.00	22.00	35.00
Gunner, Postwar	9.00	15.00	20.00
Mule	12.00	18.00	24.00
29. Display Box, 1st Life Guards, 3rd Hussars, 9th Lancers, Royal West Surrey Infantrymen, marching and on guard,			
1903-1910, 41 pieces	1000.00	2200.00	2800.00
Officer, Royal West Surrey, late	8.00	12.00	16.00
Trooper, Royal West Surrey, late	7.00	10.50	14.00
30. (9137) Drums and Bugles of the Line, 1908-1912 8 pcs.	100.00	150.00	200.00
Late 1930s, 1940 (seven pcs)	90.00	125.00	150.00
Postwar (7 and later 6 pcs)	65.00	87.50	115.00

#27 1st slot arm, #27 3rd.

#27 Metal drum.

#27 Early.

*#27 Straight arm,
white facings.*

#28 Early. Courtesy Phillips.

*Many Britains soldiers have a number of variations. These are all from early to late Number 28 Mountain
Battery sets. At left is the first version and next to him a variation of that first version, and after that a second
variation of that first version and then a third variation of that first version. After that, the pre-WWII second
version, and finally the post-WWII version. Courtesy Tom Loback. Photo by Sato Studios.*

Variations of the mounted officers from the Number 28 Mountain Battery, from left: First version, second version (circa 1924), third version (early postwar) and finally a variation of that figure. Courtesy Tom Loback. Photo by Sato Studios.

Mules from early to late versions of the No. 28 Mountain Battery Set. From left: First version, variation of the first version, second version and finally the post-WWII version. Courtesy Tom Loback. Photo by Sato Studios.

#30 Early.

#30 2nd version. Boy Bugler.

#30 L to R: 4th version bent arm, blue facing; Drummer boy.

#33 1st version.

	G	VG	EXC

31. First (Royal) Dragoons,
 officer on rearing horse,
 other horses walking,
 5 pieces, first version
 (tin sword) 150.00   270.00   350.00
   Second version, "1902"
 (on horse belly) 110.00   165.00   220.00
   1935 officer 22.00   34.50   50.00
   1935 Trooper 17.00   28.00   35.00

32. (9210) The Royal Scots Greys
 (2nd Dragoons), 5 pieces
 with officer "1902,"
 2nd version 100.00   150.00   200.00
   Postwar 60.00   90.00   120.00
   Prewar officer 14.00   22.00   30.00
   Prewar Trooper 12.00   18.00   24.00
   1960 officer 12.00   20.00   25.00
   1960 Trooper 10.00   16.00   22.00

#35 3rd version.

#32 L to R: 2nd version, 3rd version, 4th version. Note bear-skins and tin swords.

#35 L to R: 7th version, 6th version, 3rd version, 2nd version.

33. 16th/5th Lancers, mounted
 at halt, five pieces, Prewar 105.00   200.00   300.00
   Postwar 5 pcs. 80.00   125.00   165.00
   1950 officer 15.00   22.50   30.00
   1950 Trooper 12.00   18.00   24.00

34. Grenadier Guards, standing
 firing, 8 pieces, Postwar 65.00   97.50   125.00
   Trooper firing, Postwar 6.00   8.00   11.00
   First version 90.00   150.00   200.00

#36 4th version.

#34 1st version, 2nd version, 3rd version.

35. (9140) The Royal Marines
 at slope arms, with officer,
 8 pieces, 1920s 90.00   135.00   180.00
   Postwar 75.00   105.00   140.00
   Officer Postwar 10.00   18.00   23.00
   Troop Postwar 7.00   12.00   16.00

#36 Left: 1st version; Right: last version.

#37 1st version, slot arms.

#37 1930 version.

*#38 3rd version
moveable arms.*

	G	VG	EXC
36. (9142) Royal Sussex Regiment, slope arms, Mounted Officer, 1910 version, 7 pieces (white helmets)	130.00	220.00	300.00
Postwar	65.00	97.50	130.00
Prewar officer	12.50	18.75	25.00
Prewar Troop	10.00	15.00	20.00
Postwar officer	10.00	14.00	18.00
Postwar Troop	7.50	11.00	14.00
37. Full Band of Coldstream Guards, 21 pieces, 1st version (round base, plug-in arms)	350.00	550.00	800.00
Prewar, late 1930s	300.00	450.00	700.00
Postwar	225.00	350.00	500.00
Postwar, per standard figure	10.00	16.00	22.00

#39A

*#39
Early.
Note
gun,
limber,
pack on
horses'
backs.*

	G	VG	EXC
38. Dr. Jameson and the South African Mounted Infantry, c1896-1908, 5 pieces, fixed arm (see name change of set, following)	400.00	650.00	900.00
1st version Trooper	40.00	80.00	120.00
1st version officer with pistol	50.00	100.00	150.00
38. South African Mounted Infantry, moveable arms after 1911 (same as #6 but grey hat)	250.00	500.00	750.00
39. (9419) Royal House Artillery, with gun and limber, 13 pieces, 1895, 6-horse team, large collar on horse's neck, twisted wire traces. Blue uniform	450.00	625.00	900.00
Postwar	200.00	350.00	550.00
39A. Royal Horse Artillery (active service) khaki uniforms	550.00	950.00	1400.00
40. Display Box, 1st Dragoons, Somerset Light Infantry, 14 pieces, Prewar only	200.00	375.00	600.00
41. (9210) The Royal Scots Greys (2nd Dragoons) and the Grenadier Guards, 14 pieces (13 pieces Prewar)	120.00	200.00	250.00
42. Display Box, 1st Life Guards, Royal Sussex Regiment, 12 pieces	280.00	420.00	560.00
43. 2nd Life Guards, five pieces, Trumpeter, four Troopers at gallop, with rifles	125.00	250.00	350.00
Trumpeter	25.00	42.50	60.00
Trooper	20.00	35.00	50.00

#43 1st version.

#43 Last version.

	G	VG	EXC
44. The Queen's Bay (2nd Dragoon Guards), 5 pieces, galloping bay horses, Troopers with lances, officer on trotting horse or Bugler on trotting horse (the latter more common), 1901 version	100.00	200.00	250.00
Late 1930s	110.00	165.00	220.00
Postwar	110.00	165.00	220.00
Officer, late 1930s	25.00	37.50	50.00
Lancer, late 1930s	20.00	30.00	40.00
Officer, Postwar	20.00	30.00	40.00
Lancer, Postwar	16.00	24.00	32.00

#44 L to R: Postwar, 2nd version.

	G	VG	EXC
45. 3rd Madras Cavalry, 5 pieces, Trumpeter, 4 Troopers, with swords early thick-sword version, lt. Bluejacket	200.00	350.00	450.00
Trumpeter, 1930s	24.00	36.00	48.00
Trooper, 1930s	22.00	33.00	44.00

#45 1st version.

	G	VG	EXC
46. Hodson's Horse, 5 pieces, with lances, includes Bugler, 1896-1940, dk. blue jacket	125.00	187.50	250.00
Bugler	22.00	33.00	44.00
Lancer	18.00	27.00	36.00
47. 1st Bengal Cavalry, 5 pieces, includes Bugler, with lances 1896-c1934, khaki jacket	105.00	215.00	280.00
Bugler	25.00	37.50	50.00
Trooper	21.00	31.50	42.00

	G	VG	EXC
47. (9261) Skinner's Horse (1st Duke of York's Own Lancers), same as above, yellow jacket, c1934-1966, Prewar	105.00	200.00	250.00
Postwar, 5 pieces	90.00	125.00	160.00
Postwar Bugler	17.50	26.25	35.00
Postwar Trooper	15.00	22.50	30.00

#47 1st version.

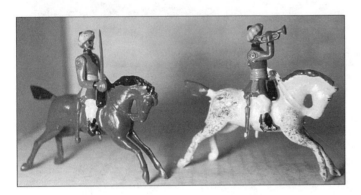

#47 1st version.

	G	VG	EXC
48. (9265) Egyptian Camel Corps, 6 pieces, 6 riders on camels, 1896-1940	270.00	350.00	550.00
Postwar cast tail (3 riders and camels)	80.00	200.00	300.00
Camel and Rider	25.00	47.50	70.00

#48 Early, wire tail.

#48 Postwar, molded tail.

	G	VG	EXC
49. South Australian Lancers, 5 pieces, early version has slouch hats, 1896?	650.00	1100.00	1500.00
(Later redone with spiked helmet, through 1941)			
1930 version	250.00	500.00	750.00
Late 1920s-early 1930s officer	35.00	65.00	85.00
Late 1920s-early 1930s Trooper	25.00	50.00	70.00

#49 1st version.

#49 Last version.

	G	VG	EXC
50. (9305) The Life Guards and the 4th Hussars, 10 pieces, double-box, Prewar	250.00	375.00	500.00
Postwar	150.00	300.00	400.00
51. Display Box 16th Lancers, 11th Hussars, mounted at halt, 10 pieces, Prewar only	300.00	550.00	800.00
52. Display Box 5th Lancers, 2nd Life Guards, mounted at halt, produced through 1937, 10 pieces	350.00	600.00	900.00
53. 4th Hussars with Trumpeter, Royal Horse Guards with officer, Grenadier Guards with Side Drummer and officer, 18 pcs.	250.00	500.00	700.00
54. Display Box, 1st Life Guards, 2nd Dragoon Guards, 9th Lancers, mounted at halt, 15 pcs.	350.00	800.00	1200.00
55. Scots Greys, 3rd Hussars, 16th Lancers at Halt, 15 pieces	350.00	800.00	1200.00
56. Grenadier Guards, East Kent Regiment, 15 pcs.	300.00	550.00	800.00

	G	VG	EXC
57. 1st Dragoon Guards (not standard size), 12 pcs.			No Price Found
58. Display Box, Royal Horse Guards, Scots Greys, Mounted Infantry (not standard size), 21 pcs.			No Price Found
59. Scots Greys, 10 pcs.	200.00	400.00	600.00
60. 1st Bombay Lancers, 15 pcs, 1896-c1935	350.00	800.00	1200.00
61. 3rd Madras Cavalry, 15 pcs, 13 Troops, Bugler, officer, 1896-1935	350.00	800.00	1200.00
61. 7th Light Cavalry, c1936 or c1937, same as above			No Price Found
62. 1st Bengal Cavalry, 10 pcs., 1896 to about 1934	250.00	550.00	800.00
Officer	30.00	45.00	60.00
Trooper	25.00	37.50	50.00
62. Skinner's Horse (1st Duke of York's Own Lancers), same as above, c1934-40, 10 pcs.	250.00	500.00	700.00
63. 10th Bengal Lancers, 10 pcs., officer, Bugler included, 1896-1940	300.00	600.00	850.00
64. 2nd Madras Lancers (5), plus 7th Bengal Infantry (8), 1896-c1938, 13 pcs.	350.00	600.00	900.00
Infantry	12.00	20.00	30.00
Lancer	22.00	35.00	50.00
64. 16th Light Cavalry (5), 7th Bengal Infantry (8), same as above, c1938-1940	300.00	500.00	750.00

	G	VG	EXC
66. (9262) 13th Duke of Connaught's Own Lancers, same as above with blue tunic, 1953-66	80.00	120.00	160.00
Trumpeter	17.00	25.00	34.00
Lancer	16.00	24.00	30.00

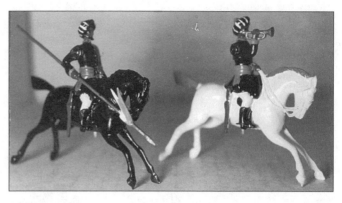

#66 Postwar.

	G	VG	EXC
67. First Madras Native Infantry at trail, officer with sword, 8 pcs., 1896-1918;			
1st version, at trail	200.00	350.00	450.00
Later version, 1929 at slope	150.00	250.00	300.00
Officer, 1st version	25.00	37.50	50.00
Troop, 1st version	20.00	30.00	40.00
Officer, later version	20.00	30.00	40.00
Trooper, later version	15.00	22.50	30.00

#67 1st version at trail.

#67 Rare white turban.

#64 Early version as 2nd Madras Lancers.

#64 Last version 7th Bengal Inf.

	G	VG	EXC
65. Display Box, Russian Cavalry and Infantry, 13 pcs.	400.00	750.00	1200.00
66. 1st Bombay Lancers, 5 pcs., 1896-1937, green tunic	175.00	275.00	400.00
Trumpeter	30.00	45.00	60.00
Trooper	25.00	37.50	50.00

#67 1st officer, 3rd version at slope.

	G	VG	EXC
68. Second Bombay Native Infantry, at the trail, with axes, officer, till 1918	300.00	450.00	600.00
Officer	40.00	60.00	80.00
Troop, later version	30.00	45.00	60.00
68. Second Bombay Native Infantry, at the slope, no other types	150.00	225.00	300.00
Troop	16.00	24.00	32.00
68. 2nd Battalion Fourth Bombay Grenadiers (King Edward's Own) mid 1930s-40s, 8 pcs.	100.00	205.00	250.00

#71

#68 1st version, officer & pioneer with ax.

#68 Last.

	G	VG	EXC
72. Life Guards at Waterloo, moveable arm, 12 pcs.	1400.00	2800.00	3500.00
73. (9407) Royal Artillery, 2nd Life Guards, 17th Lancers, Royal Welsh Fusiliers, Scots Greys, Band of the Line, Gordon Highlanders, General officer, 73 pcs., Prewar	750.00	1200.00	1800.00
Postwar, 67 pieces	500.00	850.00	1200.00
Black Watch at slope	10.00	15.00	20.00
Black Watch officer	13.00	19.50	26.00
Gordon Highlander	5.00	7.50	10.00
17th Lancers officer	40.00	60.00	80.00
17th Lancer	35.00	52.50	70.00

#72 2nd version.

	G	VG	EXC
69. Pipes of Scots Guards, 6, 7, 8 pieces	100.00	165.00	225.00
Pre-1930 Piper	12.00	18.00	24.00
Pre-1942 Piper	11.00	16.50	22.00
70. Scots Guards, running, 7 pieces, Mounted Officer	170.00	300.00	400.00
Officer	25.00	47.50	65.00
Troop	20.00	30.00	40.00

#69 L to R: 1st version, 2nd version, last version.

#70 Running at trail.

	G	VG	EXC
71. Turkish Cavalry, 5 pieces, Prewar	150.00	350.00	450.00
Officer	40.00	60.00	80.00
Trooper	25.00	40.00	55.00
72. Life Guards at Waterloo "Past and Present" fixed arms with tin sword	1800.00	3500.00	5000.00

#73 17th lancer postwar.

	G	**VG**	**EXC**
74. (9144) Royal Welsh Fusiliers, slope arms, goat mascot, officer,			
8 pieces, 1st version 300.00	450.00	700.00
Prewar 130.00	195.00	260.00
Postwar 60.00	95.00	115.00
Prewar at slope 6.00	11.00	14.00
Postwar at slope 5.00	9.00	12.00

#74   *#74 1st version.*

75. (9126) Scots Guards, slope arms, officer, Piper, 8 pcs.,

1893-1910 (round base) 150.00	225.00	300.00
Postwar, 7 pcs. 50.00	70.00	90.00
1st version officer 20.00	30.00	40.00
1st version Troop 15.00	22.50	30.00
Pre and Postwar officer 7.00	11.00	14.00
Pre and Postwar Troop 6.00	9.00	11.00

#75 1st version.

#75 2nd version.

#75 L to R: 1st, 3rd, 4th. Note backpacks.

	G	**VG**	**EXC**
76. (9136) Middlesex Regiment, marching at slope, officer,			
8 pcs. 1st version 150.00	250.00	400.00
Prewar 75.00	100.00	130.00
Postwar 55.00	75.00	110.00
Officer 10.00	14.00	18.00
Troop 6.00	9.00	12.00

#76 1st at trail & last version.

77. (9131) Gordon Highlanders, with Piper, no officer,

slope arms, 8 pcs., Prewar 90.00	120.00	150.00
1st version, 7 pcs., officer, 2 Pipers, 4 running, plug-in head 350.00	500.00	700.00
Postwar, 8 pcs. 70.00	105.00	130.00
Postwar, 6 pcs. 40.00	60.00	80.00
Round base Piper early Prewar 12.00	18.00	24.00

#77 1st version.

#77 L to R: 2nd version, 3rd version, postwar.

#77 2nd version with backpack.

#77 Last version.

#77 Piper post-war.

	G	VG	EXC
Round base Troop early Prewar	10.00	15.00	20.00
Postwar Piper	9.00	13.50	18.00
Postwar Troop	6.00	9.00	12.00

78. Bluejackets running at trail, 8 pcs., Petty officer,

	G	VG	EXC
1897-1941; 1930 set	100.00	200.00	300.00
Late 1930s set	100.00	200.00	275.00
Petty officer, very early	11.00	20.00	30.00
Bluejacket, very early	10.00	20.00	25.00
Late 1930s Petty officer	15.00	22.50	30.00
Late 1930s Bluejacket	11.00	16.50	22.00

#78 Petty officer.

#78 2nd version.

#79 Postwar.

	G	VG	EXC
79. (9455) Royal Navy Landing Party with Gun, limber, 11 pcs. (9 figures), 1898-41, has officer, semi-oval base until c1920, caps have blue tops, Prewar	185.00	325.00	475.00
Postwar set	150.00	250.00	400.00
80. Whitejackets running at slope, 8 pcs., Petty officer, after 1920 (approximately), sailors run at trail	120.00	220.00	325.00
Running at trail	12.00	22.00	28.00

#80 3rd version running at trail.

#80 2nd version running at slope.

	G	VG	EXC
81. 17th Lancers, trotting and cantering, 5 pcs., 1903	300.00	500.00	750.00
"1903" Trooper	40.00	75.00	100.00
Early 1930s Trooper	30.00	50.00	75.00
82. Scots Guards, Colours and Pioneers with axes, 7 pcs., Prewar	110.00	175.00	250.00
Postwar	80.00	155.00	190.00
Officer with Flag	20.00	30.00	45.00
Pioneer with Axe	13.00	20.00	25.00
83. Middlesex Yeomanry trotting horse, 5 pcs.	250.00	550.00	800.00
Trooper	35.00	60.00	100.00
84. Display Box, 2nd Life Guards, 7th Royal Fusiliers, (not standard size), 11 pcs.			No Price Found
85. Display Box, 5th Dragoon Guards, Scots Greys, Scots Guards, Northumberland Fusiliers, 22 pcs. (not standard size)			No Price Found
86. Lancashire Fusiliers (not standard size), 14 pcs.			No Price Found
87. 13th Hussars (not standard size, 8 pcs.)			No Price Found
88. Seaforth Highlanders, charging, 16 pcs. (2 Pipers)	160.00	250.00	400.00
1st version, plug-in hand and rifle, single figure running	18.00	28.00	40.00
89. Cameron Highlanders standing, lying firing, officer with binoculars, 30 pieces "Black Label" box 1930	350.00	500.00	850.00

#81, prewar.

Left: #81 2nd version, long lance tip; Right: #81 officer, only in pre-1914 sets (replaced by bugler).

#81 Note horse variation at right.

#82 L to R: 2nd, 3rd (note pack and bases).

#82 L to R: Pre-4th, post-4th, 1933-38 flag.

#83 Officer .

#88 1st version.

#89 Early version.

#83 Trooper green tunic .

#90

#91 Left: 1st version at slope; right: 2nd version on guard.

	G	VG	EXC

90. The Coldstream Guards
standing, kneeling,
lying firing, with 2 Officers,
drummer, Bugler, 27 pcs.

(24 later) Prewar	200.00	325.00	400.00
27 pieces, Postwar	200.00	275.00	350.00
24 piece set (Postwar)	175.00	225.00	300.00
Officer (Postwar)	10.00	14.00	18.00
Troop	8.00	10.50	12.00
Bugler	10.00	15.00	20.00

91. American Blue "Federal
Dress" on guard (fixed arm
officer early, later has
moving arm) "1906" set 400.00 600.00 800.00
"1906" officer 25.00 37.50 50.00
"1906" Troop 22.00 33.00 44.00

92. Spanish Infantry, slope, 8 pcs.,
c1898 on; 1898 version
(round base),
officer added 1914 ....350.00 650.00 900.00
Later version 175.00 280.00 350.00
1898 Troop 35.00 52.50 70.00
Later Troop 12.50 18.75 25.00

#94 1st version.

#94 3rd version, steel helmets.

#92 1st version officer.

#92 1st version at trail.

#92 2nd version at slope.

#96 Left: 1st version; Right: 3rd version white facings (collar & cuffs).

93. Coldstream Guards, Royal
Horse Guards galloping with
lances, full band, colours,
pioneers, 71 pcs. 2000.00 4000.00 7500.00
Trooper on full-stretched
horse, 1939 ....30.00 60.00 80.00
Running at trail 15.00 25.00 38.00

94. 21st Lancers, galloping,
5 pcs., has Trumpeter 300.00 450.00 650.00
Trumpet 40.00 75.00 100.00
Trooper 30.00 65.00 90.00

95. Display Box, Japanese Cavalry
and Infantry, 13 pcs. 800.00 1400.00 1800.00

96. York & Lancaster, infantry,
8 pcs running at trail,
Boer War active service
dress (khaki) 350.00 650.00 850.00
Whisstock box version
(red coat) 200.00 400.00 600.00
Boer War active
service dress officer 45.00 67.50 90.00

	G	VG	EXC

Boer War active
service dress Troop 40.00 60.00 80.00
Whisstock Box officer 21.00 31.50 42.00
Whisstock Box Troop 13.00 19.50 26.00

97. Royal Marine Light
Infantry running at trail,
8 pcs., first version 300.00 650.00 800.00
1910 issue 250.00 450.00 550.00
1930 issue 200.00 375.00 550.00
First version Troop 30.00 55.00 75.00
2nd version Troop 20.00 42.50 60.00
4th version Troop 15.00 25.00 35.00

98. King's Royal Rifle Corps,
running at trail, 8 pcs.,
1899-1940, 1948-52, has
officer, pre-1920s version 150.00 250.00 350.00
Set 1920-40 ....110.00 175.00 250.00
Set 1948-52 ....100.00 160.00 220.00
Troop, pre-1920s 15.00 22.50 30.00
Officer, 1920-40 ....12.50 18.75 25.00

#97 1st version.

#97 3rd version blue facings.

	G	VG	EXC
Troop, 1920-40	10.00	15.00	20.00
Postwar officer	15.00	22.50	30.00
Postwar Troop	10.00	15.00	20.00
99. 13th Hussars, pony trot			
horse, 5 pcs. "1903"	140.00	250.00	350.00
Officer, "1903"			
(on horse belly)	25.00	45.00	65.00
Trooper, "1903"			
(on horse belly)	15.00	35.00	45.00
100. 21st Lancers,			
cantering, 5 pcs.	150.00	275.00	375.00
Trumpeter	30.00	45.50	65.00
Trooper	20.00	35.00	55.00

Left: #97 after 1935; Right: #97 early.

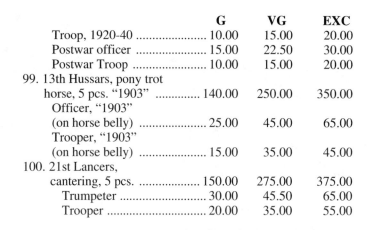

#100 Trooper.

Left: #98 Postwar; Right: #98 Early prewar.

	G	VG	EXC
101. (9406) Band of the			
Life Guards in State			
Dress, 12 pcs., Prewar	250.00	450.00	550.00
Postwar	150.00	300.00	400.00
Prewar instruments	20.00	30.00	40.00
Prewar music director	25.00	35.00	50.00
Postwar music director	20.00	30.00	40.00
Postwar instruments	18.00	25.00	35.00
102. Display Box, Grenadier,			
Scots, Irish, and			
Coldstream Guards, 32 pcs. .... No Price Found			
Irish Guard, "1901"	17.50	26.50	35.00
Irish Guard, "1905"	16.00	24.00	32.00
103. Band of the Royal Horse			
Guards, 12 pcs., moveable			
arm version rarer	1400.00	3000.00	4500.00
104. City Imperial Volunteers,			
at the ready, 10 pcs.,			
including officer, c1900	250.00	475.00	700.00

#99 Early, thick sword.

#101 Prewar drummer, arms apart.

#101 Postwar, hands crossed.

#101 Postwar.

#101 1st version, all white horses, slot arms.

#104 2nd version.

	G	VG	EXC
106. Sixth Dragoon Guards, holding carbines, mounted, with fixed arm officer, 5 pcs., 1901	220.00	400.00	550.00
107. Irish Guards, slope, 8 pcs.	110.00	175.00	250.00
Troop	9.50	14.00	20.00
108. Sixth Inniskilling Dragoons, 5 pcs., fixed arms	175.00	350.00	550.00
Trooper	30.00	60.00	80.00

	G	VG	EXC
Later Issue, 8 pcs.	200.00	410.00	520.00
c1900 officer	30.00	47.50	70.00
c1900 Troop	20.00	35.00	50.00
Later officer	20.00	30.00	40.00
Later Troop	16.00	24.00	32.00
105. Imperial Yeomanry, 5 pcs., early versions	250.00	425.00	600.00

#106 Trooper.

Left: #105 2nd version, 2 tone uniform; Right: #105 4th version, solid color uniform.

#108 3rd version, solid color uniform.

#109 1st version, smooth helmet.

#109 3rd version, wolseley helmet.

	G	VG	EXC
109. Dublin Fusiliers, at the trail, 8 pcs., "1901"	175.00	350.00	550.00
Late 1930s	125.00	250.00	300.00
Troop, "1901"	20.00	30.00	40.00
Troop, late 1930s	11.00	20.00	27.00
110. Devonshire Regiment at the trail, 8 pcs.	170.00	325.00	500.00
Troop	20.00	30.00	40.00

#110 2 variations of 1st version.

#110 2nd and last (note helmets).

#111 Two types turned head.

#111 2nd version.

#111 3rd version.

	G	VG	EXC
111. Grenadier Guards at attention, officer on swayback horse, 7 pcs. "1910"	170.00	285.00	400.00
Late version Prewar	140.00	255.00	350.00
Officer, "1910"	35.00	52.50	70.00
Troop, "1910"	20.00	30.00	40.00
Late officer	15.00	30.00	45.00
Late Troop	10.00	25.00	35.00
112. Seaforth Highlanders, slope, 8 pcs., 1940	85.00	150.00	200.00
Troop	9.00	15.00	20.00
113. East Yorkshire Regiment at attention, 8 pcs.	165.00	300.00	400.00
Troop	15.00	30.00	40.00

#112 Early.

#113 3rd version.

#114 1st & 3rd (note helmets).

#114 2nd version.

#115 Early version long lance tip.

	G	**VG**	**EXC**
114. Cameron Highlanders, at slope, 8 pcs. "1901"	120.00	210.00	300.00
Postwar	100.00	180.00	250.00
Troop, "1901," dated base	17.50	26.25	35.00
Troop, Postwar	11.00	16.50	22.00
115. (9264) Egyptian Cavalry, 4 lancers and officer with sword, 5 pcs., early 1930s	90.00	135.00	200.00
Postwar	80.00	120.00	160.00
Officer, first version	48.00	72.00	96.00
Lancer, first version	27.00	40.50	54.00
Officer, Postwar	15.00	20.00	30.00
Trooper, Postwar	10.00	18.00	24.00
116. Sudanese Infantry, 8 pcs., walking at trail, 1st version	175.00	300.00	400.00
"1901" Troop (round base)	20.00	30.00	45.00
2nd version Troop (rectangular base)	17.50	26.50	35.00
117. Egyptian Infantry, at attention, 8 pcs., Postwar	120.00	175.00	250.00
Officer pointing pistol (1957-59 sets only)	22.50	33.75	45.00
Troop	10.00	15.00	20.00
118. Gordon Highlanders, lying, firing, 8 pcs., late 1920s, Whisstock	125.00	200.00	300.00
Troop, feet together or apart	7.00	10.50	14.00

#119 L to R: 1st version, 2nd version, 3rd version.

	G	**VG**	**EXC**
119. Gloucestershire Regiment, standing firing, 9 pcs., (8 later)	150.00	350.00	500.00
Troop, later 1930s	10.00	15.00	20.00
120. (9123) Coldstream Guards, kneeling firing, with officer, 8 pcs., Prewar	75.00	125.00	150.00
Set, Postwar	60.00	95.00	120.00
Officer, kneeling	10.00	18.00	25.00
Trooper firing	7.00	9.00	12.00
121. Royal West Surrey infantrymen, 8 pcs., standing firing, officer with binoculars, early	95.00	140.00	180.00
Late 1930s set	80.00	120.00	160.00
Later officer	10.50	17.00	23.00
Later Troop	8.00	11.00	16.00

#116 1st version.

#117 Postwar officer.

#118 2 versions.

#121 2nd.

#121 3rd.

	G	**VG**	**EXC**
122. Black Watch, 8 pcs., standing, firing, "1901," 1st version	120.00	200.00	300.00
Late 1930s	100.00	190.00	270.00
Troop "1901"	12.50	18.75	25.00
Troop, later version	10.00	15.00	20.00
123. Bikanir Camel Corps, 3 pcs., men on camels, 1901-40, early camels have wire tails; 1st version	150.00	300.00	400.00
Second version, molded tail	120.00	220.00	320.00
Wire tail (1st version)	40.00	65.00	90.00
Molded tail (2nd version)	30.00	55.00	80.00

#122 1st version, round base.

#122 2nd version (note base).

#123 2nd version, tail molded to leg.

#127 Lancer.

#127 Officer.

#128 Lancer.

#130 General officer on "swayback" horse.

#134 Early lt. blue.

#134 Late '30s dark blue.

#135 In scarce dark blue, 3rd version.

#135 In scarce dark blue.

#136 Prewar.

	G	VG	EXC

124. Irish Guards lying, firing,
   8 pcs., with officer .... 100.00 — 160.00 — 200.00
   Officer .... 12.00 — 17.50 — 23.00
   Troop .... 9.00 — 14.00 — 18.00

125. Royal Horse Artillery,
   smaller version of no. 39,
   13 pcs., 1901, in blue .... 195.00 — 280.00 — 450.00
   1901 Trooper .... 9.00 — 13.50 — 18.00

126. Royal Horse Artillery
   (smaller size),
   13 pcs., in khaki .... 250.00 — 350.00 — 550.00

127. 7th Dragoon Guards galloping
   with lances, 5 pcs. .... 200.00 — 350.00 — 500.00
   Officer .... 23.00 — 37.50 — 50.00
   Trooper .... 20.00 — 33.00 — 45.00

128. 12th Lancers, 5 pcs., trotting
   and cantering, has officer,
   1903-1941; "1903" .... 150.00 — 250.00 — 350.00
   Officer .... 20.00 — 35.00 — 50.00
   Trooper .... 15.00 — 30.00 — 40.00

129. Display Box, First
   (King's) Dragoon Guards,
   12th Lancers, Royal Scots
   Greys, 11th Hussars,
   2nd Life Guards, 70 pcs. .... 1200.00 — 2400.00 — 3500.00
   Dragoon (only available
   in this set) .... 50.00 — 75.00 — 100.00
   2nd Life Guard
   with lance .... 30.00 — 65.00 — 90.00
   12th Lancer .... 22.00 — 40.00 — 55.00

130. Display Set, 118 pcs. .... 3000.00 — 7000.00 — 11,000.00
   Boy Drummer .... 10.00 — 15.00 — 20.00
   Troop .... 9.00 — 13.50 — 18.00
   Flag Bearer .... 12.00 — 18.00 — 24.00

131. Scots Guards, 275 figures,
   includes extremely rare
   Guards Camel Corps, sold
   only in this box. Presentation
   Box, Royal Horse Artillery,
   Mountain Battery, British
   Camel Corps, Scots Greys,
   11th Hussars, 5th Dragoon
   Guards, 17th Lancers, 2nd
   Life Guards, Royal Horse
   Guards, Band of Coldstreams,
   Scots Guards (firing),
   Gordon Highlanders, and
   Pipes, Worcestershire
   Regiment, Bluejackets and
   Whitejackets with 4.7
   naval gun and General
   officer (very rare) .... 5000.00 — 9000.00 — 15,000.00

132. Display Box, Royal Horse
   Artillery, Scots Greys,
   11th Hussars, 2nd Life Guards,
   Horse Guards, 7th Dragoon
   Guards, Band of the Line,
   Seaforths with pipes, Welsh
   Fusiliers, Coldstreams firing,
   East Kents, Mule Battery,
   4.7 Naval Gun, General
   officer, 167 pcs. .... No Price Found

*#133 L to R:
1st officer,
2nd at trail,
3rd at slope.*

*#133 Left: 2nd;
Right: 3rd at trail.*

	G	VG	EXC

133. Russian Infantry (Tsarist),
   officer, 8 pcs., "1904"
   version, at slope .... 140.00 — 270.00 — 360.00
   At trail .... 110.00 — 165.00 — 220.00
   Early officer .... 25.00 — 37.50 — 50.00
   Early Troop .... 20.00 — 30.00 — 40.00

134. Japanese Infantry,
   charging, 8 pcs., "1904" ...... 300.00 — 475.00 — 600.00
   1930s set .... 200.00 — 375.00 — 500.00
   Troop, "1904" .... 30.00 — 45.00 — 60.00
   Troop, 1930s .... 25.00 — 35.00 — 50.00

135. Japanese Cavalry, 5 pcs.,
   1st version with short
   carbine, 2nd version
   with long carbine;
   1st version, 1905 .... 400.00 — 600.00 — 800.00
   Long carbines .... 250.00 — 425.00 — 600.00
   Officer, 1st version .... 40.00 — 82.50 — 110.00
   Short carbine .... 30.00 — 75.00 — 100.00
   Officer, 2nd version .... 35.00 — 60.00 — 80.00
   Long carbine .... 30.00 — 52.50 — 70.00

136. (9273) Russian Cavalry,
   Cossacks, 5 pcs., 1935 issue — 115.00 — 170.00 — 225.00
   Postwar .... 80.00 — 135.00 — 180.00
   Officer, Postwar .... 15.00 — 25.00 — 35.00
   Trooper, Postwar .... 13.00 — 20.00 — 28.00

137. Royal Army Medical
   Service, doctors, nurses,
   wounded, stretcher
   bearers, 24 pcs. .... 225.00 — 450.00 — 650.00
   Doctor .... 11.00 — 18.50 — 25.00
   Stretcher Bearer .... 10.00 — 15.00 — 20.00
   Stretcher .... 3.00 — 5.00 — 6.00
   Wounded .... 7.00 — 10.50 — 14.00
   Nurse (1st version,
   Victorian dress) .... 7.50 — 11.25 — 15.00

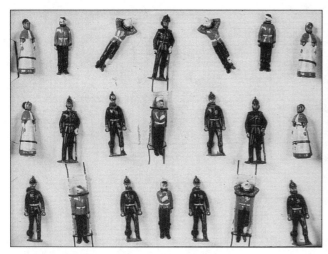

#137 Set - early.

#137 2nd version.

#137 1st version nurse.

#137 Wounded close up.

#137 Close up.

#138 1st & 2nd versions. Note small projection on 1st helmet.

	G	**VG**	**EXC**
138. (9266) French Cuirassiers with			
officer, 5 pcs., Prewar 80.00	115.00	150.00
Postwar 70.00	105.00	140.00
Postwar (1960) 4 pcs. 50.00	80.00	115.00
Officer, Postwar 14.00	21.00	28.00
Trooper, Postwar 12.50	18.75	25.00
139. French Chasseurs a Cheval,			
5 pcs. 225.00	450.00	550.00
Trooper 40.00	60.00	80.00
140. French Dragoons, 5 pcs. 225.00	450.00	550.00
Officer 45.00	67.50	100.00
Trooper 40.00	60.00	80.00

#139

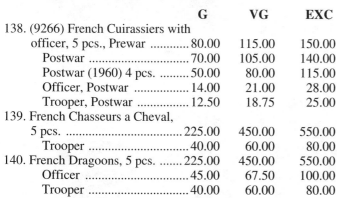

#140

#140 1st version, rifle plugged in back.

#140 2nd version.

#141 L to R:
1st lt. blue,
2nd dk. blue.

#142 Postwar.

#143 Prewar.

	G	VG	EXC
141. French infantry of the Line,			
slope, 8 pcs., 1st version	150.00	300.00	400.00
Late 1930s	120.00	215.00	270.00
Troop, first version	18.00	27.00	36.00
Troop, late version	12.00	18.00	25.00
142. (9166) Zouaves, charging,			
8 pcs., Prewar	80.00	100.00	130.00
1945-59 set, 7 pcs.,			
with mtd. officer	70.00	95.00	110.00
Troop	5.00	7.50	10.00
Officer, mtd.	10.00	15.00	20.00
143. Matelots, running at the			
trail, 8 pcs., Prewar	350.00	675.00	900.00
Postwar	300.00	550.00	750.00
Troop, Postwar	30.00	65.00	85.00
144. Royal Field Artillery,			
9 pcs., with gun and limber,			

	G	VG	EXC
officer with sword,			
6 horses, 3 drivers,			
limber with 2 seated,			
cannon with 2 seated	600.00	1000.00	1400.00
Officer, "1903"	30.00	55.00	80.00
145. The Royal Army			
Medical Corps., horsedrawn			
ambulance, 7 pcs., one			
riding "driver" on horse,			
2 seated men	150.00	300.00	400.00
145A. RAMC			
Ambulance Wagon,			
khaki uniforms	200.00	450.00	550.00
146. Army Service Corps			
Wagon, 5 pcs., 2-horse			
team and crew, early issue ...	120.00	250.00	350.00
Postwar	100.00	200.00	300.00

#144 1932-41 version. Value in Good $400.00, Excellent $850.00.

#145 2nd version prewar.

#145A Prewar late.

#146 2nd version.

#146A

	G	VG	EXC
146A. Army Service Corps Wagon, as above, but uniforms in khaki (available Prewar only)	225.00	350.00	500.00
147. (9190) Zulus of Africa, 8 pcs.	80.00	100.00	140.00
Each	7.50	11.25	15.00

#147 Postwar.

#148

148. Royal Lancaster Regiment, 13 pcs., 3 running at slope arms, 4 running at trail, running Bugler, running Flagbearer, 2 Gunners at attention with small cannon, Mounted Officer on prancing horse, with Beiser's patented display board, red jackets 1200.00   2500.00   3500.00

	G	VG	EXC
149. American Soldiers, 13 pcs., same variety of pcs. as 148, with Beiser's patented display board	600.00	1200.00	1600.00
150. (9189) North American Indians, on foot, with chiefs, 8 pcs., 7 pcs. later	55.00	85.00	120.00
Per figure	4.50	6.50	9.00

#150 With 2 versions of "Rifle at Ready."

	G	VG	EXC
151. Royal Naval Volunteer Reserve, shoulder arms fixed arm, bearded Petty officer, 1907-41, 8 pcs.	95.00	170.00	250.00
Petty officer	11.00	18.50	25.00
Single figure	8.50	13.50	18.00
152. (9289) North American Indians on horses, with rifles and tomahawks, 5 pcs., (4 pcs. later)	65.00	95.00	120.00
Per figure	9.00	14.50	20.00

#151

#152

#153

#159 1st trooper
(2 tone uniform).

#159 Last
trooper.

	G	VG	EXC
153. Prussian Hussars,			
5 pcs., "1903" 220.00	500.00	700.00
1930 ....170.00	400.00	550.00
Officer, "1903" 40.00	70.00	90.00
Trooper, "1903" 35.00	52.50	70.00
Officer, 1930 ....25.00	55.00	75.00
Trooper, 1930 ....20.00	40.00	60.00
154. Prussian Infantry,			
marching, 8 pcs. 150.00	250.00	350.00
Troop 20.00	30.00	40.00

#154 2nd and
3rd versions.

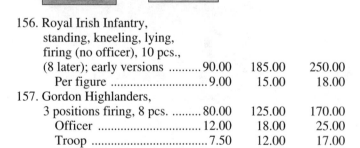

#159 Officer.

	G	VG	EXC
156. Royal Irish Infantry,			
standing, kneeling, lying,			
firing (no officer), 10 pcs.,			
(8 later); early versions 90.00	185.00	250.00
Per figure 9.00	15.00	18.00
157. Gordon Highlanders,			
3 positions firing, 8 pcs. 80.00	125.00	170.00
Officer 12.00	18.00	25.00
Troop 7.50	12.00	17.00

#157

	G	VG	EXC
159. Yeoman, Territorial Army,			
5 pcs., mounted with officer 120.00	280.00	350.00
Officer 20.00	42.00	60.00
Per figure 15.00	30.00	40.00
160. Our Territorial Infantry at			
trail, 8 pcs., 1915 issue 110.00	205.00	270.00
Last version, c1930 ....95.00	190.00	250.00
Per figure, early 1930s 11.00	18.00	25.00
161. Boy Scouts, 9 pcs., (8 from			
1939), scouts, scoutmaster ... 120.00	220.00	300.00
162. Boy Scout			
Encampment, 23 pcs. 325.00	600.00	850.00
Standing with axe 13.00	22.50	30.00
Saluter 14.00	21.00	28.00
Empty-handed 13.00	19.50	26.00
Fallen Tree 8.00	12.00	16.00
163. Boy Scout			
Signalers, 5 pcs. 140.00	280.00	400.00
Per figure 20.00	40.00	60.00
164. (9291) Arabs on Horses,			
5 pcs. 80.00	105.00	130.00
Per figure 11.50	16.50	24.00

#160 Pre-1917. Courtesy Phillips.

#160 1917-41.

#161-62 Prewar, blue shorts.

#161-62 Postwar, matching shorts.

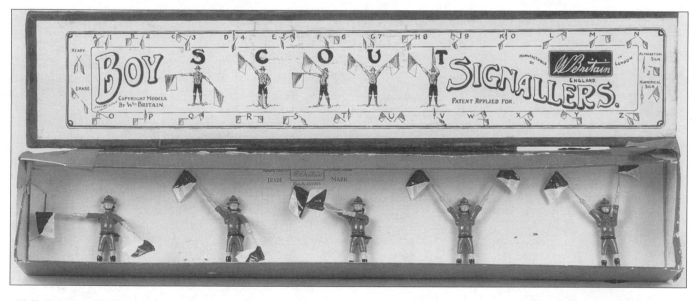

#163 Courtesy Phillips.

#164

#165 Lancer & officer.

#169

#169 Postwar.

Left: #170 Green uniform.

#170 2nd version.

	G	VG	EXC
165. Italian Cavalry,			
5 pcs., with officer 175.00	375.00	500.00
Officer 35.00	72.50	100.00
Trooper 30.00	55.00	80.00
166. Italian Infantry, slope, 8 pcs. 125.00	205.00	300.00
Troop 14.00	21.00	28.00
167. Turkish Infantry, 8 pcs. 135.00	275.00	350.00
Troop 13.00	22.00	35.00
169. (9163) The Bersaglieri,			
marching, slung rifles,			
8 pcs., Prewar 90.00	145.00	190.00
Postwar, with officer 80.00	135.00	180.00
Officer 10.00	15.00	25.00
Troop 8.00	12.00	18.00

	G	VG	EXC
170. Greek Cavalry, 5 pcs.,			
officer with sword 300.00	575.00	800.00
171. Greek Infantry, 8 pcs.,			
running at trail,			
with officer 200.00	400.00	550.00
Officer 28.00	47.50	70.00
Troop 22.00	35.00	50.00

#166 2nd version.

#167 L to R: 1st version, 2nd version.

#171 late 1930s.

#171

	G	**VG**	**EXC**

172. Bulgarians, 8 pcs., marching
at trail, officer with sword ... 220.00 415.00 620.00
    Officer 30.00 60.00 80.00
    Troop 22.00 35.00 50.00
173. Serbian Infantry charging,
8 pcs., no officer 140.00 350.00 480.00
    Troop 20.00 35.00 45.00

#172 1st version at slope.

#173

174. Montenegrin Infantry,
8 pcs., marching at slope
or walking at trail,
officer with sword 200.00 400.00 550.00
    Officer 28.00 47.50 70.00
    Troop 22.00 35.00 50.00
175. Austro-Hungarian
Lancers, 5 pcs. 300.00 600.00 800.00

#174

#174

#175

#176

*#177 3rd
version.*

	G	**VG**	**EXC**

176. Austro-Hungarian Dragoons,
5 pcs., "1902" version 280.00 525.00 660.00
    Trooper 40.00 70.00 95.00
177. Austro-Hungarian Infantry
of the Line, 8 pcs. 190.00 315.00 420.00
    Troop 20.00 33.00 44.00
178. Austro-Hungarian
Foot Guards, 8 pcs. 110.00 200.00 300.00
    Troop 16.00 30.00 40.00
179. (9288) Cowboys, 5 pcs.,
4 mounted, 1 on foot,
2 with lassos, 2 with rifles 60.00 90.00 120.00
    Mounted 8.00 12.00 15.00
    Foot 5.00 8.00 9.00
180. Boy Scout Display, 22 pcs.,
Scoutmaster, Scouts,
Signalers, Trek Carts,
Trees, Ladder 300.00 450.00 650.00

*#178 1st
& 3rd version.*

#179 & #184.

#181 Prewar, blue shorts.

#181 Postwar, khaki shorts.

#183 & #184.

	G	VG	EXC
184. Cowboys mounted and on foot, 15 pcs.	170.00	300.00	400.00
185. Wild West Display, Cowboys and North American Indians, 30 pcs.	350.00	800.00	1200.00
186. Mexican Rurales, slung rifles, officer, 1926-40, 8 pcs., early Prewar	250.00	450.00	650.00
1930s, late	180.00	350.00	450.00
Officer	30.00	45.00	60.00
Troop	27.50	41.25	55.00
187. Arabs on foot, 8 pcs.	65.00	85.00	110.00
Per figure	7.00	10.00	12.00

	G	VG	EXC
181. Boy Scouts, 45 pcs., including Scoutmaster, 6 kneeling and standing scouts with hatchets, 8 hiking, 2 signaling, 2 pulling carts, 3 standing scouts, trees, gate, hurdles, cart	600.00	800.00	1000.00
Per Scout figure	13.00	19.50	26.00
Cart, Scout pulling	37.50	56.25	75.00
182. (9114) 11th Hussars (Prince Albert's Own), dismounted with horses, 8 pcs., officer	100.00	150.00	200.00
Officer	16.00	24.00	32.00
Trooper	12.00	18.00	24.00
183. (9188) Cowboys on foot, 8 pcs., (7 later), with rifles, pistols, lassos, early version, Prewar	70.00	100.00	120.00
Postwar	60.00	85.00	105.00
Each	5.00	8.00	10.00

#186 1st version.   *#187*

	G	VG	EXC
188. Zulu Kraals with Warriors, Palm Trees	800.00	1400.00	2000.00
189. Belgian Infantry, "on guard," 8 pcs.	150.00	250.00	350.00
Per figure	10.00	16.00	21.00
190. Belgian Cavalry, with officer, 5 pcs., Prewar	110.00	215.00	280.00
Postwar	80.00	120.00	180.00
Officer, Prewar	25.00	45.00	65.00
Trooper, Prewar	18.00	30.00	45.00
Officer, Postwar	18.00	30.00	40.00
Trooper, Postwar	14.00	22.00	30.00
191. Turcos, 8 pcs.	100.00	200.00	250.00
Troop, lt. blue uniform	11.00	17.00	25.00
192. French Infantry of the Line, 8 pcs., shrapnel-proof helmets	100.00	190.00	265.00
Per figure	10.00	17.00	22.00
193. Arabs on the Desert, on Camels, 6 pcs.	210.00	350.00	450.00
Each	30.00	50.00	65.00

#182

#188 Zulu Kraal composition.

#188 Metal.

#188 2nd version with metal huts. Tied into display box with three-sided scene.

#189

#190 Trooper.

#190 Officer.

#191

#192 Late prewar, in khaki.

#193

#194 Prewar early.

#194 Late 1930s.

#195 Early prewar, sand colored helmet.

#197

#196 L to R: Prewar, red vest; Postwar, black vest.

#198

	G	VG	EXC
194. Machine Gun Section,			
8 pcs., lying 80.00	100.00	130.00
Black boots late Prewar 6.00	7.50	11.00
Brown boots early Prewar 7.00	9.00	13.00
195. Infantry of the Line at trail,			
8 pcs., with officer, Prewar 95.00	120.00	160.00
Postwar 70.00	100.00	130.00
196. (9170) Greek Evzones			
at slope, no officer, 8 pcs.			
(7 pcs. 1954-59, 6 pcs.			
1960-66); Prewar, red vest ...120.00	165.00	220.00
Postwar, 8 pcs.,			
black vest 85.00	110.00	140.00
Prewar, per figure 10.00	14.00	20.00
Postwar, per figure 8.00	12.00	17.00
197. Gurkha Rifles, marching			
at trail, 1916-30s, 1916-30s,			
1916-30s, Prewar 105.00	165.00	220.00
Postwar 90.00	125.00	175.00
Postwar, Single 9.00	13.00	16.00
198. British Machine Gunners,			
6 pcs., sitting, peak cap 90.00	150.00	200.00
Each, with gun 10.00	14.00	20.00
199. Motor Cycle Machine Gun			
Corps, 3 pcs., side car,			
machine gun,			
detachable gunner 140.00	250.00	350.00
Each 40.00	75.00	105.00
200. Despatch Riders, 1917-39,			
4 pcs., 1st version,			
fixed wheels 110.00	165.00	225.00
Per piece 20.00	30.00	45.00

#201

#201 Postwar.　　　　*#202*

	G	VG	EXC
201. Officers of the General			
Staff, mounted, 4 pcs. 100.00	160.00	210.00
Field Marshall,			
binoculars 22.00	35.00	50.00
General 18.00	30.00	40.00
202. Togoland Warriors, 8 pcs. 65.00	105.00	140.00
Each 7.00	11.00	15.00

#199

#203 2nd version.

#199

#200 1st version.

#204. Courtesy Doyle Galleries.

	G	VG	EXC
203. Pontoon Section Royal Engineers, 4 horses, 2 riders, wagon, pontoon, planking, red tunic, Review Dress	300.00	475.00	700.00
204. Pontoon Section Royal Engineers (as above), Khaki Service Dress	400.00	700.00	950.00
205. Coldstream Guards, present arms, 8 pcs.	105.00	165.00	230.00
206. Warwickshire Infantry, present arms, (8 later)	160.00	300.00	400.00
Per figure	12.00	18.50	24.00
207. Officers and Petty Officers of the Royal Navy, 8 pcs., 2 Midshipmen, 2 Admirals, 4 Petty Officers	120.00	175.00	225.00
Petty officer	9.00	14.00	20.00
Midshipman	9.00	14.00	20.00

#212   *#213*   *#214 1st version with bayonet.*

#205

#206

#215

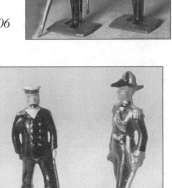

#207 L to R: 2 midshipmen (brown gloves until 1935, then white), petty officer, admiral.

208. (9389) North American Indians, 13 pcs., mounted and on foot, Chieftain

	G	VG	EXC
(11 pcs. later)	100.00	140.00	200.00
Per foot figure	5.00	7.00	9.00
Mounted figure	8.00	10.00	14.00

209. (9388) Cowboys, mounted and on foot, 13 pcs., (12 later) with lassos, rifles, pistols .... No Price Found

210. North American Indians, 15 pc., mounted on foot, trees 130.00   180.00   230.00

211. 18" Heavy Howitzer No. 2, tractor wheels, 3 shell noses, 10 horse team 600.00   1000.00   1500.00

	G	VG	EXC
212. (9145) Royal Scots, marching at slope, 8 figures, Prewar, 4 men plus Piper 1948-66;			
Prewar	100.00	150.00	220.00
Postwar	75.00	110.00	140.00
Prewar, per figure	13.00	20.00	25.00
Postwar, per figure	12.00	20.00	25.00
Piper	11.00	16.50	22.00
213. Highland Light Infantry, slope, 8 pcs.	200.00	400.00	550.00
Per figure	16.00	28.00	38.00
214. Royal Canadian Mounted Police in Winter Dress, foot, c1912-41, 8 pcs.	150.00	300.00	450.00
Each	15.00	30.00	40.00
215. French Infantry firing, 14 pcs.	120.00	220.00	300.00
Machine gunner	12.00	19.00	25.00
Troop	8.00	13.50	19.00
216. Argentine Infantry, at slope, no officer, 8 pcs. 1912-40, 1946-47, 6 pcs., 1948-49; Prewar	140.00	270.00	360.00
Postwar	100.00	160.00	210.00
Prewar Troop	18.00	27.00	36.00
Postwar Troop	17.50	26.25	35.00
217. Argentine Cavalry, 5 pcs., with officer, 1912-40, 1946-59 (4 pcs. from 1948); Prewar	150.00	225.00	300.00
Officer, early 1930s	28.00	50.00	70.00
Trooper	22.00	40.00	60.00

#216
Prewar.

#217 Blue/grey uniform.

#218

#219

#220 Dark blue uniform.

#221

#222

#225

#227 Prewar.

#228 Prewar & postwar.

#229

#230

#238

#240

#241

#242

#247

#254 White jacket in
same position.

	G	VG	EXC
218. Spanish Cavalry, 5 pcs.	300.00	600.00	800.00
Prewar officer	40.00	95.00	130.00
Prewar Trooper	35.00	80.00	105.00
219. Argentine Military School Cadets at slope, 8 pcs., no officer, 1912-40	200.00	300.00	400.00
Troop	20.00	30.00	40.00
220. Uruguayan Cavalry, 5 pcs., with officer 1912-40, 4 pcs. 1953-59; 4 pc. set	110.00	165.00	260.00
Officer, Prewar	20.00	35.00	50.00
Trooper, Prewar	18.00	30.00	40.00
221. Uruguayan Military School Cadets, at slope, no officer, 8 pcs., Prewar	230.00	345.00	460.00
Postwar version	140.00	230.00	310.00
First version Cadet	24.00	36.00	48.00
Later version Cadet	15.00	22.50	30.00
222. Uruguayan Infantry, no officer, 8 pcs.	150.00	250.00	350.00
Per figure	17.00	25.50	34.00
223. Arabs, mounted and dismounted, 13 pcs.	175.00	350.00	450.00
224. (9491) Arabs of the Desert, 2 on camels, 4 marching at slope, 2 on horses, 1 large palm tree, 2 smaller palm tree clusters, 11 pcs.	200.00	300.00	400.00
Camel and rider	30.00	45.00	65.00
Large palm	9.00	12.50	18.00
Marching	8.00	12.00	16.00
Mounted on horse	10.00	14.00	18.00
225. (9162) King's African Rifles, marching at slope, no officer, c1925-1959, 1966, 8 pcs. Prewar	100.00	130.00	165.00
Postwar, 8 pcs.	85.00	110.00	145.00
7 pc. set, Postwar	60.00	90.00	120.00
Troop	8.00	12.50	16.00
226. West Point Cadets, Winter Dress, 8 pcs.	65.00	102.50	130.00
Cadets	8.50	11.00	14.00

	G	VG	EXC
227. U.S. Infantry at slope, officer	60.00	90.00	120.00
Officer	8.00	12.00	16.00
Troop	6.50	9.75	13.00
228. (9182) U.S. Marines at slope, officer, 8 pcs., Prewar, blue caps, no officer	80.00	135.00	175.00
1940-41 version, white-topped cap	90.00	135.00	180.00
Postwar, with officer	65.00	97.50	130.00
Troop, blue cap	8.00	12.00	16.00
Troop, white-topped cap	9.00	13.50	18.00
229. U.S. Cavalry, 5 pcs., no officer	50.00	75.00	100.00
Troop	9.00	13.50	18.00
230. U.S. Sailors, Bluejackets, 8 pcs.	75.00	125.00	165.00
Each	7.00	11.50	17.50
231. Display Box, U.S. Infantry, West Point Cadets, 16 pcs.	No Price Found		
232. (9381) Display Box, U.S. Infantry, Marines and West Point Cadets, 25 pcs.	150.00	275.00	350.00
233. Display Box, U.S. Infantry, Cavalry, Marines and West Point Cadets, 29 pcs.	No Price Found		

NOTE: Few prices turn up between 238 and 500. Following World War I, there was a general turning away from war toys around the world. Because of this, Britains struggled through the 1920s as it tried to find its market. The company tried all sorts of combinations of troops in sets (most of which were short-lived), and even cut the size of some sets to seven pieces in an effort to lower prices and thus spur buying. Eventually, the firm went into the Farm, Zoo and Civilian figures in a major way, starting with the 500 series. It was the war clouds of the 1930s that triggered the renewal of interest in soldiers. (As it did in the United States with dimestore soldiers).

	G	VG	EXC
238. U.S. Girl Scouts, 8 pcs.	No Price Found		
Each	36.00	54.00	72.00
240. RAF, 8 pcs.	115.00	162.50	230.00
Prewar officer	13.00	19.50	26.00
Each	8.00	12.00	16.00

#223 Complete.

	G	**VG**	**EXC**
241. Chinese Infantry, 8 pcs.	225.00	285.00	375.00
Troop	25.00	35.00	45.00
242. U.S. Infantry, 8 pcs., slope arms, Mounted Officer	250.00	550.00	800.00
244. North American Indians, 7 pcs., mounted, foot		No Price Found	
245. Cowboys, 7 pcs., mounted, foot		No Price Found	
246. Royal Scots Greys and Scots Guards, 7 pcs.	250.00	550.00	800.00
247. Arabs, mounted and dismounted, 7 pcs.		No Price Found	
248. 1st Life guards, and Middlesex Regiment, 7 pcs.		No Price Found	
249. British Infantry and Cavalry, service dress, 7 pcs.	200.00	450.00	650.00
250. 2nd Dragoon Guards and Grenadier Guards, 7 pcs.		No Price Found	
251. 21st Lancers, Royal Fusiliers, 7 pcs.		No Price Found	
252. 3rd Madras Cavalry, 3 pcs., 1st Madras Native Infantry, 4 pcs., c1927		No Price Found	
253. Welsh Guards with Mounted officer, 8 pcs.	300.00	650.00	1000.00
254. Bluejackets and Whitejackets with Petty officer, support arms, 9 pcs., c1928-41		No Price Found	
255. Green Howards marching, officer, colours, 9 pcs.		No Price Found	
Troop	15.00	22.50	30.00
256. Cowboys mounted and foot, 17 pcs.		No Price Found	
257. North American Indians mtd. and foot, 17 pcs.		No Price Found	
258. WWI British Infantry at trail, 8 pcs., gas masks	50.00	75.00	100.00
Each	5.50	8.25	11.00
259. West Point Cadets, 16 pcs.		No Price Found	
260. U.S. Infantry Squad, 16 pcs.		No Price Found	
261. U.S. Marines, 16 pcs.		No Price Found	
262. U.S. Cavalry, 10 pcs.		No Price Found	

	G	**VG**	**EXC**
263. West Point Cadets, 24 pcs.		No Price Found	
264. Squad of U.S. Infantry, 24 pcs.		No Price Found	
265. U.S. Marines, 24 pcs.		No Price Found	
266. U.S. Cavalry, 15 pcs.		No Price Found	
267. (9380) U.S. Infantry and Cavalry, various pcs.	200.00	450.00	800.00
268. U.S. Sailors, 16 pcs.		No Price Found	

#266

#268 & #269

#267 Postwar, WWII helmets.

	G	**VG**	**EXC**
269. U.S. Sailors, 24 pcs.	250.00	750.00	1100.00
270. 11th Hussars, mounted and dismounted, at halt, 12 pcs.		No Price Found	
271. Skinner's Horse, 5 pcs., 1928 to about 1934	125.00	250.00	300.00
Each	21.00	31.50	42.00
272. (9390) North American Indians and Cowboys, mounted and on foot, 13 pcs.	150.00	300.00	450.00
273. North American Indians, Cowboys, mounted, foot, 15 pcs.		No Price Found	
274. North American Indians, 7 pcs., mounted, foot	90.00	135.00	200.00
275. Cowboys, mounted, foot, 7 pcs.		No Price Found	
276. U.S.A. Cavalry in Action, 5 pcs.	250.00	500.00	800.00
Each	22.50	33.75	45.00

#255

#258

	G	VG	EXC

277. North American Indians,
   mounted, foot .... No Price Found
278. Cowboys mounted, foot .... No Price Found
279. Display Box,
   U.S. Cavalry and Infantry .... No Price Found
280. U.S. Infantry
   and Cavalry, 17 pcs. .... No Price Found
281. North American Indians,
   8 pcs., mounted,
   foot, with Bell Tent .... No Price Found
282. Cowboys, 8 pcs.,
   mounted, foot, with tent .... No Price Found
283. U.S. Cavalry and Infantry
   with Bell Tent, 8 pcs. .... No Price Found
284. U.S. Cavalry
   and Infantry, 21 pcs. .... No Price Found
285. U.S. Cavalry
   and Infantry, 18 pcs. .... No Price Found
286. U.S. Cavalry, 10 pcs.,
   standing and action .... No Price Found
287. U.S. Cavalry
   and Infantry, 7 pcs. .... No Price Found
288. U.S. Marines
   and Sailors, 16 pcs. .... No Price Found
289. Girl and Boy
   Scouts, 13 pcs., 8 pcs. .... No Price Found
290. U.S. Cavalry
   and Infantry, 13 pcs. .... No Price Found
291. U.S. Cavalry
   and Infantry, 26 pcs. .... No Price Found
292. Arabs on horse and foot .... No Price Found
293. Girl and Boy
   Scouts, 16 pcs. .... No Price Found
294. U.S. Infantry
   and Marines, 16 pcs. .... No Price Found
295. U.S. Infantry and Cavalry .... No Price Found
296. Arabs on horse and foot .... No Price Found
297. North American Indians,
   mounted, foot .... No Price Found
298. Cowboys, mounted, foot .... No Price Found
299. (9178) West Point Cadets,
   summer dress, slope arms,
   8 pcs. 65.00   92.50   150.00
      Each 9.00   13.00   16.00
300. Arabs, mounted
   and dismounted, 17 pcs. .... No Price Found
301. Arabs, mounted and
   dismounted, with
   Bell Tent, 8 pcs. .... No Price Found
302. Scots Greys and Scots
   Guards with Bell Tent, 8 pcs. .... No Price Found
303. Life Guards and
   Middlesex Regiment
   with Bell Tent, 8 pcs. .... No Price Found
304. Territorials, mounted,
   foot, Bell Tent, 8 pcs. 200.00   600.00   800.00
305. North American Indians
   10 pcs. mounted, foot .... No Price Found
306. Cowboys, 10 pcs.,
   mounted, foot .... No Price Found
307. Arabs, mounted, foot, 10 pcs. .... No Price Found
308. U.S. Cavalry
   and Infantry, 10 pcs. .... No Price Found

#271

#272

#272

#272

#276

#299
Postwar.

#312 Postwar.

#314

#313 From left: first two - 1st version; the rest in helmets - 2nd version.

#315

#317

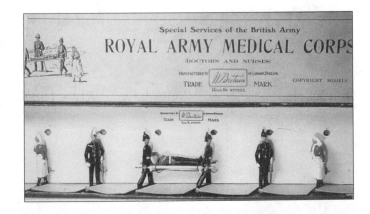

#318

	G	VG	EXC
309. Scots Greys and Scots Guards, 10 pcs. .... No Price Found			
310. Life Guards and Middlesex Regiment, 10 pcs.	200.00	500.00	700.00
311. Territorials, 10 pcs., mounted and foot .... No Price Found			
312. (9121) Grenadier Guards, winter overcoats, slope arms, officer, 8 pcs.	85.00	120.00	150.00
Officer	10.00	15.00	20.00
Troop	7.00	12.00	14.00
313. Team of Gunners, Royal Artillery 8 pcs. 1st	100.00	175.00	250.00
2nd	150.00	250.00	400.00
Troop with Ramrod	15.00	25.00	35.00
314. Coldstream Guards at Ease, officer, 8 pcs.	95.00	150.00	230.00
Officer	12.00	20.00	28.00
Troop	8.00	16.00	20.00
315. 10th Royal Hussars at halt, 5 pcs.	240.00	360.00	500.00
Each	30.00	50.00	75.00
316. Royal Horse Artillery, 9 pcs., review order, horses at halt	1000.00	1700.00	2500.00

	G	VG	EXC
317. Royal Field Artillery, review dress, 9 pcs., horses at halt	1000.00	1700.00	2500.00
318. Gun of Royal Artillery (model 1201) with limber and horse team, 17 pcs.	1200.00	1900.00	2700.00
319. Police, 7 pcs., mounted, foot, traffic	150.00	350.00	500.00
320. Royal Army Medical Corps, 8 pcs.	110.00	250.00	400.00

#320 2nd version, 1935-41.

#321 (first three); #322, scarce thin drums.

#329 Prewar grenadier guard, postwar scots guard.

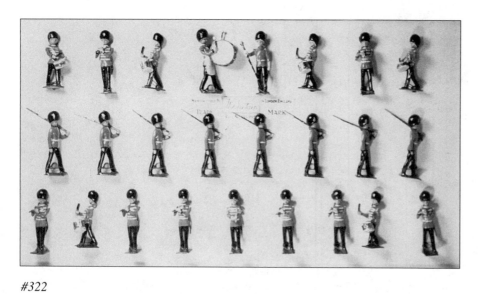

#322

#333

#399

	G	VG	EXC
321. Drum and Fife Band of the Line, 17 pcs.	650.00	1150.00	1600.00
322. Drum and Fife Band of Coldstream Guards with rank and file, 25 pcs.	700.00	1200.00	1800.00
Per figure	20.00	30.00	40.00
323. U.S. Cavalry, Artillery, Marines, Sailors (in action), Infantry of the Line, West Point Cadets, 73 pcs.		No Price Found	
324. U.S. Marines, Sailors, Infantry of the line, West Point Cadets, 81 pcs.	1500.00	3000.00	4000.00

	G	VG	EXC
325. Cowboys, mounted, 5 pcs.		No Price Found	
326. Indians Mounted, 5 pcs.		No Price Found	
327. Cowboys Mounted, 7 pcs.		No Price Found	
328. Indians Mounted, 7 pcs.		No Price Found	
329. (9426) Sentry Box with Sentry, 2 pcs.	14.00	20.00	28.00
Sentry Box	7.00	10.50	14.00
Sentry	6.00	8.50	12.00
330. U.S. Aviation, 8 pcs., Officers, in short coats		No Price Found	
Officer	22.50	33.75	45.00
331. U.S. Aviation, Officers in overcoats, 8 pcs.	250.00	550.00	800.00

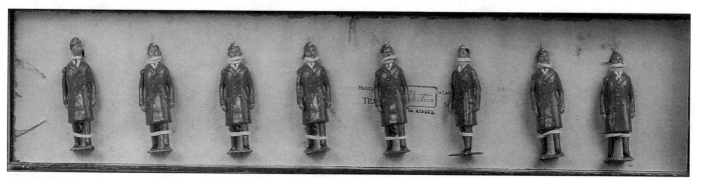

#331 In box.

332. U.S. Aviation, Aviators in
flying kit, short coats, 8 pcs. 250.00 550.00 800.00
    Per figure 22.50 33.75 45.00
333. U.S. Aviation, Aviators
in flying kit, 8 pcs. 250.00 550.00 800.00
334. U.S. Aviation, Privates
in peak cap, 8 pcs. 350.00 650.00 1000.00

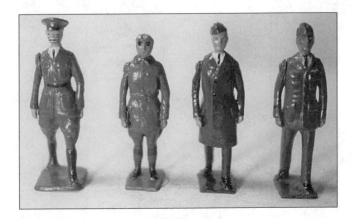

L to R: #334, #332, #331, #330.

335. U.S.A. Airforce, 8 review
order, 8 at slope, 16 pcs. .... No Price Found
336. U.S.A. Airforce, 8 Officers
in long coat, and
8 Officers in short coat .... No Price Found
337. U.S.A. Airforce, 8 Privates
peaked cap, 8 Officers .... No Price Found
338. British Infantry, Service
Dress, Gas Masks, 16 pcs. ...250.00 550.00 800.00
339. U.S. Cavalry Squad, 6 pcs. .... No Price Found
340. U.S. Cavalry, service dress .... No Price Found
341. British Army Machine Gun
Section lying, 16 pcs. .... No Price Found
342. Argentine Cavalry and Infantry .... No Price Found
343. Argentine Cavalry
and Infantry, 26 pcs. .... No Price Found
344. Life Guards
and Middlesex Regiment .... No Price Found
345. Scots Greys and Scots Guards .... No Price Found
346. U.S. Cavalry with Tent, 6 pcs. .... No Price Found
347. U.S. Infantry with Tent, 10 pcs. .... No Price Found
348. West Point Cadets
with Tent, 10 pcs. .... No Price Found
349. U.S. Marines with Tent, 10 pcs. .... No Price Found
350. North American Indians
with Bell Tent, 10 pcs. .... No Price Found
351. U.S.A. Airforce, 2 Aviators
in flying kit, 2 pilots,
2 privates, 2 Officers in
overcoat, 1 officer in
short coat .... No Price Found
352. U.S.A. Infantry, 1 marching
peak cap, 10 Privates
slouch hat, khaki,
marching at slope .... No Price Found
353. West Point Cadets,
winter dress, 11 pcs. .... No Price Found

354. West Point Cadets,
winter dress, 12 pcs. .... No Price Found
355. Life Guards,
Sussex Regiment, 7 pcs. .... No Price Found
356. Yeomanry
U.S.A. Infantry, 7 pcs. .... No Price Found
357. North American
Indians, 10 pcs. .... No Price Found
358. Cowboys, 10 pcs. 120.00 175.00 250.00
359. U.S. Machine Gunners,
lying firing, 8 pcs. .... No Price Found
360. Togoland Warriors,
in 1931 catalog only .... No Price Found
361. Infantry, Cuirassiers,
1914, 12 pcs. .... No Price Found
362.-384. UNKNOWN .... —
385. Types of the USA Forces,
16 pcs., West Point Cadets
in summer dress at slope .... No Price Found
386. Royal Canadian Mounted
Police in Winter Dress
(same as 214), 1931, 8 pcs. ...... No Price Found
387. Togoland Warriors, 8 pcs. .... No Price Found
388. Types of the French Army .... No Price Found
389. Scots Guards, 10 pcs. .... No Price Found
390. Middlesex Regiment, 10 pcs. .... No Price Found
391. 4th Bombay
Grenadiers, 10 pcs. .... No Price Found
392. Black Watch, 10 pcs. .... No Price Found
393. Royal Scots Greys, 6 pcs. .... No Price Found
394. Arabs, 6 pcs. .... No Price Found
395. 16th Light Cavalry
(Indian Army), 6 pcs. .... No Price Found
396. 11th Hussars, 6 pcs. 300.00 650.00 1000.00
397. 16th/5th Lancers, 6 pcs. .... No Price Found
398. Life Guards, 6 pcs. 300.00 650.00 1000.00
399. U.S. Marines, 8 pcs.,
khaki, marching 350.00 800.00 1200.00
400. (9205) The Life Guards,
winter dress, 5 pcs., Prewar . 100.00 145.00 185.00
    Postwar 90.00 135.00 175.00
    Troop 12.00 22.00 25.00
401. Argentine Infantry
and Cavalry, 13 pcs. .... No Price Found
402. Spanish Cavalry, 10 pcs. .... No Price Found

#400

	G	VG	EXC

403. Uruguayan Cavalry
and Cadets, 13 pcs. .... No Price Found

404. Argentine Cadets,
Cavalry and Cadets, 21 pcs. .... No Price Found

405. Uruguayan Infantry,
Cavalry and Cadets, 21 pcs. .... No Price Found

406. Spanish and Uruguayan
Cavalry, 18 pcs. .... No Price Found

407. Display Box, Royal Navy, White
jackets and Bluejackets at trail,
16 pcs., 2 Petty Officers, 1931 .... No Price Found

408. Royal Navy Bluejackets at the double,
16 pcs., Petty officer, 1931-32 .... No Price Found

409. Whitejackets at the double, 16 pcs.,
Petty officer, 1931-32 .... No Price Found

410. Argentine Cadets
and Infantry, 16 pcs. .... No Price Found

411. Argentine Infantry, 16 pcs. .... No Price Found

412. Argentine Military
School Cadets, 16 pc.
version of 219, no officers .... No Price Found

413. Uruguayan Cavalry, 10 pcs. .... No Price Found

414. Uruguayan Cavalry, 15 pcs. .... No Price Found

415. Argentine Infantry and
Uruguayan Cavalry, 12 pcs. .... No Price Found

416. Argentine Infantry and
Uruguayan Cavalry, 20 pcs. .... No Price Found

417. Admiral with Squad of Bluejackets,
running, 16 pcs., 1931-32, at trail .... No Price Found

418. Admiral with Squad of Bluejackets,
running at trail, 24 pcs., 1931-32 .... No Price Found

419. Gordon Highlanders, 16 pcs. .... No Price Found

420. Gordon Highlanders, 24 pcs. .... No Price Found

421. North American Indians, 10 pcs. .... No Price Found

422. North American Indians, 15 pcs. .... No Price Found

423. Boy Scouts .... No Price Found

424. West Point Cadets, winter
and summer dress, 16 pcs. .... No Price Found

425. Spanish Cavalry and
Infantry, double box, 13 pcs. .... No Price Found

426. Ideal Flower Support, for real or
artificial flowers, one piece .... No Price Found

427. French Cuirassiers and
Infantry of the Line, 13 pcs. .... No Price Found

428. United States of America
Police, 8 pcs. .... No Price Found

429. (9306) Scots Guards
and the Life Guards in

	G	VG	EXC
Winter Dress, 13 pcs.	135.00	270.50	350.00
Officer mounted	12.50	18.00	25.00
Troop, on foot	8.50	12.00	14.00

430. Life Guards, summer
dress and Life Guards
winter dress, 10 pcs. .... No Price Found

431. Scots Guards summer
dress and Scots Guards
winter dress, 16 pcs. .... No Price Found

432. (9169) German Infantry,
slope arms, officer,

	G	VG	EXC
8 pcs., Prewar	90.00	115.00	140.00
8 pcs., Postwar	70.00	100.00	125.00
Troop, Postwar	8.50	11.00	15.00

	G	VG	EXC

433. Monoplane, 2 pcs.,
pilot and hangar,
square wingtip version .... 850.00 | 1300.00 | 1800.00

434. RAF Monoplane with
pilot and hangar,
6 aircraftsmen, 8 pcs. .... 1200.00 | 3000.00 | 4500.00

#432 Prewar.

#432 Postwar dark green tunic.

#433 Rare camouflage version.

#433 With pilot.

L to R: #433, #434. Photo by Tim Oei.

	G	VG	EXC
435. U.S. Aviation Monoplane with pilot and hangar, 3 pcs.	900.00	1500.00	3000.00
436. U.S. Monoplane with hangar and 6 aircraftsmen, 8 pcs.	1000.00	2800.00	4000.00
437. Gordon Highlanders Officers, walking, 5 pcs., one mounted, c1930	150.00	275.00	350.00

#437

	G	VG	EXC
438. Grenadier Guards, parade series, 9 pcs.			No Price Found
Officer	7.50	11.25	15.00
Troop	6.00	9.00	12.00
439. Middlesex Regiment, parade series, 9 pcs.			No Price Found
440. 7th Royal Fusiliers, parade series, 9 pcs.			No Price Found
441. Gordon Highlanders, parade series, 9 pcs.			No Price Found
442. British Infantry, 9 pcs., khaki, parade series			No Price Found
443. West Point Cadets, 9 pcs., parade series			No Price Found
444. U.S. Marines, 9 pcs., parade series			No Price Found

	G	VG	EXC
445. U.S. Infantry, 9 pcs., parade series			No Price Found
446. Scots Guards, 13 pcs., parade series			No Price Found
447. Royal West Surrey Regiment, 13 pcs., parade series			No Price Found
448. 7th Royal Fusiliers, 13 pcs., parade series	250.00	500.00	750.00
449. Black Watch, 13 pcs., parade series			No Price Found
450. British Infantry, 13 pcs., khaki, parade series			No Price Found
451. West Point Cadets, 13 pcs., winter dress, parade series			No Price Found
452. U.S. Marines, 13 pcs., parade series			No Price Found
453. U.S. Infantry, 13 pcs., parade series			No Price Found
454. West Point Cadets, 9 pcs., summer dress, parade series			No Price Found
455. West Point Cadets, 13 pcs., summer dress, parade series			No Price Found
456. U.S. Sailors, 9 pcs., parade series			No Price Found
457. U.S. Sailors, 13 pcs., parade series			No Price Found
458. U.S. Infantry and Cavalry, 21 pcs., parade series			No Price Found
459. U.S. Infantry and Cavalry, 13 pcs., parade series			No Price Found
460. Colour party and Standard Bearer of Scots Guards (1st version was Grenadier Guards, no price found)			
7 pcs.	120.00	275.00	400.00
Officer with flag	22.00	40.00	55.00
Sergeant at slope	15.00	32.00	40.00

#460. Courtesy Phillips.

	G	VG	EXC

461. German Infantry, 16 pcs. .... No Price Found
462. Cowboys and North
American Indians, 18 pcs. .... No Price Found
463. Cowboys, 21 pcs. .... No Price Found
464. Cowboys, 26 pcs.,
10 mounted, 16 foot 350.00   650.00   850.00

#464

465. U.S.A. Infantry
and Cavalry, 26 pcs. .... No Price Found
466. U.S.A. West Point
Cadets, 32 pcs. .... No Price Found
467. U.S.A. Marines, 32 pcs. .... No Price Found
468. U.S.A. Bluejackets, 32 pcs. .... No Price Found
469. U.S.A. Infantry, 32 pcs. .... No Price Found
470. U.S.A. Cavalry, 20 pcs. .... No Price Found
471. U.S.A. Infantry
and Cavalry, 34 pcs. .... No Price Found
472. U.S.A. West Point
Cadets, 40 pcs. .... No Price Found
473. U.S.A. Marines
and Bluejackets, 40 pcs. .... No Price Found
474. U.S.A. Cavalry, 25 pcs. .... No Price Found
475. U.S. Cavalry and
Machine Gunners, 19 pcs. .... No Price Found
476. Arabs, 18 pcs. .... No Price Found
477. Lifeguards, Royal Sussex
Regiment, 12 pcs. .... No Price Found
478. French Cavalry
and Infantry, 18 pcs. .... No Price Found

	G	VG	EXC

479. U.S. Marines and Sailors,
parade series .... No Price Found
480. Black Watch with Pipers
and Mounted officer,
parade series .... No Price Found
481. Middlesex Regiment
Buglers, Drummers
and Mounted Officers,
parade series .... No Price Found
482. Gordon Highlanders,
Pipes and Mounted
Officers, parade series .... No Price Found
483. U.S. Infantry, mounted
and foot Officers,
parade series .... No Price Found
484. West Point Cadets,
parade series .... No Price Found
485. U.S. Infantry mounted
and foot, parade series .... No Price Found
486. U.S. Infantry and
Cavalry with foot
officer, parade series .... No Price Found
487. U.S. Infantry and
Cavalry with foot
officer, parade series .... No Price Found
488. U.S. Marines and Sailors,
parade series .... No Price Found
489. West Point Cadets .... No Price Found
490. Middlesex
Regiment with Buglers .... No Price Found
491. U.S.A. Infantry
and Cavalry, 12 pcs. .... No Price Found
492. U.S.A. Infantry
and Cavalry, 12 pcs. .... No Price Found
493. U.S.A. West Point
Cadets, 15 pcs. .... No Price Found
494. U.S. Marines
and Bluejackets, 15 pcs. .... No Price Found
495. U.S.A. Infantry, 15 pcs. .... No Price Found
496. Gordon Highlanders, 10 pcs. .... No Price Found
497. Royal Scots, 10 pcs. .... No Price Found
498. U.S.A. Cavalry, 6 pcs. 200.00   350.00   500.00
499. U.S.A. West Point
Cadets, 10 pcs. .... No Price Found
500. Lifeguards, winter dress .... No Price Found
1201. (9715) Gun of Royal
Artillery, 5-1/4" long 15.00   25.00   40.00

#1201

	G	VG	EXC

1202. Carden-Loyd Tank
with Driver .... No Price Found

1203. Carden-Loyd Tank driver,
machine-gunner, detachable
machine gun, 1932-1940,
with rubber tracks 105.00   150.00   220.00

#1203

1204. Chinese Infantry, 10 pcs. .... No Price Found
1205. French Infantry, 10 pcs. .... No Price Found
1206. Kings
African Rifles, 10 pcs. .... No Price Found
1207. Zulus, 10 pcs. .... No Price Found
1208. West Point
Cadets, 10 pcs. 300.00   600.00   800.00
1209. Irish Guards, 10 pcs. .... No Price Found
1210. Mexican Infantry, 10 pcs. .... No Price Found
1211. Drums and Bugles
of the Line, 10 pcs. .... No Price Found
1212. German Infantry, 10 pcs. .... No Price Found
1213. Turcos, 10 pcs. .... No Price Found
1214. Argyll and Sutherland
Highlanders, 10 pcs. .... No Price Found
1215. Royal Sussex
Regiment, 9 pcs. .... No Price Found
1216. Royal West Surrey
Regiment, 10 pcs. .... No Price Found
1217. UNKNOWN .... —
1218. French Cuirassiers, 10 pcs. .... No Price Found
1219. Twenty-First Lancers at the
Halt, 5 pcs., late 1920s .... No Price Found
1220. Imperial Yeomanry, 6 pcs. .... No Price Found
1221. Imperial Yeomanry, 6 pcs. .... No Price Found
1222. 6th Dragon Guards, 6 pcs. .... No Price Found
1223. North American
Indians, 20 pcs. .... No Price Found
1224. North American
Indians, 16 pcs. .... No Price Found
1225. Cowboys, 16 pcs. .... No Price Found
1226. UNKNOWN .... —
1227. U.S.A. Air Force, 10 pcs. .... No Price Found
1228. U.S.A. Air Force, 10 pcs. .... No Price Found
1229. U.S.A. Air Force, 10 pcs. .... No Price Found
1230. French Mule Battery, 13 pcs. .... No Price Found
1231. UNKNOWN .... —
1232. Nurses .... No Price Found
1233-34. UNKNOWN .... —
1242-43. UNKNOWN .... —
1244. 7th Royal Fusiliers, 10 pcs. .... No Price Found
1245. York and Lancaster
Regiment, 10 pcs. .... No Price Found
1246. Italian Infantry, 10 pcs. .... No Price Found

	G	VG	EXC

1247. Argentine Infantry, marching,
large set, late 1920s .... No Price Found
1248. Argentine Cavalry, 10 pcs. .... No Price Found
1249. French Dragoons, 6 pcs. .... No Price Found
1250. Royal Tank Corps,
marching 8 pcs., Prewar
with mustaches, 1st
version with rifles
at trail 175.00   400.00   600.00
    2nd version 150.00   375.00   450.00
    Late Prewar, no
    mustaches 2nd version 110.00   325.00   400.00
    Earlier figure 12.50   19.00   25.00
    Later figure 10.00   16.50   22.00
1251. U.S. Infantry, 9 pcs.,
standing, kneeling,
lying, with officer 160.00   300.00   400.00
    Troop 15.00   28.00   38.00
1252. Cowboys on foot, 8 pcs.,
standing, kneeling, firing ... 125.00   250.00   350.00
1253. (9184) U.S. Sailors,
Whitejackets, with
officer, at slope, 8 pcs.,
(7 in 1960) Prewar set 80.00   125.00   180.00
    Postwar set 65.00   100.00   150.00
    Officer, Prewar 10.00   16.00   20.00
    Sailor, Prewar 8.00   12.00   17.00
    Officer Postwar 8.00   12.00   17.00
    Sailor, Postwar 7.00   10.00   15.00
1254. Pontoon Section Royal
Engineers, same as 204 ...... 500.00   900.00   1450

#1250 2nd version.

#1253   *#1257*

#1251

	G	VG	EXC
1255. U.S.A. Bluejackets			
and Whitejackets, 10 pcs.			No Price Found
1257. (9300) Beefeaters			
with officer	87.50	131.25	175.00
Officer	12.50	18.75	25.00
Prewar Troop	7.50	11.25	15.00
Postwar Troop	5.00	7.50	10.00
1258. (9497) Knights in Armour,			
with Squires, Herald and			
Marshal set	125.00	225.00	300.00
Mounted	15.00	30.00	40.00
Foot	15.50	25.25	35.00
Marshal	20.00	45.00	60.00
Herald	15.00	25.00	32.00

#1258

#1258

	G	VG	EXC
1259. UNKNOWN			—
1260. Infantry with Flat Caps,			
firing, 9 pcs.	125.00	225.00	300.00
Lying firing,			
first version	10.00	18.00	24.00
Kneeling firing,			
first version	10.00	18.00	24.00
Lying firing, later version	7.00	13.50	18.00
Kneeling firing,			
later version	7.00	13.50	18.00

#1260

	G	VG	EXC
1261-62. UNKNOWN			—
1263. (9700) Gun of Royal			
Artillery, 3-3/4" long	12.00	18.00	25.00
1264. (9730) 4.7 Naval Gun			
(catalog designation begun			
1933, unnumbered previously,			
shield added sometime			
before 1930), 7-3/4" long,			
1st version (unpainted)	40.00	75.00	120.00
No shield	35.00	65.00	90.00

#1263

#1264 With shield.

#1265

#1266 (Postwar #2107).

	G	**VG**	**EXC**
1265. 18" Heavy Howitzer for No. 2 mounted for Garrison work,			
1st version (unpainted)	65.00	100.00	140.00
Later version	40.00	70.00	100.00

	G	**VG**	**EXC**
1266. Heavy Howitzer, 18", 7" long, with wheels	60.00	90.00	130.00

#1283

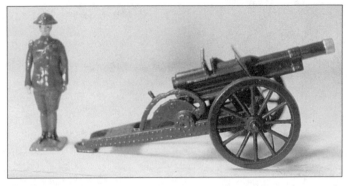

#1292 Figure for size compare to #1201.

#1284

#1284

#1293 Dark khaki.

#1293 Officer.

#1294

#1287. Courtesy Phillips.

	G	VG	EXC

1267. Display Box, Royal Scots, Scots Guards with Pipers, Gordon Highlanders, Scots Greys, Middlesex Regiment, 12th Lancers, Life Guards, 11th Hussars, 83 pcs. .... No Price Found

1268. Life Guards, Middlesex Regiment .... No Price Found

1269. Scots Greys and Seaforths .... No Price Found

1270. UNKNOWN .... —

1271. Territorials, 6 pcs. .... No Price Found

1272. North American Indians, 6 pcs. .... No Price Found

1273-1275. UNKNOWN .... —

1276. U.S.A. Bluejackets, 7 pcs. .... No Price Found

1277. U.S.A Infantry, 7 pcs. .... No Price Found

1278. U.S.A. Infantry Marines, 41 pcs. .... No Price Found

1279. U.S.A. Infantry, Cavalry, West Point Cadets, Machine Gunners, 64 pcs. .... No Price Found

1280. U.S.A. Infantry, Cavalry, Marines, Bluejackets and Whitejackets, 80 pcs. .... No Price Found

1281. U.S.A. Infantry, Cavalry, Marines, West Point Cadets, Sailors, 111 pcs. .... No Price Found

1282. U.S.A. Infantry, Cavalry, Marines, West Point Cadets, Machine Gunners, 126 pcs. .... No Price Found

1283. (9122) Grenadier Guards, standing, kneeling, lying,
8 Prewar	60.00	90.00	120.00
Postwar	50.00	80.00	100.00
Each Postwar	7.00	10.00	13.00

1284. The Royal Marines, 8 marching and 8 running at trail arms, with officers,
16 pcs., Postwar set	175.00	320.00	450.00
Officer, running at trail	14.00	24.00	30.00
Troop, running at trail	10.00	17.00	22.00

1285. Territorials, Yeomanry and Infantry, 13 pcs. .... No Price Found

1286. Infantry, Peak Caps, firing, 25 pcs. .... No Price Found

1287. British Military Band,
| 21 pcs. | 300.00 | 550.00 | 700.00 |
| Per figure | 16.00 | 24.00 | 32.00 |

1288. Royal Marine Band,
| blue tunics, 21 pcs. | 250.00 | 400.00 | 550.00 |

1289. Gun of R.A. (1201) with Team of Gunners
| and Officers, 8 pcs. | 200.00 | 550.00 | 800.00 |

1209. Band of the Line,
| Service Dress (12 pcs.) | 300.00 | 450.00 | 600.00 |

1291. Royal Marine Band, 11 instrumentalists
| and drum major, 12 pcs. | 180.00 | 370.00 | 450.00 |
| Per piece | 12.00 | 20.00 | 28.00 |

1292. (9710) Gun of Royal Artillery, 4-3/4" long,
| Prewar | 12.00 | 16.00 | 20.00 |
| Postwar | 10.00 | 14.00 | 18.00 |

	G	VG	EXC

1293. Durban Light Infantry,
| 1934-41, slope arms, 8 pcs. | 500.00 | 800.00 | 1200.00 |

1294. British Infantry in Tropical Dress, same as above with lighter
| shade of khaki, 8 pcs. | 250.00 | 500.00 | 700.00 |
| Each | 22.00 | 45.00 | 75.00 |

1295-1298. UNKNOWN .... —

1299. Zulus and Palm Tree, 9 pcs. .... No Price Found

1300. RAMC Hospital, Marquee and Doctors, 42 pcs. .... No Price Found

1301 Military Band (U.S.A.) 11 instrumentalists
| and Drum Major, 12 pcs. | 160.00 | 350.00 | 450.00 |

1302. U.S. Military Band
| (21 pcs) | 400.00 | 900.00 | 1200.00 |

1303. Knights, 17 pcs. .... No Price Found

1304. Knights, 8 pcs. .... No Price Found

#1303

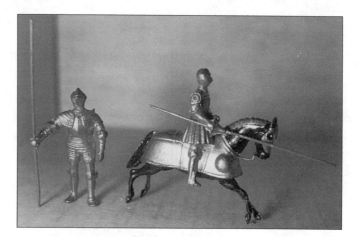

#1303, #1304, #1307, #1308.

1305. U.S.A. Infantry, Cavalry, 14 pcs. .... No Price Found

1306. Landing Party U.S.A. (box 79 painted U.S.A. uniforms) .... No Price Found

	G	VG	EXC

1307. (9398) Knights, mounted
and on foot, 16th Century,
6 mtd., 3 ft. (11 pcs.
1962-66); 9 pc. set 70.00 85.00 125.00
    Mounted 7.00 10.50 14.00
    Foot 4.00 6.00 8.00
1308. Knights Mounted
and on Foot,
16th Century, 11 pcs. 150.00 400.00 600.00
1309. UNKNOWN .... —
1310. Royal Welsh Fusiliers and
Scots Guards, marching
with officer, c1933, 8 pcs. .... No Price Found
1311. Cowboys and North
American Indians with
Chief, 8 pcs., all foot .... No Price Found
1312. North American Indians,
mounted and Cowboys,
mounted 5 pcs. .... No Price Found
1313. Eastern People (Sand
Tray Models), 12 pcs. 500.00 750.00 1200.00

#1313

1314. Eastern People (Sand
Tray Models), 20 pcs. .... No Price Found
1315. Salvation Army Band,
12 pcs., in red, bandmaster,
2 cornets, 2 euphoniums,
1 bass tuba, 2 trombones,
1 side drummer, 1 bass
drummer, 1 tenor horn,
1 double bass tuba, 1933-? .... No Price Found
1316. Salvation Army Band,
1933-?, 24 pcs., in blue,
bandmaster, 3 cornets,
2 euphoniums, 1 bass tuba,
2 trombones, 1 side drummer,
3 tenor horns, 1 double bass,
tuba, standard bearer,
2 Officers, 2 men, 2 women,
woman with tambourine,
woman with "War Cry" .... No Price Found
1317. Salvation Army Band,
25 pcs., red tunic,
bandmaster, 7 cornets,
4 euphoniums, 2 bass
tubas, 3 trombones,
1 side drummer, 1 bass
drummer, 3 tenor horns,
3 double bass tubas,
1 standard bearer 1933-? ..1400.00 2500.00 3500.00

#1317   *#1317*

#1317

#1318 Prewar & postwar.

	G	VG	EXC

1318. (9149) Machine Gun
Section, 7 pcs., lying
and sitting, Prewar 65.00 90.00 130.00
1319. Machine Gun Section,
lying and sitting, 14 pcs. .... No Price Found
1320. Infantry, Peak Caps,
with officer, 9 pcs.,
lying and firing 125.00 250.00 350.00
Officer, kneeling
with field glasses 20.00 40.00 55.00

*Above and
right: #1320*

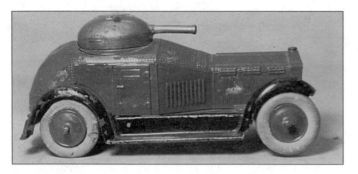

#1321 1st version.

#1328

#1328

	G	VG	EXC
1321. Armoured Car with Swiveling Gun, 1 piece	180.00	350.00	425.00
1322. Carden-Loyd Tank, 7 pcs., squad of Royal Tank Corps walking, 1934-40	150.00	250.00	400.00
Officer	11.00	17.00	22.00
Troop	8.50	13.00	17.00
1323. (9345) The Royal Fusiliers, the Seaforth Highlanders, and the Royal Sussex Regiment, with mounted and foot Officers, 23 pcs.	180.00	260.00	325.00
Fusilier	7.50	10.00	13.00
1324. Scots Guards with Pipers, Middlesex Regiment Officers and Royal Scots, 24 pcs.			No Price Found
1325. Gordon Highlanders firing, lying, standing, kneeling, 16 pcs.	125.00	250.00	350.00
1326. Irish Guards, Gordon Highlanders, with officer and Piper, 16 pcs.			No Price Found
1327. Grenadier Guards, 16 pcs., firing, lying, standing, kneeling (14 pcs. 1960-66), Pre-1960	95.00	130.00	170.00
1328. British Infantry Active ervice with Peak Caps, firing, 18 pcs.			No Price Found

	G	VG	EXC
1329. Royal Army Service Corps, rider, two walking horses, two open wagons (some sets may have galloping horses)	350.00	800.00	1150
1330. Royal Engineers General Service Wagon. Connecting 2-2 wheel wagons, horse drawn. Review dress, red tunic. Horses at gallop	150.00	250.00	350.00
Same, horses at walk	200.00	300.00	450.00

#1330 At walk.

#1327 Postwar.

#1331 At gallop.

	G	VG	EXC

1331. Royal Engineers General
    Service Wagon. (As above)
    Active Service Dress,
    khaki. Horses at walk 250.00   500.00   700.00
    (Note: there also is known
            to exist a rare steel
            helmeted version) .... No Price Found
1332. Girl Guides
    with Guider, 9 pcs. 350.00   700.00   1050.00

#1332

1333. Army Lorry Caterpillar
    type with driver, 2 pcs. 125.00   200.00   300.00
1334. Lorry, Army, with driver,
    2 pcs., 4 wheels, Prewar 105.00   155.00   200.00
    Postwar, early 85.00   125.00   170.00
1335. Lorry, Army, with driver,
    2 pcs., 6 wheels, Prewar 130.00   185.00   250.00
    Postwar 115.00   165.00   230.00

#1334 Prewar, square nose.

#1334 Postwar, rounded nose.

#1335 Prewar.

	G	VG	EXC

1336. UNKNOWN .... —
1337. Miniature Golf .... No Price Found
1338. Miniature Golf .... No Price Found
1339. Royal Horse Artillery
    (Active service order),
    khaki, 13 pcs., at gallop 1000.00   1700.00   2500.00
1340. Miniature Archery .... No Price Found
1341. Royal Irish Regiment,
    kneeling, review order,
    c1933, 8 pcs. .... No Price Found
1342. 7th Rajput
    Regiment, 8 pcs. 250.00   500.00   700.00
1343. Royal Horse Guards,
    winter dress, 5 pcs. 100.00   150.00   225.00
    Trooper 15.00   25.00   35.00

#1342

#1343 Dark blue cloak.

1344. Miniature Archery .... No Price Found
1345. Scots Greys,
    Scots Guards, 10 pcs. .... No Price Found
1346. Scots Greys and
    Gordon Highlanders, 10 pcs. .... No Price Found
1347. Cowboys, 9 pcs. .... No Price Found
1348. North American
    Indians, 9 pcs. .... No Price Found
1349. (9256) The Royal Canadian
    Mounted Police, mounted,
    summer dress, officer,
    5 pcs. 1934-66 ....70.00   105.00   135.00
    Officer 14.00   20.00   25.00
    Trooper 10.00   15.00   20.00

#1349

	G	VG	EXC
1350. Display Box, Gordon Highlanders and Scots Guards, Royal Scots, Life Guards and 11th Hussars, 64 pcs.			No Price Found
1351. U.S.A. Infantry, 20 pcs.			No Price Found
1352. Knights, 10 pcs.			No Price Found
1353. Knights, 6 pcs.			No Price Found
1354. Knights, 11 pcs.			No Price Found
1355. 4th Hussars with officer, Royal Horse Guards with officer, Grenadier Guards with Standard Bearer; Side Drummer and officer, 18 pcs.			No Price Found
1356. Coldstream Guards standing, kneeling, lying, firing, Officers, drummer, Bugler, standard bearer, 27 or 28 pcs.			No Price Found
1357. French Infantry of the Line, 16 pcs.			No Price Found
1358. Belgian Infantry, review order, 16 pcs.			No Price Found
1359. French Infantry, steel helmets, 16 pcs.			No Price Found
Troop	5.00	7.50	10.00
1360. Zouaves (review order), 16 pcs.			No Price Found
1361. French Infantry, 16 pcs.			No Price Found
1362. Belgian Infantry, review order, 24 pcs.			No Price Found
1363. Zouaves, 24 pcs.			No Price Found
1364. French Infantry, khaki, 24 pcs.			No Price Found
1365. French Cuirassiers and Infantry of the Line (review order), 21 pcs.			No Price Found
1366. French Infantry and Machine Gunners, active service, 7 pcs.	175.00	350.00	500.00
Troop	9.00	13.50	18.00
1367. Japanese Infantry and Cavalry, 21 pcs.			No Price Found
1368. Italian Bersaglieri and Cavalry (review order), 13 pcs.			No Price Found
1369. Highlanders, 8 pcs., assorted positions, Infantry officer, c1933			No Price Found

	G	VG	EXC
1370. Gordon Highlanders, 16 pcs. (or Knights at Arms)			No Price Found
1371. U.S.A.A.S.C. (Box 1460 painted with U.S.A. uniforms)			No Price Found
1372. U.S. Horsedrawn Ambulance, 7 pcs.			No Price Found
1373. U.S. Army Pontoon System, c1935, 7 pcs.	1400.00	2700.00	3500.00
1374. U.S.A. 18 pdr. gun, 1 pc.	225.00	630.00	750.00
1375. Gordon Highlanders, 10 pcs.			No Price Found
1376. Gordon Highlanders, 10 pcs.			No Price Found
1377. Coldstream Guards, 10 pcs.			No Price Found
1378. Coldstream Guards, 10 pcs.			No Price Found
1379. Belgian Cavalry, Active Service Order, 5 pcs.			No Price Found
1380. Belgian Cavalry, Service Order, 10 pcs.			No Price Found
1381. Belgian Cavalry, Service Order, 15 pcs.			No Price Found
1382. Belgian Cavalry and Infantry, Service Order, 13 pcs.			No Price Found
1383. Belgian Infantry, 14 pcs., lying, standing, kneeling, with Machine Gunner, steel helmets, 14 pcs.	150.00	300.00	450.00
Machine Gunner	10.00	20.00	30.00
Troop	8.00	14.00	20.00
1384. Belgian Infantry firing, with machine gunners, 21 pcs.	260.00	450.00	620.00
1385. French Cavalry, Chasseurs and Dragoons, 10 pcs.			No Price Found
1386. French Cavalry, Chasseurs, Dragoons and Cuirassiers, 15 pcs.			No Price Found
1387. French Infantry, firing, with Machine Gunners, 21 pcs.			No Price Found
1388. French Infantry, Turcos and Dragoons, 21 pcs.			No Price Found
1389. Belgian Infantry, 8 pcs., service order, slope arms	125.00	250.00	300.00
Troop	10.00	25.00	30.00

#1383 & #1384.

#1389

1390. Belgian Infantry and
Cavalry, service order,
18 pcs. .... No Price Found
1391. Model Fort in
stiff cardboard .... No Price Found
1392. Civilian Autogiro with
pilot, 1935-1940, 2 pcs. 1200.00   1800.00   2500.00

#1400

#1392

1393. Speed Record Car, 1 pc. .... No Price Found
1394. Model Fort with Royal
West Surrey Regiment,
7th Fusiliers, 16 pcs. 2500.00   6000.00   9000.00
1395. The King's Own Scottish
Borderers, slope arms,
8 pcs., no officer or
Piper, c1936-40 .... 175.00   350.00   500.00

#1395

*#1407
Scarce
bugler.*

1396. Marching Board Soldiers,
the Grenadier Guards,
8 pcs., c1935 .... No Price Found
1397. Model Fort with Infantry
of the Line, active service,
firing, 18 pcs. .... No Price Found
1398. Sports Open Tourer
Motor Car, 1 pc. 300.00   550.00   850.00
1399. Two-seater Coupe
Model Motor Car, 1 pc. 350.00   600.00   900.00
1400. Speed Record Car,
1 pc., "The Bluebird" 125.00   250.00   350.00
1401. Middlesex,
3rd Hussars, 9 pcs. .... No Price Found

	G	VG	EXC

1402. Scots Guards,
Life Guards, 9 pcs. .... No Price Found
1403. Gordon Highlanders,
11 pcs. .... No Price Found
1404. Territorials and
21st Lancers, 9 pcs. 50.00   100.00   150.00
1405. 7th Fusiliers, 9 pcs. .... No Price Found
1406. "Bluebird"
(with special painting) .... No Price Found
1407. Display Box, 21st Lancers,
galloping, Territorial
Yeomanry, Territorial
Infantry, 72 pcs. 1800.00   4000.00   6000.00
1408. Life Guards, 10 pcs. .... No Price Found
1409. Gordon Highlanders, 16 pcs. .... No Price Found
1410. Irish and
Coldstream Guards, 16 pcs. .... No Price Found
1411. Coldstream Guards, 10 pcs. .... No Price Found
1412. Welsh Fusiliers and
Middlesex Regiment, 8 pcs. .... No Price Found
1413. Police Car with
Two Officers 350.00   600.00   900.00

#1413

1414. U.S.A. Infantry
and Cavalry, 14 pcs. .... No Price Found
1415. Buck Rogers, 6 pcs., Buck,
Wilma, Killer Kane, Ardala,
Dr. Huer, robot (Mekkano
Man), sold in stores and as
Cream of Wheat premiums,
c1935-40. Not marked
"Britains" 750.00   1400.00   2000.00
    Buck (A) 150.00   300.00   400.00
    Wilma (B) 110.00   250.00   350.00
    Killer Kane (C) 110.00   250.00   350.00
    Ardala Valmar (D) 110.00   250.00   350.00
    Dr. Huer (E) 110.00   250.00   350.00
    Robot (F) 110.00   250.00   350.00

#1415 L to R: (C), (D), (E), (B), (F).

	G	VG	EXC
1416. Buck Rogers, 10 or 8 pcs., same as above, extra robots	No Price Found		
1417. Royal Irish Regiment, 8 pcs.	No Price Found		
1418. Middlesex Regiment, 8 pcs.	No Price Found		
1419. U.S.A. Infantry, 8 pcs.	No Price Found		
1420. Knights, 5 pcs.	No Price Found		
1421. Line Regiment O. drummers, 8 pcs.	No Price Found		
1424. Bodyguard of the Emperor of Ethiopia, at attention, 8 pcs.	175.00	375.50	500.00
Prewar Troop	20.00	32.50	40.00
Postwar Troop	18.00	30.00	37.00
1425. Ethiopian Tribesmen, slope, 8 pcs.	95.00	145.00	185.00
Troop	9.00	14.50	20.00
1426. St. John Ambulance Brigade, 8 pcs.	500.00	850.00	1200.00
Nurse (only in this set)	25.00	32.50	100.00
Male Nurse	25.00	32.50	50.00
Stretcher-Bearer	12.50	18.75	25.00
Stretcher	5.00	7.50	10.00

#1425, #1424.

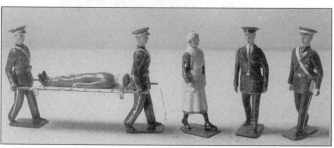

#1426

#1432

#1433 Prewar.

#1433 Early postwar version (light on top of fender, right door opens).

#1433 Postwar, last version.

	G	VG	EXC
1431. Military Autogiro, 1935-39, 2 pcs. 1500.00		3000.00	4000.00
1432. Army Tender, covered, 10 wheel, driver, 2 pcs. 125.00		200.00	325.00
1433. Army Tender (truck), 2 pcs., with driver, door opens, back drops 95.00		150.00	200.00
1434. Abyssianian Royal Bodyguard and Tribesmen, 16 pcs. 300.00		550.00	950.00
1435. Italian Infantry, slope arms, no officer, 8 pcs., Prewar 100.00		160.00	220.00
Postwar 75.00		125.00	175.00
1436. Italian Infantry, colonial service dress, 8 pcs. 140.00		265.00	350.00
Per Troop 14.00		26.00	35.00
1437. Italian Carabinieri, 8 pcs. (7 Postwar), Prewar set, no officer 110.00		195.00	260.00
Postwar set, with officer ...90.00		135.00	180.00
Prewar Troop 14.00		21.00	28.00

#1448 L to R: 1st version, 2nd version.

#1448 3rd version.

#1448 4th version.

#1435

L to R: #1436, #1437.

	G	VG	EXC
1438. Italian Infantry, colonial service dress, 16 pcs. 400.00		800.00	1200.00
1440. Royal Artillery (late R.H.A.) with gun, active service order, 9 pcs. 450.00		875.00	1300.00
1448. Staff Car, with officer and driver, 1st version, smooth white tires, black fenders 175.00		310.00	385.00
2nd version, white tires, all-khaki body 165.00		300.00	375.00
3rd version-1948-50, rectangular windshield, rubber tires 145.00		265.00	325.00
4th version-1951-57, lead tires, painted gray, split windshield 150.00		285.00	350.00
5th version-1958-59, black plastic tires 125.00		225.00	300.00

	G	VG	EXC
1449. Scots Guards (Special Painting), 2 pcs.		No Price Found	
1450. RAMC with Ambulance Wagon (Active Service Order), 7 pcs. 300.00		650.00	1000.00
1451. Scots Guards (Special Painting), 1 pc.		No Price Found	
1452. Gordon Highlanders (Special Painting), 1 pc.		No Price Found	
1453. Gordon Highlanders (Special Painting), 1 pc.		No Price Found	
1454. Scots Guards (Special Painting), 1 pc.		No Price Found	
1455. Argentine Cadets and Cavalry, 21 pcs.		No Price Found	
1456. Argentine Cadets and Cavalry, 18 pcs.		No Price Found	
1457. 3rd Hussars, 7 Fusiliers, 19 pcs.		No Price Found	
1458. Middlesex Regiment Band lemon-yellow facings, 18 pcs.		No Price Found	
1459. 10th and 11th Hussars, Grenadier Guards, 16/5th Lancers, Yorkshire Regiment, 59 pcs.		No Price Found	
1459. 10th and 11th Hussars, Grenadier Guards, 16/5th Lancers, Yorkshire Regiment, 59 pcs.		No Price Found	
1460. Army Service Corps (with wagon), Active Service Order, 5 pcs. 250.00		450.00	650.00

##1462

#1470

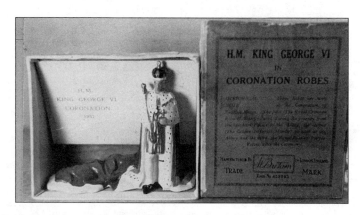

#1473 With box.

#1474

#1475

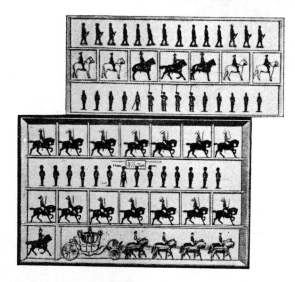

#1477 Box & insert tray.

#1503

	G	VG	EXC

1461. 21st Lancers, 5th
Dragoon Guards, 23 pcs. .... No Price Found
1462. Covered Lorry, R.A. Gun,
drivers, 5 pcs. 150.00   350.00   450.00
1464. 4th Hussars, Royal Horse
Guards, Grenadier Guards,
16 pcs. .... No Price Found
1465. Royal Fusiliers, Royal
Sussex Regiment, Seaforth
Highlanders, 18 pcs. .... No Price Found
1466. Coldstream Guards, 24 pcs. .... No Price Found
1467. Cameron Highlanders, 24 pcs. .... No Price Found
1469. Cowboys and North
American Indians, 26 pcs. .... No Price Found
1470. (9401) State Coach of
England drawn by
8 horses, 11 pcs., with
riders, Prewar 135.00   275.00   375.00
    Postwar, 11 pcs. 100.00   225.00   325.00
1471. Single figure of
George VI in copper .... No Price Found
1472. Single figure of George VI,
same as above, but in gilt .... No Price Found
1473. Same as above, painted 35.00   70.00   95.00
1474. Coronation Chair, 2 pcs.,
(gray stone under seat) 20.00   26.50   35.00
1475. (9404) Display Box,
Yeoman of the Guard,
Walking Outriders,
Footmen, (19 pcs.) 150.00   250.00   350.00
    Walking outrider 8.00   12.00   17.00
1476. State Coach and Yeomen
of the Guard, Outriders,
Footmen, 29 pcs. 300.00   650.00   850.00
1477. State Coach
and Procession, 75 pcs. 650.00   1000.00   1700.00
1478. Cinderella Coach 350.00   650.00   1000.00
1479. Royal Artillery Limber
(short-pole pattern), 1 pc. 55.00   90.00   125.00

#1479

1493. UNKNOWN .... —
1494. Army of Argentina;
Mounted Grenadiers .... No Price Found
1496-1502. UNKNOWN .... —
1503. Miniature State Coach 20.00   35.00   50.00
1504. Queen Elizabeth in copper .... No Price Found
1505. Same as above, in gilt 35.00   65.00   100.00
1506. Same as above, painted 35.00   70.00   95.00
1507. UNKNOWN .... —

#1506

#1510

	G	VG	EXC

1508. Texas Rangers, 5 mounted
cowboys (based on 1936
"Texas Rangers" film
with Fred MacMurray) .... No Price Found
1509. Texas Rangers, Cowboys,
mounted and on foot,
5 mounted, 8 foot, as above,
inspired by movie
"The Texas Rangers" .... No Price Found
1510. British Sailors regulation
dress, 8 pcs., no weapons
or officer, 1937-41,
1946-59; Prewar 80.00   120.00   160.00
    Postwar 62.50   93.75   125.00
    Prewar Sailor 6.50   9.75   13.00
    Postwar Sailor 5.50   8.25   11.00
1511. Mounted Police, 5 pcs. 270.00   405.00   540.00
1512. Army Ambulance, motor
type, 4 pcs., with driver,
wounded man, stretcher,
6" long, Prewar 110.00   165.00   220.00
    Postwar 90.00   145.00   200.00

#1512 Prewar.

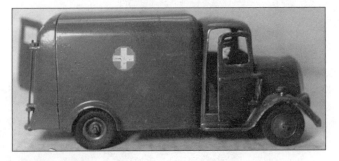

#1512 Postwar.

	G	VG	EXC
1513. Volunteer Corps Motor Tyre Ambulance, 4 pcs., with wounded man and stretcher, all doors open, 6" long (available unpainted)	350.00	550.00	800.00
1514. Corporation Motor Ambulance, 4 pcs., driver, wounded and stretcher	350.00	600.00	850.00

#1519

#1514

1515. (9124) Coldstream Guards at the Slope, 8 pcs.	70.00	90.00	120.00
Officer	8.00	12.00	16.00
Trooper	7.00	10.50	14.00
1516. Line Infantry of 1815, carrying pikes, 8 pcs.	135.00	265.00	325.00
1517. Highlanders, 1815, pikes, 8 pcs.	155.00	285.00	350.00
1518. Line Infantry, 1815, muskets, 9 pcs.	125.00	225.00	300.00
Troop	12.00	20.00	28.00

Britains box lid from set No. 1519, Waterloo Highlanders, w/muskets. Photo by Gary J. Linden.

	G	VG	EXC
1519. Highlanders, 1815, muskets, 8 pcs.	145.00	245.00	320.00
Officer	20.00	30.00	45.00
Troop	14.00	22.00	30.00
1520. "Short" Monoplane Flying Boat, 1937-39, 1 pc.	1000.00	1800.00	2500.00
1521. Model Biplane with Pilot and Hangar, 3 pcs.	1500.00	3000.00	4000.00
1522. 4-1/2" Anti Aircraft Gun, working model, 1 pc.	250.00	450.00	650.00
1523. RAF Band, 11 pcs.			No Price Found
1525. U.S.A. Biplane with pilot and hangar, 3 pcs.			No Price Found

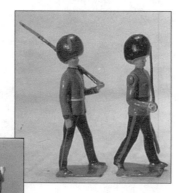

#1515

#1520

#1518 Postwar & prewar.

#1521

#1522

#1540

#1540

	G	VG	EXC
1541. Territorials, present arms, 8 pcs., green uniform	300.00	600.00	900.00
1542. Infantry with officer (New Zealand) at slope, 8 pcs., Prewar	120.00	200.00	275.00
Postwar set, 8 pcs.	85.00	165.00	220.00
Officer, Prewar	13.50	20.00	30.00
Troop, Prewar	10.00	16.00	22.00
Officer, Postwar	12.00	18.50	24.00
Troop, Postwar	9.00	13.00	18.00
1543. New Zealand. Infantry Service Kit, present arms with officer, 8 pcs.	300.00	650.00	850.00
1544. Australian Infantry at slope, officer, 8 pcs., Prewar	150.00	280.00	360.00
Postwar	105.00	225.00	300.00
Troop, Postwar	16.00	24.00	32.00

	G	VG	EXC
1527. RAF Band, 12 pcs.	250.00	500.00	700.00
1529. U.S.A. Cavalry, Infantry, Artillery, etc., 29 pcs.			No Price Found
1530. Display Set, Mounted Marshal, Knights with plumes, Squires and Heralds, 19 pcs.			No Price Found
1531. U.S.A. Infantry, 16 pcs.			No Price Found
1532. U.S.A. Infantry, 24 pcs.			No Price Found
1533. U.S.A. Infantry and Cavalry, 26 pcs.			No Price Found
1534. U.S.A. Infantry, Cavalry and Artillery, 41 pcs.			No Price Found
1535. U.S.A. Infantry and Cavalry, 80 pcs.			No Price Found
1536. Colonials at Present, 8 pcs.			No Price Found
1537. Territorials (slope, blue uniform), 8 pcs.	350.00	650.00	1000.00
1538. Territorials (slope, green uniform), 8 pcs.	350.00	650.00	1000.00
Officer	35.00	70.00	85.00
Troop	25.00	50.00	70.00
1540. Territorials, present arms, 8 pcs., blue uniform	300.00	600.00	900.00

#1542

#1543

#1545

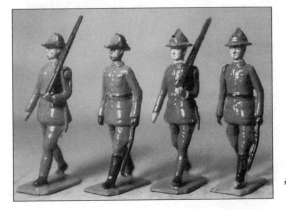

#1544

	G	VG	EXC
1545. Australian Infantry, service kit, present arms with officer, 8 pcs.	150.00	350.00	550.00
First version Troop	25.00	45.00	70.00
Second version officer (has plume)	30.00	55.00	80.00
1553. UNKNOWN			—
1554. (9156) Royal Canadian Mounted Police in summer dress, on foot, 1937-66, 8 pc. set	95.00	135.00	165.00
7 pc. set	70.00	115.00	135.00
Mounted officer	18.00	27.00	32.00
Prewar, no-gloves version	8.50	11.00	14.00
Postwar, gloves	7.00	9.00	12.00
1555. (9424) The Changing of the Guard at Buckingham Palace, 83 pcs.	500.00	1000.00	1500.00

#1554

#1554

#1555. Courtesy Phillips.

1556-1602 are the Famous Regiments of the British Army series: Uniform facings (collar and cuffs) are shown in parentheses. All consist of eight marchers, including Officer. Boxes are especially important in this series, which is rare.

	G	VG	EXC
1556. Lincolnshire Regiment (White)	300.00	650.00	1000.00
1557. East Yorkshire Regiment (White)	300.00	650.00	1000.00
1558. Bedfordshire and Hertfordshire Regiment (White)	300.00	650.00	1000.00
1559. Lancashire Fusiliers (White)	300.00	650.00	1000.00
1560. East Lancashire Regiment (White)	300.00	650.00	1000.00
1561. East Surrey Regiment (White)	300.00	650.00	1000.00
1562. South Staffordshire (White)	300.00	650.00	1000.00
1563. Welsh Regiment (White)	300.00	650.00	1000.00
1564. Loyal North Lancashire Regiment (White)	300.00	650.00	1000.00
1565. Manchester Regiment (White)	300.00	650.00	1000.00
1566. North Staffordshire Regiment (White)	300.00	650.00	1000.00

	G	VG	EXC
1567. York and Lancashire Regiment (White)	300.00	650.00	1000.00
1568. Essex Regiment (White)	300.00	650.00	1000.00
1569. Duke of Cornwall's Light Infantry (White)	300.00	650.00	1000.00
1570. Oxford and Bucks Light Infantry (White)	300.00	650.00	1000.00
1571. Royal West Surrey Regiment (Blue)	300.00	650.00	1000.00
1572. Royal Lancaster Regiment (Blue)	300.00	650.00	1000.00
1573. Royal Warwickshire Regiment (Blue)	300.00	650.00	1000.00
1574. Kings Regiment (Liverpool) (Blue)	300.00	650.00	1000.00
1575. Royal Sussex Regiment (Blue)	300.00	650.00	1000.00
1576. Royal Berkshire Regiment (Blue)	300.00	650.00	1000.00

	G	VG	EXC
1577. Royal West Kents (Blue) ...300.00	650.00	1000.00
1578. Somerset Light Infantry (Blue) 300.00	500.00	800.00
1579. Kings Own Yorkshire Light Infantry 300.00	500.00	800.00
1580. King's Shropshire Light Infantry (Blue) 300.00	500.00	800.00
1581. Royal Irish Fusiliers (Blue) 300.00	500.00	800.00
1582. The Buffs (Buff) 300.00	500.00	800.00
1583. West Yorkshire Regiment (Buff) 300.00	500.00	800.00
1584. Cheshire Regiment (Buff) ..300.00	500.00	800.00
1585. Prince of Wales Volunteers (South Lancashire Regiment); (White) 300.00	500.00	800.00
1586. Northamptonshire Regiment (White) 300.00	500.00	800.00
1587. Wiltshire Regiment (Buff) .300.00	500.00	800.00
1588. Royal Norfolks (Yellow) ...300.00	500.00	800.00
1589. Suffolk Regiment (Yellow) 300.00	500.00	800.00
1590. Border Regiment (Yellow) .300.00	500.00	800.00
1591. Hampshire Regiment (Yellow) 300.00	500.00	800.00
1592. Gloucestershire Regiment (White) 300.00	500.00	800.00
1593. Devonshire Regiment (Lincoln Green) 300.00	500.00	800.00
1594. Sherwood Foresters (Lincoln Green) 300.00	500.00	800.00
1595. Green Howards (Grass Green) 300.00	500.00	800.00
1596. South Wales Borderers (Grass Green) 300.00	500.00	800.00
1597. Dorsetshire Regiment (Grass Green) 300.00	500.00	800.00
1598. Worcesters (White) 300.00	500.00	800.00
1599. Royal Northumberland Fusiliers (Gosling Green) ...300.00	500.00	800.00
1600. Durham Light Infantry (Dark Green) 300.00	500.00	800.00
1601. Leicestershire Regiment (White) 300.00	500.00	800.00
1602. Duke of Wellington's Regiment (Scarlet) 300.00	500.00	800.00
1603. Irish Infantry, slope, officer, 8 pc. set, Prewar 120.00	225.00	300.00
1st version, Postwar, slope 100.00	205.00	280.00
2nd version, Postwar, trail 100.00	170.00	220.00
1604. Argentine Cavalry and Infantry, 34 pcs. .... No Price Found
1605. Knights, 6 pcs. .... No Price Found
1606. Knights, 10 pcs. .... No Price Found
1607. Full Company of the Royal Scots Greys, the Scots Guards, Standard Bearer, Piper, and officer, Sentry Boxes with Sentries and the Scots Guards' Band (45 pcs.) 2500.00	5000.00	8000.00
Fifer 15.00	22.50	30.00

#1603 1st version.

#1603 Postwar 2nd version.

	G	VG	EXC
1608. British Infantry and Cavalry, with Dispatch Riders and Machine Gunners (lying, sitting, service dress), 43 pcs. 650.00	1200.00	1650.00
1609. State Coach with Escort and Band, 57 pcs. 1200.00	2500.00	3500.00
1610. Royal Marines (present arms) 8 pcs. 120.00	200.00	280.00
Troop 13.50	20.00	28.00

#1610

#1610 Officer.

	G	VG	EXC
1611. British Infantry, service dress, gas masks prone, 8 pcs. 150.00	275.00	400.00
Troop 6.00	8.50	12.00
1612. British Infantry, service dress, gas masks, bomb throwers, 8 pcs. 55.00	80.00	100.00
Troop 6.50	9.50	12.00
1613. (9146) British Infantry (in action, charging with fixed bayonets) in gas masks, with officer, 7 pcs. (6 pcs. 1960) 50.00	75.00	105.00
6 pc. set 45.00	70.00	95.00
Officer 7.50	11.50	15.00
Troop 6.50	9.50	12.00

	G	VG	EXC
1614. (9346) British Infantry, action poses, officer, 24 pcs.	135.00	185.00	260.00
Officer	8.00	12.00	16.00
Digging	8.00	12.00	16.00
Troop	5.00	7.50	10.00
1615. British Infantry, charging and prone, throwing grenades, digging, officer, 15 pcs.	150.00	250.00	400.00
1616. British Infantry in action, assorted positions, 15 pcs.	200.00	400.00	550.00

	G	VG	EXC
1617. Line Regiments, Regular and Territorial Army, blue walking out dress, 8 pcs.	300.00	500.00	750.00
1618. Rifle Regiments, Regular and Territorial Army, 8 pcs., green walking out dress	300.00	500.00	750.00
1619. Royal Marines at slope, 8 pcs., tropical dress	400.00	850.00	1300.00
Each	25.00	45.00	65.00

#1612-16

#1613

L to R: #1619, #1620.

#1621

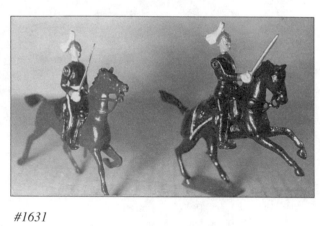

#1631

#1632

#1633

#1634 Red plume, left side.

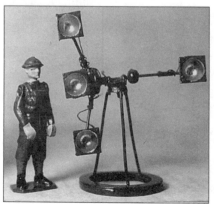

#1638

#1639

#1640

	G	VG	EXC
1620. Royal Marine Light Infantry, 8 pcs., at the slope	400.00	850.00	1200.00
Officer	30.00	60.00	80.00
Troop	25.00	45.00	60.00
1621. Twelfth Frontier Force Regiment, 3rd Battalion Sikhs, 1937-39, 8 pcs., no officer, at slope	250.00	500.00	700.00
Each	22.50	45.00	65.00
1622. Band of the Royal Marine Light Infantry, 21 pcs.	2000.00	3500.00	4500.00
1623. U.S. Infantry, 8 pcs., gas mask, prone	No Price Found		
Each	4.00	6.00	8.00
1624. U.S. Infantry, 8 pcs., gas masks, bomb throwing	100.00	200.00	300.00
Each	7.00	10.00	12.00
1625. U.S. Infantry, 7 pcs., gas masks, charging	No Price Found		
1626. U.S. Infantry in Action, gas masks, 24 pcs.	300.00	550.00	800.00
1627. U.S. Infantry in Action, gas masks, 15 pcs.	No Price Found		
Prewar Troop	7.00	10.00	12.00
1628. U.S. Infantry in Action, gas masks, 15 pcs.	No Price Found		
1629. Lord Strathcona's Horse 5 pcs., trotting, 1938, officer on rearing horse	500.00	1000.00	1500.00
Officer	70.00	180.00	250.00
Troop	60.00	135.00	200.00
1630. Royal Canadian Dragoons, 5 pcs., at the walk, 1938	500.00	1000.00	1500.00
1631. Governor-General's Horse Guards (Canadian), trotting horses, officer, 5 pcs.	70.00	120.00	150.00
Officer	15.00	22.50	30.00
Trooper	11.00	16.00	24.00
1632. Royal Canadian Regiment, 8 pcs. slope arms	250.00	450.00	700.00
1633. (9157) Princess Patricia's Canadian Light Infantry, officer, slope arms, 8 pcs.	80.00	120.00	160.00
Officer	10.00	12.00	16.00
Troop	7.00	10.50	14.00
1634. (9159) Governor-General's Footguards, at slope (Canadian), with officer, 8 pcs.	85.00	125.00	170.00
1635. Lord Strathcona's Horse and Royal Canadian Regiment, 13 pcs.	No Price Found		
1636. Princess Pat's Light Infantry and Royal Canadian Dragoons, 13 pcs.	No Price Found		
1637. (9356) Governor-General's Horse Guards and Foot Guards, with officers, 13 pcs.	120.00	180.00	250.00
1638. Sound Locator, with operator, 2 pcs.	20.00	40.00	65.00

	G	VG	EXC
1639. Army Range Finder with operator, 2 pcs.	15.00	25.00	35.00
1640. (9764) Model Searchlight, uses battery, 1 pc.	35.00	75.00	100.00
1641. Lorry, underslung, heavy duty, with driver, 18 wheels, 10-1/2" long, 2 pcs.	200.00	350.00	550.00
1642. Heavy Duty Lorry, 5 pcs., underslung, with driver, searchlight, battery and lamp (combined 1640 and 1641)	300.00	500.00	700.00
1643. Heavy Duty Lorry, underslung, with driver, AA Gun, 3 pcs.	600.00	900.00	1200.00

#1642

#1643

	G	VG	EXC
1646. Royal Canadian Mounted Police, 13 pcs.	No Price Found		
1647. Naval Display, 56 pcs.	No Price Found		
1648. Navy Landing Party Display Set, 51 pcs., c1940	1000.00	2000.00	3000.00
1649. Argentine Infantry, 7 pcs.	No Price Found		
1650. Line Drums and Bugles, 17 pcs.	No Price Found		
1651. Coldstream Guards, 21 pcs.	No Price Found		
1652. British Action Infantry, 38 pcs.	No Price Found		
1653. British Infantry and Cavalry, 52 pcs.	No Price Found		
1655. Coldstream Guards, 10 pcs.	No Price Found		
1657. Dublin Fusiliers, 9 pcs.	No Price Found		
1659. (9492) Knight with Mace, mounted	30.00	50.00	70.00
1660. (9493) Knight with Sword, mounted	30.00	50.00	70.00

	G	**VG**	**EXC**

1661. (9494) Knight with Lance,
 charging and mounted 30.00   50.00   70.00
1662. (9495) Knight with
 Standard mounted 42.50   70.00   100.00
1663. (9496) Knight with
 Lance, rearing, mounted 30.00   50.00   70.00
1664. (9392) Knights On Foot
 with Lances, Swords,
 Battle-axes and Mace,
 5 pcs. 80.00   140.00   185.00
   Each 15.00   25.00   35.00
1665. Kings Royal
 Rifle Corps. 7 pcs. .... No Price Found
1666. Yorkshire Regiment, 7 pcs. .... No Price Found
1667. Yorkshire and Lancashire
 Regiment, 7 pcs. .... No Price Found
1668. Warwickshire
 Regiment, 7 pcs. .... No Price Found
1669. Royal Irish Regiment, 8 pcs. .... No Price Found
1670. West Surrey Regiment, 8 pcs. .... No Price Found
1671. Somerset Light Infantry, 8 pcs. .... No Price Found
1672. British Infantry, khaki, 7 pcs. .... No Price Found
1673. Scot Guards, 7 pcs. .... No Price Found
1674. Grenadier Guards, 7 pcs. .... No Price Found
1675. Grenadier Guards, 8 pcs. .... No Price Found
1676. Coldstream Guards, 7 pcs. .... No Price Found
1677. Coldstream Guards, 7 pcs. .... No Price Found
1678. Welsh Fusiliers, 7 pcs. .... No Price Found
1679. British Sailors, 7 pcs. .... No Price Found
1680. Royal Marines, 7 pcs. .... No Price Found
1681. Royal Marines, 7 pcs. .... No Price Found
1682. Action Infantry, 6 pcs. .... No Price Found
1683. Action Infantry, 7 pcs. .... No Price Found
1684. Zulus, 7 pcs. .... No Price Found
1685. Khaki Infantry, 7 pcs. .... No Price Found
1686. Royal Canadian
 Mounted Police, 7 pcs. .... No Price Found
1687. New Zealand
 Infantry, 7 pcs. .... No Price Found
1688. Cowboys, 7 pcs. .... No Price Found
1689. North American
 Indians, 7 pcs. .... No Price Found
1690. Scots Greys,
 Grenadier Guards, 13 pcs. .... No Price Found
1691. 1st Dragoons, Somerset
 Light Infantry, 13 pcs. .... No Price Found
1692. Khaki Infantry, 14 pcs. .... No Price Found
1693. Buffs and Grenadier
 Guards, 15 pcs. .... No Price Found
1694. Scots Guards,
 Grenadier Guards, 14 pcs. .... No Price Found
1695. Life Guards,
 Scots Guards, 12 pcs. .... No Price Found
1696. Royal Canadian Dragoons,
 Canadian Light Infantry,
 12 pcs. .... No Price Found
1697. Infantry, khaki, firing, 16 pcs. .... No Price Found
1698. Cowboys and North
 American Indians, 12 pcs. .... No Price Found
1699. Cowboys, 12 pcs. .... No Price Found
1700. Scots Guards, Life Guards, 5 pcs. .... No Price Found
1701-1709. UNKNOWN .... —

#1659

#1662

#1663

#1664

#1664

#1664

#1664

#1664

	G	VG	EXC

1710. Royal Canadian
Mounted Police, 5 pcs. .... No Price Found
1711. (9167) The Foreign Legion
at slope with mounted
Officers, 7 pcs.,
(6 in 1960) ....75.00 | 102.50 | 140.00
Officer ....13.00 | 18.50 | 25.00
Troop ....8.00 | 12.00 | 16.00

#1711

#1711 Officer.

*#1719 Front & back
view.*

1712. French Foreign Legion with
Mounted officer, 15 pcs. ....350.00 | 650.00 | 950.00
1715. (9706) 2-pounder Light
Anti-Aircraft Gun,
base diameter 2" ....12.50 | 16.50 | 22.00
1716. Chassis for rigid or mobile
mounting for 2 pdr.
AA gun and searchlight ....90.00 | 120.00 | 155.00
1717. (9735) Mobile Unit,
2-pounder Light
Anti-Aircraft Gun,
4-1/2" long, 2 pcs. ....30.00 | 50.00 | 70.00
1718. (9765) Searchlight, on
Screw Jack chassis, uses
battery, 2 pcs. ....30.00 | 50.00 | 70.00
1719. Stretcher Party Unit
of R.A.M.C., 4 pcs.,
2 bearers, stretcher,
wounded ....65.00 | 110.00 | 150.00

#1720

	G	VG	EXC

1720. (9312) The Band of the
Royal Scots Greys (2nd
Dragoons), with Kettle
Drummer, 7 pcs.,
all mounted .... 170.00 | 300.00 | 400.00
1721. Band of Royal Scots
Greys, mounted, 12 pcs. ..... 500.00 | 800.00 | 1200.00
Cymbalist .... 40.00 | 60.00 | 80.00
Clarinetist .... 40.00 | 60.00 | 80.00
Cornetist .... 40.00 | 60.00 | 80.00
1722. Drums and Pipes Band of
the Scots Guards, 21 pcs. ... 300.00 | 500.00 | 800.00
Piper .... 12.00 | 18.00 | 24.00
1723. Royal Army Medical Corps.
Unit, 9 pcs., 2 stretchers,
4 bearers, 2 nurses,
1 wounded, SET .... 85.00 | 125.00 | 180.00
Nurse .... 7.00 | 10.00 | 12.00
Stretcher Bearer .... 8.00 | 12.00 | 16.00

#1717 Prewar combines #1715 & #1716.

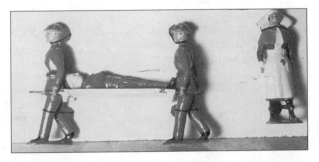

#1723 Early.

	G	VG	EXC

1724. AA Units of the British Army,
15 pcs., Searchlight, Sound
Locator, Spotting Chairs,
Tent and Tenwheel tender ..350.00 650.00 1000.00

1725. (9725) 4-1/2" Howitzer,
1939-40s, Prewar red box 12.50 20.00 30.00
    Postwar, thin box 9.50 12.50 18.50

1726. Regulation Type Limber 15.00 22.50 26.00

1727. Complete Mobile Howitzer
Unit, 4 pcs., with Limber
and Caterpillar Tractor 300.00 550.00 750.00

1728. Predictor, with Operator
(AA defense), 2 pcs. 14.50 20.00 32.00

1729. Height Finder, 2 pcs., with
Operator, Prewar 18.00 30.00 45.00
    Postwar 14.00 20.00 35.00

1730. (9148) Gun Detachment,
7 pcs., 2 kneeling, 2 kneeling
with shell, 2 at attention,
1 standing with shell 90.00 125.00 165.00
    Postwar, 7 pcs. 80.00 115.00 145.00
    Officer, Prewar, late 12.00 18.00 24.00
    Officer 1950s 10.00 15.00 20.00
    Troop, 1950s 8.00 12.00 16.00

1731. Spotting Chair (Swiveling)
with man to lie down,
2 pcs., Pre- and Postwar 15.00 25.00 40.00

1732. Standard Type Army Hut ...500.00 850.00 1200.00

1733. Nissen Type Army Hut 500.00 850.00 1200.00

1734. Guard Room 500.00 850.00 1200.00

1735. Gun Shed for housing
guns 1643 and 1717 ....500.00 850.00 1200.00

1736. Gun Shed to house
3 Guns and Lumbers 650.00 1000.00 1400.00

1737. Army Transport Shed,
to garage 3 vehicles 600.00 900.00 1300.00

1738. Stable to hold 6 horses 500.00 850.00 1200.00

1739. Gunners Quarters 500.00 850.00 1200.00

#1725

#1728

#1729

#1730

#1731

#1732

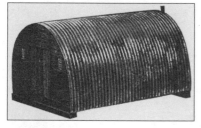

#1733

#1734

#1738

	G	VG	EXC
1740. Flight of Steps	150.00	250.00	400.00
1741. UNKNOWN			—
1742. Field Gun Emplacement	200.00	300.00	400.00
1743. Field Gun Emplacement, open type			No Price Found
1744. Machine Gun Emplacement with Corrugated Roofs and Sandbags	150.00	400.00	600.00

#1744

	G	VG	EXC
1745. Machine Gun Emplacement (sandbagged) to take two machine guns	150.00	375.00	480.00
1746. French Type sandbagged (advance position), Gun Emplacement	150.00	300.00	450.00
1747. Barrack Buildings with Parade Ground			No Price Found
1748. Barrack Buildings with Parade Grounds and two (2) Guard Huts	1600.00	3200.00	5000.00
1749. Balloon with Winch, 2 pcs., 1939	900.00	1500.00	2000.00
Winch	50.00	75.00	100.00
1750. Action Infantry, 9 pcs.			No Price Found
1751. North American Indians, 16 pcs.			No Price Found
1752. 5th Dragoon Guards, 9th Lancers, 12 pcs.			No Price Found
1753. Middlesex Regiment, 7th Fusiliers, 20 pcs.			No Price Found
1754. British Infantry and cavalry, 27 pcs.			No Price Found
1755. British Infantry and cavalry, 38 pcs.			No Price Found
1756. U.S.A. Forces, 31 pcs.			No Price Found
1757. Balloon Barrage Unit (balloon, winch, lorry, 1641), 1939	700.00	1000.00	1600.00
1758. Fire Fighters of the RAF, 8 pcs.	150.00	350.00	500.00
1759. A.R.P. National Service Stretcher Party, 9 pcs.	200.00	450.00	600.00
1760. Balloon only (barrage balloon) 1939	350.00	700.00	1000.00
1761. Hiker's or Boy Scout Tent			No Price Found
1762-63. UNKNOWN			—
1764. Cameron Highlanders, 21 pcs.			No Price Found
1765. Arabs, 12 pcs.			No Price Found
1766. Highlanders, 7 pcs.			No Price Found

#1757

#1758

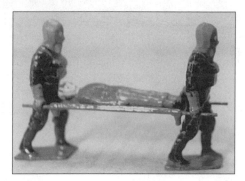

#1759

	G	VG	EXC
1767. Seaforth Highlanders, 7 pcs.			No Price Found
1768. Black Watch, 7 pcs.			No Price Found
1769. Royal Scots, 7 pcs.			No Price Found
1770. Governor General Foot Guards, 7 pcs.			No Price Found
1771. Canadian Light Infantry, 7 pcs.			No Price Found
1772. Royal Canadian Regiment, 7 pcs.			No Price Found
1773. Scots Guards, Colours and Pioneers, 6 pcs.			No Price Found
1774. Machine Gunners, 8 pcs.			No Price Found
1775. Gordon Highlanders, 14 pcs.			No Price Found
1776. Seaforth Highlanders, 14 pcs.			No Price Found
1777. Grenadier Guards, and Life Guards, 12 pcs.			No Price Found
1778. UNKNOWN			—
1779. Life Guards and Royal Sussex Regiment, 12 pcs.			No Price Found
1780. Grenadier Guards and Royal Scots Greys, 13 pcs.			No Price Found
1781. Grenadier Guards Buffs, 16 pcs.			No Price Found
1782. Irish Guards, Gordon Highlanders, 14 pcs.			No Price Found
1783. Grenadier Guards 16 pcs.			No Price Found
1784. Coldstream Guards, 22 pcs.			No Price Found

1785. Scots Guards and
Middlesex Regiment, 21 pcs. .... No Price Found
1786. Black Watch, 7 pcs. .... No Price Found
1787. Grenadier Guards, 6 pcs. .... No Price Found
1788. Gordon Highlanders, 7 pcs. .... No Price Found
1789. Royal Marines Band, 19 pcs. .... No Price Found
1790. Black Watch, Seaforth
Highlanders, 21 pcs. .... No Price Found
1791. (9153) Royal Corps
of Signals, dispatch riders,
motorcyclists, 4 pcs. 90.00   140.00   180.00
    Officer on foot
    (replaces one piece in
    1960 version) 10.00   16.50   22.00
    Dispatch Rider 15.00   25.00   35.00
1792. Mobile Traffic Police
on Motor Cycles, 4 pcs. .... No Price Found
1793. Motor Machine Gun
Corps, sidecar with driver
and gunner, 2 pcs., Prewar 80.00   120.00   160.00
2nd version 45.00   67.50   90.00
1794. Detachment of Infantry,
8 pcs., service dress,
to operate Searchlight 100.00   225.00   300.00
    Troop, late 1930s 7.50   11.25   15.00

#1791 Postwar.

#1794

1795. Life Guards
galloping, 6 pcs. .... No Price Found
1796. 12th Lancers, 6 pcs. .... No Price Found
1797. Cowboys and North
American Indians, 6 pcs. .... No Price Found
1798. Prince of Wales
Volunteers, at slope, 10 pcs. .... No Price Found
1799. Seaforth Highlanders
marching, active service order .... No Price Found
1800. Cameron Highlanders,
Active Service Order,
at slope (10 pcs.,
no officer) c1940 .... No Price Found
1801. Grenadier Guards, 10 pcs. .... No Price Found
1802. Grenadier Guards, 10 pcs. .... No Price Found
1803. East Kent Regiment, 9 pcs.,
on guard, officer, drummer .... No Price Found
1804. Kings Own Royal
Regiment, 10 pcs. .... No Price Found
1805. Royal Norfolk
Regiments, 10 pcs. .... No Price Found
1806. Bluejackets,
U.S.A., 10 pcs. .... No Price Found

1807. U.S.A. Action
firing, 10 pcs. .... No Price Found
1808. U.S.A. Action
firing, 10 pcs. .... No Price Found
1809. Cowboys and North
American Indians, 10 pcs. .... No Price Found
1810. Life Guards
and Grenadier Guards, 16 pcs. .... No Price Found
1811. 11th Hussars,
S. Lancaster Regiment, 16 pcs. .... No Price Found
1812. 21st Lancers, King's Own
Royal Regiment, 16 pcs. .... No Price Found
1813. Life Guards, Royal
Norfolk Regiment, 16 pcs. .... No Price Found
1814. Seaforth Highlanders,
12th Lancers, 16 pcs. .... No Price Found
1815. Gordon Highlanders,
21st Lancers, 16 pcs. .... No Price Found
1816. U.S.A. Cavalry
and Infantry, 16 pcs. .... No Price Found
1817. Band of the Line, 14 pcs. .... No Price Found
1818. Scots Greys, Scots Guards,
Welsh Fusiliers, c1940 .... No Price Found
1819. Gordon Highlanders,
Royal Scots Greys, 26 pcs. .... No Price Found
1820. U.S.A. Infantry
and Cavalry, 27 pcs. .... No Price Found
1821. Winch, 1 pc. .... No Price Found
1822. Cowboys mounted
and on foot, 16 pcs. .... No Price Found
1823. British Infantry
and AA Units, Khaki, 31 pcs. .... No Price Found
1824. British Service Units, 36 pcs. .... No Price Found
1825. Colonial and Empire
Troops, 41 pcs. .... No Price Found
1826. German, French, Belgian,
Russian and Italian
Troops, 42 pcs. .... No Price Found
1827. Mechanized Army
Troops, 22 pcs. .... No Price Found
1828. Infantry of the Battle
Line, steel helmets,
at ease, 8 pcs. 200.00   450.00   650.00
1831. R.A. Gun 1201, with
Short Pole Pattern
Gun Limber, 2 pcs. .... No Price Found
1832. 10 Wheel Lorry with
2 pdr. AA Gun
on chassis, 4 pcs. 350.00   700.00   1000.00

#1828

	G	VG	EXC		G	VG	EXC

1833. 10 Wheel Lorry with Searchlight on Chassis, 4 pcs. ..... 200.00 / 450.00 / 675.00

1834. Scots Guards at slope, steel helmets, 8 pcs., c1940 .... 800.00 / 1500.00 / 2100.00

1835. Argentine Naval School Cadets, at slope, has officer, 1939, 1948-49, 8 pcs. .... 250.00 / 650.00 / 850.00
    Officer .... 35.00 / 60.00 / 80.00
    Cadet .... 20.00 / 40.00 / 60.00

1836. Argentine Military Cadets, at slope, with officer, 1948-49, 8 pcs. .... 450.00 / 850.00 / 1200.00

1837. Argentine Infantry, 8 pcs., at slope .... 300.00 / 600.00 / 850.00

1838. Argentine Army, 13 pcs. .... No Price Found

1839. Argentine Army, 13 pcs. .... No Price Found

1840. Argentine Army, 16 pcs. .... No Price Found

1841. Argentine Army, 21 pcs. .... No Price Found

1842. Argentine Army, 18 pcs. .... No Price Found

1843. Army of Argentina, Mounted Grenadiers and Infantry with Steel Helmets, officer with sword, on horseback, 9 mounted lancers, 8 foot infantry, c1939 .... 1400.00 / 2800.00 / 4000.00

1844. Argentine Army, 26 pcs. .... No Price Found

1845. Argentine Army, 31 pcs. .... No Price Found

1846. Argentine Military Cadets, 16 pcs. .... No Price Found

1847. Argentine Naval Cadets, 16 pcs. .... No Price Found

1848. Argentine Infantry Khaki, 16 pcs. .... No Price Found

1849. Argentine Forces, 36 pcs. .... No Price Found

1850. Netherlands Infantry, 8 pcs., slope arms .... 350.00 / 950.00 / 1400.00

1851. Netherlands Infantry, 16 pcs. .... No Price Found

1852. Argentine Cavalry, 20 pcs. .... No Price Found

1853. Argentine Cavalry, 15 pcs. .... No Price Found

1854. Militiamen, 8 pcs., slope arms, forage caps ...... 175.00 / 400.00 / 600.00

1855. Miniature Balloon Barrage Unit with Lorry. Winch and Balloon (less than half the size of the standard balloon) 1940. 1946 .... 125.00 / 250.00 / 350.00

1856. Polish Infantry, 8 pcs., slope arms (has officer Postwar) Prewar .... 170.00 / 300.00 / 450.00
    Postwar .... 140.00 / 230.00 / 320.00
    Officer .... 25.00 / 42.50 / 60.00
    Troop, c1939 .... 18.00 / 30.00 / 45.00
    Trooper, Postwar .... 16.00 / 25.00 / 35.00

1857. Barracks with Soldiers, 41 pcs. .... No Price Found

1858. British Infantry (steel helmets), 8 pcs., slung rifles, officer, Bren Gunner .... 85.00 / 115.00 / 150.00
    Officer .... 10.00 / 14.00 / 18.00
    Bren Gunner .... 10.00 / 12.00 / 16.00
    Troop .... 7.00 / 9.00 / 12.00

#1832

#1833

#1834

#1836

#1835

#1856

L to R: #1855, #1879.

	G	VG	EXC
1859. Sentry Box with Sentry, active service, 2 pcs.	30.00	55.00	75.00
1860. Sand bags			No Price Found
1861. Camouflaged Netted Field Emplacement for Heavy Artillery	700.00	1500.00	2200.00
1862. Camouflaged Netted Machine Gun Emplacement			No Price Found
1863. Concrete Pill Box for Heavy Artillery			No Price Found
1864. Concrete Pill Box with Detachable Machine Gun Positions	400.00	900.00	1500.00
1865. Bayonet Practice Frame with 3 hanging sandbags	700.00	1500.00	2200.00
1866. Circular Sandbag Emplacement for AA Gun, searchlight	400.00	900.00	1500.00
1867. Open Field Shelter with Camouflage Roof	400.00	900.00	1500.00
1868. A.R.W. Post with Gas Detector Platform	1500.00	3500.00	5000.00
1869. RAMC Casualty Cleaning Section	900.00	2000.00	2500.00
1870. Historical Series sold in 1940 at F.A.O. Schwarz, 16 foot figures from 91, 134, 141, 192, 196, 219, 226, 227, 228, 299, 399, 432, 1251, 1253, 1435, 1437	600.00	1000.00	1500.00
1871. Historical Series sold in 1940 at F.A.O. Schwarz, 16 foot figures from 16, 34, 36, 74, 75, 78, 80, 97, 111, 206, 207 (all 3 types), 312, 1510, 1619	400.00	800.00	1200.00
1872. Historical Series sold in 1940 at F.A.O. Schwarz, 16 foot figures from 15, 19, 69, 77, 114, 117, 122, 214, 225, 1293, 1518, 1519, 1542, 1545, 1633			No Price Found
1873. Historical Series sold in 1940 at F.A.O. Schwarz, 10 mounted figures from 1, 32, 94, 99, 100, 105, 108, 159, 229, 400	600.00	1000.00	1500.00
1874. Historical Series sold in 1940 at F.A.O. Schwarz, 10 mounted figures from 38, 45, 49, 94, 105, 108, 115, 159, 229, 1630			No Price Found
1875. Historical Series sold in 1940 at F.A.O. Schwarz, 5 mounted figures, 8 foot from 1, 32, 99, 100, 400, 160, 338, 1260, 1611, 1612, 1613, 1730 kneeling, 1828			No Price Found
1876. Bren Gun Carrier with Full Crew, 4 pcs., (3 soldiers), Prewar	35.00	65.00	80.00
Postwar	30.00	55.00	70.00

#1858

#1859

#1861

#1863

#1866

#1876

#1877 Postwar.

	G	VG	EXC

1877. Beetle Lorry and Driver,
4 pcs., light Troop transport
or General Service Truck,
5" long, Prewar 60.00   95.00   135.00
    Postwar 50.00   85.00   125.00

1878. King's African Rifles, 16 pcs. .... No Price Found

1879. Lorry, miniature, pulling
trailer loaded with
hydrogen gas cylinders
for 1855 Barrage Unit,
1940, 1946, 2 pcs. 115.00   165.00   210.00

1880-1884. UNKNOWN .... —

1885. Soldiers in Action,
in gas masks crawling,
digging, throwing grenades .... No Price Found

1886. Historical Series sold in
F.A.O. Schwarz, 15 foot
figures from 76, 104, 109,
142, 178, 186, 189, 194,
216, 222, 241, 1250,
1568, 1850, 1854 .... No Price Found

1887. Historical Series sold in
1940 at F.A.O. Schwarz,
15 foot figures from 7,
36, 90 (Officer with
binoculars), 107, 113,
118, 121 (two firing poses),
124, 137, 157, 1541, 1719
(wounded, khaki stretcher,
one stretcher bearer) 350.00   750.00   1000.00

1888. Historical Series sold in
1940 at F.A.O. Schwarz,
16 foot figures from 18
(kneeling), 98, 110, 119,
205, 212, 1515, 1542,
1554, 1597, 1621, 1630,
1633, 1858, 1906 .... 350.00   750.00   1000.00

1889. Historical Series sold in
1940 at F.A.O. Schwarz,
16 foot figures from 17
(standing), 74, 82, 88,
120 (Officer and man),
157, 172, 182, 314, 1424,
1436, 1617, 1711, 1856 ...... 350.00   750.00   1000.00

1890. Historical Series sold in
1940 at F.A.O. Schwarz,
10 mounted figures from
24, 31, 46, 106, 128,
164, 220, 315, 1711 .... 350.00   750.00   1000.00

1891. Historical Series sold in
1940 at F.A.O. Schwarz,
10 mounted figures from
3, 12, 33, 43, 44, 81, 83,
315, 1343, 1631 .... 350.00   750.00   1000.00

1892. Indian Infantry, 8 pcs., at
trail, has officer, 1940 .... 300.00   500.00   700.00

1893. Royal Indian Army Service
Corps, 7 pcs., officer,
4 infantry, mule and
handler 1940 .... 100.00   190.00   250.00
    Officer 16.00   24.00   30.00
    Troop 12.00   20.00   24.00
    Mule or handler 13.00   22.00   27.00

#1893

	G	VG	EXC

1894. Pilots or RAF in Full
Flying Kit with Women's
Auxiliary Air Force,
6 pilots, 2 WAAFs 250.00   500.00   700.00
    Per figure 12.00   25.00   35.00

1895. Pilots of the German
Luftwaffe in Full
Flying Kit, 8 pcs. 350.00   650.00   1000.00
    Per figure 30.00   55.00   75.00

#1894

#1895 Grey suit,
dark straps.

1896. RAMC Stretcher Party,
8 pcs., service order 250.00   550.00   800.00

1897. Motor Ambulance with
doctor, wounded, nurses,
orderlies, 18 pcs. 175.00   325.00   450.00
    Wounded 10.00   15.00   20.00
    Nurse 10.00   15.00   20.00
    Orderly 10.00   15.00   20.00

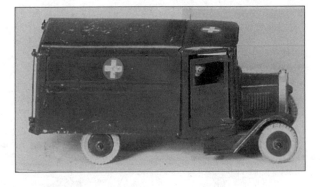

#1897 Ambulance, prewar.

#1897

#1898. L to R: Late flak helmet; early version.

	G	VG	EXC
1898. (9147) British Infantry (steel helmets) with rifles and Tommy guns, officer in battle dress, 8 pcs.	50.00	75.00	100.00
Officer	5.00	8.00	10.00
Troop	4.00	6.00	8.00
1899. Military Autogiro, with pilot, 2 pcs.	1500.00	3000.00	4500.00
1900. Regiment Louw Wepener, 8 pcs., slope, officer, 1939-41, 1948-49	300.00	650.00	900.00
Officer	35.00	65.00	90.00
Troop	30.00	55.00	80.00
1901. Capetown Highlanders, slope, officer, 8 pcs., 1939-41, Prewar	115.00	165.00	200.00
Postwar	100.00	140.00	175.00
Officer	13.00	20.00	28.00
Troop	8.00	15.00	22.00

#1900

#1901

	G	VG	EXC
1902. Union of South Africa Defense Force, 8 pcs., 1940-41	350.00	700.00	1100.00
Troop	35.00	65.00	90.00
1903. Indian Mountain Battery with Gun, gunners, mules, Mounted Officer, officer has sword held up, 1940, 12 pcs.	650.00	1000.00	1500.00
1904. U.S. Army Air Corps officer and Men, 8 pcs.			No Price Found
1905. U.S. Army Air Corps, Pilots, Officers and Men, 16 pcs.			No Price Found
Pilot	60.00	90.00	120.00
Man	20.00	30.00	40.00
1906. RAF Pilots, ground staff, and fire fighters, 16 pcs.			No Price Found
1907. British Army (Active Service Order), staff Officers with dispatch rider, 5 pcs.	115.00	165.00	225.00
Officer with swagger stick	13.50	20.00	30.00
Officer with binoculars	13.50	22.00	35.00
1908. Officers of the General Staff, the Guards, Line Infantry, Light Regiments, Fusiliers and Rifle Regiments, Number of pieces not known	800.00	1500.00	2100.00
1909. RAMC Doctors, Nurses, Orderlies, Wounded, Stretchers, Hospital Tent, Ambulance, Car and Lorry, 28 pcs.			No Price Found

#1907

#1908

	G	VG	EXC
1910. RAMC Field Hospital Staff with Wounded (Battle Dress), 24 pcs.			No Price Found
1911. Officers and Petty Officers of the Royal Navy, 7 pcs., 1940, 1946-59	125.00	187.50	250.00
Officer, coat over arm	15.00	32.50	40.00
Officer in shorts	12.00	27.50	35.00
Officer	10.00	17.50	22.00
Petty officer	10.00	14.50	20.00
1913. Cameronians marching (Scottish Rifles), 7 pcs.	900.00	1700.00	2400.00
Troop	50.00	100.00	150.00
1914. A.R.P. Wardens, 8 pcs. regulation uniforms	350.00	650.00	1000.00
1915. U.S. Infantry, 24 pcs.			No Price Found
1916. Reported to be a steel helmeted U.S. Army Band			Sold at 4500.00
1917. U.S. Cavalry, 3 row set	1000.00	2500.00	3500.00

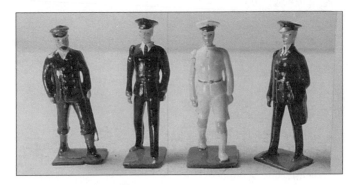

#1911

#1913

#1917 U.S. Cavalry, 15-piece non-cataloged set in steel helmet.

#1918

#2002-2004

	G	VG	EXC
1918. The Home Guard, slung rifles, 8 pcs.	125.00	250.00	400.00
Troop	12.50	22.00	40.00
1921-2001. UNKNOWN (Games and toys through 1999)			—
2002. Bell Tent, 4-1/2" Base			No Price Found
2003. Bell Tent, 5-1/2" base			No Price Found
2004. Bell Tent, 6-1/2" base			No Price Found
2005. Marquee or Hospital Tent, 5-1/2" long base	10.00	18.00	24.00
2006. Marquee or Hospital Tent, 7-1/2" long base			No Price Found
2007. Marquee or Hospital Tent, 9" long base			No Price Found
2008. 4-1/2" Howitzer and Limber	100.00	165.00	225.00
2009. Belgian Grenadiers in Greatcoats, 8 pcs.	100.00	150.00	200.00
Troop	8.00	12.00	16.00
2010. Parachute Regiment, 8 pcs., 1948-59 (7 in 1960)	90.00	135.00	180.00
7 pc. set	80.00	120.00	160.00
Officer	10.00	18.00	25.00
Slung Rifle	8.00	12.00	18.00
Bren Gun	10.00	16.50	24.00
2011. Display Box, Officers, flight sergeant, pilots, WRAF, Dispatch Rider and RAF Regiment Officers and men, 23 pcs.	240.00	360.00	500.00
Fire fighter, asbestos unit	10.00	20.00	25.00
WRAF	11.00	18.50	22.50

#2009

#2010

#2011

#2013

	G	VG	EXC
Bren Gun	11.00	16.50	22.00
Rifle	11.00	16.50	22.00
Officer Swagger Stick	12.00	19.50	26.00
Aircraftsman	9.00	15.00	20.00

2012. Royal Australian Air Force marching, red berets, 8 pcs. .... No Price Found
2013. Indian Mounted Army, 12 pcs. .... No Price Found
2014. Band of U.S. Marine Corps, 21 pcs. 700.00 1300.00 1800.00
2015. Soviet Cavalry and Soviet Guards, 13 pcs. .... No Price Found

	G	VG	EXC
2016. Japanese Imperial Guards, 13 pcs.		No Price Found	
2017. Ski Troups, four, 1948-57	220.00	400.00	600.00
Troop	45.00	65.00	130.00
2018. Danish Army, Guard Hussar Rgt., 8 pcs., with officer and Trumpeter	280.00	500.00	800.00
Officer and Trumpeter	35.00	65.00	100.00
Hussar	25.00	50.00	80.00
2019. Danish LivGarde, 7 pcs.	120.00	210.00	275.00
Troop	14.50	22.50	30.00
2020. Portuguese Native Infantry, 8 pcs.		No Price Found	
2021. (9183) U.S. Military Police (Snowdrops), 8 pcs., (7 in 1960), no officer	70.00	95.00	125.00
Troop	7.00	9.00	11.00
2022. (9371) Swiss Papal Guards with officer, 9 pcs.	120.00	200.00	275.00
Officer	13.50	22.00	30.00
Guard	10.00	18.50	25.00
2023. Covered Wagon, 6 pcs.		No Price Found	
2024. Light Goods Van with driver, various colors, 2 pcs.	250.00	450.00	600.00

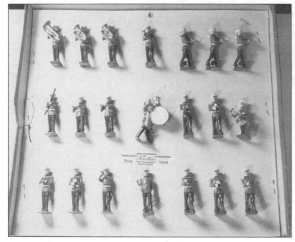

#2014 Boxed.

#2015

#2019

#2017

#2021

#2022

#2018

#2024

#2025

#2026

#2027

#2028

#2029

	G	VG	EXC
2025. (9334) Cameron Highlanders, firing, with Pipers, 18 pcs.	150.00	225.00	350.00
Officer	12.50	24.00	30.00
Piper	10.00	15.00	20.00
Troop	9.00	13.00	18.00
2026. (9705) 25 pdr. Howitzer	7.00	10.50	14.00
2027. (9172) Red Army Guards in greatcoats, 8 pcs., has officer	75.00	112.50	150.00
Officer	10.00	15.00	20.00
Troop	7.00	10.50	14.00
2028. Red Army Cavalry at parade halt, 5 pcs.	100.00	155.00	230.00
Officer	14.00	27.50	35.00
Trooper	12.00	23.50	30.00
2029. (9105) Life Guards, mounted at halt and foot sentries, 6 pcs.	65.00	95.00	125.00
Mounted	10.00	15.00	20.00
Foot	8.00	12.00	16.00
2030. Australian Infantry in Blue Ceremonial Dress, has officer, 1949-59, 8 pcs.	100.00	150.00	200.00
Officer	12.00	18.00	28.00
Troops	10.00	15.00	20.00
2031. Australian Infantry in Battle Dress, at slope, 8 pcs., 1949-59	85.00	125.00	160.00
Officer	10.00	15.00	20.00
Trooper with slouch hat	8.00	12.00	16.00
2032. Red Army Infantry, summer infantry, summer uniforms, marching in review	95.00	130.00	180.00
Troop	8.00	12.00	16.00
2033. (9180) U.S. Infantry marching, steel helmets, with officer, 8 pcs., (7 in 1960)	55.00	80.00	105.00
Officer	6.50	9.75	13.00
Troop	5.00	7.50	10.00
2034. Covered Wagon, 4 horses, pioneer, wife, 7 pcs.	105.00	150.00	200.00

#2030

#2031

#2032

#2033

#2035

	G	VG	EXC
2035. (9175) Svea (Swedish) Lifeguards, 8 pcs., slope with officer	100.00	160.00	220.00
Officer	12.00	18.00	24.00
Troop	10.00	15.00	20.00
2036. (9311) Scots Greys, Scots Guards, Black Watch, 19 pcs. (12 in 1960)	145.00	280.00	350.00
12 pc. set	120.00	200.00	260.00
2037. Ski Trooper, 1pc.	40.00	70.00	125.00
2038. Scots Guards at ease, 8 pcs.	No Price Found		
2039. Colours of the Scots and Coldstream Guards, 8 pcs., 4 color bearers, 4 color sergeants	No Price Found		

	G	VG	EXC
2040. Pipers and Royal Scots, 4 pcs.	No Price Found		
2041. Trailer, Universal Clockwork Unit with key	35.00	60.00	90.00
2042. Covered Wagon Set and attacking Indians, 13 pcs.	400.00	900.00	1300.00
2043. Rodeo Set, 13 pcs.	275.00	450.00	700.00
Stockade fence (wood and metal)	25.00	40.00	60.00
Figure Bucking Horse	30.00	65.00	100.00
Seated Cowboys	25.00	30.00	40.00
2044. (9179) U.S. Air Corps, 1949 pattern blue uniform, marching, slung carbines, 8 pcs.	65.00	105.00	125.00
Officer	8.50	11.50	15.00
Troop	7.00	10.00	12.50
2045. Clockwork Van, driver, 2 pcs.	300.00	650.00	1000.00
2046. (9391) Arab Display, mounted, foot, 12 pcs.	175.00	300.00	400.00
Running, foot	12.50	18.75	25.00
Mounted	8.00	12.00	16.00
Marching	5.00	7.50	10.00
2047. Knights in Armor, 6 pcs.	No Price Found		
2048. Lorry, 25 pdr. and clockwork trailer	140.00	210.00	280.00
2049. Life Guards and Scots Guards in Review Order, 20 pcs.	900.00	1500.00	2000.00

#2043 Partial.

#2043 Partial.

#2044

#2046

	G	VG	EXC
2050. Foreign Legion, Zouaves, Cuirassiers, 20 pcs., Legion marching (6) with mtd. officer, (8) Zouaves charging, (5) Cuirassiers with officer	700.00	1100.00	1500.00
2051. Uruguayan Military School Cadets, at slope, with officer, 1953-59, 8 pcs.	180.00	270.00	360.00
Officer	25.00	37.50	50.00
Cadet	20.00	30.00	40.00
2052. (9448) Anti-Aircraft Unit, 2 predictors, Height Finder, AA Gun and Searchlight, 15 pcs.	300.00	550.00	800.00
2053. Corral 18" square	No Price Found		
2055. (9286) "1862" Confederate Cavalry, officer, 5 pcs.	75.00	100.00	125.00
1960, 4 pc. set	50.00	70.00	85.00
Officer	11.00	16.50	22.00
Trooper	10.00	15.00	20.00

#2058

#2060

#2059

#2051

#2055

2056. (9287) "1862" Union Cavalry, 5 pcs., has Bugler, officer	80.00	105.00	130.00
1960, 4 pc. set	55.00	75.00	90.00
Officer	10.00	15.00	20.00
Bugler	10.00	15.00	20.00
Trooper	9.00	13.50	18.00
2057. (9487) "1862" Union Artillery with Gunners, 3 pcs.	35.00	65.00	85.00
Gunner	12.50	18.50	25.00

	G	VG	EXC
2058. (9486) "1862" Confederate Artillery with Gunners, 3 pcs.	35.00	65.00	85.00
2059. (9187) "1862" Union Infantry, 7 pcs.	65.00	85.00	115.00
Officer	7.50	10.00	13.00
Troop	6.50	8.50	10.00
2060. (9186) "1862" Confederate Infantry, 7 pcs.	65.00	85.00	115.00
Officer	7.50	10.00	13.00
Flagbearer	5.50	9.50	11.00
Bugler	5.50	9.50	11.00
Troop	6.50	8.50	10.00
2061. Wild West Display, 90 pcs.	1000.00	2000.00	2800.00

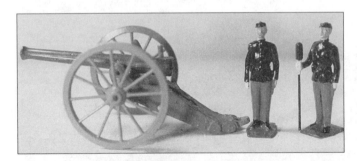

#2057

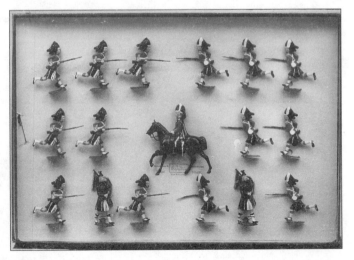

#2062

	G	VG	EXC
2062. (9332) Seaforth Highlanders charging, with Pipers, 17 pcs. (15 1960-61, 12 as 9332)	165.00	225.00	300.00
Mounted officer	22.50	35.00	55.00
Foot	9.00	12.50	16.00
2063. (9133) Argyll & Sutherland Highlanders, firing, 6 pcs. (5 in 1960)	70.00	115.00	150.00
Troop	8.50	12.75	17.00
2064. (9745) 155mm Gun	35.00	65.00	100.00
2065. (9400) H.M. Queen on horseback, saluting	20.00	35.00	55.00
2066. Royal Canadian Mounted, one piece, Mounted Officer	20.00	30.00	45.00
2067. The Sovereign's Standard of the Life Guards and Escort, 7 pcs (contents vary)	130.00	250.00	400.00
Farrier	15.00	28.00	40.00
Trumpeter	13.00	25.00	35.00
2068. (9386) "1862" Confederate Cavalry and Infantry, 12 pcs.	125.00	200.00	275.00
2069. (9387) "1862" Union Cavalry and Infantry, 12 pcs.	125.00	200.00	275.00

#2067

	G	VG	EXC
2070. "1862" Display Box, 30 pcs.	600.00	1000.00	1500.00
2071. Royal Marines, present arms, 7 pcs., (6 in 1960)	70.00	105.00	140.00
2072. King's Royal Rifle Corps, walking at trail, 1953-59	115.00	200.00	275.00
2073. RAF, slope, 8 pcs., officer, 1953-59	115.00	205.00	280.00

#2065

#2065 Canadian version, white horse.

#2071

#2072

#2066

#2073

	G	VG	EXC
2074. (9212) First (King's) Dragoon Guards, walking, cantering and trotting horses, officer, 5 pcs.	105.00	150.00	200.00
1960, 4 pc. set	70.00	105.00	150.00
Officer	14.00	22.50	30.00
Trooper	12.00	18.00	24.00
2075. (9214) 7th Queen's Own Hussars, 5 pcs.	115.00	165.00	226.00
Officer	15.00	27.00	35.00
Troop	12.00	22.00	28.00
2076. (9217) 12th Lancers, trotting and cantering, 5 pcs.	100.00	135.00	195.00
Officer	14.00	24.00	32.00
Trooper	12.00	21.00	28.00
2077. Kings Troop, R.H.A., Gun and Limber, 8 pcs.	275.00	400.00	550.00
2078. Irish Guards, present arms, 7 pcs., 1953-59	100.00	130.00	190.00
Troop	10.00	15.00	22.00
2079. (9302) Royal Company of Archers, 13 pcs.	250.00	350.00	500.00
Archer	15.00	25.00	32.00

#2078

#2079

	G	VG	EXC
2080. Sailors Royal Navy, at slope, 1953-61, officer, 8 pcs. (7 in 1960)	95.00	135.00	200.00
Officer	11.50	16.00	25.00
Sailor	9.50	13.00	18.00
2081. The Sovereign's Escort, Coronation of Queen Elizabeth, 211 pcs., which made a display bout 15 ft. long	2900.00	4200.00	5500.00
2082. (9125) Coldstream Guards, attention, officer, 8 pcs.	70.00	105.00	140.00
Officer	8.00	12.00	16.00
Troop	6.50	9.75	13.00

#2074

#2075 Officer.

#2076

#2080

#2082

	G	VG	EXC
2083. (9127) Welsh Guards, at ease, with Mounted Officer, 7 pcs.	90.00	135.00	180.00
Officer	11.00	16.50	22.00
Troop	8.00	12.00	16.00
2084. Colour Party of the Scots Guards, 6 pcs.	150.00	225.00	300.00
Sergeant	12.00	18.50	25.00
2085. (9405) Musical Ride of the Household Cavalry, 23 pcs.	700.00	1100.00	1500.00
Single Lancer	25.00	45.00	65.00

	G	VG	EXC
2086. (9339) Royal West Surrey Infantry, standing, kneeling, prone firing, 16 pcs.	125.00	225.00	280.00
Troop	8.50	11.00	14.00
2087. Dismounted 5th Iniskilling Dragoon Guards, has officer, 1954-59, 8 pcs.	135.00	235.00	300.00
Guard	13.00	22.00	32.00

#2083

#2083

#2084

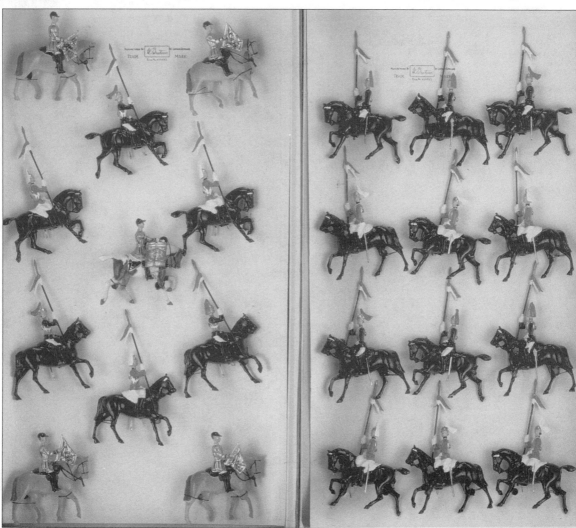

#2085 Set arranged in correct order. Courtesy William Doyle Appraisals & Consulting.

#2087

#2089

	G	VG	EXC
2090. Royal Irish Fusiliers, at attention, officer, 1954-59, 8 pcs.	145.00	260.00	325.00
Officer	18.00	28.00	40.00
Troop	13.50	24.50	32.00
2091. Rifle Brigade, at trail, officer, 8 pcs., 1954-59	135.00	235.00	300.00
Officer	14.00	24.50	35.00
Troop	13.50	22.00	28.00
2092. Parachute Regiment, at left slope, officer, 8 pcs., 1954-59	110.00	215.00	280.00
Officer	12.50	22.50	30.00
Troop	11.00	20.00	26.00
2093. Band of the Royal Berkshire Regiment, 25 pcs., 1954-59, plastic drums after 1955	800.00	1450.00	1800.00
2094. (9402) State Open Landau with team of 6 Windsor Greys, Queen Elizabeth, Prince Phillip, 11 pcs.	170.00	250.00	400.00
2095. (9366) French Foreign Legion in Action, 14 pcs.	160.00	220.00	350.00
12 pc. set, 1960-61	125.00	215.00	270.00
13 pc. set, 1962	135.00	245.00	300.00
Mounted officer	13.00	18.50	24.00
Officer kneeling with binoculars	12.50	22.50	27.50

	G	VG	EXC
2088. Duke of Cornwall's Light Infantry, 8 pcs., marching at trail, has officer, 1954-59	110.00	205.00	270.00
2089. Gloucestershire Regiment, at left slope, has officer, 1954-59, 8 pcs.	135.00	235.00	300.00
Officer	14.00	24.50	35.00
Troop	12.00	22.00	28.00

#2090   #2091 Note brown gloves.   #2092

#2095

#2093 Dark blue uniforms trimmed in red.

	G	VG	EXC
Machine Gunner	11.50	18.50	24.00
Charging	10.50	17.50	22.00
Standing Firing	8.00	12.00	16.00

2096. (9428) Drum and Pipe Band
of the Irish Guards, 12 pcs. 350.00 / 600.00 / 900.00

2097. French Foreign Legion
and Arabs, 26 pcs. 450.00 / 850.00 / 1250

2098. Venezuelan Military
School Cadets, 7 pcs.,
6 men, officer with
furled flag, 1955-59 125.00 / 265.00 / 350.00

Officer	15.00	22.50	40.00
Cadet	12.00	18.00	30.00

#2096 Tenor drum.

#2096

#2098

2099. Venezuelan Military
School Cadets, 15 pcs.,
13 men, Flagbearer,
officer, 1955-59 175.00 / 400.00 / 550.00

2100. (9375) Venezuelan Cadets,
Infantry, Sailors, 23 pcs.
(sailors in no other set),
1 officer, 7 sailors,
8 cadets, 7 infantry
(20 pcs. from 1960 on) 200.00 / 450.00 / 700.00

1960 set 150.00 / 400.00 / 650.00

2101. (9482) U.S. Marines
Color Guard Party, 4 pcs. 125.00 / 165.00 / 225.00

Flagbearer	20.00	35.00	50.00
Troop	10.00	15.00	20.00

	G	VG	EXC
2102. (9760) Austin Champ (jeep-like vehicle)	30.00	50.00	65.00

2103. Life Guards, Scots Greys,
Scots Guards, Welsh
Fusiliers, Coldstream
Guards Band, 32 pcs.,
SELFRIDGES SPECIAL ...... No Price Found

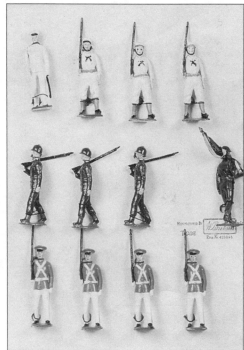

#2100 Note blue trim on flap.

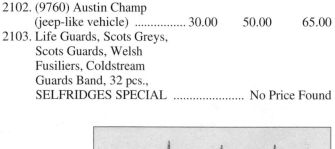

#2100

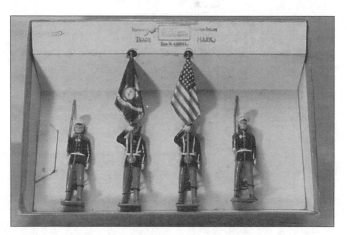

#2101 Boxed.

#2102

	G	VG	EXC
2104. Venezuelan Infantry, 7 pcs., officer with flag, 1955-59	115.00	175.00	250.00
Officer	25.00	37.50	50.00
Troop	12.50	18.75	25.00

#2105

#2106

#2109

	G	VG	EXC
2105. Venezuelan Infantry, 15 pcs., officer, Officer-flagbearer included, 1955-59	200.00	365.00	450.00
Officer-flagbearer	25.00	37.50	50.00
Officer	15.00	22.50	30.00
Troop	12.50	18.75	25.00
2106. 18" Heavy Howitzer Mounted for Garrison Work	45.00	70.00	100.00
2107. (9740) 18" Heavy Howitzer Mounted on Tractor Wheels	45.00	70.00	100.00
2108. Drums and Fifes of the Welsh Guards, 12 pcs.	400.00	750.00	1000.00
2109. (9435) Highland Pipe Band of the Black Watch, 20 pcs.	300.00	650.00	1000.00
2110. (9478) U.S. Military Band, full dress, 25 pcs.	800.00	1400.00	2000.00
2111. Black Watch Colour Party, 6 pcs.	225.00	375.00	600.00
2112. U.S. Marine Corps Band, summer dress, 25 pcs.	700.00	1400.00	2000.00
Drum Major	45.00	72.50	100.00
Sousaphone	35.00	60.00	80.00
Other	30.00	55.00	75.00
2113. Full Band of Grenadier Guards, 25 pcs.	800.00	2200.00	2800.00
Per figure	35.00	75.00	100.00
2114. Band of the Line (plastic drums) 12 pcs.	200.00	400.00	600.00

#2110

#2111

#2111

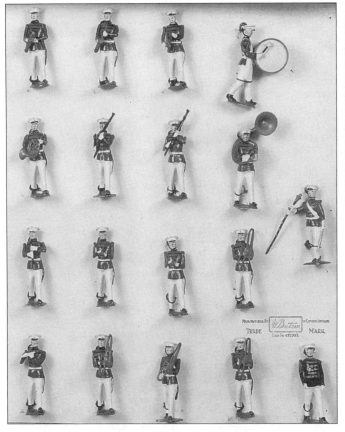

#2112 Boxed.

#2115

#2117

#2117

	G	VG	EXC
2115. Drums and Bugles of the Royal Marines, 12 pcs.	250.00	500.00	800.00
2116. Band of the RAF, 12 pcs.	200.00	400.00	550.00
2117. Band of the U.S.A. Army, khaki, 12 pcs.	300.00	550.00	850.00
Drum Major	25.00	45.00	65.00
Others	15.00	30.00	40.00

2118 to 2147 are half-sets

	G	VG	EXC
2118. Life Guards, 3 pcs., mounted, dismounted	$95.00	$150.00	$225.00

	G	VG	EXC
2119. The Second Dragoons (Royal Scots Greys), 3 pcs., officer on cantering horse, 2 dismounted Troopers at attention with drawn swords	110.00	175.00	250.00
2120. 3rd Kings Own Hussars, 3 pcs.	150.00	250.00	375.00
2121. Grenadier Guards, 4 pcs.	65.00	110.00	175.00
Officer	7.50	11.25	15.00
Troop	4.00	6.00	8.00
2122. Scots Guards, 4 pcs.	65.00	110.00	175.00
2123. Irish Guards, 4 pcs.	125.00	300.00	400.00
2124. Welsh Fusiliers, 4 pcs., at attention, 1957-59	100.00	200.00	275.00
2125. Loyal North Lancashire, 4 pcs., 2 standing, 1 kneeling, officer standing with binoculars	100.00	200.00	275.00
Kneeling	11.00	16.50	22.00
2126. Black Watch, 3 pcs.	100.00	200.00	300.00
Mounted officer	35.00	52.50	70.00
2127. Royal Marines, 4 pcs.	100.00	200.00	275.00
2128. Life Guards and Scots Guards, 3 pcs.	100.00	200.00	275.00
2129. Royal Artillery Gun Detachment, 1957-59, 4 pcs.	75.00	112.50	150.00
2130. Infantry in Battle Dress, 4 pcs., 1957-59	75.00	112.50	150.00

#2127

#2149

	G	VG	EXC
2131. Medium Machine Gunners, 3 pcs.	75.00	112.50	150.00
2132. Royal Army Medical Corps., 5 pcs.	85.00	150.00	225.00
2133. Canadian Governor-General's Horse and Foot Guards, 3 pcs.	75.00	125.00	200.00
2134. Royal Canadian Mounted Police, 3 pcs.	75.00	125.00	200.00
2135. Danish Hussar and Life Guards, 3 pcs.	100.00	175.00	250.00
2136. French Foreign Legion, 3 pcs.	100.00	175.00	250.00
2137. French Foreign Legion in Action, 4 pcs.	100.00	175.00	250.00
2138. French Tirailleurs, 3 pcs.	75.00	200.00	300.00
2139. U.S. Cavalry and Infantry, 3 pcs.	65.00	110.00	150.00
2140. Union Cavalry, 3 pcs.	100.00	200.00	275.00
2141. Confederate Cavalry, 3 pcs.	100.00	200.00	275.00
2142. Union Infantry, 4 pcs.	100.00	200.00	275.00
2143. Confederate Infantry, 4 pcs.	100.00	200.00	275.00
2144. Soviet Russian Infantry and Cavalry, 3 pcs.	65.00	120.00	200.00
2145. Cowboys, mounted and on foot, 3 pcs.	65.00	110.00	150.00
2146. North American Indians, 3 pcs.	65.00	110.00	150.00
2147. Arabs, 3 pcs.	65.00	120.00	200.00

End half-boxes

2148. (9158) Canadian Fort Henry Guards with goat mascot, 7 pcs.	$65.00	$85.00	$115.00

	G	VG	EXC
2149. Gentleman at Arms, with officer, 9 pcs.	350.00	800.00	1200.00
2150. (9770) Centurion Tank	175.00	290.00	400.00
2151. Mounted Kettle Drummer, Life Guards, 1 pc.	20.00	40.00	55.00
2152. (9499) Waterloo Gunners with Gun, 3 pcs.	50.00	85.00	125.00

#2152

2153. Band of the Royal Marines (plastic drums) 12 pcs.	200.00	400.00	550.00
2154. Centurion Tank, painted for Desert Warfare	250.00	450.00	600.00
2155. U.N. Infantry, 1957-60, 8 pcs.	250.00	600.00	900.00
Officer	15.00	40.00	60.00
Slung Rifle	12.00	22.00	30.00
Bren Gun at Trail	15.00	25.00	45.00

#2148

#2155

	G	VG	EXC
2156. H.M. Queen Elizabeth (Picture Box Souvenir)			No Price Found
2157. Mounted Kettle Drummer, Life Guards (Picture Box Souvenir), 1 pc.			No Price Found
2158. Royal Canadian Mounted Police (Picture Box Souvenir) 1 pc.			No Price Found
2159. (9460) Fort Henry Guard, Sentry and Box, 2 pc.	65.00	100.00	150.00
2160. Fort Henry Guard, 1 pc.			No Price Found
2161. Knights of Agincourt, mounted and foot	175.00	265.00	325.00

2162-2167 are solidcast in non-lead alloy for export to Australia, 1954. Only marked "England."

	G	VG	EXC
2162. Cowboys and Indians, 8 pcs.			No Price Found
2163. Cowboys and Indians, 16 pcs.			No Price Found
2164. Infantry in Action, 8 pcs.			No Price Found
2165. Infantry in Action, 16 pcs.			No Price Found
2166. Guards and Infantry of the Line, 8 pcs.			No Price Found
2167. Guards and Infantry of the Line, 16 pcs.			No Price Found

End of non-lead exports to Australia

	G	VG	EXC
2168. Gordon Highlanders, officer Mounted, 1 pc. (Picture Box Souvenir)	$30.00	$50.00	$65.00

#2168

	G	VG	EXC
2169. 12th Lancers, Mounted Officer at the halt, 1 pc. (Picture Box Souvenir)			No Price Found
2170. Mounted Trumpeter of Life Guards Band, 1 pc. (Picture Box Souvenir)			No Price Found
2171. RAF Colour Party, (extremely rare, semi-unique)	1000.00	2400.00	3000.00
2172. Algerian Spahi (en grande tenue), Review Order, 5 pcs.	300.00	650.00	900.00
Standard Bearer	50.00	100.00	150.00
Trooper	40.00	75.00	120.00
2173. (9720) Batallion Anti-Tank Gun	9.50	13.50	18.00

	G	VG	EXC
2174. (9750) Batallion Anti-Tank Gun with Towing Vehicle	75.00	150.00	200.00
2175. (9748) 155mm Gun, Mounted on Centurion Tank Body	200.00	350.00	500.00

#2172

#2172

#2173

#2175

	G	VG	EXC

2176. Greek Royal Guards
at slope, no officer
(c1959), 4 pcs. 100.00   200.00   300.00

2177. (9154) Band of the Fort
Henry Guard, 5 pcs. 90.00   150.00   225.00

#2177   *#2177*

2178. Fort Henry Guards,
Fife and Drums, 10 pcs. 175.00   300.00   450.00

2179. Highland Pipe Band of the
Black watch, plastic drums,
1959-60, 9 pcs. 225.00   450.00   650.00

2180. Fort Henry
Band Drum Major, 1 pc. .... No Price Found

2181. Papal Guards .... No Price Found

2182. Fort Henry Guard Pioneer,
1 pc. This is the last
completely new lead alloy
figure made by Britains 15.00   25.00   32.00

2183. Fort Henry Cannon, 1 pc. .... No Price Found

2184. Bahamas Police at
Attention, 8 pcs., native
sergeant, white officer 700.00   1200.00   2000.00
     Per piece 35.00   57.50   80.00

2185. Bahamas Police Band,
12 or 13 pcs. 1200.00   2500.00   3500.00
     Per piece 35.00   70.00   100.00

2186. Bahamas Police Band, 26 pcs. .... No Price Found
     Per piece 35.00   70.00   100.00

2187. (9174) Red Army Guards
Infantry in Greatcoats and
Summer Uniform,
Mounted Officer, 6 pcs. 210.00   350.00   500.00

2188. Anti-Aircraft Personnel
with Predictor, Range
Finder and Height
Finder, 6 pcs. 105.00   175.00   250.00

2189. (9721) 18th Century
Cannon, plus
6 cannon balls 10.00   20.00   30.00

2190. (9192) Knights
of Agincourt, foot, 4 pcs. 50.00   80.00   105.00

9104. Attendants to the State
Coach, 6 pcs., (1475) 70.00   105.00   135.00

9155. Fort Henry Guards, War
of 1812, 49th Foot, 7 pcs.,
(6 later), no officer 60.00   90.00   120.00

9160. Fort Henry Guards, War
of 1812, 89th Foot, 6 pcs.,
no officer 60.00   90.00   120.00

#9160

9302. Attendants to the State
Coach, 12 pcs. (1475) .... No Price Found

9345. Ninth Lancers, mounted
at halt, with officer, Royal
Fusiliers at slope,
no officer, 11 pcs. .... No Price Found

9392. Knights of Agincourt,
mounted and foot,
9 pcs. (2161) 120.00   185.00   250.00

#2182   *#2184*   *#2186*

Picture Packs

Britains military Picture Packs did not follow any logical numbering sequence. When introduced in the 1954 catalog, they were grouped by subjects rather than number. The range was unchanged until discontinued in 1959. Picture Packs listed are shown in the order of their appearance in the catalog. Generally only found in "EXC" or better.

LIFE GUARDS

	Boxed Excellent
37B Trooper, Full Dress	$30.00
1325B Trumpeter, Regimental Dress	60.00
1270B Farrier, Full Dress	55.00
1268B Corporal Major with Standard, Full Dress	60.00
645B Officer, Full Dress	30.00
1269B Trumpeter, State Dress	45.00
477B Drummer, State Dress	45.00
116B Trooper, Cloak	35.00
1333B Trumpeter, Cloak	60.00
1334B Farrier, Cloak	60.00
1335B Corporal Major with Standard, Cloak	60.00
844B Officer, Cloak	35.00
1198B Trooper Dismounted	25.00

ROYAL HORSE GUARDS

	Boxed Excellent
1336B Trooper, Full Dress	$30.00
1337B Trumpeter, Regimental Dress	60.00
1338B Farrier, Full Dress	55.00
1339B Corporal Major with Standard, Full Dress	60.00

	Boxed Excellent
218B Officer, Full Dress	35.00
1340B Trooper, Dismounted	40.00

11th HUSSARS (Prince Albert's Own)

	Boxed Excellent
883B Trooper, Full Dress	$50.00
1345B Trumpeter, Full Dress	60.00
647B Officer, Full Dress	50.00
48B Trooper, Dismounted	25.00

12th ROYAL LANCERS (Prince of Wales)

1346B Trooper, Lance at Carry	$50.00
1347B Trooper, Lance Slung	50.00
1348B Trumpeter, Full Dress	60.00
1439B Officer, Full Dress	50.00

#1345B 11th Hussars.

#1347B Royal Lancers.

1st KING'S DRAGOON GUARDS

1279B Trooper, Full Dress	$50.00
1341B Trumpeter, Full Dress	60.00
1342B Standard, Full Dress	60.00
1278B Office, Full Dress	50.00
1343B Trooper, Dismounted	35.00

#37B Life Guards.

#1335B Life Guards.

#1198B Life Guards.

#1339B Royal Horse Guards.

#1341B 1st King's Dragoon Guards.

#1342B 1st King's Dragoon Guards.

ROYAL SCOTS GREYS (2nd Dragoons)

41B Trooper, Full Dress $40.00
1344B Trumpeter, Full Dress 60.00
668B Officer, Full Dress 45.00

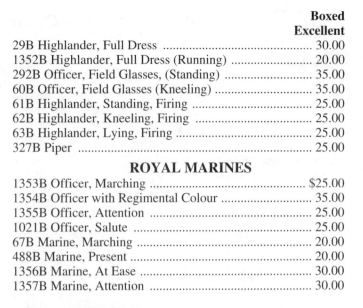

#1344B Royal Scots Greys.

SCOTS GUARDS

666B Officer, Marching $25.00
915B Officer, Marching, Drawn Sword 25.00
239B Queen's Colour Bearer, (Carry) 35.00
240B Regimental Colour Bearer, (Carry) 35.00
340B Queen's Colour Bearer (Slope) 35.00
1006B Officer, Salute 25.00
1350B Officer, Attention 25.00
899B Officer, Greatcoat 25.00
914B Colour-Sergeant, Slope Arms 30.00
339B Pioneer 20.00
28B Guardsman, Marching, Slope Arms 20.00
1005B Guardsman, Present 20.00
778B Guardsman, Attention 30.00
906B Guardsman, At Ease 30.00
898B Guardsman, Greatcoat 20.00
14B Piper 30.00
768B Side Drummer 30.00
1351B Bugler 30.00

GORDON HIGHLANDERS

845B Mounted Officer, Full Dress $65.00
461B Officer, Full Dress 40.00

#461B Gordon Highlanders.   *#845B*

29B Highlander, Full Dress 30.00
1352B Highlander, Full Dress (Running) 20.00
292B Officer, Field Glasses, (Standing) 35.00
60B Officer, Field Glasses (Kneeling) 35.00
61B Highlander, Standing, Firing 25.00
62B Highlander, Kneeling, Firing 25.00
63B Highlander, Lying, Firing 25.00
327B Piper 25.00

ROYAL MARINES

1353B Officer, Marching $25.00
1354B Officer with Regimental Colour 35.00
1355B Officer, Attention 25.00
1021B Officer, Salute 25.00
67B Marine, Marching 20.00
488B Marine, Present 20.00
1356B Marine, At Ease 30.00
1357B Marine, Attention 30.00

L to R: #488B, #1021B. Royal Marines.   *#1357B Royal Marines.*

ROYAL NAVY

1290B Officer, Marching $30.00
1289 Bluejacket, Marching, Slope Arms 25.00
429B Bluejacket, Marching 20.00

ROYAL AIR FORCE

1081B Air Commodore $65.00
1276B Officer, No. 1 Dress 30.00
1277B Airman, Marching 30.00
1054B Pilot, Full Equipment 30.00
66B Pilot, Sidcot Suit 30.00
587B Fire Fighter 40.00

#1081B   *#587B*

	Boxed Excellent
1055B WRAF	35.00
1149B Officer (RAF Regiment)	30.00
1151B Bren-gunner (RAF Regiment)	30.00
1150B Airman (RAF Regiment)	30.00

YEOMAN OF THE GUARD

219B Officer	$35.00
1138B Yeoman	25.00

UNITED STATES OF AMERICA

39B Cavalry, Galloping	$60.00
31B Cavalry, Walking	35.00
1205B Infantry officer	25.00
1206B Infantry Colour Bearer	40.00
1204B Infantry Private	20.00
1157B Officer Marine Corps	25.00
20B Marine	20.00
1226B Air Corps	20.00
107B West Point Cadet	20.00
1190B Military Policeman	20.00

AMERICAN CIVIL WAR, 1862-1865
Union Forces Cavalry

1358B Officer	$60.00
1359B Trumpeter	60.00
1360 Trooper	40.00

Infantry

1249B Officer	$30.00
1361B Officer, Field Glasses	50.00
1250B Standard	30.00
1251B Bugler	25.00
1253B Standing, Firing	20.00
1252B Standing, On Guard	20.00
1255B Kneeling, Firing	20.00
1254B Kneeling on Guard	20.00
1362B Zouave, Charging	30.00

Confederate Forces Cavalry

1363 Officer	$60.00
1364B Trumpeter	60.00
1365B Trooper	40.00
1366B Officer, Field Glasses	50.00

L to R: #1364B, #1366B, #1361B. Civil War Union & Confederates.

	Boxed Excellent
Infantry	
1237B Officer	$30.00
1366B Officer, Field Glasses	50.00
1238B Standard	30.00
1239B Bugler	25.00
1241B Standing, Firing	20.00
1240B Standing, On Guard	20.00
1243B Kneeling, Firing	20.00
1242B Kneeling, On Guard	20.00

#1240B Two versions: slouch hat; campaign or Montana hat.

FRENCH FOREIGN LEGION

1329B Officer, Full Dress (Mounted)	$35.00
1367B Officer, Full Dress (On Foot)	45.00
1035B Officer, Service Dress (Mounted)	35.00
561B Legionnaire, Marching	20.00
1368B Charging	30.00
1369B Standing, Firing	25.00
1371B Lying, Firing	25.00
1372B Machine Gunner	30.00

ARABS (All very rare in Picture Pack)

1232B Mounted, with Spear	$40.00
40B Mounted, with Scimitar	40.00
829B Mounted, with Rifle	40.00
53B Marching	25.00
1229B Running, with Scimitar	35.00
1231B Running, with Rifle	35.00

COWBOYS

34B Mounted, with Pistol	$25.00
1180B Mounted, with Rifle	25.00

#1219B Cowboy.

#275B Cowboy.

	Boxed Excellent
35B Mounted, with Lasso	25.00
1219B Mounted, on Bucking Bronco	95.00
275B Standing, Firing	20.00
274B Crouching, Firing	20.00
55B Standing, with Pistol	20.00
356B Standing, with Lasso	20.00
25B Walking, with Rifle	20.00

NORTH AMERICAN INDIANS

	Boxed Excellent
33B Mounted, with Rifle	$25.00
32B Mounted, with Tomahawk	25.00
23B Chief, with Tomahawk	20.00
22B Chief, with Knife	20.00
24B Chief, with Tomahawk	20.00

	Boxed Excellent
1216B Chief, with Rifle	20.00
1217B Brave, with Rifle	20.00
74B Brave, with Rifle	20.00
1179B Brave, Crawling with Knife	20.00
143B Brave, with Knife and Tomahawk	20.00

ROYAL CANADIAN MOUNTED POLICE

	Boxed Excellent
1373B Mounted with Lance	$85.00
271B Mounted, with Rifle	30.00
1267B Officer Mounted	40.00
591B Regulation Dress, Marching	20.00
1374B Regulation Dress, Attention	40.00
52B Winter Dress, Marching	45.00

#1373B

#271B

#591B

#1374B

#52B

Farm Series

	VG	EXC		VG	EXC
501. Farmer	$5.50	$7.50	504. Carter, plain arm	6.00	8.00
502. Farmer's wife, with basket	6.50	8.50	505. Carter with whip	6.75	9.00
503. Farmer's wife, with umbrella	6.50	8.50	506. Shire Horse	7.00	9.50
			507. Shire Colt	4.50	6.00
			508. Cows (assorted colours)	3.00	4.00

L to R: #501, #502, #503.

#506

#507

L to R: #504, #505.

#508

	VG	EXC
509. Calves (assorted colours) standing	2.50	4.00
Walking	2.75	4.00
510. Sheep, walking	2.00	3.00
511. Sheep, feeding	2.00	3.00
512. Lamb	3.00	4.00
513. Dogs (assorted colours)	3.00	4.00

L to R: #510, #511.

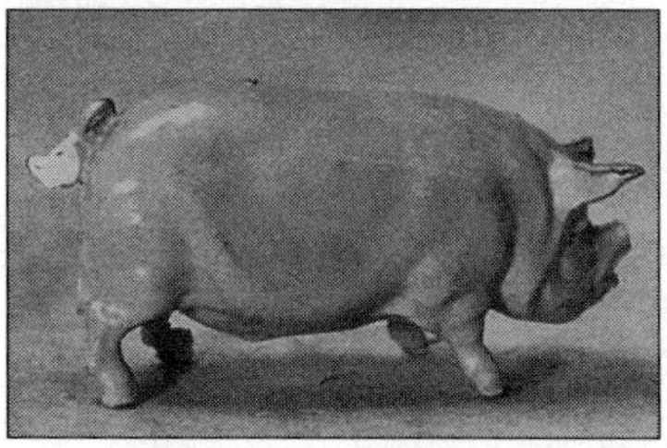

#514

#513

	VG	EXC
514. Pig (assorted colours)	3.00	4.00
515. Turkey	3.40	4.50
516. Fowls, Cocks and Hens (assorted colours)	3.00	4.00
517. Fowls, Cocks and Hens (white) each	2.25	3.00
518. Fowls, Cocks and Hens (yellow) each	2.25	3.00
519. Angry Gander	3.00	4.50
520. Goose	3.00	4.00
521. Oak Trees, each	15.00	20.00

L to R: #517, #518.

#520

#519

	VG	EXC
522. Cedar Trees, each	18.75	25.00
523. Elm Tree	15.00	20.00
524. Fir Tree	13.50	18.00
525. Fallen Tree, Prewar only	12.00	16.00
526. Shrub	5.25	7.00
527. Hurdle, 2-1/2" long	1.50	2.00
528. Large Troughs, each	3.00	4.00
529. Small Trough	2.25	3.00
530. Sheep, lying	3.00	4.00
531. Milkmaid, Pail on Head, early 1920s-40s	9.50	15.00
532. Milkmaid carrying pail	6.75	9.00
533. Ducks and Drakes (assorted colours), Ducks each	2.50	3.50
Drakes each	3.00	4.00

#523

#524

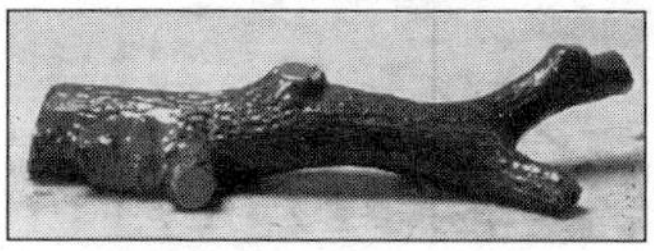

#525

#526

#527

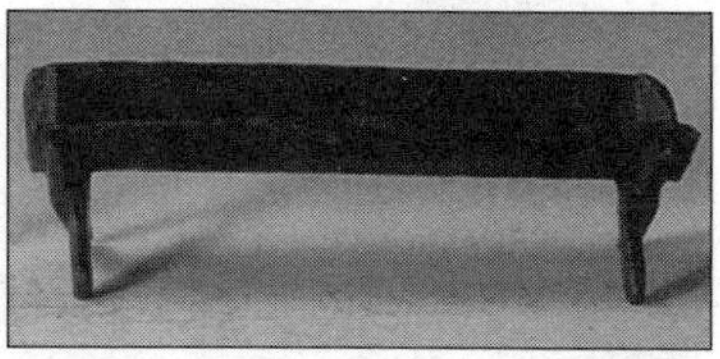

#528

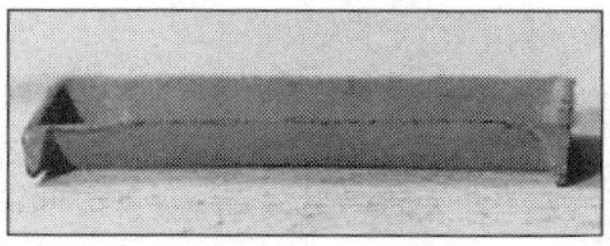

#529

#530

#531

#532

	VG	EXC		VG	EXC
534. Calf, lying	2.50	3.50	550. Cob	3.75	5.00
535. Landgirl	11.00	18.00	551. Scarecrow, detachable hat	8.50	11.50
536. Sheep and lamb lying together	5.00	6.50	552. Donkey	5.25	7.00
537. Milkmaid, milking	5.25	7.00	553. Sheaves of Wheat, single bundle (2 types exist)	5.00	6.50
538. Cow, lying	3.75	5.00	554. Farmer's son, sitting, c1920s-1940	24.00	32.00
539. Cow, feeding	5.25	7.00	555. Aged Villager, Man, sitting	8.50	12.00
540. Goat	3.00	4.00	556. Aged Villager, Woman, sitting	8.50	12.00
541. Cart Horse	7.50	10.00	557. Village Girl, walking c1920s-40	22.50	30.00
542. Wheatsheaf, stacked	4.00	5.50	558. Village Boy, walking, with stick, c1920s-40	22.50	30.00
543. Horse, feeding	4.25	6.00	559. Young Lady, walking	16.50	22.00
544. Chicks (assorted positions)	2.25	3.00	560. Farm Hand, sitting, for driving farm machine	9.00	12.00
545. Hens sitting (assorted colours)	2.25	3.00	561. Farmer's Daughter, sitting, c1920s-40	12.50	16.50
546. Piglets (assorted colours and sizes)	2.00	2.50			
547. Man and Wheelbarrow	9.00	12.00			
548. Hedges and Field Gate	21.00	28.00			
549. Hedges and Garden Gate	14.50	24.00			

#533

L to R: #534, #509.

#535 Prewar.

#538

#539

#540

#541

#542

#543

#547

#550

#551

#552

#554

#555 & #556 (sitting on #567).

#557

#558

#560 sitting on #568.

#561

	VG	EXC		VG	EXC
562. Golfer, c1920s-1940s	44.00	60.00	583. Signpost (two directions)	8.50	11.00
563. Stable Lad, walking	9.00	12.00	584. Signpost (three directions)	8.50	11.00
564. Man and Swing Water Barrow	10.00	14.00	585. UNKNOWN		—
565. Goslings, each	3.00	4.00	586. Fencing, per piece 3" long	2.00	3.00
566. Field Hayrack	7.50	10.00	587. Village Idiot, 1920s-1940	145.00	190.00
567. Log Seat	3.75	5.00	588. Milk Churn	2.50	4.00
568. Garden Seat	6.75	9.00	589. Blacksmith with Anvil	13.00	17.50
569. Dog Kennel	5.00	6.50	590. Pail	1.50	2.00
570. Dog Kennel with Baseboard	35.00	50.00	591. Dairyman with Yoke and Pails	15.00	20.00
571. Dog, lying (assorted colours)	4.00	5.50	592. Curate, c1920s-40	55.00	75.00
572. Dog, for Kennel,			593. Country Clergyman	10.00	13.00
sitting (assorted colours)	5.00	6.50	594. Shepherd with Lamb	19.50	26.00
573. Bull (assorted colours)	7.00	9.50	595. Shepherd Boy with Lantern	24.00	32.00
574. Telegraph Pole	9.00	13.00	596. Berkshire Pigs (boars and sows,		
575. Dove Cote	8.00	11.00	assorted colours) each	3.75	5.00
576. St. Bernard Dog	5.25	7.00	597. Exmoor Horn Sheep (ewes		
577. Shepherd with Crook	9.50	13.00	and rams in full fleece) each	3.75	5.00
578. Automobile Association			598. Gentleman Farmer, mounted	16.50	21.00
Scouts, c1920s-40, each	50.00	75.00	599. Jersey Cow (Champion)	3.75	4.50
579. Automobile Association			600. Boy on Shetland pony	24.00	32.00
Sign (destination)	22.00	30.00	601. Hampshire Down Ram	3.75	5.00
580. Automobile Association			602. Foal	2.25	3.00
Sign (Caution)	22.00	30.00	603. Rabbit	3.75	5.00
581. Rustic Stile	9.00	11.00	604. Cat	8.00	10.50
582. Signpost (one direction)	8.50	11.00	605. Greyhound, standing	15.00	20.00

#562

#563

#564

#566

L to R: #569, #571, #572.

L to R: #574, #575.

#577

#578

#581

#582

#586 3" long.

#587

#588

#589

	VG	**EXC**		**VG**	**EXC**
606. Greyhound, running	15.00	20.00	624. English Flint Wall straight section	13.00	17.50
607. Girl Guides and Guider, c1920s-40, Girl Guide	50.00	80.00	625. English Flint Wall round corner section	13.00	17.50
Guider	55.00	85.00	626. Stile	21.00	28.00
617. Folding Table	27.00	36.00	627. Flint Wall, gate post section	10.00	15.00
618. Seesaw, with boy and girl	66.00	88.00	628. Flint Wall, short cross section	10.00	15.00
Girl	18.75	25.00	629. Flint Wall, square corner section	11.00	17.00
Boy	18.75	25.00	630. Five Barred Gate, large	8.00	12.00
Seesaw	27.50	38.00	631. Five Barred Gate (small)	5.50	9.00
619. Garden Swing, with Boy	45.00	65.00	632. Tryst Gate Frame (rare)	33.00	46.00
620. Hare, running	3.50	4.50	633. English Flint Wall-Stone Pier	8.50	11.00
621. Traffic Policeman	11.50	16.50	634. English Flint Wall-Stone Pier for Gate	8.50	11.00
622. Swan and 5 Cygnets, set	10.00	13.00			

#596 Sow.

#591

#592

#593

#594

#595

#597

#598

#599. The 599 at right is the rare variation with bell. Its value is $40.00 in very good and $65.00 in excellent condition.

L to R: #605, #606.

#599 Note metal export tag on leg.

#600

#602

#619

#620

#621

#626

	VG	EXC		VG	EXC

635. Lithographed Pond (never appeared
    in catalogs), swan and 2 cygnets 300.00   400.00
636. Rabbit, sitting up 8.50   11.00
637. Dog, begging 33.00   44.00
638. Spiteful cat 30.00   40.00
639. Assorted Shrubs (two types) .... No Price Found
640. Tree 6.75   9.00
641. Motorcycle with Sidecar, c1920s-40 ..... 700.00   1250.00
642. Rhode Island Reds (prize poultry),
    assorted cocks and hens, each 2.50   4.00
643. White Leghorns (prize poultry),
    assorted cocks and hens, each 2.50   4.00
644. Black Plymouth Rocks (prize
    poultry), assorted cocks and hens 3.00   4.50
645. Navvy with Pick Axe 33.75   45.00
646. Navvy with Shovel 30.00   40.00
647. Highland Cattle 7.00   9.50
648. Field Horse 6.00   8.00
649. Field Horse 6.00   8.00
650. Blacksmith (no anvil) 8.25   11.00
651. Anvil 2.50   3.50
652. Milk Roundsman 13.00   17.50
653. Man on Motorcycle, c1920s-40 .... 500.00   900.00
654. UNKNOWN ....   —

655. Assortment of Farm Animals
    (3 dozen) .... No Price Found
656. Assortment of the Larger
    Farm Animals (1 dozen) .... No Price Found
657. Assortment of Farm People (2 dozen) ..... No Price Found
658. Assortment of the smaller size
    Farm Animals (3 dozen) .... No Price Found
659. Policeman, peak cap 11.50   15.50
660. Prize Poultry, assorted cocks
    and hens, feeding, each 2.00   4.00
661-662. UNKNOWN ....   —
663. Cafe Table with Sun Shade .... No Price Found
664. Assortment of Farm Animals (3 dozen) ... No Price Found
665. UNKNOWN ....   —
666. Stone Pier for Stone Walling .... No Price Found
667. Garden Roller 2.50   5.00
668. Crazy Paving, per piece .... .50   1.00
669. Sundial 6.00   10.00
670. Wheelbarrow 2.50   5.00
671. Stone Walling 4.50   6.00

L to R: #636, #637.

#638

L to R: #633, #624, #634, #631, #625.

L to R: #645, #646.

#640

#641

#647

#648

#649

#652

#653

#659

	VG	EXC		VG	EXC
672. Fencing	No Price Found		752-755. UNKNOWN		—
673. Lawn Mower	15.00	20.00	756. Wild Horse	6.00	10.00
674. Stone Balustrading	9.00	12.00	757. UNKNOWN		—
675. Cold Frame	23.00	31.00	758. Bullock Running	7.50	10.00
676. Hose Reel	23.00	31.00	759-768. UNKNOWN		—
677. Pond	82.50	110.00	769. Field Horse (leg down)	9.00	12.00
678. Man for Wheelbarrow	6.00	8.00	770. UNKNOWN		—
679. Man for Mower	6.50	9.00	771. Esso (yellow pump with red lettering),		
680. Man for Roller	6.50	9.00	Motor and Road series (very rare)	No Price Found	
681-714. UNKNOWN		—	772-774. UNKNOWN		—
715. Man with Garden Roller	11.50	15.50	775. Police Mounted	37.00	49.50
716-743. UNKNOWN		—	776. Policeman with Helmet	13.50	18.00
744. Farmhand Sowing Seed	12.00	16.00	777-778. UNKNOWN		—
745. Women's Land Army,			779. Ladder	15.00	25.00
single figure, Postwar	16.50	22.00	780. Painter carrying Ladder	75.00	110.00
746. Berkshire Sow, with litter of Piglets	16.00	30.00	781. House Painter	75.00	110.00
747. Girl, with Feeding Bucket	9.50	16.00	782. Suffolk Mare	31.50	42.00
748. Shell (red pump with red			783. Suffolk Foal	26.50	35.00
lettering), Motor and Road series	18.75	25.00	784. Ayrshire Bull	40.00	70.00
749. Shellmax (red pump with red			785. Ayrshire Cow	45.00	75.00
lettering), Motor and Road series	16.50	22.00	786. Ayrshire Calf	40.00	70.00
750. BP (green pump with black			787. Garage Hand	75.00	100.00
lettering), Motor and Road series	16.50	22.00	788-799. UNKNOWN		—
751. Power (yellow pump with green					
lettering) Motor and Road series	16.50	22.00			

#746

#744

#745

#679 with #673 (grass catcher detaches).

#715

L to R: #748, #750, #751.

#756

L to R: #747, #744.

#758

L to R: #775, #776.

L to R: #779-780, #781.

#782

#787

#783

L to R: #786, #785, #784.

MODEL HOME FARMS SERIES (Boxed)

	VG	EXC
1F Model Home Farm, 23 pcs.	$175.00	$250.00
2F Model Home Farm, 19 pcs.	No Price Found	
3F Model Home Farm, 73 pcs.	No Price Found	
4F Tumbrel Cart, with Farm Hand and Horse, removable Hay Racks and Backboard	40.00	50.00

#4F

	VG	EXC
5F Farm Wagon with Farm Hand, 2 horses, removable backboard	125.00	160.00
6F General Purpose Plough with Farm Hand and 2 Horses	95.00	125.00
7F Tree and Gate	65.00	95.00
8F Farm Rake, with Driver and Horse, lever	45.00	70.00
9F Farm Roller with Farm Hand and Horse	45.00	70.00

	VG	EXC
10F Shepherds with flock of Sheep and Lambs	No Price Found	
11F Milkmaids with Cows	No Price Found	
12F Timber Wagon, with Farm Hand and 2 horses, real log	175.00	250.00
13F Village Group, villagers on garden seat, lady and gentleman riders, boy on pony, dog	No Price Found	
14F Farmyard Display, cows, geese, ducks, turkey, milkmaids	No Price Found	

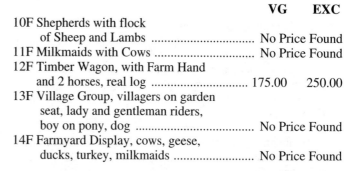

#7F

#8F

#9F

	VG	EXC
15F Cattle Display, sheep, cows, pigs, shepherd and boy, man and barrow	No Price Found	
16F Stable Display, shire horses, colts, cob, stable lad, dog	No Price Found	
17F Farm Display, bull, pigs, piglets, donkey, goat, drover, boy	No Price Found	
18F Farmyard Display, fowls, sheep, lambs, cow and calf, dog, feeding trough, farmer, wife	No Price Found	
19F Tree and Gate with Swing	125.00	175.00
20F Farmer's Gig	150.00	200.00

#19F

#20F

	VG	EXC
21F English Flint Wall	350.00	500.00
22F Flint Wall Assortment, 18 pcs.	300.00	450.00
23F-25F UNKNOWN	—	
26F Farm Cart and Horse	24.00	32.00
27F Assortment of pigs, geese, small shrubs and trees, milkmaid carrying pail, Jersey cow	No Price Found	
28F Assortment of pigs, small shrubs and trees, carter, dog, chicken, cob	No Price Found	

	VG	EXC
29F Assortment of small shrubs, trees, carter, dog, chicken, cob	No Price Found	
30F Fencing with Gate	250.00	350.00
31F-35F UNKNOWN	—	
36F Farmyard Display, stable lad, cow, calf, Berkshire pig, collie, cob, sheep	40.00	60.00
37F Sheep, walking and feeding, farmer, cow, pigs, piglets, lambs, trees, and shrubs	No Price Found	
38F Farmyard Display, 14 pcs.	No Price Found	
39F Farmyard Display, sheep walking and feeding, milkmaid, cow feeding, farm hand, cob, geese, fowls, lambs, piglets, small trees and shrubs, 26 pcs.	275.00	375.00
40F Farm Cart and Horse	25.00	35.00
41F-42F UNKNOWN	—	
43F A Country Cottage, farmer, farmer's wife, villagers, poultry, pig, trees, seat, flower bed	No Price Found	
44F A Country Cottage in natural colors, with imitation thatched roof	700.00	1000.00
45F Milk Float and Horse	25.00	35.00
46F-51F UNKNOWN	—	
52F Large Presentation Box, animals, sheep, pigs, cows, etc., farm people, horse rake with driver, farm wagon with driver	No Price Found	

#40F

#44F

53F Model Home Farm, Farmer,
Farmer's Wife, sheep, horse,
lambs and piglets, 9 pcs. 65.00   100.00
54F Model Home Farm, Land Girl,
Exmoor horn ram and ewe, horse,
Jersey cow, pigs, 7 pcs. 75.00   120.00
55F Model Home Farm, 10 pcs. 82.50   110.00
56F Model Home Farm, 13 pcs. 150.00   220.00
57F UNKNOWN .... —
58F Fully modeled tree, 5" high 65.00   100.00
59F 4-wheeled Lorry with Driver,
body tips, 6" long 150.00   250.00

#59F (Common driver wears peak cap) Postwar.

60F 6-wheeled Lorry with Driver 300.00   400.00
61F 10-wheeled Lorry with Driver 550.00   800.00
62F Farmyard Display, 23 pcs. 175.00   250.00
63F Farmyard Display, trees and shrubs,
hurdles, cows, prize poultry, sheep
feeding, walking, dog, shire horse,
stable lad, milkmaid, 23 pcs. .... No Price Found
64F-65F UNKNOWN .... —
66F Farmhouse Scene, cottage and bridge
for display of farm animals .... No Price Found
67F Model Home Farm, stock, farm hands ..... No Price Found
68F UNKNOWN .... —
69F Farm Assortment, sheep, Rhode Island
Red, pig, cow feeding, 2 trees .... No Price Found
70F Farm Assortment, sheep standing,
sheep feeding, sheep lying,
Jersey cow, 2 trees .... No Price Found
71F Farm Assortment, horse feeding, calf
lying, calf, Rhode Island Red, 2 trees ...... No Price Found
72F Farm Assortment, cow, calf, sheep,
pig, 2 trees .... No Price Found
73F Farm Assortment, horse, colt, foal,
sheep, pig, 2 trees .... No Price Found
74F Farm Assortment, cow, calf, goose,
goat, 2 trees .... No Price Found
75F-76F UNKNOWN .... —
77F Farm Assortment, horse, foal, cow,
sheep, pig, goose, 2 trees .... No Price Found
78F-89F UNKNOWN .... —
90F Builders Lorry with builder's
name on sides, driver .... No Price Found
91F Builders Lorry, 6-wheeled,
builder's name on sides .... No Price Found
92F Builders Lorry, 10-wheeled,
builder's name on sides .... No Price Found

93F UNKNOWN .... —
94F Farmhouse, natural roof 1900.00   2500.00
95F Large Barn and Cart-Shed for farm
wagon and tumbrel .... No Price Found
96F Stable with 2-horse box
compartments, open section for cart 800.00   1200.00
97F Country Cottage 600.00   950.00
98F Store Shed, corrugated roof 350.00   500.00
99F Cowshed, for 4 cows .... No Price Found
100F Pigsty 52.50   70.00
101F Rabbit Hutch 550.00   800.00
102F Chicken House and Run, wire fence 550.00   800.00
103F Barn, mansard type, large sliding door ... No Price Found
104F-110F UNKNOWN .... —
111F Farmyard Presentation Box, 50 pcs.,
includes farmhouse, barn, people,
animals, shrubs, fencing .... No Price Found
112F Greenhouse 250.00   350.00
113F Garden Shelter 300.00   400.00

#113F (seated #560).

114F-119F UNKNOWN .... —
120F Farmyard Display, 14 pcs. 100.00   150.00
121F Farmyard Display, 16 pcs. .... No Price Found
122F Farmyard Display, 12 pcs. 100.00   150.00
123F Farmyard Display, 7 pcs., pigs, turkey,
angry gander, goat, feeding horse, cob 33.00   44.00
124F Farmyard Display, sheep walking,
feeding, sheep and lamb lying,
dog, lamb, 7 pcs. 45.00   65.00
125F Farmyard Display, cows standing,
feeding, calves standing and lying,
dog, 7 pcs. 60.00   85.00
126F Rubber Tyred Farm Cart 20.00   27.00
127F Fordson Tractor, metal wheels, driver 85.00   120.00
128F Fordson Major Tractor,
with driver, rubber tires 75.00   100.00
129F Timber Trailer with real log 50.00   75.00
130F Farm Trailer, with racks 20.00   30.00
131F Horse-Drawn Milk Float,
milkman, 2 churns 50.00   75.00
132F Farmyard Display, 23 pcs.,
includes tumbrel cart, trough 187.50   250.00

#128F

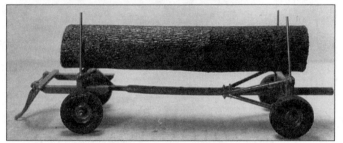

#129F

#134F In box.

	VG	EXC
133F Farmyard Display, 7 pcs.	52.50	70.00
134F Tractors and Implements Set, "Fordson Major" tractor, rubber tyres, "Fordson Major" tractor, metal wheels, Timber Trailer, Tipping Trailer, Roller and Disc Harrows	350.00	500.00
135F Disc Harrow	10.00	15.00
136F Roller	10.00	15.00
137F Clockwork Set, "Fordson Major" tractor with driver, mechanical clockwork trailer, tipping haycart with removable hay racks	350.00	450.00
138F Four-Furrow Tractor Plough	No Price Found	
139F Clockwork Set "Fordson Major" tractor with driver and mechanical trailer	No Price Found	

	VG	EXC
140F-141F UNKNOWN		—
142F Single Horse General Purpose Plough, with Ploughman	35.00	50.00

#142F

	VG	EXC
143F UNKNOWN		—
144F Haystack, papier-mâché, 6" x 3-1/2" x 4"	40.00	60.00
145F Tractor and Implements Set, Muledozer, 3-Furrough Plough and Tipping Trailer, 4pcs.	No Price Found	

#172F With attached #174F (#560 driver added).

	VG	EXC
146F Tractors and Implements Set, 2 Power Major Tractors, Roller, Muledozer, 3-Furrow Plough, Tipping and Timber Trailers, 7 pcs.	360.00	480.00
147F Farmyard Display, 5 pcs.	45.00	70.00
148F Farmyard Display, 6 pcs.	No Price Found	
149F Farmyard Display, 9 pcs.	No Price Found	
150F Farmyard Display, 10 pcs.	No Price Found	
151F Farmyard Display, 8 pcs.	No Price Found	
152F Farmyard Display, 10 pcs.	80.00	120.00
153F Farmyard Display, 11 pcs.	No Price Found	
154F Farmyard Display, 12 pcs.	No Price Found	
155F Farmyard Display, 13 pcs.	No Price Found	
156F Farmyard Display, 21 pcs.	No Price Found	
157F Farmyard Display, 21 pcs.	No Price Found	
171F "Fordson Power Major" Tractor	No Price Found	
172F "Fordson Power Major" Tractor, no driver	75.00	100.00
173F Three-Furrow Plough	11.00	16.00
174F Muledozer	No Price Found	
175F Cultivator	No Price Found	
176F Acrobat Rake	No Price Found	
1495 Housepainters, 4 pcs., 2 carrying ladder, 3rd with paintbrush raised, 1954-59	450.00	600.00

Hunt Series

	G	VG	EXC		G	VG	EXC
608. Huntsman, mounted (assorted colours)	$10.00	$15.00	$20.00	243. Huntsmen and Huntswomen, with Hounds, in 1934 catalog			No Price Found
609. Huntswoman, mounted, sidesaddle, at halt	10.00	15.00	20.00	1235. Huntsman, mounted, hounds, 3 pcs.			No Price Found
610. Huntsman, mounted, galloping	10.00	15.00	20.00	1236. Huntswoman mounted sidesaddle, hounds, 3 pcs.			No Price Found
611. Huntswoman, mounted, galloping	10.00	15.00	20.00	1237. Huntsman mtd. galloping, hounds, 3 pcs.			No Price Found
612. Huntsman, standing, dismounted	6.00	9.00	12.00	1238. Huntswoman mtd. galloping, hounds, 3 pcs.			No Price Found
613. Huntswoman, standing, dismounted	6.00	9.00	12.00	1239. Huntswoman astride, hounds, 3 pcs.			No Price Found
614. Hounds, standing (assorted positions)	4.00	5.75	8.00	1240. Huntsman mounted walking, hounds, 3 pcs.			No Price Found
615. Hounds, running	3.00	4.50	6.00	1241. Gentleman Farmer, standing hounds, 3 pcs.			No Price Found
616. Fox	7.50	11.25	15.00	1445. Huntsmen, mounted and dismounted, 11 pcs.			No Price Found
623. Huntswoman, mounted, astride	20.00	50.00	75.00	1446. (9650) "The Meet," 11 pcs., huntsmen, mounted and dismounted, 11 pcs.			No Price Found

(Note: Hats may vary from derby to top hat, and jacket colors can be red, black, grey)

	G	VG	EXC
234. (9655) "The Meet," Huntsmen mounted and foot, with hounds, 18 pcs.	200.00	350.00	500.00
235. (9656) Huntington Series, "Full Cry," 20 pcs.	200.00	350.00	500.00
236. Hunting Series, display box, 38 pcs.	350.00	600.00	850.00

	G	VG	EXC
1447. (9651) "Full Cry," 10 pcs., huntsmen mounted with hounds and fox	55.00	90.00	120.00

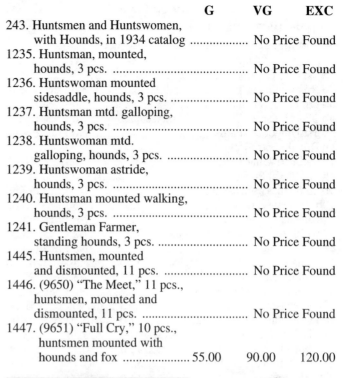

#610

L to R: #612, #613.

#608

#609

#611

#623

#236 Box art.

L to R: #614, #615, #616.

#236 Bottom layer.

2nd Quality Military

"B" SERIES

1896-1907 Round Base, 1907-1914 Square Base, 44mm high, sold in sets. Price is per piece.

	G	VG	EXC
1b 1st Life Guards	$10.00	$15.00	$20.00
2b Royal Horse Guards			No Price Found
3b 5th Dragoon Guards			No Price Found
4b Scots Guards			No Price Found
5b 1st Dragoon Guards			No Price Found
6b Royal Scots Greys	6.00	9.00	12.00
7b 2nd Life Guards	10.00	15.00	20.00
8b 7th Royal Fusiliers			No Price Found
9b 13th Hussars			No Price Found
10b 11th Hussars	9.00	13.50	18.00
11b Japanese Cavalry			No Price Found
12b 16th Lancers (active service)	7.50	11.25	15.00
13b 17th Lancers			No Price Found
14b Russian Cavalry (Cossacks)	15.00	22.50	30.00
15b Mounted Infantry	15.00	22.50	30.00
16b Coldstream Guards			No Price Found
17b Lancashire Fusiliers			No Price Found
18b Grenadier Guards	11.00	16.50	22.00
19b Dublin Fusiliers	9.00	13.50	18.00
20b Manchester Regiment	4.50	6.75	9.00
21b Northumberland Fusiliers	3.50	5.25	7.00
22b Bluejackets, R.N.	4.00	6.00	8.00
23b Cameron Highlanders (active service)	10.00	15.00	20.00
24b Whitejackets, R.N.	7.00	11.00	15.00
25b Japanese Infantry	15.00	22.00	30.00
26b Russian Infantry			No Price Found
125 Royal Horse Artillery (review order with outriders)			No Price Found
126 Royal Horse Artillery (active service order with outriders)			No Price Found

"W" SERIES

1912-1940 45mm, sold in sets by F.W. Woolworth chain only at first, 2nd grade painting. 5 pieces mtd., 8 pcs. foot. Average price $8 in Very Good for mounted, $6 for foot, boxed sets average $50 in Very Good.

Left: "W" size; Right: Standard size.

British Army and Navy

11w Grenadier Guards
12w Highlanders
28w Highlanders
8w Hussars
30w Hussars
14w Hussars (gilt)
10w Infantry of the Line
9w Lancers
15w Lancers (gilt)
7w Life Guards, The
13w Life Guards (gilt)
29w Life Guards, The
19w Sailors (Bluejackets), R.N.
26w Sailors (Bluejackets), R.N.
20w Sailors (Whitejackets), R.N.
25w Sailors (Whitejackets), R.N.
18w Scots Greys, The
27w Scots Greys, The

"P" SERIES

C1932-1935 (Changed to "N" series in 1936). Standard size 54mm, bulk series, sold by the dozen to retail singly. Second grade painting. No prices found, except where noted.

#2P

	G	VG	EXC
1p Boy Scouts			No Price Found
2p Buffs, khaki			No Price Found
3p Buffs, review order			No Price Found
4p Cowboys, kneeling			No Price Found
5p Cowboys, on foot, with Pistol			No Price Found
6p Cowboys, on foot, standing, firing			No Price Found
7p Highlanders, charging	$12.50	$18.75	$25.00
8p Highlanders, marching	15.00	22.50	30.00
9p Infantry, British, kneeling, firing			No Price Found
10p Infantry, British, lying, firing			No Price Found
11p Infantry, British, standing, firing			No Price Found
12p Machine Gunner, lying, with Gun			No Price Found
13p Machine Gunner, sitting, with Gun			No Price Found
14p North American Indian, Chief			No Price Found
15p North American Indian, crawling			No Price Found
16p North American Indian, with Knife and Hatchet			No Price Found

	G	VG	EXC
17p North American Indian, standing	No Price Found		
18p Rifles, The	No Price Found		
19p Sailors, British	No Price Found		
20p Sussex Regiment	No Price Found		
21p Zulus	No Price Found		

#21P

"D" SERIES--1-3/4"

The "D" Series contained smaller size pieces used for games and novelties. 29d-31d were added during the 1930s and available in six different colors. They were flat models, able to stand erect and were suitable for board games. All were discontinued in 1940. 44d and 86d were gold-painted souvenir items added to commemorate the 1953 coronation. No prices found, except where noted.

1d Life Guards, The	No Price Found		
2d Hussars	No Price Found		
3d Lancers	No Price Found		
26d Gun, mounted on wheels	No Price Found		
27d Armoured Car	No Price Found		

L to R: #27d, #26d

	G	VG	EXC
29d Racing Motor	No Price Found		
30d Yacht	No Price Found		
31d Cyclist	No Price Found		
86d Coronation Chair	$10.00	$15.00	$20.00
44d Her Majesty's State Coach	40.00	60.00	80.00

"N" SERIES

Standard size, 54mm. Sold in bulk for retailing singly. The painting was 2nd grade. This series was available just before WWII, and it contained many distinctive action poses not found in the main range. It replaced the "C" and "P" series which had been phased out earlier. No price found except where noted.

	G	VG	EXC
1N Boy Scouts			
2N East Kent Regiment, The Buffs, khaki, On Guard position	$6.00	$9.00	$13.00
3N East Kent Regiment, The Buffs, review order, On Guard position	No Price Found		

	G	VG	EXC
4N Cowboys, crouching, firing Pistol	No Price Found		
5N Cowboys, on foot, with Pistol	5.00	7.00	10.00
6N Cowboys, standing, firing Pistol	No Price Found		
7N Highlanders, khaki, charging with Bayonet, shrapnel proof helmet	3.00	4.50	6.00
8N Highlanders, review order, marching, slope arms	No Price Found		
9N British Infantry, khaki, with peak caps, kneeling, firing	No Price Found		
10N British Infantry, khaki, with peak caps, lying, firing	No Price Found		
11N British Infantry, khaki, with peak caps, standing, firing	No Price Found		
12N British Infantry, machine gunner, khaki, lying position, with Gun	No Price Found		
13N British Infantry, machine gunner, khaki, sitting position, with Gun	No Price Found		
14N North American Indian Chief	No Price Found		

#13N

#14N

	G	VG	EXC
15N North American Indian, crawling, with Hatchet	5.00	8.00	11.00
16N North American Indian, standing, with Knife and Hatchet	No Price Found		
17N North American Indian, standing, with Rifle	No Price Found		
18N The King's Royal Rifle Corps., running position, with Rifle	8.00	12.00	16.00
19N British Sailor	6.00	9.00	12.00
20N The Royal Sussex Regiment, review order, marching, slope arms	No Price Found		
21N Zulus with Shield and Knobkerrie	No Price Found		

#17N

#19N

#20N

	G	VG	EXC

22N U.S.A. Army, Infantry, slouch hat, marching, slope arms .... 2.50 · 3.75 · 5.00

23N U.S.A. Army, Infantry, slouch hat, standing, firing position .... No Price Found

24N U.S.A. Army, Infantry, slouch hat, charging with Bayonet .... No Price Found

25N U.S.A. Army, Infantry, slouch hat, kneeling, firing position .... No Price Found

26N U.S.A. Army, Infantry, slouch hat, lying, firing position .... No Price Found

27N U.S.A. Army, Infantry officer, peak cap .... No Price Found

28N British Foot Guards, review order, marching, slope arms .... No Price Found

29N British Infantry, khaki with peak cap, running position .... No Price Found

#28N

#29N

30N British Foot Guards, review order, lying, firing position .... No Price Found

31N British Foot Guards, review order, kneeling, firing position .... No Price Found

32N Highlander, khaki, lying, firing position .... 4.00 · 7.00 · 9.00

33N Highlander, khaki, kneeling, firing position .... No Price Found

34N Highlander, khaki, standing, firing position .... No Price Found

35N U.S.A. Army Infantry, peak caps, running position ..... 4.50 · 6.75 · 9.00

36N U.S.A. West Point Cadet, winter dress .... No Price Found

#33N

#36N

	G	VG	EXC

37N U.S.A. West Point Cadet, summer dress .... No Price Found

38N U.S.A. Navy, bluejacket .... No Price Found

39N U.S.A. Navy, Marine, blue uniform .... No Price Found

40N British Infantry officer, khaki, peak cap .... 5.00 · 8.00 · 10.00

41N The Queen's Royal Regiment, West Surrey, review order, kneeling, firing .... No Price Found

42N The Queen's Royal Regiment, West Surrey, review order, lying, firing .... No Price Found

43N The Queen's Royal Regiment, West Surrey, review order, standing, firing .... No Price Found

44N British Foot Guards, review order, standing, firing position .... No Price Found

45N U.S.A. Navy, Whitejacket .... No Price Found

46N U.S.A. Navy, Marine, service dress .... No Price Found

47N U.S.A. Army, Machine Gunner, sitting position, with Gun .... No Price Found

48N U.S.A. Army Machine Gunner, lying position, with Gun .... No Price Found

49N Royal Navy, Bluejacket, shoulder arms .... No Price Found

50N Royal Navy, Whitejacket, shoulder arms .... No Price Found

51N Royal Navy, Midshipman .... No Price Found

52N British Cavalry, The Life Guards, review order .... No Price Found

53N British Cavalry, The Lancers, review order, with Lance, movable arm .... No Price Found

54N British Cavalry, The Lancers, review order, with Sword, movable arm .... No Price Found

55N British Cavalry, The Royal Scots Greys, 2nd Dragoons, review order .... No Price Found

#55N

56N British Cavalry, khaki, service dress .... No Price Found

57N British Cavalry, The Lancers .... No Price Found

#58N

#61N

	G	VG	EXC
58N British Cavalry, khaki with shrapnel helmet		No Price Found	
59N British Cavalry, 1st Royal Dragoons, review order	6.00	9.00	12.00
60N British Cavalry, Royal Horse Guards, review order		No Price Found	
61N British Cavalry, The Hussars, review order		No Price Found	
62N U.S.A. Army, Cavalry, with peak cap		No Price Found	
63N North American Indian on Horseback, with Hatchet		No Price Found	
64N Cowboy on Horseback, with Pistol		No Price Found	
65N U.S.A. Army, Cavalry, with slouch hat		No Price Found	
66N North American Indian, galloping, on grey horse		No Price Found	

#63N

#64N

#71N

L to R: #88N, #93N.

	G	VG	EXC
67N Arab on Horseback, with Scimitar		No Price Found	
68N Egyptian Camel Corps		No Price Found	
71N Highlanders, running, khaki	5.00	7.50	10.00
72N British Infantry, marching, slope arms, khaki	3.00	4.50	6.00
73N British Army Drummer Boy, with peak hat		No Price Found	
74N British Army Bugler Boy, with peak hat		No Price Found	
87N Battle Dress Officer		No Price Found	
88N Battle Dress man, charging	4.00	6.00	8.00
89N Battle Dress man, on guard	5.00	7.50	10.00
90N Battle Dress man, standing, firing		No Price Found	
91N Battle Dress man, kneeling, firing		No Price Found	
92N Bluejacket, new regulation		No Price Found	
93N Tommy-gunner		No Price Found	
69N Assorted Box, containing three dozen well assorted (12 different kinds) "N" Infantry		No Price Found	
70N Assorted Box containing one dozen (12 different kinds), "N" Cavalry		No Price Found	

Note: There may be more in this series.

"H" SERIES

C1930(?)-1940. Large-size 70mm bulk series for retailing singly. Painting grade usually was between "Best Quality" and Second Grade.

Left: "H" size;
Right: Standard
54mm size.

	G	VG	EXC
4h Infantry of the Line		No Price Found	
5h Foot Guards	$7.00	$11.00	$15.00
6h Highlanders	7.00	11.00	15.00

In addition to the military pieces, certain novelty items were designated "H" Series. These are all from the period 1930-1940. Numbers 16h through 21h were manufactured through special license from Walt Disney-Mickey Mouse LTD. Numbers 12h and 22h were for Garden Ornament use.

	G	VG	EXC
7h Terrier Dog, 4-1/2" long	80.00	120.00	160.00
9h Pug Dog, 2-3/4" long		No Price Found	
10h Stag, 4" long	45.00	67.50	90.00
11h Doe, companion model to 10h		No Price Found	
12h A large scale model of a Seagull with wings outstretched, 4-1/4" across the wing tips	10.00	15.00	20.00

	G	VG	EXC
16h Mickey Mouse			No Price Found
17h Minnie Mouse			No Price Found
18h Pluto			No Price Found
19h Donald Duck			No Price Found
20h Clarabelle the Cow			No Price Found
21h Goofy			No Price Found
22h Large scale model of a Seagull with wings folded, 2-1/4" tall to beak	14.00	21.00	28.00

FORT RANGE--S AND P

These were Britain's Postwar second-grade figures (simplified painting with no details). All were in 54mm. They were first introduced in the 1950 "New Lines" section of the catalog. Later in 1956, the series was upgraded and became the "New Crown Range." The "P" Series was designed to offer individual pieces from counter displays. All second grade ranges were discontinued in 1959. No prices found except where noted. There may be more in this series. Price per figure.

"Fort Range"
(single row boxes)

	G	VG	EXC
94S British Foot Guards, marching at slope arms, review order, 6 pcs., per Troop	$5.00	$7.50	$10.00
95S British Line Regiments, marching at slope arms, review order, 6 pcs., per Troop	5.00	7.50	10.00
96S Highlanders, marching at slope arms, review order, 6 pcs.			No Price Found
97S British Foot Guards, standing, kneeling, lying firing, review order, 6 pcs.			No Price Found

#97S

	G	VG	EXC
98S Highlanders, standing, kneeling and lying firing, active service, khaki, 6 pcs.			No Price Found
100S Cowboys, mounted and on foot, assorted positions, 5 pcs.			No Price Found
101S North American Indians on foot, assorted positions, 5 pcs.			No Price Found
103S Sailors, Royal Navy, 6 pcs.			No Price Found
104S North American Indians, mounted and on foot, assorted positions, 5 pcs.	3.00	5.00	7.00
105S Cowboys, on foot, assorted positions, 6 pcs.	3.00	5.00	7.00

#119S

	G	VG	EXC
119S Infantry, Battle Dress, assorted positions: at the ready, standing and kneeling, firing and with Tommy Guns, 6 pcs.	5.00	7.50	10.00
123S Infantry of the Line, on guard, review order, 6 pcs., per Troop	5.00	7.50	10.00
144S French Infantry of the Line, on guard, review order, 6 pcs.			No Price Found
145S Belgian Infantry of the Line, on guard, review order, 6 pcs.			No Price Found
149S Foot Guards and Life Guards, marching, review order, 5 pcs.			No Price Found
150S French Infantry with Mounted Officer, review order, 5 pcs.			No Price Found
201S Foot Guards, standing firing, kneeling firing, lying firing, 5 pcs.			No Price Found
202S Life Guard and Foot Guards, 4 pcs.			No Price Found
203S Highlanders, 5 pcs.			No Price Found
204S Cowboys, 4 pcs.			No Price Found
205S North American Indians, 4 pcs.			No Price Found
206S Scots Grey and Highlanders, 4 pcs.			No Price Found
207S Infantry of the Line, 5 pcs.			No Price Found
208S Infantry in Battle Dress, 5 pcs.			No Price Found
209S French Infantry and Zouave, 4 pcs.			No Price Found
210S Union Infantry, 1862, 4 pcs.	3.00	5.00	7.00
211S Confederate Infantry, 1862, 4 pcs.	3.00	5.00	7.00

"Duofort" Range
(double row boxes)

106S Infantry and Cavalry, Line Regiments and Highlanders, assorted positions, khaki, 10 pcs.

108S North American Indians and Cowboys, mounted and on foot, assorted, 10 pcs.

109S British Life Guards, Foot Guards and Highlanders, review order, 9 pcs.

110S British Foot Guards and Line Regiments in assorted positions, review order, 12 pcs.

111S Scots Greys and Foot Guards, in
assorted positions, review order, 9 pcs.
120S Infantry in Battle Dress, assorted
positions, with officer, 12 pcs.
146S Belgian Grenadiers and Chasseurs
a'Pied, review order, 12 pcs.
147S French Zouaves and Infantry of the
Line, with Mounted Officer, review
order, 11 pcs.
212S Cowboys and Indians, 7 pcs.
213S U.S. Sailors and West Point Cadets, 9 pcs.
214S Hussars and Infantry of the Line, 7 pcs.
215S Foot Guards, 8 pcs.
216S Scots Greys and Highlanders, 7 pcs.
217S Infantry in Battle Dress, 9 pcs.
218S French Infantry and Zouaves, 8 pcs.
219S Confederate Cavalry and Infantry,
1862, 7 pcs.
220S Union Cavalry and Infantry, 1862, 7 pcs.
221S Cowboys, 7 pcs.
222S North American Indians, 7 pcs.
237S Foot Guards, 9 pcs.

"Trifort" Range
(treble row boxes)

	G	VG	EXC
112S Highlanders and Scots Greys, various positions, assorted, khaki and review order, 15 pcs.			No Price Found
114S North American Indians and Cowboys, mounted and on foot, in various positions, 14 pcs.			No Price Found
115S British Foot Guards, standing, kneeling and lying, firing and marching, slope arms, review order, 18 pcs.			No Price Found
116S Infantry of the Line and Hussars, assorted positions, review order, 15 pcs.			No Price Found
117S Life Guards, Highlanders and Foot Guards, various positions, review order, 14 pcs.			No Price Found
148S Belgian Horse Gendarmes, Chasseurs a'Pied and Infantry of the Line, review order, 15 pcs.			No Price Found
223S Scots Greys and Highlanders, 10 pcs.			No Price Found
224S Cowboys and Indians, 10 pcs.			No Price Found
225S Foot Guards, 12 pcs.			No Price Found
226S Hussars and Infantry of the Line, 10 pcs.			No Price Found
227S French Cavalry, Infantry and Zouaves, 10 pcs., set	$37.50	$56.25	$75.00
228S Confederate Cavalry and Infantry, 1862, 10 pcs., price for Cavalry	5.00	8.00	10.00
229S Union Cavalry and Infantry, 1862, 10 pcs., price for Cavalry	5.00	8.00	10.00
230S Infantry in Battle Dress, 14 pcs.	5.00	8.00	10.00

"Super-Fort" Range

	G	VG	EXC
231S Life Guards and Foot Guards, 12 pcs.			No Price Found
232S Scots Greys and Highlanders, 13 pcs.			No Price Found
233S Hussars and Infantry of the Line, 13 pcs.			No Price Found
234S Cowboys and Indians, 14 pcs.			No Price Found
235S Infantry in Battle Dress, 16 pcs.	$80.00	$120.00	$160.00
236S Union and Confederate Cavalry and Infantry, 1862, 14 pcs.			No Price Found

"New Crown" Range
"P" SERIES

Soldiers, Cowboys and Indians, packed in bulk for retailing singly. Second-quality painting, issued in 1956, 54mm high.

	G	VG	EXC
41P Foot Guard, marching, slope arms, review order	$4.00	$6.00	$9.00
42P Infantry of the Line, on guard, spike helmet, review order	5.00	8.00	10.00
43P Infantry of the Line, marching, slope arms, review order	6.00	9.00	12.00
45P Highlander, standing, firing, khaki			No Price Found

#41P   *#42P*   *#45P & #123P*

	G	VG	EXC
46P Infantry of the Line, on guard, shrapnel helmet, khaki			No Price Found
51P North American Indian, on foot, with Rifle	5.00	7.50	10.00
52P North American Indian, on foot, with Knife and Hatchet	5.00	7.50	10.00
56P Highlander, lying, firing, khaki			No Price Found
57P Highlander, kneeling, firing, khaki	5.00	7.50	10.00
58P British Foot Guard, firing, standing, review order	4.00	6.00	8.00
59P British Foot Guard, kneeling, firing, review order	5.00	7.50	10.00
60P British Foot Guard, lying, firing, review order	4.00	6.00	8.00
80P Cowboy, crouching, firing pistol			No Price Found
83P Cowboy on foot with pistol	3.00	5.00	7.00
92P U.S.A. Bluejacket	6.00	9.00	12.00

	G	VG	EXC
93P U.S. West Point Cadets, in grey uniforms, winter dress	No Price Found		
96P Cowboy on foot, firing pistol	No Price Found		
98P Highlander, marching, slope arms, review order	4.00	6.00	8.00
99P North American Indian Chief	5.00	7.50	10.00
110P Infantry officer, Battle Dress	4.50	7.00	9.00
111P Infantry, charging, Battle Dress	4.50	7.00	9.00
112P Infantry, on guard, Battle Dress	No Price Found		
113P Infantry, standing, firing, Battle Dress	4.50	7.00	9.00
114P Infantry, kneeling, firing, Battle Dress	4.50	7.00	9.00
115P Infantry, with Tommy-guns, Battle Dress	4.50	7.00	9.00
116P British Bluejacket	3.50	5.00	7.00
122P Nurse, R.A.M.C.	5.00	7.50	10.00
123P Highlander, standing, firing, review order	4.00	6.00	8.00
124P Highlander, kneeling, firing, review order	No Price Found		

	G	VG	EXC
125P Highlander, lying, firing, review order	No Price Found		
126P Zouave (French Army), charging	5.00	7.50	10.00
127P French Infantry, on guard, review order	5.00	7.50	10.00
128P French Infantry, standing, firing	5.00	7.50	10.00
129P French Infantry, kneeling, firing	5.00	7.50	10.00
130P French Infantry, lying, firing	5.00	7.50	10.00
132P Belgian Grenadier marching, review order	No Price Found		
133P Belgian Chasseur a'Pied, running	3.50	5.00	7.00
134P Belgian Line Infantry, on guard, review order	No Price Found		
136P North American Indian Chief, carrying rifle	6.00	9.00	12.00
137P North American Indian, crouching with rifle	5.00	7.50	10.00
150P Pilot in full flying kit	7.00	11.00	14.00
152P Red Army Infantry, charging	10.00	15.00	20.00
153P Royal Canadian Mounted Police on foot, slope arms	No Price Found		
154P Cowboy on foot, firing pistol	5.00	8.00	10.00
155P North American Indian on foot, swinging club	No Price Found		

#96P

#111P

#122P

#123P

#125P

#126P

#127P

#136P

#152P

#154P

"P" SERIES CAVALRY

No price found except where noted. Price per each.

	G	VG	EXC
64P Life Guard, review order	No Price Found		
65P Scots Grey, review order	No Price Found		
66P Horse Guard, review order	No Price Found		
68P Hussar, review order	$7.00	$11.00	$14.00
70P British Cavalry, shrapnel helmet, khaki	No Price Found		
72P U.S.A. Cavalry, slouch hat, khaki	7.00	11.00	14.00
117P North American Indian, mounted with hatchet	No Price Found		
118P Cowboy, mounted with pistol	No Price Found		
121P Royal Canadian Mounted Police	7.00	10.00	14.00
135P Belgian Horse Gendarme	10.00	15.00	20.00

#64P

#118P

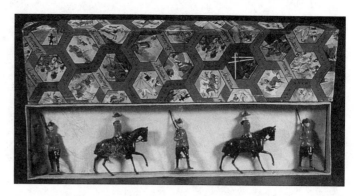

Britains box cover and contents from No. 57S Royal Canadian Mounted Police. Photo by Gary J. Linden.

	G	VG	EXC
151P Red Army Cossack			No Price Found
156P Highland officer, mounted with white tropical helmet			No Price Found
120MP Assorted Infantry Pack of 48 pcs. (8 different kinds)			No Price Found
121MP Assorted Pack of 24 Cavalry Models (8 different per box)	7.00	11.00	14.00
123MP Assorted Pack of 30 pcs., consisting of 6 Cavalry and 24 Infantry			No Price Found
124MP Assorted Pack of 3 dozen			No Price Found
148P Motorcycle Dispatch Rider	4.50	6.75	9.00

#148P

	G	VG	EXC
149P Speed Cop			No Price Found
51S Highland Infantry, Mounted Officer, review order, 6 pcs.			No Price Found
52S Hussars, mounted with Infantry of the Line, review order, 5 pcs.			No Price Found
53S The Scots Greys, with Highland Infantry, review order, 5 pcs.			No Price Found
54S British Foot Guards, firing, review order, 7 pcs.			No Price Found
55S The Life Guards, mounted, and Foot Guards, review order, 5 pcs.			No Price Found
56S Infantry in Battle Dress, with officer, 7 pcs.			No Price Found
57S Royal Canadian Mounted Police, mtd. and foot, full dress, 5 pcs.			No Price Found
58S North American Indians, mtd. and foot, 6 pcs.			No Price Found
59S Cowboys, mtd. and foot, 5 pcs.			No Price Found
60S French Infanterie, with Mounted Officers, review order, 5 pcs.			No Price Found

	G	VG	EXC
61S The Scots Greys, with British Foot Guards, review order, 11 pcs.			No Price Found
62S Infantry in Battle Dress with officer, 14 pcs.			No Price Found
63S The Scots Greys, with Highland Infantry, review order, 10 pcs.			No Price Found
64S North American Indians, mtd. and foot, 10 pcs.			No Price Found
65S Cowboys, mounted and foot, 10 pcs.			No Price Found
66S Cowboys and North American Indians, mtd. and foot, 10 pcs.			No Price Found
67S Scots Greys with British Foot Guards, review order, 17 pcs.			No Price Found
68S British Inf. in Battle Dress, with officer and machine gunner, 20 pcs.			No Price Found
69S Scots Greys, mounted with Highlanders on foot, review order, 17 pcs.			No Price Found
70S Cowboys and North American Indians, mtd. and foot, 17 pcs.			No Price Found
71S A modern type gun (with 6 shells to fire) and ass't of British Inf. in Battle Dress, 6 pcs.			No Price Found

FOOTBALL TEAMS

The Football Teams first appeared in the 1905 catalog. Numbers were not assigned at that time. These round-based models were made in positions representing Forwards, Half Backs, and Full Backs. Special Teams and color combinations could be ordered upon request--all utilizing the same figures. The line was discontinued in 1941. No prices found, except where noted. These are seldom found in mint condition.

	G	VG	EXC
258b Football			No Price Found
257b Corner flag on post			No Price Found
254b Referee			No Price Found
255b Linesman with flag	$22.00	$33.00	$45.00
256b Goalposts			No Price Found
189b Goalkeeper (green/white)	27.00	41.00	55.00

Various teams.

Typical "Racing colors" (detachable rider).

	G	VG	EXC
Unnumbered "Famous Football Teams," 18 pcs., includes goal, 3 flag markers, and ball			No Price Found
Singles	12.00	22.00	32.00

RACING COLORS

Averaged/boxed	$35.00	$70.00	$125.00

TRAFFIC SIGNS

239. Motor Patrol and Road signs	$200.00	$400.00	$600.00
1427. Traffic Signs, 8 pcs.	200.00	500.00	750.00
1428. Traffic Signs, with policeman, 16 pcs.			No Price Found
1429. Traffic Signs, with policeman, 24 pcs.			No Price Found
1430. Traffic Signs, traffic display, 22 pcs.			No Price Found
1468. Traffic Signs, 5 pcs.			No Price Found

Typical traffic signs.

Zoo Series

	G	VG	EXC
901 Indian Elephant (boxed)	$30.00	$55.00	$100.00
902 Kangaroo	3.50	5.75	8.00
903 Penguin	2.50	3.75	5.00
904 Monkey	2.50	4.75	8.00
905 Adult Hippopotamus	6.00	12.00	18.50
906 Gorilla	6.00	9.00	13.00
907 Zebra	4.00	7.50	10.00
908 Adult Rhinoceros	8.00	15.50	20.00
909 Pelican (open beak)	3.50	6.75	9.00
910 Lion	4.00	7.50	10.00

#901 1st version, rare rubber trunk.

L to R: #906, #907, #909.

L to R: #902, #903, #904.

L to R: #910, #911, #913.

#912

	G	VG	EXC
911 Lioness	3.00	5.75	8.00
912 Giraffe (adult) Prewar only	66.00	110.50	165.00
913 Pelican (spread wings)	2.50	5.25	7.00

L to R: #915, #916, #918.

	G	VG	EXC
914 Polar Bear (sitting)	7.00	11.50	15.00
915 Chimpanzee	4.00	7.50	10.00
916 King Penguin	2.00	4.50	6.00
917 Adult Nile Crocodile	10.00	21.00	28.00
918 Bactrian Camel	10.00	20.00	30.00
919 Coconut Palm	10.50	18.75	25.00
920 Date Palm	7.00	13.50	18.00
921 Guinon Monkey (walking)	3.50	6.00	9.00
922 Ostrich	3.00	7.00	10.00
923 Llama	3.50	6.50	8.50
924 Gate with Posts	10.00	16.50	22.00
925 Railing (straight section)	2.50	5.25	7.00
926 Railing (curved section)	2.50	5.25	7.00
927 Standard Post, two way (straight)	6.00	9.00	12.00
928 Straight Post, two way (right angle)	6.00	9.00	12.00
929 Standard Post, three way	6.00	9.00	12.00
930 Standard Post, four way	5.00	7.50	10.00
931 Zoo Keeper, tall version	9.00	16.50	22.00
Short version	9.00	16.50	22.00
932 Zoo Keeper (for seating astride elephant)	50.00	85.00	140.00
933 Eland Bull	4.25	6.38	8.50
934 Brown Bear	4.50	6.50	9.00
935 American Bison	14.00	22.00	30.00
936 Cub bears, sitting, walking	3.50	5.25	7.00
937 Giant Tortoise	6.00	9.00	12.00
938 Howdah for Elephant	15.00	25.00	40.00
939 Boy or Girl for Howdah	11.00	16.50	24.00
940 Baby Hippopotamus	3.00	5.50	7.00
941 Tiger (walking)	4.50	6.50	12.00
942 Wild Boar	3.00	5.75	8.00
943 Baby Camel	3.00	5.75	8.00
944 Baby Elephant	3.50	6.50	9.00
945 Sable Antelope	4.00	7.50	10.00
946 Stork	2.00	4.50	6.00
947 Flamingo	2.50	5.25	7.00
948 Wart Hog	2.50	4.00	5.50
949 Malay Tapir	2.75	5.00	6.50
950 Baby Kangaroo (Wallaby)	2.00	4.00	5.50
951 Baby Rhinoceros	3.00	6.00	8.00

#920

L to R: #921 (many colors), #922, #923.

L to R: #931 Short, #933.

#934

L to R: #936, #940, #941.

L to R: #938 & #939 on #901 2nd version, #931 Tall.

	G	VG	EXC
952 Young Indian Elephant	9.00	14.50	20.00
953 Bactrian Camel with Boy Rider	65.00	105.00	155.00
954 Gorilla with Pole	6.50	9.50	12.50
955 Wolf	7.00	12.00	16.00
956 Walrus	3.00	4.50	7.00
957 Red Deer	6.50	12.00	16.00
958 Young Crocodile	8.00	13.00	17.50
959 Young Hippopotamus	4.25	7.50	10.50
960 Young Rhinoceros	4.00	7.25	10.00
961 Young Giraffe	9.00	16.00	21.00
962 Lion Cub	2.50	4.75	7.00
963 Gazelle	3.50	5.75	8.00
964 Sea Lion	3.50	5.75	8.00
965 Himalayan Bear (sitting)	4.00	7.00	10.00
966 Polar Bear (walking)	4.00	7.50	12.00
967 Polar Bear (standing)	4.00	7.50	12.00

#937

L to R: #942, #943.

#944

#945

L to R: #946, #947.

#948

#949

L to R: #951, #950.

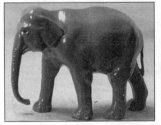

#952

#953

#954

#955

#956

#957

#958

#959

	G	VG	EXC
968 Indian or Water Buffalo	5.00	10.00	16.00
969 Giant Panda	4.00	7.50	10.00
970 Baby Panda (two positions) sitting, on all fours, each	2.50	4.00	6.00
971 The Panda Family (969-970) boxed	60.00	145.00	200.00
972 Assortment of Zoo animals, 37 pieces			No Price Found
973 Assortment of Zoo animals, 24 pieces			No Price Found
974 Assortment of Zoo animals, 12 pieces			No Price Found
975 UNKNOWN			—
976 Boy Rider for Camel or Elephant	15.00	25.00	40.00
977 UNKNOWN			—

	G	VG	EXC
978 Baby Chimpanzee	6.50	14.00	20.00
979-985 UNKNOWN			—
986 Panther, Postwar only	15.00	30.00	50.00
987 Baboon, Postwar only	10.00	20.00	30.00
988 Springbuck, Postwar only	13.00	25.00	33.00
989 Bushbuck, Postwar only	16.50	30.00	37.50
990 Vulture, Postwar only	11.00	20.00	27.50
991 King Cobra	6.50	12.50	16.50
992 Tiger (sitting)	8.00	13.00	17.50
993 Curved railing section	4.00	7.50	10.00
994 Straight railing section	6.00	10.00	14.00
995-999 UNKNOWN			—
1Z Boxed Zoo Set, lion, lioness, zebra, gorilla, 2 monkeys, 2 pelicans, 2 penguins, 10 pieces	65.00	100.00	150.00

#960

#961

L to R: #962, #963, #964.

#968

#969

L to R: #965, #967.

#970

#978

#986

#987

L to R: #988, #989.

#991

#992

	G	VG	EXC

2Z Boxed Zoo Set, lion, lioness, camel, zebra, polar bear, kangaroo, 2 monkeys, 2 pelicans, 4 penguins, 15 pieces .... No Price Found

3Z Boxed Zoo Set, camel, polar bear, lion, lioness, zebra, kangaroo, chimpanzee, gorilla, monkey, 2 pelicans, 2 penguins, 2 date palms and 1 coconut palm, 16 pieces 125.00 225.00 325.00

4Z Boxed Zoo set, elephant, rhinoceros, hippo, giraffe, crocodile, camel, lion, lioness, polar bear, llama, kangaroo, zebra, gorilla, ostrich, chimpanzee, monkeys, 2 penguins, 2 pelicans, 2 date palms and 2 coconut palms, 24 pieces .... No Price Found

5Z Boxed Zoo Set, camel, crocodile, eland bull, polar bear, ostrich, llama, bison, brown bear, lioness, lion, kangaroo, giraffe, zebra, hippo, rhinoceros, 2 date palms, 2 coconut palms, 19 pieces .... No Price Found

6Z Boxed Zoo Set, brown bear, 2 monkeys, chimpanzee, eland bull, ostrich, 2 bear cubs, bison, llama, 10 pieces .... No Price Found

11Z Boxed Zoo Set, eland bull, crocodile, sable, antelope, monkey, zebra, walrus, llama, ostrich, rhinoceros, hippopotamus, giraffe, elephant, 11 pieces 100.00 180.00 250.00

17Z Boxed Zoo Set, eland bull, crocodile, ostrich, boar, pelican, gorilla, 9 pieces .... No Price Found

18Z Mammal House, rhino, water buffalo, eland bull, 2 zebras .... No Price Found

19Z Polar Bear Pool, cave, sitting, standing and walking Polar Bears 250.00 450.00 650.00

20Z Large Pool enclosure, rock formation sides, penguins, tortoise, walrus, sea lions .... No Price Found

21Z Monkey Hill, a natural layout with variety of monkeys including chimpanzees and gorilla .... No Price Found

22Z Animal Houses, with enclosure, assorted animals (art hogs, Malay tapirs, wild boars) .... No Price Found

23Z Rock Pool with trees, pelican, storks and flamingos .... No Price Found

24Z Box Zoo Set, Elephant with keeper, Howdah and children, camel with boy and baby camel, llama, zebra, eland bull, tiger, wart hog, wild boar, giant tortoise, panda and 2 cubs, date palm, fencing, 55 pieces 350.00 650.00 1000.00

25Z Elephant with Keeper, Howdah, Boy, Girl 100.00 150.00 200.00

26Z Display Box, contains Hippo, Rhinoceros, Elephant, Giraffe, Lioness, Zebra, Leopard, Gorilla and Eland Bull .... No Price Found

27Z Display Box, contains Elephant, Hippo, Zebra, Crocodile, Leopard, Baby Elephant, Chimpanzee, Gazelle, Giraffe, Sable Antelope, Gorilla, Guenon Monkey, Ostrich, Lion, Lioness, Rhinoceros, Bush Buck .... No Price Found

28Z Display Box, contains Elephant, Hippo, Zebra, Crocodile, Leopard, Baby Elephant, others, 17 pieces (1960 catalog) .... No Price Found

32Z Box Zoo Set, 2 Date Palms, Camel, Kangaroo, Gorilla, Zebra, Lion, Lioness, Monkey, Chimpanzee, Penguin, Polar Bear, Coconut Palm 125.00 225.00 300.00

#Prewar box set (No. 2Z).

#25Z

Mammoth Circus
(Individual Pieces)

L to R: #449B, #448B.

#450B

	G	VG	EXC
351B Prancing Circus Horse	$18.00	$30.00	$36.00
352B Trotting Circus Horse	18.00	30.00	36.00
353B Circus performer on stilts	16.00	27.00	34.00
354B Clown with Hoop	18.00	25.00	35.00
355B Circus Equestrienne	18.00	28.00	35.00
356B Circus Cowboy Performer with Lasso (probably Prewar only)			No Price Found
357B Circus Ringmaster	16.00	27.00	32.00
358B Clown, Standing	14.00	25.00	30.00
359B Circus Elephant with blanket on black and hole in head to fit equestrienne or clown with hoop	18.00	28.00	40.00
446B Tub	6.50	9.00	12.00
447B Boxing Clown	15.00	25.00	35.00

L to R: #450B on #446B, #448B.

L to R: #451B, #447B.

#1439 Roundabout with six riders (1936-39). Swings round with a spin of the fingers. No mechanism to get out of order. Beautifully finished (assorted colourings). Measures 5-1/2" diam., by 5" high. Value about $4500.00 as shown. Courtesy Arnold Rolak.

#1441 The Flying Trapeze. A working model, comprising Clown with Umbrella and Fairy. The model is so constructed that as the performers travel along a stretched wire the umbrella twirls. The effect is very realistic. Sufficient wire is supplied to stretch across a normal room. Measures 8" high.

#1539

	G	VG	EXC
448B Lion Tamer	16.00	27.00	32.00
449B Performing Tiger	8.00	12.50	16.00
450B Performing Elephant (without tub)	20.00	37.50	50.00
451B Boxing Kangaroo	15.00	25.00	35.00
? Circus Ring, red, pressed wood, 7" diameter	20.00	30.00	40.00
1439 Circus Roundabout	See photo for price.		
1441 Circus--The Flying Trapeze a high wire act, 3 pieces	600.00	1000.00	1500.00

	G	VG	EXC
1442 Mammoth Circus, 6 pieces, 1936-40	No Price Found		
1443 Mammoth Circus, 10 pieces, 1936-40	No Price Found		
1444 Mammoth Circus, 14 pieces, 1936-40	350.00	750.00	1200.00
1539 Mammoth Circus, 23 pieces, 1937-41; 1948-61	375.00	750.00	1000.00
2054 Mammoth Circus, 1951-61, 12 pieces	200.00	400.00	600.00

Railway

L to R: #800 with #811, #801.   *#800 with #811.*

	G	VG	EXC
800 Porter to push trolley	$7.00	$13.50	$18.00
801 Porter to carry luggage	10.00	18.00	24.00
802 Station Master	8.00	15.00	20.00
803 Guard with Flag	12.00	27.50	50.00
804 Guard with Lamp	12.00	20.00	28.00
805 Ticket Collector	8.00	15.00	20.00
806 Lady Passenger, Prewar, 1st ...	20.00	30.00	40.00
807 Gentleman Passenger, Prewar .	20.00	30.00	40.00
808 Policeman	9.00	14.00	18.00
809 Engine Driver	12.00	22.50	30.00
810 Stoker with separate shovel	30.00	45.00	66.00
811 Trolley	5.00	8.00	12.00
812 Trunk	3.50	6.00	9.00
813 Dress Basket	3.50	6.00	9.00
814 Portmanteau	4.50	7.25	13.00

	G	VG	EXC
815 Golf sticks	5.00	8.00	14.00
816 Rugs and Sticks	4.50	7.00	12.50
817 Yachtsman	20.00	45.00	65.00

STATION STAFF AND SUNDRIES
NO. "0" GAUGE

	G	VG	EXC
818 Platelayers (assorted), each	No Price Found		
819 Golfer	$20.00	$30.00	$40.00
820 Guard with Flag	No Price Found		
155 Railway Staff, 12 pieces "1908"	150.00	300.00	400.00
158 Railway Station Staff, 25 pieces	400.00	600.00	800.00
168 Civilians, 8 pieces	200.00	450.00	700.00
1256 Station Figures, 17 pieces ...	250.00	500.00	850.00
1422 "0" Gauge Railway, 9 pieces	No Price Found		
1423 Station Staff, 9 pieces	200.00	350.00	600.00
1-R Station Set, 20 pieces (1954-59 only)	No Price Found		

#801 (cupped hands).   *#801 with #816.*   *#802*

#803

L to R: #804, #805 Empty handed.

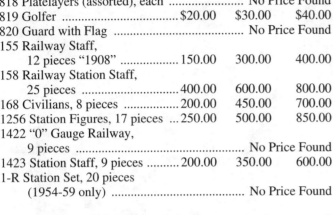

"Lady Passengers." L to R: 1st version, 2nd version, postwar set #1R, #1R with umbrella.

"Gentleman Passengers." L to R: 1st version, postwar set #1R, set #168, #817.

#819

#808 Red & white wristband.   *#810*

Chauffeur without lamp. Value $80.00 in very good condition.

#155 (Circa 1920-25).

#168 First version (1912).

Set #1256.

Miniature Gardening

The Miniature Gardening Series was available in the 1930s. The flowers were made with a special alloy of almost pure lead. This allowed bending of the stems and flowers to give a three-dimensional effect. The series was dropped from the 1940 catalog, due, in part, to critical shortages of lead during the early years of WWII, but some pieces were added to the Farm section in that year and are noted with an asterisk and the "New" Farm number. No prices found except where noted.

	G	VG	EXC
01 Flower Bed with grass border, straight section	$4.00	$6.00	$8.00
02 Flower Bed with grass border, finishing circular section	4.00	6.00	8.00
03 Flower Bed with grass border, return square section	4.00	6.00	8.00
04 Flower Bed with grass border, return circular section	4.00	6.00	8.00
05 Flower Bed with grass border, half straight section	3.00	5.00	7.00
06 Flower Bed with grass border, finishing corner section	3.00	5.00	7.00
*07-666 Post for Stone Wall	5.00	8.00	11.00
*08-667 Garden Roller			
*09-668 Crazy Paving, per 10 pieces	3.50	5.25	7.00
*010-669 Sundial on pedestal	5.00	8.00	10.00
*011-670 Garden wheelbarrow	3.00	5.00	7.00
*012-671 Stone wall	6.00	9.00	13.00
013 Pergola Section, used with rambler roses or similar plants	12.00	18.00	24.00
014 Rustic arch	12.00	18.00	24.00

#07

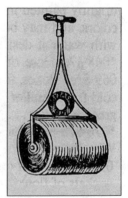

#08

"Amydst ye
Flowers
I tell ye
Houres."

#010

	G	VG	EXC
015 Mound, for mounting single plants, rose bushes, rustic arch or pergola	2.50	3.75	5.00
016 Coloured vase, holds conifer or any single plant	2.50	3.75	5.00
017 Garden seat, white			
*018-672 Interlaced board fence with trellis	8.00	12.00	16.00
019 Rambler Rose, varied colors	5.00	7.50	10.00
020 Lobelia (L. Gacilis, L. Erinus) a beautiful blue border flower	.10	.20	.30
021 Geranium, reds, whites, pinks, packet of 10 pieces	2.00	3.00	4.00
022 Torch Lily, (Knipholia), red hot poker, packet of 5 pieces	2.00	3.00	4.00
023 Conifer, dwarf trees, used in pots and tubs	2.00	3.00	4.00
024 Sunflower (helianthus)	4.50	6.00	9.00
025 Poppy (Papaver) large range of colors, packet of 6 pieces	2.50	3.75	5.00
026 Lupin (Lupinus) beautiful colored spikes of flowers, per 5 pieces	2.50	3.75	5.00
027 Half Standard Rose, a variety in which the branches are only allowed to grow from a single stem some height above the ground			
028 Rose Bush, various colors	2.50	3.75	5.00
029 Aster, excellent for borders	2.00	3.00	4.00
030 Hollyhock, double (Althaea rosea), pinks, yellows, whites, good for background	2.50	3.75	5.00
031 Antirrhinum (Snap-dragon), various colors, packet of 10 pieces	2.00	3.00	4.00
032 Dahlia, double, packet of 4 pieces	2.00	3.00	4.00
033 Dahlia, single	2.00	3.00	5.00
034 Gladioli, lily-like flowers, packet of 10 pieces	2.00	3.00	4.00
035 Wallflower (Cheiranthus), suitable for beds or borders			
036 Foxglove (Digitalis), packet of 10 pieces	2.00	3.00	4.00
037 Chrysanthemum, packet of 5 pieces	2.50	3.75	5.00
038 Full Standard rose			
039 Delphinium, packet of 5 pieces	2.00	3.00	4.00
040 Hyacinth (Hyacinthus), various colors	2.00	3.00	4.00
041 Tulip, various colors, packet of 8 pieces	2.00	3.00	4.00
042 Crocus, various colors, packet of 13 pieces	4.00	6.00	8.00
043 Snowdrop (Galanthus), packet of 11 pieces	2.00	3.00	4.00
044 Daffodil, of the Narcissus family, yellow			

	G	VG	EXC
045 Narcissus, border plant, white with yellow/orange centers	2.00	3.00	4.00
046 Sweet Alyssum (a Maritimum) white border, packet of 10 pieces	2.00	3.00	4.00
047 Square Tub, holds conifer or any single plant	2.00	3.00	4.00
048 Small flower bed, holds 7 plants	3.00	4.50	6.00
049 Lawn Section 1-3/4"x1-3/4", colored green, representing well kept lawn	1.00	2.00	3.00
*050-673 Lawn Mower with removable grass box	37.00	56.00	75.00
*051-679 Man for lawn mower			
*052-680 Man for Garden roller			
053 Greenhouse, with windows, unbreakable and staging for flower pots	100.00	150.00	200.00
054 Rockery, straight section (2 kinds, each with varying rock arrangements)	9.00	13.00	18.00
055 Rockery, inner return corner	9.00	13.00	18.00
056 Rockery, outer corner	9.00	13.00	18.00
057 Rockery, upper steps	9.00	13.00	18.00
058 Rockery, lower steps	9.00	13.00	18.00
059 Flower Pots, large, medium and small for greenhouse, etc.	2.00	3.00	4.00
060 Blocks (wooden, 1-3/4"x1-3/4x7/8", for varying levels or terracing, per each	4.00	6.00	8.00
*061-674 Balustrading, long section	12.00	18.00	24.00
062 Balustrading, short section	7.00	11.00	14.00
063 Post for balustrading	2.00	3.00	5.00
*064-675 Cold Frame, to open	27.00	41.00	55.00
065 Round bed, without grass verge	6.00	9.00	13.00

#050

#062

#068

	G	VG	EXC
066 Square bed, without grass verge	6.00	9.00	12.00
*067-677 Lily Pond, very brightly painted in natural colors, and may be filled with water if desired	55.00	82.00	110.00
*068-676 Hose on reel	30.00	45.00	60.00
069 Seed Boxes, for use in cold frame and/or greenhouse	6.00	9.00	12.00

*070-678 Man for Wheelbarrow

071 Assortment of 2 dozen packets of flowers. Appeared first in 1938 catalog

Miniature Garden Display Sets

Each set is complete in itself and will make up into various designs, the larger ones being more variable than the smaller.

1MG A collection of flower beds and flowers to form a complete circular bed

2MG A similar layout as 1MG but with different flowers

3MG A collection of flower beds and flowers to form a completed square bed

4MG A collection of various flower beds and other accessories with flowers

5MG A collection of flower beds and flowers forming a large oval or circular bed, etc.

6MG A similar collection as 5MG with different flowers to form square, oblong or other beds

7MG A collection of various flower beds, accessories and flowers making a nice display

8MG A larger collection as 7MG including crazy paving, capable of a number of variations

9MG A collection of pieces with flower beds, crazy paving, stone walling, rustic arch, etc. and flowers, permitting many pleasing variations of design

10MG A collection of flower beds, flowers, crazy paving, stone walling, fencing and with Rambler Roses, makes a number of designs

11MG A collection of flower beds, crazy paving with lawn and sundial and variety of flowers making a large layout with many variations

12MG A collection of flower beds and accessories, including fencing and stone walling and varieties of flowers, giving extremely pleasing layouts.

13MG A large collection of pieces and flowers permitting many ideal layouts.

14MG A collection of flower beds and bulbs making a well-filled circular section

15MG A similar collection as 14MG, but to form a square bed.

16MG A variety of flower beds and bulbs, making some very attractive layouts.

Nos. 17MG through 22MG are small beds well filled with flowers and suitable as beginners sets, or for placing on Miniature Garden Lawns to form Center beds. Each in an attractive box.

17MG Round bed filled with Hyacinths and Crocuses.

18MG Round bed filled with Tulips and Crocuses

19MG Round bed filled with geraniums, gladioli, foxglove, and red hot poker

20MG Round bed filled with geraniums, aster and delphiniums

21MG Square bed filed with lobelia, sweet alyssum and chrysanthemums

22MG Square bed filed with lobelia, gladioli and bush rose

23MG A large collection of rockery with blocks for terracing, flowers and flower beds, crazy paving, lawn, balustrading, etc.

24MG A collection on similar lines to 23MG, but not as large

25MG A collection of rockery pieces and accessories

26MG A varied assortment of rockery with flower beds and a good range of flowers

27MG A collection on similar lines to 26MG but with variation of pieces and flowers

28MG Garden shelter, measures 4-1/4" long

29MG A large well-fitted presentation box, containing cottage and varied collection of miniature gardening pieces, flowers, etc.

30MG A larger collection than the preceding, containing cottage, rockery, greenhouse, garden shelter, cold frames, lily pond, flowers, lawn, crazy paving, etc.

31MG A fully modeled tree, in which the foliage fits on to a central trunk. Perfectly natural from all angles of view, measures 5" high.

"1938" Display Sets listed below are in cellophane-wrapped boxes and attractively displayed with brightly colored labels.

32MG Containing a selection of plants, flower beds, crazy paving, lawn, conifers in pots, stone walling and posts.

33MG Containing a selection of plants, flower beds, crazy paving, lawn, rustic arch, stone walling and posts, similar to 32MG but a larger selection.

34MG Containing a selection of plants, flower beds, crazy paving, lawn, stone walling, balustrading, sundial, arch and colored vases.

35MG Containing a larger selection of plants, flower beds, rockery, balustrading and posts, crazy paving, lawn, wooden terracing blocks, sundial, man, garden roller, lawn mower, wheelbarrow, garden seat, rustic arch, pergolas, stone walling, cold frame and seed boxes.

Miscellaneous

	G	VG	EXC
1546-49 UNKNOWN	....		—
1550 Noah's Ark (25 pcs.)	$1500.00	$2500.00	$3500.00
1644 Mickey Mouse at the cinema	.... No Price Found		
1645 Mickey Mouse set (6 pcs.)	.... No Price Found		
1654 Snow White and Seven Dwarfs, 8 pcs.	200.00	525.00	750.00
Each	20.00	60.00	80.00
1526 All Metal Flower Holder, 5-1/4" wide, 1 pc.	.... No Price Found		
1552 Royal Mail Van, 2 pcs. with driver	.... No Price Found		
1656 John Cobb's Railton Wonder Car	200.00	350.00	500.00
1658 John Cobb's Railton Wonder Car (Chromium Plated Body)	150.00	275.00	400.00

	G	VG	EXC
1912 Historical Figures, (issued November 1940) includes:			
T-1 King Henry VIII	35.00	60.00	90.00
T-3 Little Red Riding Hood	.... No Price Found		
T-4 Queen Elizabeth	35.00	60.00	90.00
T-5 Cinderella	35.00	60.00	90.00

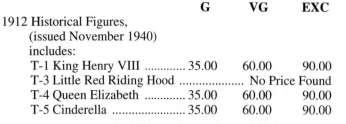

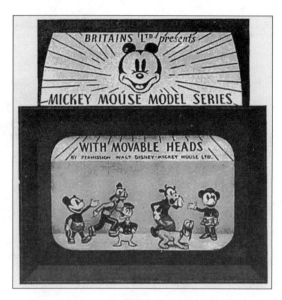

#1644 MICKEY MOUSE AT THE CINEMA. This is an ingenious display box containing Mickey Mouse, Minnie Mouse, Pluto, Donald Duck, Clarabelle and Goofy, and so designed to represent a cinema show. The characters are arranged behind the title screen, which can then be drawn up so that the figures appear as seen at the Cinema. Provides lots of fun. Measures 12" x 8-3/4".

#1550 NOAH'S ARK, with Noah and His Wife and the following animals in pairs: elephants, rhinoceroses, polar bears, lions, llamas, wolves, monkeys, storks, kangaroos, brown bears, penguins. Ark measures: length 12"; breadth 5-3/4"; height 6". 25 pieces.

#1654

#1552

T-1

T-3

	G	**VG**	**EXC**
1919 Historical Figures,			
(issued December 1940)			
includes 86D Chair			No Price Found
T-1 King Henry VIII	35.00	60.00	90.00
T-4 Queen Elizabeth	35.00	60.00	90.00

(Note: 1912 and 1919 were made up of figures done special for Madame Tussaud's Wax Museum)

	G	**VG**	**EXC**
Unnumbered, Madame Tussaud,			
bronze painted bust	35.00	70.00	100.00
1920 Set of Chessmen,			
with board, 25 pcs.	120.00	250.00	400.00
1921-1989 UNKNOWN			

(Used in part for Horton's Toys. See "Reno" Sports Games) .... —

	G	**VG**	**EXC**
1990 Chess Set			No Price Found
Unnumbered, Mikado String			
pull spins parsal, c1900.			
Offered in 1993,			
mint in the box for 1000.00			
Unnumbered, Life Boatman	25.00	35.00	55.00
Unnumbered, Sir Kreemy Knut	50.00	75.00	100.00
Cricketeer, rare, prewar only	25.00	50.00	100.00
31 Folding Ladder	10.00	20.00	35.00
1413 Mobile police with two			
Officers, prewar only	200.00	400.00	700.00
U.S. Policeman directing			
traffic, rare	25.00	75.00	125.00

T-4

T-5

Gilt bust of Edward VII.

Bust of General Booth.

Madame Tussaud.

Mikado with original box. Courtesy Arnold Rolak.

Life Boatman.

Sir Kreemy Knut.

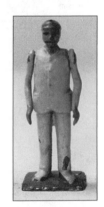

Cricketeer

#31

#1400 Blue Bird Race Car. Detachable body from chassis. 6-3/8" long.

#1413

U.S. Policeman directing traffic.

#475 Extremely rare Victorian family. Boy not shown in photograph. Value $7,000-$10,000.

Early Britains Mechanical Equestrienne. Offered with box top in 1993 for $2300.00 in excellent-plus condition.

Unnumbered Mandarin. Offered in 1993 in excellent condition for $450.00. Courtesy Phillips.

The Fountain Top (1880), with the original printing block used to show this toy in the Britains 1880 catalog. Value about $950.00. Courtesy Arnold Rolak.

The New Mechanical Galloping Donkey (1860-1870). Value about $1750.00 with box. Courtesy Arnold Rolak.

Britains Crane, very early (1870s?). Purchased from the London Toy and Model Museum. Value $1500.00. Courtesy Arnold Rolak.

The General (1880), with original box. Value $4500.00 with box (only boxed one known). Courtesy Arnold Rolak.

The Boomerang Top (1880), with original box. Value $1100.00 with box. Courtesy Arnold Rolak.

Walking Elephant (1880). Value $2750.00. Courtesy Arnold Rolak.

The Clown (1880). Only one known. Value as shown $1650.00. Courtesy Arnold Rolak.

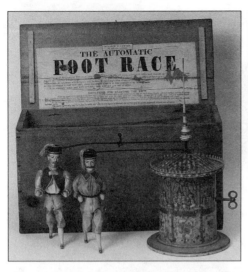

The Automatic Foot Race (1880). This is the only complete set known. Value with box is $12,500.00. Courtesy Arnold Rolak.

#Britains Road Roller (1870s?). Value $850.00. Courtesy Arnold Rolak.

The Miniature London Road Roller (1880) with original box. Value with box $4250.00. Courtesy Arnold Rolak.

The Waltzers (1880). Value $3450.00 with original box. Courtesy Arnold Rolak.

Don Quixote and the Windmill (1880) with original box. Only two known. Value about $4,750.00 as shown, with box. Courtesy Arnold Rolak.

RACING GAME MODELS

It is believed these models date from 1905. Sometime during the 1920s, they were assigned catalog numbers. After being out of production from 1946 through 1953, they were reintroduced in 1954. The Milton Bradley Company issued a horse racing board game that included these figures. They were discontinued in 1959.

	G	VG	EXC
19D Jockey on horse, assorted colors, 2-1/4" long	$14.00	$21.00	$28.00
123b Jockey for Race Games, assorted colors, 3-3/4" long, reassigned number 96D in 1954			No Price Found

#96D, $20.00-35.00-55.00.

CADBURY COCOCUBS

These delightful and colorful characters were given as a sales promotion with Cadbury Cocoa during the mid 1930s. In addition to the figures, club members were sent Cococub Newsletters and issued badges in the shape of a star. Only pieces with bases are stamped "Cpryt Britains Cadbury." The smaller figures averaged 40mm tall, while the larger were almost 80mm. The numbering system included here has been designed by V.J. Medcalf for ease of identification. S = Small, L = Large.

	G	VG	EXC
S1a Dumpty Doo Duck, open beak, large hat			No Price Found
S1b Dumpty Doo Duck, half open beak, bowler hat			No Price Found
S1c Dumpty Doo Duck, half open beak, cap			No Price Found
S1d Dumpty Doo Duck, closed beak, very small hat	$14.00	$21.00	$28.00
S2 Dan Crow	12.00	18.00	25.00
S3 Silas Slink (fox)	12.00	18.00	25.00
S4 Freddie Frog	14.00	21.00	28.00
S5 Monty Monkey	14.00	21.00	28.00
S6 Gussie Robin	10.00	15.00	20.00
S7 Tom Kitten	11.00	16.00	22.00
S8 Timothy Tortoise			No Price Found
S9 Tubby Bear	11.00	16.00	23.00

S5

L to R: S3, S6, S2, S18, L1.

L to R: S1b, S15.

	G	VG	EXC
S10 Pat Pelican	No Price Found		
S11 Mrs. Cacklegoose	12.00	18.00	25.00
S12 Captain Kangaroo	13.00	19.00	26.00
S13 Will Mouse	11.00	16.00	22.00
S14 Percy Parrot	11.00	16.00	22.00
S15 Granny Owl	12.00	18.00	24.00
S16 Bill Badger	No Price Found		
S17 Mrs. Henrietta Fussy Feathers	12.00	18.00	25.00
S18 Nutty Squirrel	12.00	18.00	25.00
S19 Piglet	11.00	16.00	22.00
S20 Brother Rabbit	11.00	16.00	22.00
S21 Percy Penguin	13.00	19.00	26.00
L1 Jonathan (boy)	75.00	112.00	150.00
L2 Peter Pum (poodle)	17.00	25.00	34.00
L3 Whiskers Rabbit	No Price Found		
L4 Mr. Pie Porker	11.00	16.00	22.00
L5 Mrs. Pie Porker	No Price Found		
L6 Tiny Tusks (elephant)	No Price Found		
L7 Squire Rooster	20.00	30.00	40.00
L8 "Name Unknown," boy eating chocolate, wearing blue Edwardian sailor suit	No Price Found		

LILLIPUT

Lilliput figures were first issued in the 1950 catalog supplement and finally entered into the main catalog in 1954. They were manufactured by W. Horton LTD (established in 1832), under license from Britains LTD. They were distributed in the United Kingdom by Horton, while Britains handled all export orders. A foot figure in this series is 13/16" or 21 mm in height. This was compatible with "00" and "HO" scales. No prices found except where noted.

"Farm"

	G	VG	EXC
LB/513 Tree	No Price Found		
LB/514 Shire horse	No Price Found		
LB/515 Farmer	$3.50	$5.00	$7.00
LB/516 Farmer's Wife	3.50	5.00	7.00
LB/517 Nurse and Child	10.00	15.00	20.00
LB/518 Foal	3.00	4.50	6.00
LB/519 Cob	3.00	4.50	6.00
LB/520 Standing Cow	3.00	4.50	6.00
LB/521 Feeding Cow	3.00	4.50	6.00
LB/522 Calf, lying	2.00	3.00	4.00
LB/523 Collie Dog	1.00	2.00	3.00
LB/524 Goose	2.50	3.75	5.00
LB/525 Sheep, standing	2.00	3.00	4.00
LB/526 Sheep, feeding	3.00	4.50	6.00
LB/527 Pig	2.00	3.00	4.00
LB/528 Lamb	3.00	4.50	6.00
LB/529 Ducks and Drakes	2.00	3.00	4.00
LB/530 Hurdle	.50	1.00	2.00
LB/531 Stable Lad	3.50	5.25	7.00
LB/532 Land Girl	3.50	5.25	7.00

"Railway"

	G	VG	EXC
LB/533 Porter with Barrow	$7.00	$10.50	$14.00
LB/534 Guard	4.00	6.00	8.00
LB/535 Station Master	4.00	6.00	8.00
LB/536 Civilian	No Price Found		
LB/537 Porter with luggage	5.00	7.50	10.00
LB/538 Newsvendor	1.50	3.00	4.00
LB/539 Lady with case	5.00	7.50	10.00
LB/540 Man with book	5.00	7.50	10.00
LB/541 Man with umbrella	5.00	7.50	10.00
LB/542 Lady with hatbox	5.00	7.50	10.00
LB/543 Golfer	2.00	4.00	5.50
LB/544 Barrel	No Price Found		
LB/545 Hamper	No Price Found		
LB/546 Large packing case	3.50	5.25	7.00
LB/547 Small packing case	3.00	4.50	6.00
LB/548 Telegraph Boy	No Price Found		
LB/549 Electric Trolley	4.00	6.00	8.00
LB/550 Speed Cop	No Price Found		

"Hunting Series"

LB/559 Huntsman, mounted, galloping, top hat	No Price Found		
LB/560 Huntswomen, mounted, galloping, top hat	No Price Found		
LB/561 Hounds, running, legs outstretched	No Price Found		
LB/562 Hounds, running, legs closed	No Price Found		
LB/563 Fox, running	No Price Found		
LB/564 Huntswoman, mounted, galloping, bowler hat	No Price Found		
LB/565 Huntsman, mounted, galloping, cap	No Price Found		

"LILLIPUT WORLD"

(Picture Packs)

"Farm"

LP 501 4 standing sheep, 4 feeding sheep, 3 lambs	No Price Found		
LP 502 3 standing cows, 3 feeding cows	No Price Found		

	G	VG	EXC
LP 503 12 Hurdles	$7.50	$11.25	$15.00
LP 504 5 cobs, 2 foals	20.00	30.00	40.00
LP 505 4 geese, 6 ducks, 1 land girl	32.00	48.00	65.00
LP 506 4 shire horses, 1 stable lad, 1 collie dog			No Price Found
LP 507 2 feeding cows, 3 standing cows, 2 lying calves			No Price Found
LP 508 8 pigs, 1 farmer, 1 collie dog			No Price Found
LP 509 1 farmer, 1 farmer's wife, 2 land girls, 2 stable lads, 1 collie dog	21.00	31.50	42.00

"Railway"

LP 510 Guard, station master, porter for trolley, porter with luggage, newsvendor, two-wheeled trolley, 6 pcs.

LP 511 Lady with attaché case, man with book, man with umbrella, lady with hat box, golfer, nurse with child, 6 pcs.

LP 512 Electric trolley, two-wheeled trolley, 2 barrels, 2 hampers, 2 large packing cases, 2 small packing cases, 10 pcs.

LP 513 18 trees (this later changed to the Hunt Picture Pack in 1958 which contained huntsman, huntswomen, 3 dogs (assorted positions), 1 fox

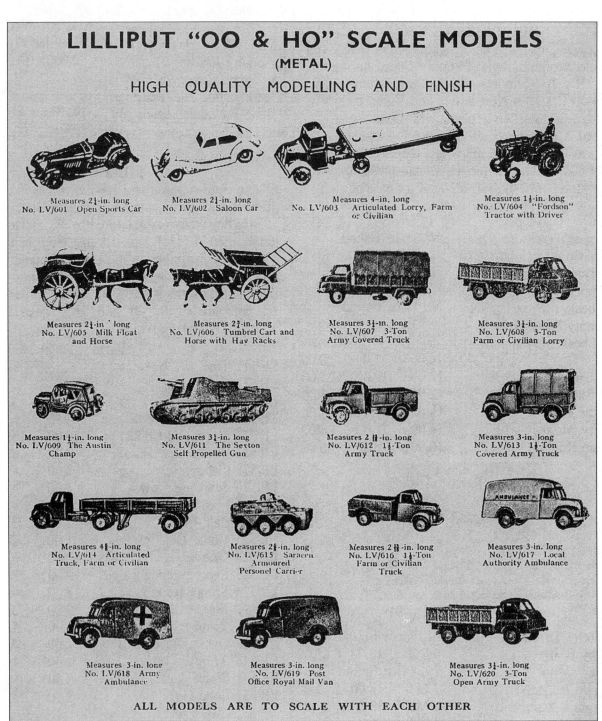

LILLIPUT "OO & HO" SCALE MODELS
(METAL)
HIGH QUALITY MODELLING AND FINISH

Measures 2¼-in. long
No. LV/601 Open Sports Car

Measures 2¼-in. long
No. LV/602 Saloon Car

Measures 4-in. long
No. LV/603 Articulated Lorry, Farm or Civilian

Measures 1½-in. long
No. LV/604 "Fordson" Tractor with Driver

Measures 2¼-in long
No. LV/605 Milk Float and Horse

Measures 2¾-in. long
No. LV/606 Tumbrel Cart and Horse with Hay Racks

Measures 3¼-in. long
No. LV/607 3-Ton Army Covered Truck

Measures 3¼-in. long
No. LV/608 3-Ton Farm or Civilian Lorry

Measures 1½-in. long
No. LV/609 The Austin Champ

Measures 3¼-in. long
No. LV/611 The Sexton Self Propelled Gun

Measures 2⅛-in. long
No. LV/612 1¼-Ton Army Truck

Measures 3-in. long
No. LV/613 1¼-Ton Covered Army Truck

Measures 4⅛-in. long
No. LV/614 Articulated Truck, Farm or Civilian

Measures 2⅝-in. long
No. LV/615 Saracen Armoured Personel Carrier

Measures 2⅛-in. long
No. LV/616 1¼-Ton Farm or Civilian Truck

Measures 3-in. long
No. LV/617 Local Authority Ambulance

Measures 3-in. long
No. LV/618 Army Ambulance

Measures 3-in. long
No. LV/619 Post Office Royal Mail Van

Measures 3¼-in. long
No. LV/620 3-Ton Open Army Truck

ALL MODELS ARE TO SCALE WITH EACH OTHER

"Lilliput Vehicles"

	G	VG	EXC
LV/601 Open Sports Car	$20.00	$30.00	$40.00
LV/602 Saloon Car	20.00	30.00	40.00
LV/603 Articulated Lorry	20.00	30.00	40.00
LV/604 Fordson Tractor with driver	20.00	30.00	40.00
LV/605 Milk Float and horse with milkman	22.00	33.00	45.00
LV/606 Tumbrel Cart and horse with hay racks and carter	20.00	30.00	40.00
LV/607 Army covered 3 ton truck with removable plastic top, khaki	25.00	38.00	50.00
LV/608 3 Ton farm lorry. Spare wheel fitted, ass't colors, measures 3-1/4" long	No Price Found		
LV/609 The Austin "Champ," all purpose vehicle with removable hood	No Price Found		

LV/610 Centurion tank	25.00	38.00	50.00
LV/611 The Sexton. A fine model of the most modern self-propelled gun. Not fitted to fire, measures 3-1/4" long	27.00	41.00	55.00
LV/612 1-1/2 Ton Army truck, with spare wheel, measures 2-13/16" long	No Price Found		
LV/613 1-1/2 Ton covered Army truck with spare wheel, measures 3" long	No Price Found		
LV/614 Articulated truck with spare wheel, measures 4-5/8" long	No Price Found		
LV/615 "Saracen" Armoured personnel carrier, measures 2-5/8" long	No Price Found		
LV/616 1-1/2 Ton Farm or Civilian truck with spare wheel, measures 2-13/16" long	No Price Found		
LV/617 Local authority ambulance, cream, measures 3" long	8.00	15.00	20.00
LV/618 Army ambulance, measures 3" long	No Price Found		
LV/619 Post Office Royal Mail Van, measures 3" long	No Price Found		
LV/620 3 Ton open Army truck with spare wheel, measures 3-1/4" long	No Price Found		

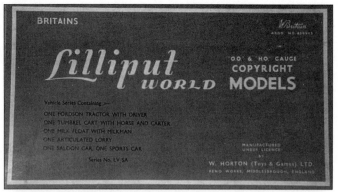

LV/SA

	G	VG	EXC
LV/SA Boxed set containing: 1 LV/601, 1 LV/602, 1 LV/603, 1 LV/604 with driver, 1 LV/605 with Milkman, 1 LV/606, with accessories and Carter as listed in the 1951 Catalog Supplement	65.00	125.00	200.00

"Lilliput World"
(Window Packs)

	G	VG	EXC
L1 Shire horse; 1 land girl; 1 standing cow; 1 standing sheep; 1 feeding sheep; 2 ducks	$5.00	$10.00	$15.00
L2 1 Cob; 1 farmer; 1 goose; 1 pig; 1 farmer's wife; 1 feeding cow	5.00	10.00	15.00
L3 1 Duck; 1 pig, 1 land girl; 1 standing cow; 1 stable lad, 1 goose; 1 lying calf	5.00	10.00	15.00
L4 1 farmer; 1 foal; 1 shire horse; 1 collie dog; 1 feeding sheep; 1 stable lad; 1 standing sheep			
L5 1 feeding cow; 1 farmer's wife, 2 lying calves; 1 land girl; 1 standing cow	12.00	18.00	25.00
L6 1 standing cow; 1 goose; 1 pig; 1 lamb; 1 collie dog; 1 duck; 1 cob; 1 standing sheep	5.00	10.00	15.00

	G	**VG**	**EXC**

L7 Lilliput Display Box containing Saloon Car, tractor, tumbrel cart and milk float, farmer, farmer's wife, stable lad, farm girl and dog, horses, cows and calf, sheep and lamb, pig, geese, hurdles and tree, 28 pcs. 75.00   150.00   250.00

L8 Roadside Inn or Country House .... No Price Found

L9 Two country cottages, back and front elevations are different .... No Price Found

L10 Typical Barn and cart stable .... No Price Found

L11 Lilliput Railway Personnel and Vehicles: saloon car, lorry, sports car, articulated lorries, Austin "Champ," motorcyclists, station trolleys, packing cases, barrels, hampers, porters with trolleys, guards, station master, porters with luggage, newsvendor, general public asst., 43 pcs. .... No Price Found

L12 Scenic Display containing 8 battledress soldiers in various attitudes .... No Price Found

	G	**VG**	**EXC**

LL14 Wallet Pack; 8 battledress soldiers; khaki color only .... No Price Found

L51 Land Girl, stable lad and 11 assorted animals, 13 pcs. .... No Price Found

L52 Hurdles, 2 standing sheep, 2 feeding sheep; 1 collie dog, 1 farmer, 1 standing cow, 1 shire horse, 2 lying calves .... No Price Found

L53 2 Feeding sheep; 2 standing sheep, 2 lambs, 1 collie dog, 2 foals, 1 standing cow, 1 feeding cow, 2 lying calves, 2 geese .... No Price Found

L101 2 geese; 2 lambs; 1 standing sheep; 1 farmer; 1 feeding sheep; 2 standing cows, 2 ducks, 2 lying calves, 1 farmer's wife, 1 foal, 1 shire horse, 2 feeding cows, 1 land girl, 1 stable lad, 2 pigs .... No Price Found

L102 2 pigs; 2 standing sheep, 2 feeding sheep, 2 cobs; 4 lambs; 2 geese, 2 shire horses, 2 foals, 1 farmer, 1 land girl, 1 stable lad .... No Price Found

L7

L8

L9

L10

✕ **Britains Plastic** ✕

by Joseph Saine

Plastic soldiers in the Britains line began in 1954 with Herald. The Herald figures are noted for their stocky appearance. This line was to be a mainstay of the Britains catalog through 1977.

In 1960, Britains launched its very popular Swoppet line. These figures began with the "War of the Roses" knights and soon branched off into western and military figures, as well. They are very complicated figures, with separate pieces that can be swopped (thus the name). These remained on Britains' sales list until 1977.

1961 saw the introduction of a new range of Britains plastic: "Eyes Right," known for their plug-in heads, moving arms and separate square bases. These were largely ceremonial figures and band figures. They were sold both singly and in boxed sets in varying sizes.

No new innovations in the plastic ranges (other than packaging or lack of) was to happen until "Deetail" exploded upon the marketplace in 1975. These plastic figures plugged into a square metal base and are still being marketed today (albeit, manufactured in China since 1993). These were to prove so popular (and profitable) that they ran the gamut of historical periods: Waterloo, 15th Century, Foreign Legion and Arabs, Western, Civil War and--the mainstay--the many armies of World War II. Britains later began a line of military die-cast vehicles that added play value to the WWII armies, much like its hollowcast lead forerunners. To collect the entire Britains plastic line (with all the packaging and mold variations) could be a lifetime venture. But it would be an affordable and satisfying venture, to be sure.

Prices are for individual mint figures. No scuffs, worn or flaking paint; Swoppets must be complete with all parts. *Divide prices by one half for Very Good and take 80% off for Good.* Most collectors do not want poor examples, other than for converting or repainting. Many thanks go to Jeff Anusbigian and Rick Berry for opening their homes to have their collections photographed.

(According to *The Plastic Warrior Guide to U.K. Makers of Plastic Toy Figures*, Roy Selwyn-Smith sculpted "many of the best known Herald figures." Kay Fido also sculpted some. George Ford designed the Eyes Right series and the American Civil War Swoppets. George Musgrave also worked on Herald and "designed the prototype Swoppet cowboys." Charles Biggs was the originator "of the Deetail concept," and Cameron sculpted "the bulk of the Deetail range.")

Herald

HERALD ROMANS & TROJANS
(Drawings courtesy Bob Bard)

		MINT
4590	Roman Chariot (driver, 2 horses)	$25.00
4594	Mounted Trojan General	8.00
4595	Trojan Warriors, 6 pieces	25.00
	Price Per individual figure in mint	3.00
7599	Trojan Warriors, 25 pieces, made in Britain	175.00
7599	Trojan Warriors, 25 pieces, made in Hong Kong	100.00
594	Mounted Trojan General	6.00
595	Warrior with Spear	3.00
596	Warrior Defending with Shield	3.00
597	Warrior attacking with Sword	3.00
598	Archer	3.00
599	Warrior standing	3.00

#594

Top, L to R: #596, #597; Bottom, L to R: #595, #598, #599.
Herald Trojans. Photo by Gary J. Linden.

HERALD KNIGHTS (all made in Hong Kong)
MINT
4406	Knights, 6 pieces	$18.00
4415	Standing Knights, 6 different	5.00
4420	Mounted Knights, 4 different	70.00
7404	Knights, 11 pieces	70.00
7406	Knights, 14 pieces	85.00
7409	Knights, 26 pieces	150.00
	Foot knights, per figure	5.00
	Mounted knights, per figure	15.00

HERALD CIVIL WAR & 7TH CAVALRY
H431	Confederate officer, advancing	$3.00
H432	Confederate Bugler	3.00
H433	Confederate Infantryman, advancing	3.00

MINT
H434	Confederate Infantryman, standing firing	3.00
H461	Federal officer, advancing	4.00
H462	Federal Bugler	4.00
H463	Federal Infantryman, advancing	4.00
H464	Federal Infantryman, standing firing	4.00
	7th Cavalry (made in Hong Kong) mounted, per mint figure	4.00
	7th Cavalry foot figures each	3.00

Top, L to R: #H463, #H463, #H461; Bottom: #H464, #H464,
#H462. Herald Civil War. Photo by Gary J. Linden.

HERALD COWBOYS AND INDIANS
(Drawings courtesy Bob Bard)

H600	Standing firing	$3.00
H601	Standing firing two pistols	3.00
H602	Cowboy, lassoing, foot, made in Britain	3.00
H602	Cowboy, made in Hong Kong	2.00
H603	Cowboy, kneeling firing, made in Britain	3.00

#H602

Top, L to R: #H433, #H433, #H431; Bottom, L to R: #H434,
#H434, #H432. Herald Civil War. Photo by Gary J. Linden.

L to R: #H603, #H600, #H605, #H601, #H???, #H603. Photo
by Joseph F. Saine.

	MINT
H603	Cowboy, made in Hong Kong 2.00
H604	Cowboy, clubbing with rifle, foot, made in Britain 3.00
H604	Cowboy, made in Hong Kong 2.00
H605	Cowboy, firing twin guns, made in Britain 3.00
H605	Cowboy, made in Hong Kong 2.00
H620	Cowboy, throwing lasso, mounted, made in Britain 3.00
H620	Cowboy, made in Hong Kong 2.00
H621	Cowboy, masked bandit, firing six-shooter, mounted, made in Britain 3.00
H621	Cowboy, made in Hong Kong 2.00
H500	Chief with spear and shield 2.50
H501	Indian, crawling with knife 2.50
H502	Indian, with tomahawk, foot, made in Hong Kong 2.50
H503	Indian, firing rifle, foot, made in Hong Kong 2.50
H504	Indian, with bow and arrow, foot, made in Hong Kong 2.50
H504(A)	Chief standing firing 2.50
H505	Indian Chief, pointing, foot, made in Hong Kong 2.50
H506	Indian Chief, sitting 2.50
H507	Squaw, nursing Papoose 2.50

#L to R: #H506, #H510, #H509, #H511, #H507. Photo by Joseph F. Saine.

#H520

#H521

	MINT
H508	Indian Chief, standing 2.50
H509	Camp Fire 2.50
H510	Totem Pole 2.50
H511	Teepee (Wigwam) 2.50
H520	Indian Chief with spear and shield, mounted, made in Hong Kong 2.50
H521	Indian Brave with bow and arrow, mounted, made in Hong Kong 2.50

HERALD GORDON HIGHLANDERS

H100	Highlander officer, mtd. $5.00
H101	Highlander, at attention, made in Britain 3.00

#H620

#H621

#H502

#H503

#H504

#H505

#H100, #H120

#H101

#H102, #H122

		MINT
H101	Highlander made in Hong Kong	2.00
H102	Highlander, marching at the slope, made in Britain	3.00
H102	Highlander, made in Hong Kong	2.00
H103	Officer with sword, marching, made in Britain	3.00
H103	Officer, made in Hong Kong	2.00
H104	Piper, marching, made in Britain	3.00
H104	Piper, made in Hong Kong	2.00
H105	Drummer with side drum, marching, made in Britain	3.00
H105	Drummer, made in Hong Kong	2.00
H106	Drummer with bass drum, marching, made in Britain	3.00
H106	Drummer, made in Hong Kong	2.00
H107	Drum Major, marching, made in Britain	3.00
H107	Drum Major, made in Hong Kong	2.00

#H103, #H123   #H104, #H124

#H105, #H125   #H106, #H126   #H107, #H127

HERALD BLACK WATCH

H120	Highlander officer, mounted	$5.00
H122	Highlander, marching at the slope, made in Britain	3.00
H122	Highlander, made in Hong Kong	2.00
H123	Officer with sword, marching, made in Britain	3.00
H123	Officer, made in Hong Kong	2.00
H124	Piper, marching, made in Britain	3.00
H124	Piper, made in Hong Kong	2.00
H125	Drummer with side drum, marching, made in Britain	3.00
H125	Drummer, made in Hong Kong	3.00
H126	Drummer with bass drum, marching, made in Britain	3.00
H126	Drummer, made in Hong Kong	2.00
H127	Drum Major, marching, made in Britain	3.00
H127	Drum Major, made in Hong Kong	2.00

HERALD ROBIN HOOD

		MINT
H1490	Robin Hood	$25.00
H1491	Maid Marian	25.00
H1492	Friar Tuck	25.00
H1493	Little John	25.00
H1494	Sheriff of Nottingham, mounted	25.00

L to R: #H1490, #H1491, #H1482, #H1493, #H1494. Photo by Joseph F. Saine.

HERALD KNIGHTS

Mounted Knights, various, price each $10.00

Herald mounted knights. Photo by Joseph F. Saine.

HERALD GUARDS

(Herald British drawings courtesy Bob Bard)

H200	Officer, mtd.	$5.00
H201	Guardsman, at attention at the slope, made in Britain	3.00
H201	Guardsman, made in Hong Kong	2.00
H202	Guardsman, marching at the slope, made in Britain	3.00
H202	Guardsman, made in Hong Kong	2.00
H203	Officer with sword, marching, made in Britain	3.00
H203	Officer, made in Hong Kong	2.00

#H200   #H201   #H203

		MINT
H204	Guardsman, at ease, made in Britain	3.00
H204	Guardsman, made in Hong Kong	2.00
H205	Guardsman, presenting arms, made in Britain	3.00
H205	Guardsman, made in Hong Kong	2.00
H206	Queen's Colour Bearer	
	(Red Standard) marching, made in Britain	6.00
H206	Queen's Colour Bearer, made in Hong Kong	5.00
H207	Regimental Colour Bearer	
	(Blue Standard), marching, made in Britain	6.00
H207	Regimental Colour Bearer, made in Hong Kong ...	5.00
207	Standing Firing	3.00
208	Kneeling Firing	3.00
209	Lying Firing	3.00

#H204

#H205

#H206

HERALD ROUNDHEADS

402	Mounted officer	$50.00
407	Pikeman, foot	40.00
408	Trooper, foot	30.00

HERALD CAVALIERS

412	Mounted officer	$50.00
417	Trooper, foot	30.00
418	Musketeer, foot	30.00

HERALD FARM FIGURES
(Drawings courtesy Bob Bard)

2045	Shepherd	$4.00
2046	Labourer with rake	4.00
2047	Labourer with hoe	4.00
2048	Labourer with broom	4.00
2049	Labourer with pitchfork	4.00
2050	Farmer	4.00
2051	Farmer's Daughter	4.00
2052	Landgirl	4.00
2053	Girl Milking	4.00
2054	Man with sack	4.00
2055	Rider for horse or tractor	4.00

HERALD KHAKI INFANTRY (in Battle Dress)
(Drawings courtesy Bob Bard)

H301	Infantryman, at attention, made in Britain	$3.00
H301	Infantryman, made in Hong Kong	2.00
H302	Infantryman, charging, made in Britain	3.00
H302	Infantryman, made in Hong Kong	2.00

L to R: #407, #408, #417, #418. Photo by Joseph F. Saine.

L to R: #412, #402. Photo by Joseph Saine.

#2045
Shepherd.

#2046

#2050
Farmer.

#2051
Farmer's
daughter.

#2052
Landgirl.

#2053 Girl
milking.

#H301

	MINT
H303 Infantryman, kneeling firing, made in Britain 3.00
H303 Infantryman, made in Hong Kong 2.00
H304 Infantryman, standing firing, made in Britain 3.00
H304 Infantryman, made in Hong Kong 2.00
H305 Infantryman, throwing grenade, made in Britain ... 3.00
H305 Infantryman, made in Hong Kong 2.00
H306 Officer with pistol, advancing, made in Britain 3.00
H306 Officer, made in Hong Kong 2.00

Top: L to R: #H306, #H307, #H303; Bottom, L to R: #H305, #H304. Herald Khaki Infantry. Photo by Gary J. Linden.

H307 Radio Operator (Walkie-Talkie),
     kneeling, made in Britain 3.00
H307 Radio Operator, made in Hong Kong 2.00
H308 Infantryman with fixed bayonet,
     attacking, made in Britain 3.00
H308 Infantryman, made in Hong Kong 2.00
H309 Infantryman, falling wounded, made in Britain 3.00
H309 Infantryman, made in Hong Kong 2.00
H311 Infantryman, with bazooka 3.00
H312 Infantryman, with mine detector 3.00
H313 Infantryman, crawling 3.00
4307 Khaki Infantry, howitzer, 5 men .... No Price Found
4312 British Assault Craft, boat, 2 figures 12.00

#H308   #H309

	MINT
4315 Khaki Infantry, 6 different 40.00
4316 Khaki Infantry, 6 different, Hong Kong 25.00
7309 Khaki Infantry, howitzer,
24 infantry, 2 sentry boxes 90.00

HERALD ANTARCTIC
(Drawings courtesy Bob Bard)

H5299 Sledding Team $60.00
H1299 Polar Skier .... No Price Found

#H5299

#H1299

HERALD SIKH INFANTRY

401   Indian Infantryman (Sikh)
       in Parade Uniform, at attention $6.00

HERALD BRITISH LIFE, HORSE AND SCOTS GUARDS
(Drawings courtesy Bob Bard)

801   Life Guard Standard Bearer,
       mounted, made in Britain $6.00
801   Life Guard made in Hong Kong 4.00
802   Life Guard Trumpeter, mounted,
       made in Britain 6.00
802   Life Guard made in Hong Kong 4.00

#H801, #H901   #H802, #H902

803	Life Guard Trooper with sword, mounted, made in Britain	6.00
803	Life Guard made in Hong Kong	4.00
804	Life Guard Standard Bearer, dismounted, made in Britain	3.00
804	Life Guard, made in Hong Kong	2.00
805	Life Guard, Trumpeter, made in Britain	3.00
805	Life Guard, made in Hong Kong	2.00
806	Life Guard Trooper with sword, dismounted, made in Britain	3.00
806	Life Guard made in Hong Kong	2.00
901	Horse Guard Standard Bearer, mounted, made in Britain	6.00
901	Horse Guard made in Hong Kong	4.00
902	Horse Guard Trumpeter, made in Britain	6.00
902	Horse Guard made in Hong Kong	4.00
903	Horse Guard Trooper with sword, mounted, made in Britain	6.00
903	Horse Guard made in Hong Kong	4.00
904	Horse Guard Standard Bearer, dismounted, made in Britain	3.00
904	Horse Guard made in Hong Kong	2.00
905	Horse Guard Trumpeter, dismounted, made in Britain	3.00
905	Horse Guard made in Hong Kong	2.00
906	Horse Guard Trooper with sword, dismounted, made in Britain	3.00
906	Horse Guard made in Hong Kong	2.00
H903	Horse Guard Trooper Mounted	20.00
4120	Mounted Scots Guard officer	15.00
4206	Scots Guards, 5 foot, sentry box	50.00
4215	Scots Guards, 5 figures	42.00
	Price per individual figure	8.00
4806	Life Guards, 6 pieces	35.00
	Price per figure, Britain	5.00
	Price per figure, Hong Kong	3.00
4906	Horse Guards, 6 pieces	35.00
	Price per figure, Britain	5.00
	Price per figure, Hong Kong	3.00
4815	Regimental Soldiers, 8 figures	45.00
	Price per mint standing figure, Britain	5.00
	Price per mint standing figure, Hong Kong	3.00
4820	Mounted Life Guards, 6 pieces, Britain	65.00
4820	Mounted Life Guards, 6 pieces, Hong Kong	30.00
4920	Mounted Horse Guards, 6 pieces, Britain	65.00
4920	Mounted Horse Guards, 6 pieces, Hong Kong	30.00
7209	Guards Set, 28 pieces, 24 foot, 1 mounted, 2 sentry boxes	120.00
7804	Horse and Life Guards, 11 pieces	70.00
7806	Horse and Life Guards, 14 pieces	14.00
7809	Horse and Life Guards, 22 pieces	150.00

HERALD ENEMY TROOPS
(Dark Green Helmets)

H352	Charging	$3.00
H353	Kneeling firing	3.00
H354	Standing firing	3.00
H355	Throwing grenade	3.00
H356	Officer with pistol	3.00
H357	Radio operator	3.00
H358	Attacking with bayonet	3.00
H359	Falling wounded	3.00

#H803, #H903

#H804, #H904

#H805, #H905

#H806, #H906

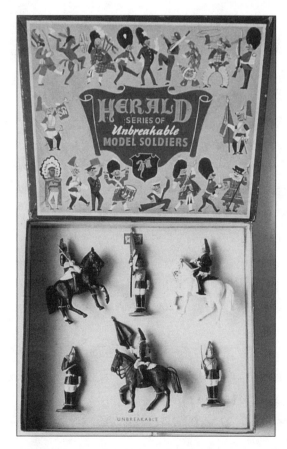

#H7903 Horse Guard box. Earliest box version. Value $100.00. Photo by Joseph F. Saine.

Swoppets

SWOPPET KNIGHTS
(Drawings courtesy Bob Bard)

		MINT
1450	Mounted with Standard	$25.00
1451	Mounted Charging with Lance	25.00
1452	Mounted Attacking with Sword	25.00
1453	Mounted Defending with Lance	25.00
1470	Foot Standing with Lance	13.00
1471	Foot Attacking with Sword	13.00
1472	Foot Standing Firing Longbow	13.00
1473	Foot Attacking with Pike	13.00
1474	Foot attacking with Axe	13.00
1475	Foot Kneeling Firing Crossbow	13.00
7479	Set of all 6 foot	90.00
7481	3 mounted, 5 foot	180.00

#1450. Photo by Joseph Saine.

#1451. Photo by Joseph F. Saine.

#1471

#1452. Photo by Joseph F. Saine.

#1453. Photo by Joseph F. Saine.

L to R: #1470, #1471, #1472, #1473, #1474, #1475. Photo by Joseph F. Saine.

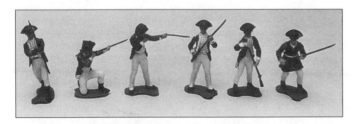

Swoppets Revolutionary War British. L to R: #360, #361, #362, #363, #364, #365. Photo by Joseph F. Saine.

REVOLUTIONARY WAR

		MINT
360	British Infantry Marching	$7.00
361	British Infantry Kneeling Firing	7.00
362	British Infantry Standing Firing	7.00
363	British Infantry On Guard	7.00
364	British Infantry Loading	7.00
365	British Infantry Charging	7.00
380	American Infantry Marching	7.00
381	American Infantry Kneeling Firing	7.00
382	American Infantry Standing Firing	7.00
383	American Infantry On Guard	7.00
384	American Infantry Loading	7.00
385	American Infantry Charging	7.00
7364	1776 British Infantry, per figure	7.00
7384	1776 Colonial Infantry, per figure	7.00

SWOPPET WORLD WAR II BRITISH INFANTRY
(Drawings courtesy Bob Bard)

330	Marching in Full Field Pack	$5.00
331	Charging with Rifle and Bayonet	5.00
332	Kneeling Firing	5.00
4336	Stretcher Party, 6 pieces	30.00
4340	Mortar Team, 4 pieces	30.00

Swoppets Revolutionary War Americans. L to R: #380, #381, #382, #383, #384, #385. Photo by Joseph F. Saine.

#330

#331

#332

#4336. Photo by Joseph F. Saine.

#4340. Photo by Joseph F. Saine.

SWOPPET COWBOYS AND INDIANS
(Drawings courtesy Bob Bard)

		MINT
530	Mounted Medicine Man	$14.00
531	Mounted Chief with Spear	14.00
532	Mounted Brave with Bow	14.00
533	Mounted Chief with Dagger	14.00
534	Mounted Brave with Bow and Arrow	14.00
535	Mounted Brave with Tomahawk	14.00
550	Foot Medicine Man	8.00
551	Foot Chief with Spear	8.00
552	Foot Brave Standing Firing Bow	8.00
553	Foot Chief with Dagger	8.00
554	Foot Brave Kneeling Firing Bow	8.00
555	Foot Brave with Tomahawk	8.00
630	Mounted Sheriff	12.00
631	Mounted Bank Robber	12.00
632	Mounted Cowboy Throwing Lasso	12.00
633	Mounted 2-Gun Cowboy	12.00

		MINT
634	Mounted Cowboy Firing Rifle	12.00
635	Mounted Wounded Cowboy	12.00
636	Mounted Cowboy Holding Lasso	12.00

#530

#531. Photo by Joseph F. Saine.

#534. Photo by Joseph F. Saine.

#535

#550

#551

#553

#554

#630

#631

#634

#635

#650

#651

#652. Photo by Paul Stadinger.

#654.
Photo by
Paul
Stadinger.

CIVIL WAR

		MINT
420	Mounted Confederate officer	$20.00
421	Mounted Confederate Standard Bearer	20.00
422	Mounted Confederate Bugler	20.00
423	Mounted Confederate Trooper	20.00
425	Confederate Infantry officer, foot	12.00
426	Confederate Infantry Standard Bearer	12.00
427	Confederate Infantryman Advancing	12.00
428	Confederate Standing Firing	12.00
429	Confederate Kneeling Firing	12.00
430	Confederate Prone Firing	12.00
450	Mounted Union officer	20.00

		MINT
637	Mounted Mexican on Guard	12.00
638	Mounted Mexican Resting	12.00
639	Mounted Cowboy Knifefighter	12.00
640	Mounted Cowboy Prisoner	12.00
641	Mounted Cowboy Firing Pistol	12.00
650	Foot Sheriff	8.00
651	Foot Bank Robber	8.00
652	Foot Cowboy Throwing Lasso	8.00
653	Foot 2-Gun Cowboy	8.00
654	Foot Cowboy Firing Rifle	8.00
655	Foot Wounded Cowboy	8.00
656	Foot Cowboy Gunslinger	8.00
657	Foot Mexican on Guard	8.00
658	Foot Cowboy Resting	8.00
659	Foot Cowboy Knifefighter	8.00
660	Foot Cowboy Tied to Tree	8.00
661	Foot Cowboy Firing from behind keg	8.00

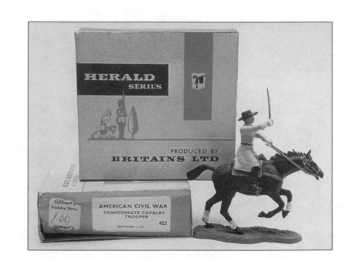

#423

Swoppet Confederates. L to R: #425, #426, #427, #428, #429, #430. Photo by Joseph F. Saine.

Swoppet Union Troops. L to R: #455, #456, #457, #458, #459, #460. Photo by Joseph F. Saine.

		MINT
451	Mounted Union Standard Bearer	20.00
452	Union Mounted Bearer	20.00
453	Mounted Union Trooper	20.00
455	Union officer, foot	12.00
456	Union Standard Bearer, Infantry	12.00
457	Union Infantry Advancing	12.00
458	Union Infantry Standing Firing	12.00
459	Union Infantry Kneeling Firing	12.00
460	Union Infantry Prone Firing	12.00

		MINT
4435	Confederate Gun Crew and Gun, 5 pieces	45.00
4465	Union Gun Crew and Gun, 5 pieces	45.00

Swoppet Civil War Gun: #4435 as Confederate; #4465 as Union. Photo by Joseph F. Saine.

Swoppets Civil War display box. Photo by Joseph F. Saine.

Eyes Right

EYES RIGHT SCOTS GUARDS

H226	Queen's Color Bearer	$6.00
H227	Regimental Color Bearer	6.00
H228	Officer	4.00
H233	At Slope	4.00
H234	At Ease	4.00
H242	Piper	4.00
H243	Drum Major	6.00
H244	Bass Drummer	6.00
H245	Side Drummer	6.00
H246	Trombone	6.00
H248	Coronet	6.00
H249	Fife	6.00
H250	Bassoon	6.00
H251	Clarinet	6.00
H252	French Horn	6.00
H253	Double Bass	6.00
H254	Tenor Horn	6.00

H255	Cymbals	6.00
H256	Saxophone	6.00

EYES RIGHT ROYAL MARINES

H268	Officer	$6.00
H273	At Slope	6.00
H283	Drum Major	6.00
H284	Bass Drummer	6.00
H285	Side Drummer	6.00
H286	Trombone	6.00
H288	Coronet	6.00
H289	Fife	6.00
H290	Bassoon	6.00
H291	Clarinet	6.00
H292	French Horn	6.00
H293	Double Bass	6.00

	MINT
H295 Cymbals	6.00
H296 Saxophone	6.00

EYES RIGHT MIDDLESEX REGIMENT

H148 Officer	$4.00
H153 Marching at Slope	4.00
H163 Drum Major	4.00
H164 Bass Drummer	4.00
H165 Side Drummer	4.00
H166 Bugler	4.00

EYES RIGHT R.C.M.P.

695 Marching	$7.00
699 Mounted	12.00

EYES RIGHT CIVIL WAR, CONFEDERATES

	MINT
420 Mounted officer	$20.00
421 Mounted Standard Bearer	20.00
422 Mounted Bugler	20.00
423 Mounted Trooper	20.00

EYES RIGHT CIVIL WAR, UNION

450 Officer	$20.00
451 Standard Bearer	20.00
452 Bugler	20.00
453 Trooper	20.00

Eyes Right Civil War Confederates. L to R: #420, #421, #422, #423. Photo by Joseph F. Saine.

Eyes Right Civil War Union Troops. L to R: #450, #451, #452, #453. Photo by Joseph F. Saine.

Eyes Right #7466 Marine Color Party. Value $40.00 for the group. Photo by Joseph F. Saine.

Eyes Right #7499 U.S. Marine Corps Full Band. Value $120.00. Photo by Joseph F. Saine.

Deetail

CONTEMPORARY BRITISH TROOPS

7250 Scots Guards, 6 different	$25.00
Individual figures, price for each	2.50
7256 Scots Guards, 6 different	25.00
Individual figures, price for each	4.00

CIVIL WAR-7TH CAVALRY

435 Confederate officer	$4.00
436 Confederate Standard Bearer	4.00
437 Confederate Bugler	4.00
438 Confederate Troop with sword	4.00
439 Confederate Troop with pistol	4.00
440 Confederate Troop with rifle	4.00
465 Union officer	4.00
466 Union Standard Bearer	4.00
467 Union Bugler	4.00
468 Union with sword	4.00
469 Union with pistol	4.00
470 Union with rifle	4.00

7422 Confederate Forces, 3 mounted, 9 foot, accessory	50.00
7423 Confederate Patrol, Gatling Gun, 5 foot	50.00
7426 Confederate, foot, 7 figures	25.00
7427 Confederate, 6 foot, 2 accessories	35.00

Civil War Gun Team and Limber. #7434 as Confederate, #7464 as Union. Value for either $75.00. Photo by Joseph F. Saine.

		MINT
7428	Confederate, 2 mounted, 3 foot	25.00
7439	Confederate Cavalry, 6 different	40.00
	Individual figures, price for each	6.00
7440	Confederates, foot, 6 different	26.00
	Individual figures, price for each	4.00
7449	Federal (Union) Cavalry, 6 different	40.00
	Individual figures, price for each	5.00

#7483. Photo by Joseph F. Saine.

#7449. Photo by Joseph F. Saine.

#7484. Photo by Joseph F. Saine.

		MINT
7450	Federal (Union) foot, 6 different	26.00
	Individual figures, price for each	4.00
7452	Federal (Union) Forces, 2 mounted, 3 foot, accessory	40.00
7456	Federal (Union), 3 mounted, 9 foot, 2 accessories	80.00
7457	Federal (Union), 6 foot, accessory	35.00
7462	Confederate and Federal Forces, 6 mounted, 12 foot, 2 accessories	135.00
7470	Confederate Gatling Gun	15.00

		MINT
7483	7th Cavalry, mounted, 6 different, price for each	4.00
7484	7th Cavalry, foot, 6 different, price for each	2.50
7489	7th Cavalry, mounted, 6 different	45.00
	Individual figures, price for each	7.00
7490	7th Cavalry foot, 6 different	35.00
	Individual figures, price for each	5.00

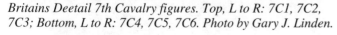

Britains Deetail 7th Cavalry figures. Top, L to R: 7C1, 7C2, 7C3; Bottom, L to R: 7C4, 7C5, 7C6. Photo by Gary J. Linden.

Britains Herald 7th Cavalry figures. Top, L to R: 7C1, 7C2, 7C3; Bottom, L to R: 7C4, 7C5, 7C6. Photo by Gary J. Linden.

COWBOYS, INDIANS, MEXICANS, APACHES

580	Mounted Indian with bear headdress	$5.00	584	Mounted Indian chief with rifle	5.00
581	Mounted Indian brave with bow	5.00	585	Mounted Indian brave with tomahawk	5.00
582	Mounted Indian chief with spear	5.00	680	Mounted Mexican	5.00
583	Mounted Indian brave with rifle	5.00	681	Mounted buffalo hunter	5.00

	MINT
682	Mounted sheriff 5.00
683	Mounted cowboy with lasso 5.00
684	Mounted cowboy bank robber 5.00
685	Mounted Cowboy firing pistol 5.00
7519	Mounted Mexicans, 6 different 75.00
	Individual figures, price for each 7.00
7520	Mexicans, foot, 6 different 35.00
	Individual figures, price for each 4.00
7539	Mounted Indians, 6 different 20.00
	Individual figures, price for each 3.00
7540	Foot Indians, 6 different 26.00
	Individual figures, price for each 4.00
7547	Indians, 12 figures, 2 accessories 75.00
7549	Mounted Apaches, 6 different 70.00
	Individual figures, price for each 10.00
7550	Foot Apaches, 6 different 65.00
	Individual figures, price for each 2.00
7557	Apaches and Mexicans,
	12 figures, 2 accessories 75.00
7639	Mounted Cowboys, 6 different 20.00
	Individual figures, price for each 3.00
7640	Foot cowboys, 6 figures, price for each 2.00
7647	Cowboys, 12 figures, 2 accessories 85.00
7650	Foot Cowboys, 6 different 15.00
	Individual figures, price for each 2.00
7660	Foot cowboys, 6 figures 70.00
7670	Foot cowboys, 6 different 55.00
	Individual figures, price for each 8.00

KNIGHTS AND TURKS

7719	15th Century knights,
	mounted, 6 different, price for each $3.00
7720	Knights, foot, Swoppet type, 6 different 100.00
	Individual figures, price for each 1.50
7729	Knights, mounted, Swoppet type, 6 different 80.00
	Individual figures, price for each 12.00
7730	Knights, foot, 6 different 35.00
	Individual figures, price for each 5.00
7739	Knights mounted, 6 different 45.00
	Individual figures, price for each 7.00
7740	Knights, foot, 6 different 35.00
	Individual figures, price for each 5.00
7749	Turks mounted, 6 different 35.00
	Individual figures, price for each 3.00
7750	Turks, foot, 6 different 35.00
	Individual figures, price for each 1.50
7760	Black Knights, foot, 6 different 35.00
	Individual figures, price for each 5.00
7669	Black Knights, mounted, 6 different 45.00
	Individual figures, price for each 7.00

FOREIGN LEGION AND ARABS

	MINT
7770	Foreign Legion Gatling Gun, 2 figures, gun $14.00
	Individual figures, price for each 8.00
7775	Foreign Legion and Arabs,
	2 mounted, 4 foot, accessory 85.00

Britains Deetail Foreign Legionnaires. There are several variations of FL7, with the one shown probably the most striking. Top, L to R: FL1, FL2, FL3, FL4-6; Bottom, L to R: FL7, FL8, FL9, FL10.

Britains Deetail Arabs. Top, L to R: AR1, AR2, AR3; Bottom, L to R: AR4, AR5, AR6.

Britains Deetail Arabs. L to R: AR7, AR8, AR9, AR10, AR11, AR12.

#7370. Photo by Joseph F. Saine.

MINT

7779	Foreign Legion Cavalry, 6 different	85.00
	Individual figures, price for each	13.00
7780	Foreign Legion Infantry, 6 different	55.00
	Individual figures, price for each	8.00
7783	Foreign Legion Patrol, 5 figures, Gatling	70.00
7784	Foreign Legion, 6 foot, all different, 2 accessories	70.00
7789	Mounted Arabs, 6 different	85.00
	Individual figures, price for each	10.00
7790	Arabs, foot, 6 different	55.00
	Individual figures, price for each	7.00
7794	Arabs, 6 pieces, 2 accessories	65.00
7797	Arabs, 3 mounted, 9 foot, 2 accessories	150.00
7799	Foreign Legion and Arabs, 12 figures, 2 accessories	175.00

WATERLOO

7940	British Infantry, 6 different, price for each	$7.00
7944	British Infantry, foot, 6 pieces, 5 different	75.00
	Individual figures, price for each	7.00
7945	British Forces, 2 mounted, 4 foot, accessory	80.00
7947	British Forces, 3 mounted, 9 foot, 2 accessories	110.00
7949	British Cavalry, 6 different	100.00
	Individual figures, price for each	12.00
7950	French Infantry, foot, 6 different	80.00
	Individual figures, price for each	7.00
7954	French Infantry, 6 foot, 2 accessories	70.00
7955	French, 2 mounted, 4 foot, accessory	75.00
7957	French, 3 mounted, 9 foot, 2 accessories	120.00
7959	French Cavalry, 6 different	100.00
	Individual figures, price for each	12.00
7960	British and French, 3 mounted, 9 foot, 2 accessories	110.00
7965	British and French, 6 pieces, accessory	45.00

WORLD WAR II, AMERICAN, BRITISH, GERMAN, JAPANESE

7333	German Mortar, 3 pieces	$12.00
	Individual figures, price for each	4.00
7334	U.S. Recoilless Rifle, 3 pieces	12.00
	Individual figures, price for each	4.00
7337	Japanese Recoilless Rifle, 3 pieces	18.00
	Individual figures, price for each	6.00
7338	British Mortar, 3 pieces	15.00
	Individual figures, price for each	5.00

MINT

7339	8th Army Vickers Machine Gun, 3 figures	15.00
	Individual figures, price for each	4.00
7340	U.S. Infantry, 6 different pieces	25.00
	Individual figures, price for each	3.00
7342	British Infantry, 6 different pieces	25.00
	Individual figures, price for each	3.00
7346	British Infantry, 18 figures, 4 accessories	150.00
7347	U.S. Infantry, 18 figures, 4 accessories	50.00
7350	German Infantry, 6 different pieces	40.00
	Individual figures, price for each	3.00
7352	Japanese Infantry, 6 different, price for each	5.00
7356	Japanese Infantry, 18 figures, 4 trees	150.00
7370	German Afrika Korps, 6 different, price for each	4.00
7380	German Infantry, 6 different pieces	40.00
	Individual figures, price for each	3.00
7386	German Infantry, 7 figures	45.00
7390	British 8th Army, 6 figures	40.00
	Individual figures, price for each	3.00

SUPERDEETAIL

6016	Ballet, 4 different	$40.00
6300	Paratroopers, 4 different, price for each	2.00
6320	Marine Commandos, 7 different, per each	2.00
6330	SAS Commandos, 7 different, per each	2.00
7850	Hospital, 6 different	75.00
7851	Doctor and Patient	20.00
7852	Nurse and Patient	20.00
7853	Nurse, Mother, Baby	20.00
7854	Nursing Sister, Patient	20.00
7857	Hospital Ward	150.00
7858	Hospital X-Ray Department	150.00
7859	Hospital Maternity Unit	150.00

Equipment

(Photos by Joseph F. Saine)

9726	Civil War Cannon	$18.00
9732	German Field Pak 38	18.00
9736	Naval Cannon 18th Century with Crew	25.00
9737	Gun of the Revolution with Crew	25.00
9761	Hughes Military Helicopter	25.00
9777	Land Rover Military Longwheel	30.00
9780	Kettenkrad	25.00
9781	British Scout Car	20.00
9782	Military Land Rover Sht. Wheel	25.00
9783	Kubelwagon	20.00
9784	8th Army Scout Car	20.00
9786	U.S. Jeep	20.00
9787	Army Land Rover and Gun	20.00
9788	Kubelwagon and Gun	25.00

#9726

#9736

#9737

#9777

L to R: #9781, #9788.

#9783

Miscellaneous Plastic

(Photos by Joseph F. Saine)

		MINT
4375	Chimpanzee Tea Party	$40.00
4500	Indian Canoe	12.00
4502	Trapper Canoe	12.00
4590	Roman Chariot	20.00
4601	Cowboy Floating Raft	12.00
4675	Catapult with Two Knights	10.00
4676	Balista with Two Knights	10.00
7615	Concorde Overland Stagecoach	70.00
7616	Pioneer Covered Wagon	70.00
7617	Buckwagon	45.00

#4601

#4675

#7615

#7616

✕ Charbens ✕

by K. Warren Mitchell

Founded around 1920 by Charles and Benjamin Reid, with the name a composite of the two first names. Originally produced under contract for other makers until the late 1920s, when the company started marketing its own line of figures. Its history is intertwined with a number of other makers. Production continued until the late 1960s. The last few years were spent making plastic versions of its earlier metal items.

Charbens was prolific in its production of civilian horse-drawn vehicles that captured the world around them in the 1930s and 1940s. Also popular among collectors today is their circus group, and U.S. GIs (often confused with Timpo GIs). Charbens can usually be identified by the company's name under the base.

"X" numbers are author's code, when factory number is not available. Prices are for pieces in very good condition.

AMERICAN G.I. SOLDIERS

Cat. #	Description	VG
200	Grenade Thrower	$8.00
201	Charging	8.00
202	Lying, Firing	8.00
203	Kneeling, Firing	8.00
204	Marching	8.00
205	Walking, Wounded	8.00
206	Field Telephone Operator	8.00

L to R: Timpo, #204 (comparison). #205

#206

L to R: #200, #201.

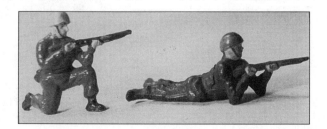

L to R: #203, #202.

#207

Cat. #	Description	VG
207	Crawling	8.00
208	Tommy Gunner	8.00
209	Mine Detector	9.00
210	Stretcher Party	25.00
211	Despatch Rider, Motor Cyclist	40.00
212	Standard Bearer	20.00
213	Walkie Talkie	8.00

L to R: #208, #209.

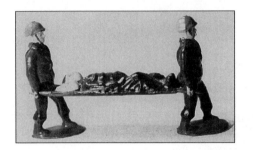

#210 (3 pieces).

#212

#213

(X-4)

L to R: #289, #291.

(X-5)

#294

Cat. #	Description	VG
(X-4)	Home Guard at Slope, prewar	10.00
(X-5)	Yeoman of the Guard	7.00
289	Life Guard mounted (late)	8.00
291	Life Guard dismounted	5.00
294	State Trumpeter	10.00

CIRCUS FIGURES (Metal)

700	Clown	$30.00
701	Clown with Hoop	30.00

Cat. #	Description	VG
214	Bazooka Operator	8.00
215	Machine Gunner	10.00
216	Mortar Man	9.00

BRITISH PARATROOPS (Red Berets)

259	Tommy Gunner	$9.00
260	Patrol Leader	11.00
261	Grenade Thrower	9.00
262	Flame Thrower	9.00
(X-1)	Kneeling Firing	9.00
(X-2)	Motorcycle Rider	35.00
(X-3)	Standing, Firing, Foot on Rock	11.00

L to R: (X-3), #260, #262.

L to R: #701, #700.

#702

702	Clown on Wheel	35.00
703	Policeman	30.00
704	Strong Man	25.00
705	Barbell	10.00

Cat. #	Description	VG
706	Fairy	25.00
707	Horse for Fairy	25.00
708	Horse, Prancing	25.00
709	Long Man, Stilts	30.00
710	Circus Dog	25.00
711	Circus Elephant	30.00
712	Tub for Elephant	10.00
713	Ringmaster	25.00

(Prewar Only)

603	Cyclist on Bike	$35.00
605	Sea Lion with Ball	35.00
609	Acrobat on Chair	40.00
613	Clown on Ladder	45.00
614	Juggler	40.00
616	Boxing Midgets (2)	45.00
(X-6)	2 Acrobats on Wire	65.00

MISCELLANEOUS

(X-7)	Goat cart with little girl, prewar	$50.00
(X-8)	Flower seller seated with separate basket, prewar	40.00

HIKER'S CAMP (Prewar)

519-1	Male hiker walking	$50.00
519-2	Female hiker walking	50.00
519-3	Male resting, supine	50.00
519-4	Female seated	50.00
519-5	Tent (metal)	65.00
519-6	Tree	20.00

"JACK'S BAND"

Cat. #	Description	VG
222/1	"Jack" conducting	$35.00
222/2	Piano and player	75.00
222/3	Saxophone	35.00
222/4	Sousaphone	35.00
222/5	Accordion	35.00
222/6	Trumpet	35.00
222/7	Cello	35.00
222/8	Violin	35.00
222/9	Banjo	35.00

(Note: Musicians came in various-color jackets, and each had separate metal chair included. Also sold as trio--piano, cello, violin).

ROAD REPAIR

811	Lamp post	$20.00
812	Man with pick	35.00
813	Man with shovel	35.00
814	Policeman directing traffic	30.00
815	Man with drill (jackhammer)	35.00
818	Trestle and poles	25.00
819	Night watchman, hut, brazier, and barrel seat	75.00
(X-9)	Sign "No Road"	25.00

CARTS AND WAGONS

500	Gypsy wagon and horse	$150.00

#703

#704 (-705)

#706 on #707.

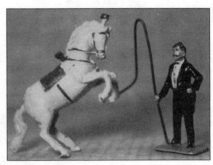

L to R: #708, #713.

#709

#710

L to R: #711, #712.

L to R: #605, #616, #614.

(X-7)

(X-8)

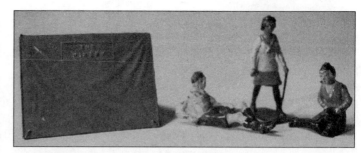

L to R: #519-5, #519-3, #519-2, #519-4.

#222 "Jack's Band."

L to R: #819, (X-9), #815, #813, #812, #818.

#501

#800

Cat. #	Description	VG
501	Gypsy caravan, wagon and horse, man, seated wife with baby, fire and kettle, clothesline	400.00
503	Farm wagon, horse and farmer	75.00
505	Hay cart and horse	65.00
506	Roller and horse	65.00
513	Tree wagon with 2 horses	75.00
521	Governess cart, donkey, 2 children	70.00
738	Milk cart "Pure Milk," horse, churn, milkman	85.00
800	Coal cart, horse, man with sack, sacks	300.00
815	Pitch boiler, horse and man	300.00
816	Railway wagon, horse, driver, crated piano	400.00
821	United Dairy van with rubber tires, horse, man	200.00
822	Express Dairy van with rubber tires, horse, man	200.00
823	Baker's van, horse, man with basket	125.00
855	Wheeled organ, donkey, organ grinder, monkey	200.00
900	Costercart, donkey, costermonger, baskets	150.00
(X10)	Steam roller (rare)	500.00

815 (-man)

816

#821

#822

#855

#900

(X10) Rare, 1 of only 5 known.

#286. Value $15.00.

⚔ Charbens Plastic ⚔

According to *The Plastic Warrior Guide to U.K. Makers of Plastic Toy Figures*, Charbens produced in plastic from about 1960 to 1976. Prindus (Prison Industries) later bought the molds, with the pieces painted by prisoners. The molds changed hands at least twice after, and Marlborough in Wales now produces some. John Ricardini, according to Plastic Warrior's publication, was the moldmaker, and some of the earlier production came from the firm's lead molds.

L to R: CBG1, CBG2, CBG3. Charbens plastic British Grenadiers, value $2.50 each. Courtesy Plastic Warrior.

L to R: CBG4, CBG5, CBG6. Charbens plastic British Grenadiers, value $2.50 each. Courtesy Plastic Warrior.

L to R: CCW1, CCW2, CCW3. Charbens plastic Civil War, value $6.00 each. Courtesy Plastic Warrior.

L to R: CCW4, CCW5, CCW6. Charbens plastic Civil War, value $6.00 each. Courtesy Plastic Warrior.

L to R: CJA1, CJA2, CJA3, CJA4. Charbens plastic WWII Japanese. Courtesy Plastic Warrior.

L to R: CRU1, CRU2, CRU3, CRU4. Charbens plastic Russians, value $6.00 each. Courtesy Plastic Warrior.

Charbens plastic women. Value $12.50 each. Courtesy Paul Stadinger - Stad's.

Charbens plastic women. Value $12.50 each. Courtesy Paul Stadinger - Stad's

✕ **Cherilea** ✕

by K. Warren Mitchell

Founded in 1946 by John Leaver and W. Cherrington, both previously employed by John Hill and Co. Merged with Flyde Co., in 1950. Purchased some molds from J. Hill. Started production of plastic in 1955, and went completely to plastic by 1961.

Its most popular lines are spacemen, knights, ballet dancers and baseball players.

Marked "Cherilea" under the base most of the time. Company numbers are used here, and prices are for very good condition.

Photos by K. Warren Mitchell

Cat. #	Model	
19/10	Guardsmen Marching	$4.00
19/11	Mounted Soldier	8.00
19/11A	Miniature Mounted Soldier	5.00
19/12	Royal Scots Grey Mounted	7.00
19/13	Lancer Moveable Arm	10.00
19/14	Middlesex Regiment	4.00

Cat. #	Model	
19/15	Guardsmen at ease	4.00
19/16	Lifeguard Marching	4.00
19/17	Lifeguard Attention	4.00
19/18	Lifeguard Mounted	4.00
19/19	Horseguard Marching	4.00
19/20	Horseguard Attention	4.00

L to R: #19/10, #19/15.

#19/13

#19/21

#19/22

#19/24

#19/25

L to R: #19/29, #19/28, #19/26.

#19/30a

Cat. #	Model		Cat. #	Model	
19/21	Horseguard Mounted	7.00	19/51	Soldier Standing at ease	5.00
19/22	Black Watch Marching	5.00	19/52	Soldier Marching at ease	5.00
19/23	Black Watch Piper	6.00	19/53	Soldier Throwing Grenade	5.00
19/24	Black Watch Glengarry	5.00	19/54	Soldier Firing Bazooka	5.00
19/25	Black Watch at ease	6.00	19/55	Soldier at charge	5.00
19/26	Knight In Armour	7.00	19/56	Soldier Mine Detecting	6.00
19/26A	Knight in Armour with plumed headdress	7.00	19/57	Soldier Flame Thrower	5.00
19/28	Crusader at ease	7.00	19/58	Soldier Machine Gunner	6.00
19/29	Crusader in Action	7.00	19/59	Machine Gun	5.00
19/30	Mounted Knight	10.00	19/60	Sailor	6.00
19/30A	Mounted Knight with plumed headdress	12.00	19/61	Marine Marching	6.00
19/31	Beefeater	6.00	19/65	Stretcher Bearer	8.00
19/33	Guardsmen Mov. Arm	5.00	19/66	Convalescent with crutches	15.00
19/35	Royal Hussar Mov. Arm	9.00	19/67	Wounded man on stretcher	8.00
19/36	Crusader at Charge	7.00	19/68	Nurse Standing	7.00
19/37	Crusader on Guard	7.00	19/69	Nurse Kneeling	7.00
19/38	Armoured Knight with Sabre	7.00	19/70	Tank	12.00
19/39	Richard Coeur-de-Lion Mounted	25.00	19/71	Artillery Man	8.00
19/41	English Archer	9.00	19/72	Howitzer	8.00
19/42	Saracen Standard Bearer	9.00	19/73	Marine Saluting	7.00
19/43	Saracen Pikeman	9.00	19/74	Marine Bugler	7.00
19/44	Saracen Swordsman	9.00	A109	WAC	9.00
19/45	Guards Band, Cornet	7.00	XC-1	Mortar Team (3 pieces)	18.00
19/46	Guards Band, Side Drum	7.00			
19/47	Guards Band, Bassoon	7.00	19/76	Ballerina Adage	30.00
19/48	Guards Band, Trombone	7.00	19/77	Ballerina En Attitude	30.00
19/49	Guards Band, Clarinet	7.00	19/78	Ballerina Pose	30.00
19/50	Soldier Marching Attention	5.00	19/79	Male Ballet Dancer	40.00

L to R: #19/41, #19/42, #19/38.

L to R: #19/53, #19/55, #19/52, #19/51.

L to R: #19/74, #19/61, #19/73. Photo by Roger W. Hocking.

L to R: #19/76, #19/77, #19/78, #19/79.

#A109

XC-1

L to R: #53, #50, #51, #50, #51, #50, #52. Plastic helmets.

#59

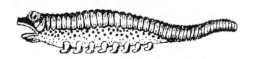

#60

SPACEMEN SERIES

Cat. #	Model	
50	Mechanical Man	$15.00
51	Spaceman with Ray Gun	22.00
52	Spaceman with Atom Gun	22.00
53	Spaceman	22.00
54	Rocketship	25.00
55	Spaceman with Atom Pistol	22.00
56	Spaceman Kneeling	22.00
57	Spaceman Crawling	22.00
58	Ant Man	25.00
59	Giant Lizard	25.00
60	Giant Worm	25.00
61	Launching Ramp for Rocket Ship	25.00
1001	Space Set, 7 pieces	300.00

#3/16

L to R: #3/30, #3/29.

Cat. #	Model	
3/10	Cowboy Kneeling	6.00
3/11	Cowboy Standing	6.00
3/12	Cowboy Mounted	9.00
3/13	Indian Kneeling	6.00
3/14	Indian Standing	6.00
3/15	Indian Mounted	6.00
3/16	War Canoe with 2 Indians	25.00
3/17	Cactus Plant	10.00
3/18	Totem Pole	15.00
3/19	Camp Fire	10.00
3/20	Witch Doctor	8.00
3/21	Dancing Indian	8.00
3/22	Indian Sitting	8.00
3/23	Indian War Drum	8.00
3/24	Galloping Mounted Cowboy	9.00
3/25	Mounted Indian Galloping	9.00
3/26	Cowboy Prone	8.00
3/27	Small Mounted Indian	8.00
3/28	Small Mounted Cowboy	8.00
3/29	Indian Brave with Rifle	6.00
3/30	Kneeling Indian with Tomahawk	6.00
3/50	Cowboy with Lasso	6.00
3/51	Cowboy Firing Six-shooter	6.00
3/52	Apache Indian Creeping	6.00
3/53	Apache Indian Running	6.00
3/60	U.S. Cavalryman Charge	10.00
3/61	Cowboy Firing Six-shooter at gallop	9.00
3/62	Davy Crockett with Pistol	25.00
3/63	Davy Crockett with Rifle	25.00
3/64	Standing Cowboy with Revolver	6.00
3/65	Standing Cowboy with Rifle	6.00
3/66	Kneeling Cowboy with Revolver	6.00
167	Baseball Set (11 pieces)	400.00
	Baseball Umpire	30.00
	Baseball Players, each	25.00

#167 Set.

#167 Umpire.

#167 Players.

A Cherilea boxed set.

Plastic
60mm (approx. 2-1/2")
54mm (approx. 2-1/4")
120mm (5")
30mm Mounted
40mm Mounted

⚔ **Cherilea Plastic** ⚔

According to Plastic Warrior magazine's separate publication on this company, their plastic production employed new molds only after extensive use of the company's original molds, plus other lead soldier molds from Hilco, Monarch, Benbros, and possibly others. Later, as part of the Sharna group, Cherilea marketed some boxed sets under the name Flexitoys. The bulk of the now-defunct firm's molds are owned today by Marksmen Models. Most of the designs, according to Plastic Warrior's editors, were by co-owner Wilfred Cherrington, with wide variation in quality. The publication lists the following plastic types in 54mm: Medieval; Cowboys; Indians; Backwoodsmen; Khaki Infantry; Guardsmen; Spacemen; Mounted Knights; Mounted Arab; Mounted Foreign Legion; Robin Hood; Cowboys; Backwoodsmen; Indians; Highlanders; Foreign Legion; Arabs; Modern Infantry; Mounted Cowboy; Mounted Indian; Mounted Cavalry Officer; Mounted Cavalry Trooper; Mounted Mexican; Mounted Mountie. 60mm types consisted of: Egyptians; Nubians; Ancient Britons; Vikings; Romans; Medieval Knights; English Civil War; Elizabethans; Execution Set; Highland Clansmen; Zulus; Victorian; Cowboys; Saloon Set; Indians; U.S. Cavalry; Canadian Mounties; Guardsmen; Life Guards; Highlanders; Eighth Army - WWII; British Infantry - WWII; German Infantry - WWII; Russians; Indian Army; Chinese/Korean Army;

Cherilea's Batman & Robin. Value $30.00 each. Courtesy Paul Stadinger - Stad's.

L to R: CFL1, CFL2, CFL3, CFL4. Cherilea's complete 54mm Foreign Legion range. Value $5.00 each.

Kings African Rifles; United Nations Troops; Mounted Knights, Cowboys; Indians; U.S. Cavalry; Mountie; Life Guard. There were also 30mm and 40mm Mounted and, near the end, swoppet types, all of which seem to have been pretty ugly.

L to R: CEX1, CEX2, CEX3, CEX4, CEX5. Cherilea's eye-catching Execution Set. Different officers (right) came with the set. 60mm. Value minimum of $100.00 for the set. Courtesy Plastic Warrior.

Cherilea Knight, value $25.00 (very hard to find). Photo by Paul Stadinger.

Cherilea's 60mm Wild West Saloon set. Value minimum of $100.00 for the set. Courtesy Plastic Warrior.

⚔ **Courtenay** ⚔

by Bob Hornung

Richard Courtenay, born in England in 1892, began making toy soldiers in 1918. However, the figures commonly associated with him weren't produced until 1928.

Although his medieval fighting knights are what he's known for, Courtenay also produced a series of ancient warriors, many historical personalities and mounted jockeys. In all, he created a total of nearly 150 different figures. Variations were possible via changing arms, heads or weapons.

Courtenay figures are known for their superb animation and exquisite painting. From the start they were painted with the heraldry of actual knights of the "Hundred Years War" period. Courtenay's painting continued to improve, so that by the late 1940s and the 1950s he was producing true works of art. Both heraldry and faces were executed with exceptional detail.

Richard Courtenay.

Richard Courtenay died in 1963, ending a long and rewarding career. His molds were first passed to miniaturist Freddy Ping. His versions of Courtenay figures continued until his death in 1977. In 1978 Peter Greenhill acquired the molds. His Courtenay-Greenhill figures are of the same outstanding quality as the finest Courtenays.

Early Courtenay figures were often unsigned. Later they normally had the name of the knight signed in gold on the base. The bottom was usually signed "Made in England" or "Made in England by R. Courtenay". The position number was often added as well. There are many copies of Courtenays. In fact, a company in New York copied nearly all of his work in the 1950s. Quality is generally very poor on these.

The following is a list of the known personalities and Ancients produced by Courtenay.

Henry VIII
Wife of Henry
Cardinal Wolsey
Queen Elizabeth
Sir Walter Raleigh
Sir Francis Drake
Mary Queen of Scots
Executioner
Lady Jane Grey
Nell Gwynn
King Charles I
King Charles II
Queen Philippa
Beefeater
King George V
Queen Mary
King George VI
Queen Elizabeth
Queen Victoria
Officer, foot guards 1664
15th Century Lady
15th Century Gentleman
17th Century Pikeman
17th Century Musketeer
H8 Jockey
H8A Jockey
H9 Jockey
AH1 Mounted Assyrian with bow
AH2 Mounted Assyrian with sword
Babylonian King
Babylonian Shield bearer
Assyrian with bow
Assyrian with trumpet
Assyrian with fan
Assyrian Lady
Persian Immortal
Philistine Spearman
Philistine Officer
Shardanu Bodyguard
Nubian Bowman

Dancing Girl
Greek Hoplite
Greek Lady
Roman Legionary
Retarius
Scutor
Pharaoh Seti I
Queen Nefertiti
Fan bearer
Queen Cleopatra
Priestess of Ishtar

The following prices are only approximate and represent a figure in very good condition. A similar figure in worse condition would bring less and one in mint condition would bring much more. These prices are provided primarily to show relative rarity.

Number	Black Base VG	Green Base VG
1-7	$150.00	$200.00
8 double		400.00
8A, 8B		300.00
9-12	150.00	200.00

#L to R: #1, #2, #3, #4, 5.

L to R: #6, #7, #8, #8.

L to R: #8A*, #8B*, #9, #10, #11.

Number	Black Base VG	Green Base VG	Number	Black Base VG	Green Base VG
13		300.00	Z5		250.00
13A	175.00	250.00	Z6-8		350.00
14-22	150.00	200.00	Z9, Z10		400.00
Z1, Z2, Z2A		250.00	Z11, Z12		450.00
Z3		300.00	Z13		No Price Found
Z4 same figure as 13		—	Z14		250.00

L to R: #12, #13*, #13A, #14.

L to R: #15, #16, #17, #18, #19.

L to R: #20, #21, #22, Order of Garter, Order of Star.

L to R: Z1, Z2, Z2A, Z5.

L to R: Z6, Z7, Z8*, Z9*.*

L to R: Z10, Z11, Z12*, Z13*.*

Number	Black Base VG	Green Base VG	Number	Black Base VG	Green Base VG
Z15, Z16		450.00	Z20		No Price Found
Z17		550.00	Archers, men at arms	150.00	200.00
Z18		No Price Found	M1, M2, M3	250.00	300.00
Z19		No Price Found			

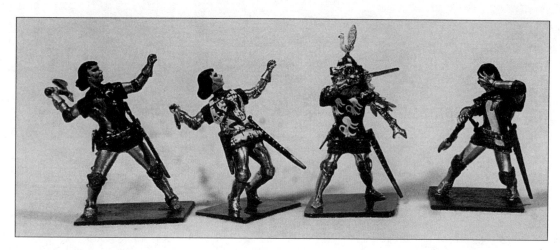

L to R: Z14, Z15*, Z16*, Z17.

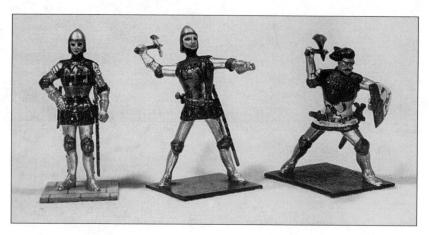

L to R: Z18, Z19, Z20.

L to R: Archer, Man at Arms, Fighting Foot Soldier*, Crusader #1, Crusader #2.

L to R: Walking Bowman, Courtenay Doran Spearman, Sir Walter Raleigh, Cardinal Wolsey, Henry VIII, Wife of Henry.

L to R: Executioner, Viking, Suctor, Retarius.

L to R: Greek Hoplite*, Persian Immortal*, Nubian Bowman*, Seti I*, Nefertiti*.

Number	Black Base VG	Green Base VG	Number	Black Base VG	Green Base VG
Tournament Knight		300.00	H5		No Price Found
Token house Knight (not pictured)		No Price Found	H6	300.00	350.00
Joan of Arc horse		300.00	H7		Figure Not Known
Richard I horse		No Price Found	H8, H8A, H9		600.00
Cruciform horse (not pictured)		400.00	H10		600.00
H1, H2, H3		350.00	H11	300.00	400.00
H4		400.00	H12		500.00

L to R: 17th Century Pikeman, Edward I and baby Prince of Wales, 15th Century Gentleman.

L to R: Tournament Knight, Joan of Arc, Richard I*.

L to R: #12 Special, X1 Special, Sir John Telfrey X1*.

L to R: M1, M2, M3.

L to R: H1, H2, H3.

Number	Black Base VG	Green Base VG
H13		500.00
H13A		No Price Found

PERSONALITIES

Henry VIII	50.00
Wife of Henry	40.00
Executioner and block	50.00
Other personalities	75.00
Pikeman and Musketeers	75.00
Ancient Warriors	150.00

Number	Black Base VG	Green Base VG
Ancient on horse		300.00
Ancient and court ladies		75.00

Special figures with unusual Heraldry or converted pieces (often numbered X1, X2, etc.) often command higher prices. Pings tend to sell for $40 to $75 in very good. Copies, especially those marked "Knights Castle" generally have little value. All photos by Bob Hornung. Those figures marked with an asterisk are actually recently cast by Greenhill from original Courtenay molds and were employed to show the pose.

L to R: H4, H5*, H6*.

L to R: H8, H8A*, H9*.

L to R: H10*, H11, H12.

L to R: H13, H13A*, Henry V.

⚔ Crescent ⚔

According to Garratt's "Encyclopaedia," Crescent began in 1921 with its cut-off date not known. It made both hollowcast lead soldiers and plastic figures. Again, according to Garratt, the company began producing military figures in 1930 and moved into plastics in 1956. It was in business through at least 1975. Following are some representative prices in today's market. According to Andrew Rose's *Toy Soldiers*, Crescent was located in Tottenham in North London, and was "operating on the fringes of the toy and novelty market since 1925."

Crescent mounted plastic knights, value $15.00 each. Photo by Paul Stadinger.

Set 1224. Value in very good condition, $300.00.

Crescent bought most of Reka's molds in 1930, and seems to have bought many or all of its other molds from other companies.

The CR coding is the author's. Numbers that follow after the code are Crescent's own. *Prices shown are for pieces in very good condition.*

African Safari set (with kangaroo!). Value in very good condition, boxed $100.00.

		VG
CR1	Knight with halberd, standing	$5.00
CR2	Knight swinging sword overhead	6.00

CR2

CR4

CR3	Knight, sword overhead, no shield	6.00
CR3A	Knight standing with Lance	6.00

L to R: CR3A, CR3.

CR4A

						VG
CR4	Mounted Knight on charging horse	10.00	CR6B	Herald		8.00
CR4A	Mounted Knight 253	10.00	CR7	Masked Bandit with gun		6.00
CR5	Mounted Knight with Lance	9.00	CR8	Masked Bandit drawing gun		6.00
CR5A	Crusader at ease 167	6.00	CR8A	Cowboy kneeling firing A221		6.00
CR6	Mounted Crusader 254	10.00	CR8B	Cowboy firing pistol		6.00
CR6A	Herald, horn angled up	8.00	CR8C	Cowboy with Lasso		6.00

L to R: CR5A, CR1, CR6.

L to R: CR6, CR5, CR1. Courtesy K. Warren Mitchell.

L to R: CR6A, CR6B.

CR8A

CR8B

L to R: CR8C, CR8D.

CR8E

L to R: CR8F, CR8G.

CR8H

L to R: CR8I, CR8J, CR8K, CR8L.

		VG
CR8D	Cowboy firing raised pistol	6.00
CR8E	Cowboy standing firing rifle	6.00
CR8F	Masked Bandit holding pistols	6.00
CR8G	Cowboy with drawn pistol, gripping another	6.00
CR8H	Cowboy playing banjo	12.00
CR8I	Cowboy in hut playing cards	15.00
CR8J	Bareheaded Cowboy playing cards	15.00
CR8K	Cowboy resting	15.00
CR8L	Cowboy and Cowgirl tied to tree	35.00
CR9	Mounted Cowboy firing pistol	8.00

CR9

		VG
CR12	Infantry standing with Tommy gun, WWII	6.00
CR13	Officer firing pistol, helmet	6.00
CR13A	Marching in cap	6.00
CR13B	Marching rifle slung over back	6.00
CR14	Infantry lying with wire cutters	14.00
CR15	Artillery piece	18.00
CR16	U.S. Marine, saluting	7.00
CR17	U.S. Marine, parade rest	7.00
CR18	U.S. Marine, marching at slope	7.00

CR9A

CR12

L to R: CR13, CR13A, CR13B.

L to R: CR9B, CR9C.

CR14

		VG
CR9A	Mounted Cowboy on charging horse firing pistol	8.00
CR9B	Cowboy on steer	10.00
CR9C	Cowboy reining in horse	10.00
CR10	Infantry kneeling firing, WWII, A243	5.00
CR10A	Lying firing A243	6.00
CR11	Infantry prone with bren gun, WWII	6.00

L to R: CR15, CR8, CR7, CR22. Courtesy K. Warren Mitchell.

CR11

L to R: CR18, CR17, CR19.

CR20

CR20A

		VG
CR24	Indian walking with rifle, headdress	6.00
CR25	Indian walking with Tomahawk	6.00
CR25A	Indian paddling canoe, 402	35.00
CR26	Crescent Stagecoach	65.00
CR26A	Milkmaid carrying buckets, 102	5.00
CR27	Milkmaid seated on separate stool, 16	8.00
CR28	Farmer with pitchfork, 51	7.00
CR29	Farmer shoveling, 52	7.00
CR29A	Farmer, foot on shovel, 40	7.00
CR29B	Groom with brush, moving arm, 30	7.00
CR30	Farmer dumping bucket	7.00
CR31	Farmer in derby with cane, 103	7.00
CR32	Butcher in straw hat, cleaver raised	20.00

L to R: CR20B, CR20C.

CR21

CR24

CR25

CR25A

CR27

CR23

		VG
CR19	U.S. Marine empty handed	7.00
CR20	Indian firing rifle, long headdress	6.00
CR20A	Indian brandishing knife	6.00
CR20B	Indian with rifle shading eyes	6.00
CR20C	Indian, rifle across chest	6.00
CR21	Indian crawling with Tomahawk	6.00
CR22	Indian kneeling with bow	6.00
CR23	Mounted Indian, shielding eyes	10.00

L to R: CR29, CR26A, CR28. Courtesy K. Warren Mitchell.

CR29A

L to R: CR29B, CR30.

L to R: CR32, CR33, CR33A.

L to R: CR34A, CR34, CR59A.

CR35

CR36

CR37

CR38

L to R: CR41, CR39, CR40, CR41A, CR41B.

CR41C

L to R: CR43, CR42, CR10. Courtesy K. Warren Mitchell.

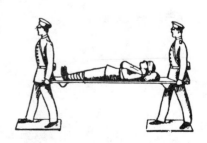

CR45

CR33	Butcher's assistant, plate in one hand, tray in other	20.00
CR33A	Butcher Shop customer, basket in hand	20.00
CR33A	Butcher Shop customer	20.00
CR34	Grenadier Guard standing firing	5.00
CR34A	Grenadier Guard at ease, A214	5.00
CR35	Grenadier Guard kneeling firing	5.00
CR36	Grenadier Guard lying firing	5.00
CR37	Life Guard at attention with sword, foot	5.00
CR38	Sailor at slope	7.00
CR39	Mountie kneeling	7.00
CR40	Mountie, rifle at foot	7.00
CR41	Mountie, marching at slope	7.00
CR41A	Mountie kneeling firing pistol	7.00
CR41B	Mountie standing firing pistol	7.00
CR41C	Mountie mounted, 267	10.00
CR42	Buffalo Bill, mounted, arm in air	25.00
CR43	Annie Oakley with shotgun, standing	20.00
CR44	Egyptian tourist, riding camel	20.00
CR45	Civilian stretcher party, 2 bearers, stretcher, injured, 1540	25.00

CR45 (part).

CR46	Doctor with stethoscope	8.00
CR47	Nurse holding towel	8.00
CR48	Nurse, hands in front	8.00

CR49	Coronation Coach, 8 horses, 4 outriders	50.00
CR50	G.I. mortar shell loader, bronze body	9.00
CR51	G.I. standing with mortar shell, bronze body	9.00

L to R: CR51, CR50.

CR52	G.I. throwing grenade	6.00
CR53	G.I. walking at trail	6.00
CR54	G.I. with flame thrower	6.00
CR55	G.I. standing with Tommy gun	6.00

L to R: CR54, CR53, CR52.

CR56	G.I. lying firing	6.00
CR57	G.I. charging with pistol	6.00
CR57A	G.I. running, arm raised	6.00
CR57B	G.I. at guard	6.00

L to R: CR48, CR47, CR46. From "Children's Hospital."

L to R: CR57A, CR55, CR57B, CR57.

CR57C

L to R: CR57D, CR57E.

L to R: CR57F, CR57G, CR10A.

		VG
CR57C	G.I. Bugler	6.00
CR57D	G.I. standing firing	6.00
CR57E	G.I. sitting at machine gun	6.00
CR57F	G.I. Radioman	6.00
CR57G	G.I. kneeling firing	6.00
CR58	Bandsman trombone player	6.00
CR59	Bandsman tuba player	6.00
CR59A	Bandsman tuba variation	6.00
CR60	Bandsman bassoon player	6.00
CR61	Bandsman cymbals player	6.00

CR58 CR59   CR60 CR61

CR62

CR63

		VG
CR62	Bandsman drummer	6.00
CR63	Bandsman cornetist	6.00
CR64	Dan Dare set	200.00
CR64A	Dan Dare with gun	25.00

CR64 boxtop. Courtesy Paul Stadinger.

CR64. Courtesy Paul Stadinger.

CR64A

		VG
CR65	Treen (space alien from Dan Dare set) standing firing	25.00
CR66	Senegalese officer carrying flag	18.00
CR67	Senegalese bugler in white bearskin	18.00
CR68	Senegalese marching at slope	18.00
CR69	French Foreign Legion marching at slope	15.00

L to R: CR68, CR66, CR67.

CR69

CR70

Crescent Policemen and horse (CR72). Photo by Gary J. Linden.

CR73

CR74

CR75 *(wrong horse).*

CR76

L to R: CR77, CR78.

CR78A

CR79

L to R: CR80, CR81, CR82, CR83.

CR84

200 ✠ Crescent

		VG				VG
CR70	700 Royal Engineers, field telephone, 2 soldiers, one has detachable reel of wire, telegraph pole, boxed	75.00		CR85	African Tribesman	15.00
				CR86	Arab with scimitar, 182	12.00
CR71	2537 Knight set, 13 pieces	125.00		CR87	African Tribesman	12.00
CR72	Policemen and horse, set	45.00		CR88	Seated Arab	12.00
CR73	Indian Lancer, formerly Reka	20.00		CR89	Maori, 246	12.00
CR74	Mounted lancer charging	12.00		CR90	Marching with telescope	15.00
CR75	State drums	20.00		CR91	WWII throwing bomb	6.00
CR76	Lifeguard at trot	12.00		CR92	WWII Bugler, A26	6.00
CR77	Guardsman saluting	6.00		CR93	Standing firing	6.00
CR78	Guardsman presenting arms	6.00		CR94	Charging, steel hat, A79	6.00
CR78A	Guardsman reining horse	12.00		CR95	WWII Officer, standing hand on hip	8.00
CR79	Guardsman at trot	12.00		CR96	WWII Bomber, A179	6.00
CR80	Highlander at slope	6.00		CR97	WWII kneeling, fixed Bayonet	6.00
CR81	Highlander Piper	6.00		CR98	RAF Pilot	15.00
CR82	Highlander kneeling firing	6.00		CR99	Officer in flying jacket with papers, B185	15.00
CR83	Highlander prone firing	6.00		CR100	RAF plane guider	15.00
CR84	Drummer, forage cap	10.00		CR101	Airman, slope arms	10.00

CR85, CR86, CR87.

CR88

CR89

CR90

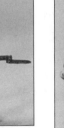

CR91

L to R: CR92, CR93, CR94.

L to R: CR95, CR96.

CR97

CR98

L to R: CR99, CR100, CR101, CR102.

CR103

		VG
CR102	RAF officer in greatcoat	10.00
CR103	RAF Infantry	10.00
CR104	Home Guard, A66	12.00
CR105	ARP kneeling with binoculars, A27	10.00
CR106	ARP plane spotter	12.00
CR107	Women's Auxiliary Territorial Service, A88	20.00

		VG
CR108	WWI kneeling nurse	6.00
CR109	WWI standing nurse	6.00
CR110	Mary feeding lamb, 38	25.00
CR111	School Days boy	8.00
CR112	School Days girl, both from set 1227, both oversize	8.00
CR113	Fish Shop assistant, from set	20.00
CR114	Cadet	6.00

L to R: CR104, CR105, CR106, CR107 (bucket missing).

CR108

CR110

L to R: CR111, CR112.

ARP Range finger, value in very good condition $15.00.

Radio operators from K703 set, value each in very good condition $15.00.

CR113

CR114

A65. Value in very good condition $10.00

101 Value $6.00.

1263 Saladin Scout Car. $40.00.

A214 mounted to tin sentry box bank. $50.00.

L to R: A5, AA1 assorted (middle three), AA2.

England
Metal, Hollowcast
54mm normally (2-1/8")

✕ **Johillco** ✕

Johillcos are the equivalent of America's dimestore toy soldiers. Since John Hill & Co. seems not to have given a hoot about aesthetics or authenticity, anyone who collects its figures can relax and simply enjoy them for what they are: toy soldiers, plain and simple. There's much to be said for that.

Despite the official name of the company, its owner was not John Hill, but George Wood. A defector from Britains, Wood set up operations about 1900. In time, his firm became Britains' greatest competitor. Almost all of Johillco's soldiers were hollowcast in a 54mm size (plastics began in 1956, according to John Garratt) and had a fairly diverse range, from ancient Romans, Ethiopians, Boers, Arabs and Mahouts, to the usual mix of British and American troops and American Indians and cowboys. Of greater interest to collectors is the fact that Johillcos were issued in far more positions than Britains, and, though quality of design varied greatly, a large number had a dynamism and zest that compare to the U.S.'s Manoil. The fact that most were sold separately, rather than in sets, probably accounts, in large part, for their individuality.

Most Johillcos are marked. The earliest bear the imprint "J. Hill & Co.," the majority are inscribed "Johillco" and some can be found that read "J. Hill" or "Jo

#1 - Open.

Postwar "Playpack" #1 - Indian Camp.

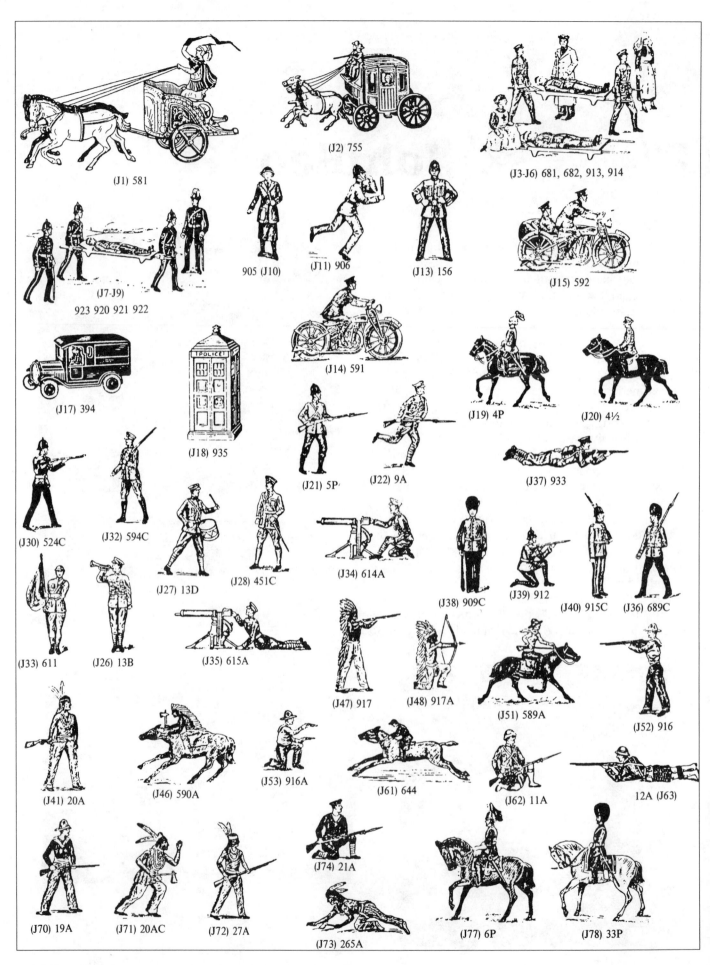

(J1) 581

(J2) 755

(J3-J6) 681, 682, 913, 914

(J7-J9)
923 920 921 922

905 (J10)

(J11) 906

(J13) 156

(J15) 592

(J17) 394

(J18) 935

(J14) 591

(J19) 4P

(J20) 4½

(J30) 524C

(J32) 594C

(J21) 5P

(J22) 9A

(J37) 933

(J27) 13D

(J28) 451C

(J34) 614A

(J38) 909C

(J39) 912

(J40) 915C

(J36) 689C

(J33) 611

(J26) 13B

(J35) 615A

(J47) 917

(J48) 917A

(J51) 589A

(J52) 916

(J41) 20A

(J46) 590A

(J53) 916A

(J61) 644

(J62) 11A

12A (J63)

(J70) 19A

(J71) 20AC

(J72) 27A

(J74) 21A

(J73) 265A

(J77) 6P

(J78) 33P

(J76) 171L (J79) 215A (J80) 215P (J81) 243A (J82) 244A (J83) 245A (J84) 535A (J90) 908

(J91) 910 (J92) 911 (J93) 924 (J94) 925 (J95) 936 (J96) 937 (J97) 938 (J98) 939 (J99) 940

(J100) 941 (J101) 942 (J102) 943 (J103) 260P (J104) 303L (J105) 304L (J106) 530A (J107) 903C

(J108) 20C (J109) 918 (J110) 904C (J111) 931 (J112) 902C (J113) 501A

(J114) 172L (J115) 105A (J116) 176P (J117) 944 (J118) 945 (J119) 569A (J120) 177P

(J121) 251L (J122) 249L (J123) 691 (J124) 677

(J125) 591D (J126) 691 (J127) 40P (J128) 692

Prewar box art.

Hill" (the plastic figures, not listed here, were marked "Hillco/Made in England").

According to Shamus O.D. Wade, only about 80% of Johillco's output is known. New figures continually turn up, to the delight of those who find them and to considerably more mixed reactions from those who don't. Although the company was in business until 1960, the destruction of its Tottenham factory during World War II seems to have been a blow from which it never quite recovered. The following listing is, of course, incomplete, but is a representative sampling of the company's output and the prices its figures bring today. For space reasons, and the fact that they turn up rarely in sales lists, only a few sets have been listed. Numbers in parentheses after code numbers are Johillco's mold numbers. *Prices listed are for pieces in very good condition.*

	VG
(J1) 581 Roman Chariot, painted, and Charioteer	$75.00
(J2) 755 Wild West Stage Coach, with driver and armed guard	25.00
(J3) 681 Nurse, standing	9.00
(J4) 681 Nurse, kneeling	11.00
(J4A) 686 Doctor in service dress	18.00
(J4B) Nurse, kneeling with bandage	22.00

	VG
(J5) 913 Stretcher with wounded soldier, two pieces	11.00
(J6) 914 Stretcher, wounded soldier, two stretcher bearers	30.00

J2

J4

L to R: J4A, J8, J9, J3.

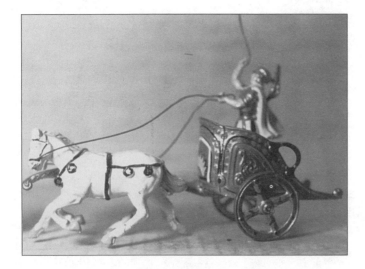

J1

J4B

J6

(J7) 920 Wounded soldier, red coat,
          on stretcher, stretcher bearers................................ 12.00
(J8) 922 Senior Medical Officer,
          Red Cross, full dress 12.00
(J9) 923 Junior Medical Officer,
          Red Cross, full dress 13.00

J18

(J18) 935 Police Box....................................... No Price Found
(J19) 4P Cavalry (Lifeguard).. 12.00
(J20) 4-1/2" Khaki Cavalry .... No Price Found
(J21) 5P Infantry 8.00
(J22) 9A Charging Infantry, khaki.. 8.00
(J23) 10A Firing Infantry, khaki.. 8.00
(J24) 11AC Kneeling Highlanders.................................... 6.00
(J25) 12AC Prone Highlanders.. 6.00
(J26) 13B Bugler, khaki.. 8.00
(J27) 13D Drummer, khaki 6.00

L to R: J9, J8, J283.

(J10) 905 Policewoman....................................... 15.00
(J11) 906 Policeman, running 12.00
(J12) 688 Policeman, small .... No Price Found
(J13) 156 Policeman....................................... 16.00
(J14) 591 Speed Cop, solo .... No Price Found
(J15) 592 Speed Cop, combination, sidecar..................... 48.00
(J16) 93 Mounted Policeman 9.00
(J17) 934 Police Van....................................... No Price Found

J20 (undersize).

L to R: J21, Variation with white helmet.

J13 (60mm).

J14

J15

J22

J26

L to R: J26A Red tunic, J27A Red tunic.

	VG		VG
(J28) 451C Officer, khaki	10.00	(J41) 20A Indian brave	6.00
(J29) 523C Firing Fusiliers	7.00	(J42) 20S Creeping Indian	No Price Found
(J29A) 10A Standing Firing	8.00	(J43) 20T Indian Chief	No Price Found
(J29B) Mounted Lancer in Cap	12.00	(J44) 27C North American Indian	No Price Found
(J29C) Infantry at Slope with Bandolier	8.00	(J45) 265C Crawling Indian	No Price Found
(J30) 524C Firing Lincolnshire Regt.	No Price Found	(J46) 590A Mounted Indian	15.00
(J31) 593AC Marching Infantry, khaki	6.00	(J47) 917 Indian firing rifle	6.00
(J32) 594C Marching Infantry, khaki	10.00	(J48) 917A Kneeling Indian firing bow and arrow	6.00
(J33) 611 Colour bearer, khaki	No Price Found	(J49) 19C Foot Cowboy with rifle	5.00
(J34) 614A Kneeling machine gunner, plain	11.00	(J50) 530C Foot cowboy, with revolver	5.00
(J35) 615A Prone machine gunner, plain	20.00	(J51) 589A Mounted cowboy	15.00
(J36) 689C Marching Fusiliers	6.00	(J52) 916 Cowboy firing rifle	5.00
(J37) 933 Infantry, prone, khaki	8.00	(J53) 916A Kneeling cowboy firing revolvers	4.00
(J38) 909C Fusilier (Attention!)	7.00	(J54) 21C Kneeling sailor	5.00
(J39) 912 Manchester Regt. kneeling	6.00	(J55) 47C Standing Sailor	8.00
(J40) 915C Liverpool Regt., slope arms	8.00	(J55A) Sailor, slope arms	8.00

J27

L to R: J28 Peak cap, J32 Peak cap.

J29A

J29B

J30

J33

J35

J36

J 51 - #589A
(smaller scale).

J41

J50

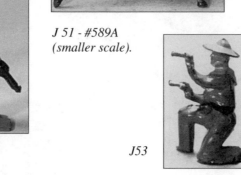

J53

L to R: J55, J54.

L to R: J55A, J55B.

J56-J75

L to R: J58, J59, J57.

	VG
(J55B) Sailor, trail arms	8.00
(J56) 106C Charging Zulu	6.00
(J57) 267PC R.A.F. pilot	9.00
(J58) 267RC R.A.F. rigger	9.00
(J59) 267MC R.A.F. mechanic	9.00
(J60) 191A Small submarine	No Price Found
(J61) 644A Racehorse and jockey	No Price Found
(J62) 11A Gordon Highlander, kneeling	No Price Found
(J63) 12A Argyle and Sutherland Highlander, prone	No Price Found

J62

L to R: J62, J168.

	VG
(J64) 16AP Black Watch	No Price Found
(J65) 523A Firing Fusilier	7.00
(J66) 524A Firing Lincolnshire Regt.	No Price Found
(J67) 614P Kneeling machine gunner	No Price Found
(J68) 615P Prone machine gunner	No Price Found
(J69) 689 Inniskilling Fusiliers, marching	No Price Found
(J70) 19A Cowboy with rifle	6.00
(J71) 10AC Indian, foot, creeping	8.00
(J72) 27A North American Brave	8.00

J70

L to R: J70, 19C, 917, 916, 916A. Last four are smaller scale, value $5.00 each.

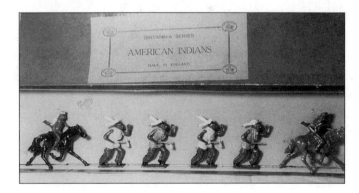

J71 and J113 in boxed set - "Britannia Series."

	VG
(J73) 265A Crawling Indian	8.00
(J74) 21A Kneeling sailor	No Price Found
(J75) 106A Zulu, charging	6.00
(J76) 171L Knight in armour, foot	6.00
(J76A) Mounted Knight, c. 1955	10.00
(J77) 6P Lifeguards	10.00
(J78) 33P Scots Greys	11.00
(J79) 215A Scots Guards, marching	6.00
(J80) 215P Piper	8.00
(J81) 243A Grenadier Guards, running	6.00
(J82) 244A Black Watch, marching	5.00
(J83) 245A Manchester Regt., running	No Price Found

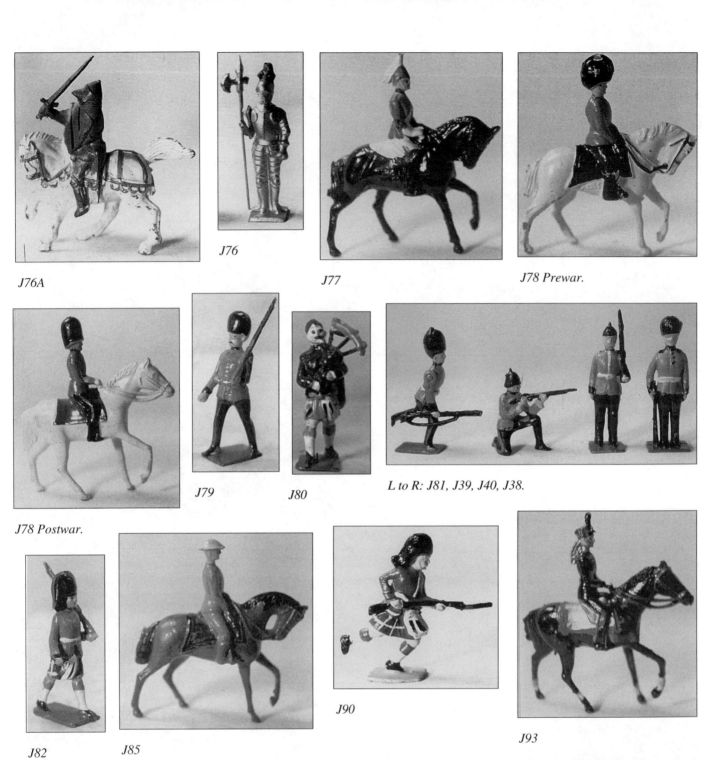

J76A

J76

J77

J78 Prewar.

J78 Postwar.

J79

J80

L to R: J81, J39, J40, J38.

J82

J85

J90

J93

L to R: J94, J120, J116. Courtesy Wilbur Bittenbender.

L to R: J94, J94A.

(J84) 535A Cavalry, service dress 12.00

(J85) 535B Cavalry,
service dress with steel helmet.............. No Price Found

(J86) 614 Machine gunner,
kneeling, service dress .... No Price Found

(J87) 615 Machine gunner,
prone, service dress .... No Price Found

(J88) 691G Gilt trumpeter, mounted .... No Price Found

(J89) 692G Gilt standard bearer, mounted........ No Price Found

(J90) 908 Black Watch, charging.. 8.00

(J91) 910 Middlesex Regt., present arms.......... No Price Found

(J92) 911 Scots Guards, standard bearer.......................... 10.00

(J93) 924 Hussar, mounted 9.00

(J94) 925 12th Lancers, Prince of Wales' Royal 11.00

(J94A) 925 12th Lancers,
Prince of Wales' Royal, officer............................ 14.00

(J95) 936 Officer (Sussex Light
Infantry) with field glasses................... No Price Found

(J96) 937 Royal Marines, captain .... No Price Found

(J97) 938 Royal Marines, marching................. No Price Found

(J98) 939 Royal Marines, bugler...................... No Price Found

(J99) 940 Infantry, marching, service uniform 6.00

(J100) 941 Infantry, captain, service uniform.................... 6.00

(J101) 942 Infantry, gun crew, kneeling
with gas mask, service uniform............................ 11.00

(J102) 943 Infantry, gun crew, standing
with gas mask, service uniform............................ 11.00

L to R: J106, J104.

J105

J101

L to R: J102, J185.

(J103) 260P Mounted Cowboy firing rifle........ No Price Found

(J104) 303L Cowboy walking with lasso 6.00

(J105) 304L Cowgirl with whip... 6.00

(J106) 530A Cowboy on foot firing pistol......................... 8.00

(J107) 903C Mounted Cowboy, firing pistol 15.00

(J108) 20C Indian Chief with hatchet................................ 6.00

(J109) 918 Mountie with rifle... 12.00

(J110) 904C Cowboy firing from behind horse................ 18.00

(J111) 931 Cowgirl on horse... 9.00

(J112) 902C Mounted Indian firing rifle 15.00

J110

J111

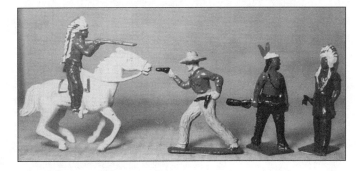

L to R: J112, J106, J41, J108.

(J113) 501A Mounted Indian with rifle 15.00
(J114) 172L Mounted knight with lance........................... 15.00

J114

J119

L to R: J128, J126.

(J115) 105A Jockey on galloping horse............ No Price Found
(J116) 176P Camel with rider 15.00
(J117) 944 Civil Air Guard, instructor............. No Price Found
(J118) 945 Civil Air Guard, pupil .... No Price Found
(J119) 569A Roman Gladiator 6.00
(J120) 177P Elephant with rider 13.00
(J121) 251L Mounted Cowboy with lasso, large 12.00

(J128) 692 Scots Greys standard bearer........... No Price Found
(J129) 191A Large submarine .... No Price Found
(J130) 261 Mounted Arab.. 17.00
(J131) 267B Airship... No Price Found
(J132) 31A Lancers, khaki, large..................... No Price Found
(J133) 213A Mounted Hussars, large 11.00
(J134) 907 Field Marshal, mounted 9.00

The following five lines are larger than the ordinary lines, being approximately 3-1/2" in height.

(J135) 562A Cowboy on foot, firing rifle......... No Price Found
(J136) 565A Indian on foot, with tomahawk $8.00
(J137) 575A Officers marching, khaki .... No Price Found
(J138) 575B Infantry marching, khaki............. No Price Found
(J139) 577A Crusaders 6.00

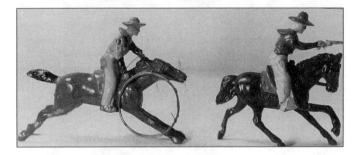

L to R: J121, J107.

(J122) 249L Cowboy riding bucking bronco.................... 18.00
(J123) 691 Range Rider with revolver and horse 11.00
(J124) 677 Sudanese Camel Corps 26.00
(J125) 591D Dispatch Rider, on motorcycle 27.00
(J126) 691 Scots Greys trumpeter.................................... 16.00
(J127) 40P Mounted Arab... 16.00

L to R: J124, J127.

J136

J139

(J140) 26A Mounted cowboy,
large, with revolver .... No Price Found
(J141) 695 Range rider with rifle and horse 11.00
(J142) 773 Royal Canadian Mounted policeman............. 16.00

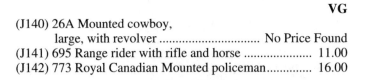

L to R: J141, J143, J123 (all detachable from saddle).

J142

(J143) 946 Texas Ranger 11.00
(J144) 678 Bedouin Arab on camel 21.00
(J145) 673 Mule carrying light mountain gun 16.00
(J145A) Mule carrying gun wheels................................... 16.00
(J145B) Mule carrying ammo boxes................................. 16.00

L to R: J145B, J145, J145A.

REGIMENTAL BANDSMEN:
GRENADIER GUARDS

(J146) 50/1 Drum Major $9.00
(J147) 50/2 Bass Drum 7.00
(J148) 50/3 Side Drum... 7.00
(J149) 50/4 Saxhorn.. 7.00
(J150) 50/5 Trumpet.. 7.00
(J151) 50/6 Trombone.. 7.00

(J152) 50/7 Clarinet 7.00
(J153) 50/8 Fife.. 7.00
(J154) 50/9 Cymbals.. 7.00

End Regimental Bandsmen

(J154A) Ethiopian, slung rifle.. $9.00
(J154B) Italian Colonial, slope arms 27.00
(J155) Ethiopian Tribesman, standing at ready 8.00
(J156-7) Ethiopian Regular Army stretcher
bearers, stretcher and wounded man
(Ethiopians in khaki uniform, barefooted)............. 30.00

Ethiopian Mountain Battery (lead soldier, J154A, has rifle strapped diagonally to back).

L to R: J154A, J154B.   *J155*

J156-7

(J158) Tommy carrying wounded on back 22.00
(J159) Scot in bearskin, large, at ready................................ 6.00
(J160) Greek Evzone... 8.00
(J161) Union Army Set, 12 pieces, each............................. 8.00
(J162) Horseguard, at walk, old.. 9.00
(J163) Unused .... —
(J164) Hussar, with sword at carry 8.00
(J165) Lifeguard, dismounted, walking 5.00
(J166) Scots Grey Standard Bearer, mounted...................... 9.00
(J167) Goat Mascot of Royal Welsh Fusiliers.................... 3.00

VG

(J168) Highlander,
   Tropical Helmet, lying firing, 12A 6.00
(J169) Highlander, marching at slope 6.00
(J170) West Point Cadet at slope 6.00
(J170A) Thinner variation of above 6.00

L to R: J170A, J170, J215B, J215.

(J171) Man hurling Stick Grenade, early 6.00
(J172) Officer kneeling with binoculars, WWI helmet 9.00
(J173) Infantryman, WWI helmet, at slope 6.00

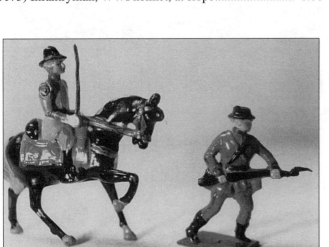

L to R: J177A, J177B.

L to R: J177G, J177H, J177I.

VG

(J174) Officer, WWI, standing firing pistol,
   one hand on hip 8.00
(J175) Beefeater 9.00
(J175A) Beefeater with Halberd 9.00
(J176) Lake, larger than 278 Pond, with printed
   card to represent water reeds, etc. 48.00
(J177) Confederate Army, price per each 8.00
   Mounted 12.00
(J178) Finn, slung rifle 30.00
(J179) Royal Scot, marching slope, 36 .... 6.00

J175   *J175A*

L to R: J177C, J177D, J177E, J177F.

L to R: J178, J179.

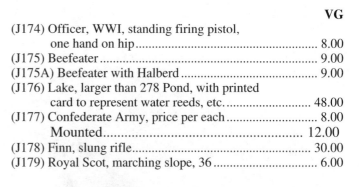

	VG		**VG**
(J180) Spotter in spotting chair, K64	22.00	(J183A) Mounted Crusader	10.00
(J181) Tommy clubbing with rifle, K65	No Price Found	(J184) Mounted Turk firing rifle	22.00
(J181A) Tommy charging with bayonet	8.00	(J185) Australian charging, slouch hat	16.00
(J182) Marching Ethiopian	24.00	(J186) Gordon Piper	11.00
(J183) Crusader knight	6.00	(J187) Highlander kneeling firing, Glengarry cap	9.00

L to R: J180, J158.

L to R: J181A, J37, J34.

J181

L to R:
J154B,
J182.

J182

J183

J183A

J184

J186

J187

L to R: J188, J160.

L to R: J189, J190, J191, J192. Postwar Indians
with bronze-colored bodies.

#667

J189A

L to R: J191, J189B.

(J188) Guard winter dress, 31 .... 6.00
(J189) 12 Chief with peace pipe, moveable arm, 664 .... 9.00
(J189A) Indian kneeling firing rifle, in headdress, 663 .... 6.00
(J189B) Indian advancing with knife, 661 .... 6.00
(J190) 9 Indian doing war dance, long headdress, 660 .... 6.00
(J191) Totem Pole, 666 .... 9.00
(J192) Indian Kneeling firing, 663 .... 6.00
(J193) Highlander, tropical helmet, kneeling firing 6.00
(J194) Marching, Gas Mask bag (15) 8.00
(J194A) K69 Officer firing pistol 9.00
(J195) Firing Bren Gun (S15) 8.00
(J196) Gun Crew Kneeling, no gas mask (S30) 8.00
(J197) At Ease (S36) 8.00
(J198) Marching, ring hand (to hold weapon) (S39) 8.00
(J199) Kneeling Firing (S42) 8.00
(J200) Kneeling Infantry (S45) 8.00
(J201) Kneeling with binoculars (S54) 8.00
(J202) Charging (56) 8.00
(J203) Standing Firing (57) 8.00
(J204) U.S.A. Standing Firing (S554) 8.00
(J205) U.S.A. Advancing (S555) 8.00

Top, L to R: J194, J195, J33, J196, J102, J197, J198; Bottom, L to R: J199, J200, J181, J158, J201, J202, J203.
Unpainted castings courtesy Ken Wittenrich, West Falls Toy Co.

J194A   J195   J197   J199   J200

J201

L to R: J204, J211, J211A.

L to R: J209, J207, J206.

J213

Top, L to R: J216, J136, J217, J218, J108; Bottom, L to R: J189, J71, J43, J219, J220, J47, J192. Unpainted castings courtesy Ken Wittenrich, West Falls Toy Co.

L to R: J109, J221, J222, J223, J224. Unpainted castings courtesy Ken Wittenrich, West Falls Toy Co.

	VG
(J206) U.S.A. Lying Firing	8.00
(J207) U.S.A. Officer (S557)	8.00
(J208) U.S.A. Flagbearer (S558)	8.00
(J209) U.S.A. Marching (S560)	8.00
(J210) U.S.A. Standing Firing (S565)	8.00
(J211) U.S.A. Advancing (S566)	8.00
(J211A) U.S.A. Kneeling Firing	8.00
(J212) U.S.A. Flag Bearer (S569)	8.00
(J213) 7th Cavalry (S572)	12.00
(J214) U.S. Sailor Marching	8.00

	VG
(J215) U.S. Marine (S199)	8.00
(J215A) U.S. Marine with bugle	10.00
(J215B) 47th New York Regiment at slope	10.00
(J216) Large Indian with Lance	9.00
(J217) Indian, mounted	8.00
(J218) Indian with Spear	6.00
(J219) Indian with scalp	9.00
(J220) Chief with Blanket	6.00
(J221) Large Cowboy Firing (S296)	9.00
(J222) Cowboy to Ride Horse	4.00

	VG		**VG**
(J223) **Marshal** (S304)	6.00	(J231) **Knight with Mace**	6.00
(J224) **Cowboy with Lasso**	8.00	(J232) **Knight with Sword, no visor**	8.00
(J225) Unused	—	(J233) **Knight with Sword, visor**	8.00
(J226) Unused	—	(J234) **Pirate with a Bottle**	12.00
(J227) Unused	—	(J235) **Pirate Playing Concertina**	12.00
(J228) **Charging WWII**	6.00	(J236) **Pirate with Hook**	12.00
(J229) **Kneeling Firing WWII**	6.00	(J236A) **Pirate with pistol and sword**	12.00
(J230) **Crawling, WWII**	6.00	(J236B) **Pirate with knife**	6.00

L to R: J228, J229, J230. Unpainted castings courtesy Ken Wittenrich, West Falls Toy Co.

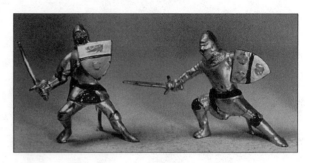

L to R: J232, J233.

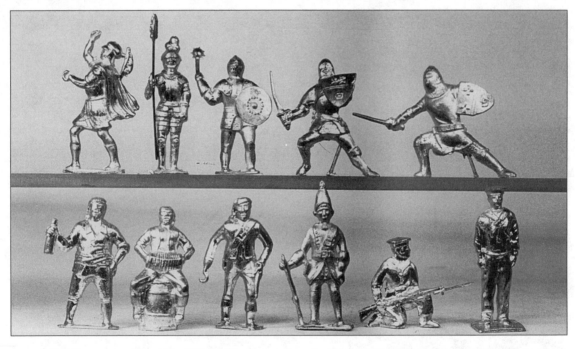

Top, L to R: J1(part), J76, J231, J232, J233; Bottom, L to R: J234, J235, J236, J237, J74, J238. Unpainted castings courtesy Ken Wittenrich, West Falls Toy Co.

L to R: J236A, J235, J236.

L to R: J236B, J236C, J236D, J236E, J236F.

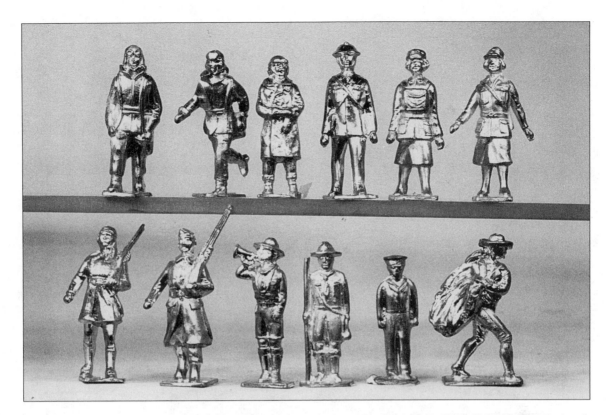

Top, L to R: J239, J240, J57, J241, J242, J243; Bottom, L to R: J160, J244, J245, J246, J247, J248. Unpainted castings courtesy Ken Wittenrich, West Falls Toy Co.

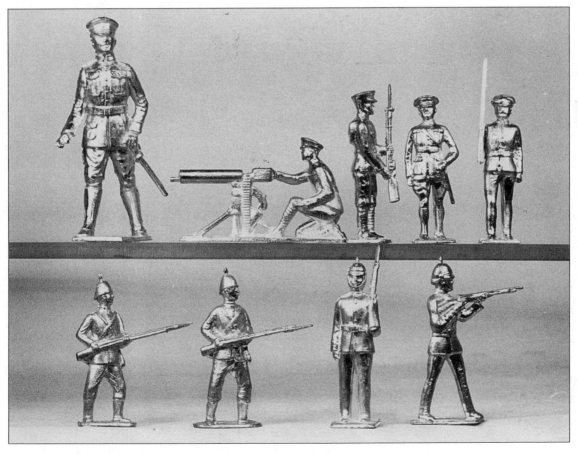

Top, L to R: J249, J34, J250, J28, J251; Bottom, L to R: J252, J253, J40, J30. Unpainted castings courtesy Ken Wittenrich, West Falls Toy Co.

	VG		**VG**
(J236C) Pirate with one leg, parrot 12.00		(J242) W.A.A.F., arms straight down (S262) 8.00
(J236D) Pirate with hook, sword 12.00		(J243) W.A.A.F., arms down at angle 8.00
(J236E) Pirate Sack 12.00		(J244) Marching in Greatcoat, cap (S359) 8.00
(J236F) Pirate with eye patch 12.00		(J245) Boy Scout Blowing Bugle (S393) 6.00
(J236G) Pirate with bottle 12.00		(J246) Boy Scout with Staff (S394) 6.00
(J237) Grenadier, 1750? 8.00		(J247) Sea Scout? (S394) 6.00
(J238) Sailor Standing (S196) 8.00		(J248) Bullfighter (S372) 8.00
(J239) Pilot Walking (S172) 8.00		(J249) Large Officer (S13) 9.00
(J240) Pilot Running (S173) 8.00		(J250) Present Arms (S49) 8.00
(J241) Air Raid Warden (S237) 8.00		(J251) Marching (S191) 8.00

Top, L to R: J254, J255, J36, J81, J256, J257, J258; Bottom, L to R: J79, J259, J260, J92, J261, J262, J263. Unpainted castings courtesy Ken Wittenrich, West Falls Toy Co.

J262A

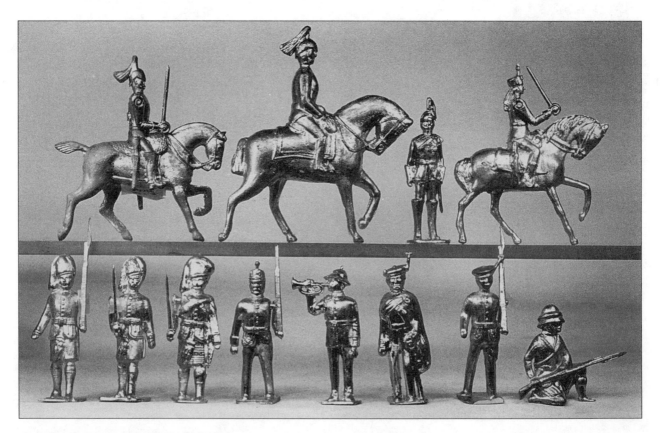

Top, L to R: J264, J265, J266, J267; Bottom, L to R: J82, J268, J269, J270, J98, J271, J179, J193. Unpainted castings courtesy Ken Wittenrich, West Falls Toy Co.

	VG			**VG**
(J252) At Ready (S19)	8.00		(J265) Large Life Guard (S76)	9.00
(J253) At Ready, larger (S20)	8.00		(J266) Life Guard (S70)	8.00
(J254) Guard Officer	8.00		(J267) Hussar (S83)	8.00
(J255) Guard Kneeling, Firing (S4)	8.00		(J268) Black Watch Officer (S136)	8.00
(J256) Guard Lying Firing	8.00		(J269) Highland Officer (S137)	8.00
(J257) Boy Guard Side Drummer (S124)	8.00		(J270) Highland Light Infantry	8.00
(J258) Guard Bandsman, tuba (S128)	8.00		(J271) Royal Scots Officer	8.00
(J259) Guard Side Drummer (S132)	8.00		(J272) Home Guard	8.00
(J260) Guard Marching, Greatcoat (S133)	8.00		(J273) Cowboy, arms extended	6.00
(J261) Guard Officer in Greatcoat (S135)	8.00		(J274) Mountie hands on hips	10.00
(J262) Guard Marching (S147)	8.00		(J275) Sentry Box, 463	No Price Found
(J262A) Guard Standing Firing	8.00		(J276) Guard in Greatcoat	8.00
(J263) Royal Welsh Fusiliers Goat Handler (S163)	9.00		(J277) At Slope	No Price Found
(J264) Horse Guard	8.00		(J278) Line Officer	8.00

J267

J272

J273

J274

J275

J276

L to R: J277, J215A, J119. Courtesy Stad's.

L to R: J278, J279, J29C.

L to R: J280, J281.

J282

J284

J285

	VG
(J279) Infantry, Present Arms	8.00
(J280) Black Watch Drummer	9.00
(J281) Black Watch Piper	9.00
(J282) U.S.M.P., moveable arm	20.00
(J283) Black Watch at slope	8.00
(J284) Black Watch at Ready, 17/7, 60mm high	8.00
(J285) 907 Field Marshal	12.00
(J286) 68/1 Scots Grey	12.00

L to R: J286, J134, J126, J77. Courtesy Wilbur Bittenbender.

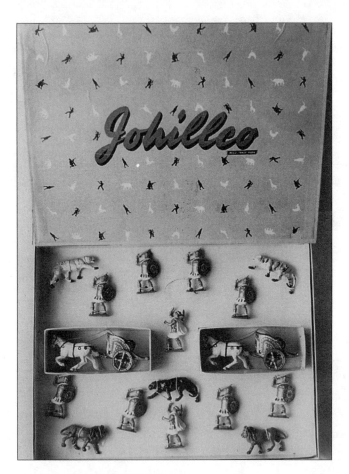

Set 21, price (VG) $275.00.

Set 19, price (VG) $225.00.

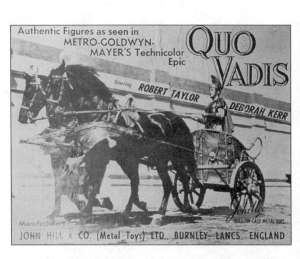

Above and right: Set 10, price (VG) $120.00.

Santa Claus
VG $60.00.

Unlisted, but style seems to be Johillco.
No price found.

JOHILLCO FARM

	VG
157 Hedge	$7.00
157A Small Oak Tree	9.00
157B Pine Tree	9.00
223 Milk Churn	5.00
246 Sign Post	7.00
246A Walnut Tree	10.00
246B Large Oak Tree	12.00
246C Fir Tree	10.00
246D Bulrushes	8.00
246E Flags or Iris	8.00
246F Footbridge	14.00
246G Gate and Gate Post	15.00
246H Hurdle	5.00
246I Stile	11.00
246J Dove Cote	9.00
246K Pigeons or Doves, each	4.00
246L River Bridge	20.00
246M Farm Ladder	5.00
246MS Haystack Ladder	6.00
246N Pig Sty	15.00

#246N

	VG
246OW Sow Pig, white	4.00
246OB Sow Pig, black	4.00
246PW Piglets, white, assorted positions, each	4.00
246PB Piglets, black, assorted positions	4.00
246Q Pig Trough	4.00
246R Beehive	10.00

L to R: #246R, #254, #246J.

	VG
246T Fencing	4.00
254 Kennel and Bulldog	15.00
254D Bulldog	8.00
258 Farmer	7.00
259 Huntsman	8.00
264 Steer	5.00
275 Rabbit Hutch	12.00
276 Large Rabbit	4.00
277 Small Rabbit	4.00
278 Pond, each in box	35.00

#278 Pond, #279 Duck, #258 Farmer.

279 Swimming Duck	4.00
280 Walking Duck	4.00
281 Duckling	4.00
282 Fowls, Cock	3.00
283 Fowls, Hen, feeding	3.00
284 Chicks, walking	4.00
285 Chicks, running	4.00
286 Fowls, Hen, sitting	3.00

	VG		VG
287 Nest Box	12.00	310 Cart-horse	8.00
288 Hen Coop	15.00	311 Colt	6.00
289 Corn Stack	22.00	312 Lamb	5.00
290 Walking Sheep	4.00	313 Calf	5.00
291 Farm Labourer	7.00	314 Windmill, each in box	65.00
292 Farm Barrow	7.00		

#288

#291-#292.

L to R: #314 Prewar, narrow blade, #316, #410, #329.

L to R: #289, #246MS, #299, #315, #410, #348.

	VG
294 Weeping Willow	12.00
295 Small Bush	10.00
296 Medium Bush	12.00
297 Large Bush	12.00
298 Fern	12.00
299 Haystack	20.00
306 Milkmaid, sitting	7.00
307 Milking Cow	5.00
308 Feeding Cow	5.00
309 Feeding Horse	6.00

#314 Postwar, wide blade.

	VG
315 Miller	8.00
316 Miller's labourer carrying flour sack	8.00
317 Cornshucks	8.00
318 Milkmaid and Yoke with two pails	7.00
328 Village Blacksmith	14.00
329 Cornbin	25.00
330 Flour Sack, full	12.00
331 Flour Sack, partly filled	10.00

#306

#309

L to R: #318, #246L, #500G.

L to R: #338, #339/#340, #342, #341. Photo by Will Beierwaltes.

#339/340

#353

#356 (apron) with #357.

#364

#366

L to R: #367, #366, #370.

#368

#370

L to R: #3755 and #3745 on #413; #3715.

#383

	VG		VG
332 Sleeping Pig	7.00	357 Gardener's Barrow	7.00
338 Forge	17.00	358 Flowerpots with plants	7.00
339 Anvil	7.00	359 Open Dovecote	9.00
340 Anvil Blacksmith	12.00	360 Miller's Labourer (for 361)	10.00
341 Blacksmith Shoeing	15.00	361 Miller's Barrow	7.00
342 Horse for shoeing	18.00	364 Shepherd and Lamb	15.00
343 Owl	6.00	365 Milking Stool	7.00
344 Crow	6.00	366 Village Bride	8.00
345 Greenhouse, each in box	65.00	367 Village Bridegroom	25.00
346 Lying Horse	6.00	368 Village Parson	12.00
347 Lying Colt	6.00	369 Village Curate	8.00
348 Traffic Sign, assorted directions, each	10.00	370 Village Bridesmaid	8.00
350 Signpost, two arms	10.00	3715 Dairymaid, sitting on stool	10.00
351 Signpost, three arms	10.00	372 Shepherd's Dog, lying	6.00
352 Signpost, four arms	10.00	373 Squirrel, sitting	5.00
353 Well, with bucket	20.00	3745 Farmer's Wife, sitting on stool	9.00
354 Pump	10.00	3755 Aged Villager, sitting on stool	9.00
355 Cattle Drinking Rack	12.00	376 Farmhouse steps	10.00
356 Gardener (for 357)	8.00	377 Punt	10.00

	VG		VG
379 Summerhouse, large	40.00	400 "Near London" Milestone	22.00
380 Summerhouse, small	30.00	401 Country Milestone	15.00
381 Summerhouse table	20.00	402 Lying Sheep	4.00
383 Golfer	18.00	403 Tramp	12.00
384 Tennis Player, male or female, each (A and B)	20.00	404 Horse Float and Horse, each in box	85.00
385 Innkeeper	12.00	405 Horse Float, Horse and Show Horse, each in box	95.00
		407 Running Fox	10.00
		410 Milk Churn and Lid	7.00
		411 Field Hurdle	5.00
		412 Level Crossing Sign	15.00
		413 Covered Country Seat	18.00
		414 Punt and Child	20.00
		415 Sitting Child	10.00
		416 Cattle Drover	12.00
		417 Tennis Players (male and female) C and D, scarce	35.00
		425 Hare	4.00

L to R: #384A, #384B, #417C, #417D.

	VG		VG
386 Child to ride Carthorse	12.00	500A Shire Horse	8.00
387 Running Pig	8.00	500B Lying Cow	6.00
388 Cattle Float and Horse, each in box	85.00	500C Lying Calf	6.00
389 Cattle Float, Horse and Show Cow, each in box	95.00	500D Standing Calf	5.00
390 Golden Eagle	9.00	500E Feeding Sheep	4.00
391 Farmer's Collie Dog	6.00	500F English Bull	10.00
392 Farm Sack Trolley	15.00	500G Swan	6.00
393 Corn Truck	15.00	500H Frog	6.00
394 Birds, Robin, Greenfinch, Chaffinch, etc.	5.00	500J Witch	50.00
395 Fox Terrier	5.00	500K Witch's Fire	10.00
396 Farm Cat	6.00	500L Witch's Cauldron	10.00
397 Fox and Duck	25.00	500M Log	12.00
398 Garden Seat	8.00	500N Goat	4.00
399 Farmer's Daughter	8.00	500O Turkey	4.00
		500P Sitting Pig	4.00
		500Q Donkey	4.00
		500R Mule	4.00
		500S Standing Horse	5.00
		500T Gander	3.00

L to R: Fallen Log #500M, #387, #246PW, #396.

L to R: #400, #403.

#385

#414

#416

L to R: #500A, #388.

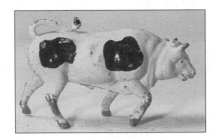

#500F

Left: #500S; Far right: #311.

	VG
500U Goose	3.00
500V Black Swan	No Price Found
919 Thatched Cottage	No Price Found
600 Ostrich	9.00
600A Lion	12.00
600B Tiger	12.00
600C Chimpanzee	8.00
600D Bison	No Price Found
600E Seal	No Price Found
600F Small Frog	No Price Found
600G Large Frog	8.00
600H Tortoise	9.00

	VG
600I Squirrel	No Price Found
600J Lying Rat	No Price Found
600K Sitting Rat	No Price Found
600L Sitting Rabbit	No Price Found
600M Eagle	No Price Found
600N Polar Bear	9.00
600O Giraffe	No Price Found
600P Grizzly Bear	6.00
600Q Elephant	No Price Found
600R Camel	9.00
600S Alligator	11.00
600T Leopard	8.00
600U Hippopotamus	No Price Found
600VG Bear Cub, Grizzly	9.00
600VP Bear Cub, Polar	No Price Found
600W Penguin	3.00
600X Rhinoceros	No Price Found
600Y Pelican	5.00
600Z Kneeling Camel	No Price Found
601A Giant Tortoise	No Price Found
601BG Bear Sitting, Grizzly	5.00
601BP Bear Sitting, Polar	No Price Found
601C Stag	6.00
601D Kangaroo	12.00
601E Baby Kangaroo	No Price Found
601F Gander	No Price Found
601G Goose	No Price Found
601H Otter	No Price Found
601J Walrus	No Price Found
601K Flamingo	No Price Found
601L Lizard	No Price Found
601M Stork	No Price Found
601N Black Swan	No Price Found
601P Panda, Sitting	No Price Found

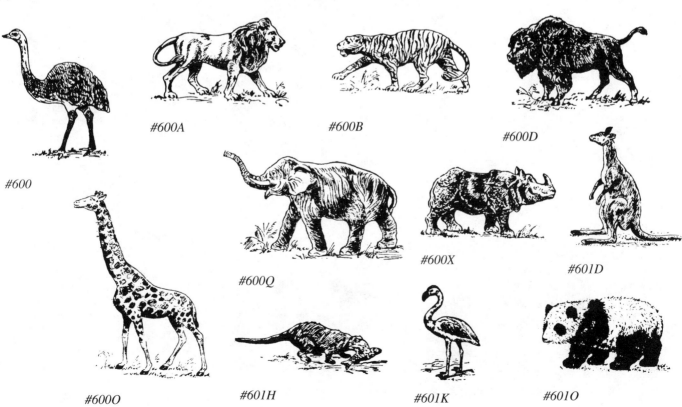

#600

#600A

#600B

#600D

#600Q

#600X

#601D

#600O

#601H

#601K

#601O

601Q Panda, lying .... No Price Found
601R Panda, sitting and Chair .... No Price Found
760 (set) Lamppost with ladder and cleaning man 70.00

#760 Set.

RAILWAY STAFF, ETC.

134 Stollworks Machine 20.00
135A Guard 12.00
135B Trolley Porter (for 135D) 10.00
135C Station Master 10.00
135D Small Luggage Trolley 7.00
135E Old Lady Passenger 10.00
135F Old Gentleman Passenger 10.00
135G Lady with Bag 10.00

135H Young Man Passenger 10.00
135I Sitting Lady Passenger 10.00
135J Sitting Gentleman Passenger 10.00
135K Girl with Basket 9.00
135L Schoolboy Passenger 9.00
135M Station Master's Dog 6.00
135N Station Cat 6.00
135O Engine Driver 10.00
135P Stoker 10.00
135Q Milk Truck Porter 10.00
135R Air Mail Pillar Box 14.00
135S Tourist 15.00
137 Fire Alarm 14.00
138 Electric Light Standard 15.00
139 Nestle's Chocolate Machine 20.00
140 Station Board 20.00
141 Weighing Machine 20.00
142 Ticket Machine 20.00
220 Lady Passenger 10.00
221 Gentleman Passenger 10.00
222 Milk Truck 20.00
223 Milk Churn with Lid, large 6.00
224 Brief Bag 5.00
225 Oval Trunk 5.00
226 Cabin Trunk 5.00
227 Rug and Umbrella 5.00
228 Porter carrying Suitcase 10.00
229 Station Seat 7.00
232 Pillar Box 15.00
239 Child sitting on Luggage 20.00

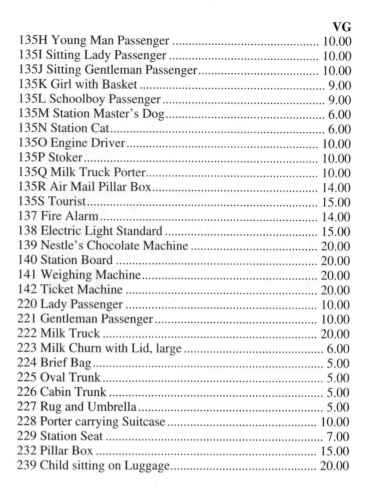

L to R: #135B with #135D, #225, #224, #226, #135P.

L to R: #135H, #135L, #135K, #239, #135J & #135I on #229.

#135R

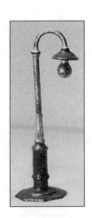

#138

L to R: #140, #135A, #221, #135F, #135G, #220.

L to R: #228, #141, #139, #142, #134, #137, #135C.

CORONATION PROCESSION SERIES

30mm foot figures

	VG
Coach with 8 horses	85.00

Mounted figures

	VG
A) Life Guard	7.00
B) Horse Guard	7.00
C) Marshal	10.00

Coach and 8 horses.

Mounted figures. L to R: A, B, C.

Each VG $5.00.

JOHILLCO SPACEMEN

No prices found on spacemen.

L to R: JA, JB, JC, JD, JE, JF.

JG, JH.

✕ **Lone Star** ✕

According to *Plastic Warrior* magazine's separate publication on Lone Star, this firm was started by Arthur Eagles, a member of the family which ran Crescent, and its plastic figures were known as the Harvey Series because they were manufactured and painted by the Harvey Toy Company for Die Cast Machine Tools Ltd. of Enfield, England. Lone Star's plastic soldiers were sold from 1955 to 1976. The company is still in business, producing die-cast tractors and guns. George Todd seems to have designed all its figures.

Many of Lone Star's figures were copies, both other firms' and Lone Star's own hollowcast lead pieces. The "Lone Star" publication by Plastic Warrior lists the following types: Knights, Robin Hood, Siege Weapons, African Natives, Afghans, Cowboys, Indians, early Indians, Davy Crockett, Western Children, the Lone Ranger and Tonto, Zorro, Civil War, Foreign Legion, Anzacs, Germans, Red Berets, Paratroopers, Royal Navy, Royal Marines, Frogmen, Midget Submarine, Foot Guards, Guards Band, Life Guard, Highlanders, Swoppets (Knights, Cowboys, Indians, horses for the Cowboys and Indians, Ski Troops with various heads and accessories, Infantry--Red Berets, U.S. Paratroops, RAF, U.N., soldiers), Dick Turpin, a Safari set, Frogmen, various vehicles and crewmen, plus buildings, a shooting game (with some of Lone Star's Indians) and non-military figures (Popeye set, Noddy set, Women fashion models, Farm animals).

Some of Lone Star's Afghans. Value $10.00 each. Courtesy Paul Stadinger - Stad's.

Some of Lone Star's Anzacs. Value $12.00 each. With flesh painted black, they were also sold as Kings African Rifles (and are valued at $10.00 each). An Anzac kneeling firing rifle, molded in white, was used as a white hunter in the Safari set. Courtesy Plastic Warrior.

Lone Star's Dick Turpin. Value $50.00. Courtesy Plastic Warrior.

231

Lone Stars tend to be stocky and vigorous-looking, but the quality of sculpting varies from striking to mediocre. Most can be identified by an underbase marking that reads "Lone Star Harvey Series Made in Gt. Britain." Average prices for common pieces range from $5 to $6 each.

Lone Star's Tonto and Lone Ranger. Value $50.00 each. Courtesy *Plastic Warrior.*

Some of Lone Star's Foreign Legionnaires. These are modified copies of American Civil War pieces. Value $12.00 each.

Lone Star's Zorro. Value $50.00. Courtesy Plastic Warrior.

Lone Star's Cowboy on Bucking Bronco. Value $8.00. Courtesy Plastic Warrior.

England
Metal, Hollowcast
54mm standard (2-1/8")

Miscellaneous English Metal

by K. Warren Mitchell

The following pieces represent a variety of makers in Great Britain, of which there were many. Due to the restriction of their line or lack of reference materials, most get little recognition but are very collectible.

"Gypsy" caravan by Morestone. Comes with driver, woman, and detachable steps. (VG) $195.00.

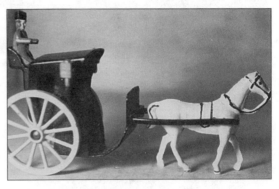

Hansom carriage by Morestone. Diecast driver. (VG) $65.00. (Undersized.)

Knights by Sacul. Chrome coated with real feather plumes and moveable visors. (VG) foot figures at $16.00 each, mounted at $24.00.

Ice cream tricycle by Morestone. (VG) $125.00.

TV characters by Sacul. Left: "Billy Bean"; Right: "Mr. Turnip." Average (VG) $25.00 each.

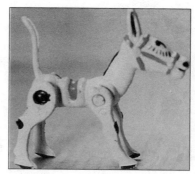

"Muffin the Mule" with moveable legs by Sacul. (VG) $20.00.

"Muffin the Mule" by Luntoy. Smaller than Sacul version and legs don't move. (VG) $20.00.

Rare Disney characters by Sacul. (VG) $100.00 each.

Arab leading camel by Noble. (VG) $35.00.

TV character "Sooty" by Luntoy (made for them by Barrett & Sons). (VG) $25.00.

Mounted by Reka (moveable arm). (VG) $20.00 each.

Left: Farm woman with buckets by Roydon. (VG) $12.00. Right: Babies, crawling and standing by Stoddart. (VG) $10.00 each.

Bersaglieri by Fry. (VG) $15.00.

Nurse by Fry. (VG) $15.00.

By Reka. (VG) $12.00 each.

"Bullock" brand artillery and searchlight by MSR. Although they made some figures, their guns are the most collectible. (W. Britains figures appear in photos for size comparison.) (VG) average $65.00 each.

England
Metal, Hollowcast
52-54mm standard
(approx. 2-1/8")

⚔ Taylor & Barrett ⚔

by K. Warren Mitchell

F.G. Taylor and the Barrett brothers (who had previously worked for Britains) formed their own company in 1920. The firm grew, employing many relatives, and prospered until metal supplies were cut off to nonessential industries at the start of World War II. The operation closed for the duration, and F.G. Taylor and A.R. Barrett divided the existing molds between them. With the end of the war, the old partners chose to go their own ways, rather than start up together again. F.G. Taylor & Sons operated until 1978, while A. Barrett & Sons existed until 1984.

Both before and after the war, the major areas of production seem to have been in civilian figures, with an extensive "zoo" line, and an interesting variety of wheeled vehicles. What with the addition of sons, expansion and split of partners, it's not always easy to tell who did what and when. For that reason, we've put everything under the one title here, "Taylor & Barrett," and given simple identification numbers to items. (They are not Taylor & Barrett's numbers, which, when given, follow after the code.)

Identification can usually be found under the base. The following is just a sampling of their more popular items.

MILITARY

XTB-1	Crawling bomber	$11.00
XTB-2	Standing firing	8.00
XTB-3	Officer saluting	9.00
XTB-4	Stand at ease	8.00
XTB-5	Present arms	8.00
XTB-6	Guard at attention	7.00
XTB-7	Marine at slope	10.00
XTB-8	Officer with binoculars	10.00
XTB-9	A.R.P. with brush and bucket	20.00

XTB-1

XTB-2

XTB-3

L to R: XTB-4, XTB-6.

L to R: XTB-8, XTB-5, XTB-7, XTB-9.

MISCELLANEOUS

XTB-100	Racing chariot	100.00
XTB-101	Rickshaw (4 pieces)	65.00
XTB-102	Indians in canoe (3 pieces)	40.00

XTB-100
Box.

XTB-100

XTB-102

XTB-103

XTB-101

XTB-104

XTB-105

XTB-106

XTB-107

XTB-108

XTB-109

*XTB-110
(1930 version,
minus hut).*

XTB-200

XTB-103	Racing sulky, driver and trotting horse	45.00
XTB-104	Window cleaner and barrow (4 pieces)	95.00
XTB-105	Baker and barrow (3 pieces)	125.00
XTB-106	Water cart (4 pieces)	225.00
XTB-107	Brewers dray (10 pieces)	350.00
XTB-108	Costermonger with cart, donkey, baskets	135.00
XTB-109	Milk float, milkman, horse, large urn	75.00
XTB-110	Donkey ride set (9 pieces)	125.00
XTB-200	Windmill	65.00
XTB-201	Rabbits and warren	50.00
XTB-202	Cat, kittens in basket	20.00
XTB-203	Blacksmith set (8 pieces)	65.00
XTB-204	Dovecoat with dove	12.00
XTB-205	Pump	12.00
XTB-206	Rabbit hutch	10.00
XTB-207	Bridge	14.00
XTB-208	Postman	15.00
XTB-209	Deck chair	65.00
XTB-210	Jazz band (11 pieces)	350.00
XTB-211	Pixie tea party (7 pieces)	100.00

XTB-201

XTB-202

XTB-203

XTB-204

XTB-205

XTB-206

XTB-207

XTB-208

Rare XTB-209.

XTB-210 With box.

ZOO

XTB-300	Seal pond (rare)	150.00
XTB-301	Girl on tortoise	40.00
XTB-302	Polar bear sitting	9.00
XTB-303	Polar bear walking	9.00
XTB-304	Polar bear cub	7.00
XTB-305	Llama cart ride (4 pieces)	100.00
XTB-306	Governess cart ride (6 pieces)	125.00
XTB-307	Girl visitor, hand in air	14.00
XTB-308	Elephant ride (7 pieces)	95.00
XTB-309	Elephant, trunk up	40.00
XTB-310	Elephant steps	35.00
XTB-311	Pay booth	30.00
XTB-312	Turnstile	30.00
XTB-313	Keeper carrying monkey	25.00

XTB-211 (still attached to card).

XTB-314	Zoo keeper	15.00
XTB-315	Tiger lying	9.00
XTB-316	Seated lioness	8.00

XTB-300 (visiting Timpo penguins).

XTB-301

Taylor & Barrett ✠ 239

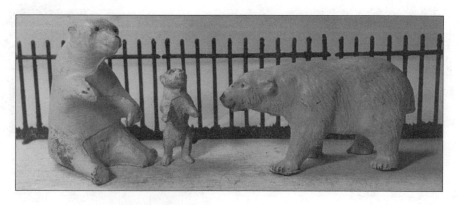

L to R: XTB-302, XTB-304, XTB-303.

XTB-305

L to R: XTB-306, XTB-307.

XTB-308

L to R:
XTB-309,
XTB-310,
XTB-314,
XTB-311.

L to R: XTB-311, XTB-314, XTB-312.

XTB-313

L to R: XTB-315, XTB-316.

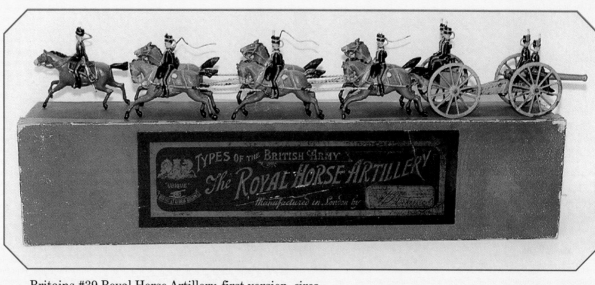

Britains #39 Royal Horse Artillery, first version, circa 1896. Courtesy Ray Haradin - Toys of Yesteryear.

Britains #2042 Prairie Schooner with escort and attacking Indians. Courtesy Ray Haradin - Toys of Yesteryear.

Britains #1521 Biplane with pilot and hangar, circa 1937. The box folds into an airplane hangar. Courtesy Ray Haradin - Toys of Yesteryear.

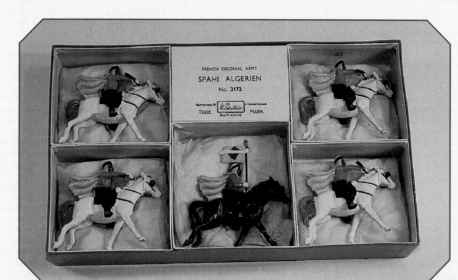

Britains #2172 Algerian Spahis. Courtesy Ray Haradin - Toys of Yesteryear.

This grouping is known variously as the Britains Family, the Edwardian Family, or the Victorian Family. Value as shown $7,000. Courtesy Arnold Rolak.

Britains unusual 2nd quality paint. Set came in a can (special promo?) with no label. Photo by Steve Balkin.

Left: Britains Two-Seater Coupe #1399 (rare); Right: Britains Mobile Police Car #1413. Courtesy Guernsey's.

Airfix U.S. Paratroopers. Value $1.50 each. Courtesy Paul Stadinger - Stad's.

L to R: CBG4, CBG5, CBG6. Charbens plastic British Grenadiers. Value $2.50 each. Courtesy *Plastic Warrior.*

L to R: CCW1, CCW2, CCW3. Charbens plastic Civil War. Value $6 each. Courtesy *Plastic Warrior.*

L to R: CJA1, CJA2, CJA3, CJA4. Charbens plastic WWII Japanese. Courtesy *Plastic Warrior.*

L to R: CRU1, CRU2, CRU3, CRU4. Charbens plastic Russians. Value $6 each. Courtesy *Plastic Warrior.*

L to R: CEX1, CEX2, CEX3, CEX4, CEX5. Cherilea's eye-catching Execution Set. Different officers (right) came with the set. 60mm. Value minimum of $100 for the set. Courtesy *Plastic Warrior*.

Cherilea Knight, value $25 (very hard to find). Photo by Paul Stadinger.

Cherilea's 60mm Wild West Saloon Set. Value minimum of $100 for the set. Courtesy *Plastic Warrior*.

Courtenay Knights.
L to R: H3, H13. Photo
by Bob Hornung.

Johillco boxed set of
Finnish ski soldiers.
Value as shown $1000.
Courtesy Bill O'Brien
and Norman Joplin.

THE
SKI·ING PATROL
Types of Finland's Heroic "Ghost" Army
MADE IN ENGLAND

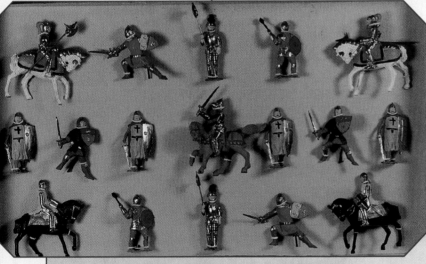

A Johillco set circa the 1950s. The box top
reads "Buckingham Cast Metal Toys–Finest
English Hand Painted Figures Made To
Scale–Made in England Expressly For Macy
Associates." The sales slip, with only a "Nov.
25" date, shows the set sold for $3.07. Photo by
William A. Hankins.

Timpo swoppet
Eskimo kayak.
Value $20.
Photo by Paul
Stadinger -Stad's.

Lucotte Foreign Cavalry, L to R: Saxon Lt. Cavalry, Westphalian Garde du Corps, Westphalian Bugler, Vistula Legion Officer, Guard of Honor of Prince Berthier, Guides of Murat Officer, Hussars of Murat. Photo by Lenoir Josey.

Lucotte French Line Cavalry, L to R: Hussars, 1st Regt. Bugler, 2nd, 3rd, 4th Elite Bugler, 5th Elite Officer, 6th Trooper. Photo by Lenoir Josey.

Mignot Zoo Diorama - monkey house (rare). Courtesy Guernsey's.

Timpo swoppet Apache. Value $8.
Photo by Paul Stadinger - Stad's.

Timpo Cossack. Value $25.
Photo by Paul Stadinger -
Stad's.

Wend-Al Toy Town figures. Originally designed by Quiralu, the molds for these figures were bought by Wend-Al. This is the second version, painted by convicts. Value as shown $400. Courtesy Joseph F. Saine. Photo by Mark Packo.

Lucotte Imperial Guard Cavalry, L to R: Horse Grenadier Flag, Bugler, and Kettledrummer;
Empress' Dragoon Kettledrummer, Bugler, and Flag. Photo by Lenoir Josey.

Mignot Indian Encampment (rare). Courtesy Guernsey's.

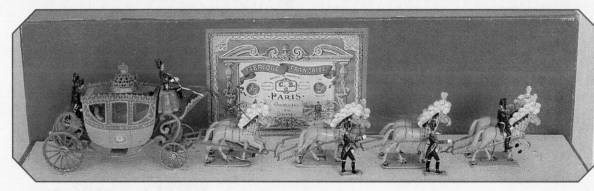

Mignot Emperor's Coach (rare). Courtesy Guernsey's.

Mignot Chariot of Ramses II with Escort. Photo by Sierotys.

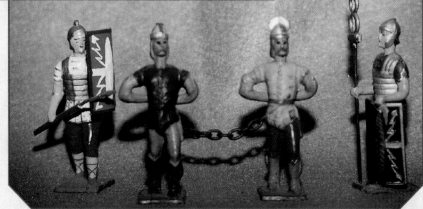

Mignot Romans with Captive Gauls. Photo by Will Beierwaltes.

Mignot vehicles, L to R: Civilian, French, U.S., Prussian. Photo by Hansens.

Superstarlux Marshal LaSalle (boxed) and Starlux Napoleon. Photo by Will Beierwaltes.

54mm aluminum soldiers by France's Quiralu. They are fastened to the card. The flagbearer is missing his flag. Photo by Robert D. Worthen.

Vertunni Napoleon Etat Major. Photo by Will Beierwaltes.

Nicely done French plastic coffee premiums. L to R: "Light Foot" and "Big Fisherman" by Café Lesal; "Robinson Crusoe" by Café Martin. Courtesy *Plastic Warrior*.

Elastolin plastic variations: Sir Gawain, L to R: 1st version, stained; 2nd version, painted; 3rd version, pink plastic. Prince Valiant, L to R: 1st version, sword down (very rare); 1st version, sword out (scarce). Courtesy Joseph F. Saine. Photo by Mark Packo.

Lineol and Elastolin personality figures. Courtesy Jack Matthews.

Collectors agree that these 13 British Grenadiers, which were imported to the U.S. by Kresge about 1937, are German-made. For some years, collectors had thought these came from Lineol, but that theory has been disputed, since they are cruder than Lineol's line. They stand about 2-1/2 inches high, and at the 1995 Chicago Toy Soldier Show, this set was sold for $275. Photo by Bill Nutting.

Heyde assorted Indian Encampment pieces. Photo by Steve Balkin.

Heyde rare Ostrich Hunt and Native Boy Crawling upon Giraffe. Photo by Steve Balkin.

Heyde assorted Polar Expedition figures. Photo by Steve Balkin.

A circa 1790s Polish revolutionary. It was made from excess plastic from toilet seat and wash basin production. Maker was Polish, but is otherwise unknown. Value $4. Courtesy Paul Stadinger - Stad's.

Durso Tarzan group. Tarzan worth about $200, the others about $125, and the tree $65. Courtesy Joseph F. Saine. Photo by Mark Packo.

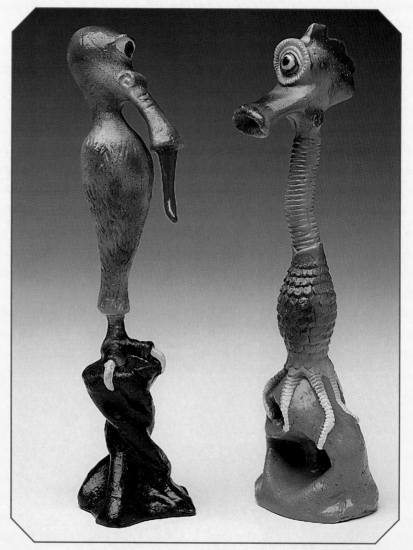

Rarely found Durso Martians, 9 inches high. Slow sales for these composition figures saw just a six-month production period in 1962. A must-have for the space collector, they are valued at $200 each. Courtesy Joseph F. Saine. Photo by Mark Packo.

MIM, L to R: Napoleon, Mounted Grenadier.
Photo by Will Beierwaltes.

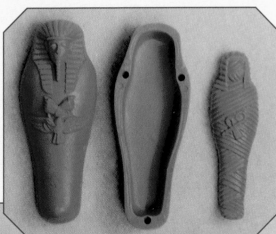

Atlantic Mummy.
Value $2.
Courtesy Paul
Stadinger - Stad's.

Atlantic Japanese. Value $2 each. Courtesy
Paul Stadinger - Stad's.

The Volkswagen from the Atlantic Hitler-S.S. set.
Hitler could stand in its back. Courtesy *Plastic
Warrior*.

SAE, L to R: From Milicast Set 1500, Swiss Infantry on
Parade 1945; From Milicast Set 2085, German African
Corps in Action 1942; From Milicast Set 1575, Albanian
Infantry Parade 1914. All 54mm. Photo by Vadis Godbey.

Three Italian Bersaglieri Musicians. SAE numbers unknown. 54mm. Photo by Vadis Godbey.

SAE. Left: C3321 - Trooper 1st Skinner's Horse; Right: C3305 - Trooper 15th Bengal Lancers. Both 54mm. Photo by Vadis Godbey.

SAE, L to R: C1781 - Trooper Polish Legion Lancers; C1760 - Napoleon Bonaparte; SAE # unknown - Royal Canadian Mounted Police. All 54mm. Photo by Vadis Godbey.

Minikin Samurai plus mounted Tamerlane. Photo by Will Beierwaltes.

Mexico's Garcia Plastics produced these plastic figures. The painted ones sell for $2 each, the unpainted $1 each. Courtesy Paul Stadinger - Stad's.

L to R: LC1, LC2, LC3. Llardo of Spain produced these striking plastic, hand-painted 100mm (approx. 4-1/4-inch) cowboys. Value $15 each. Courtesy Paul Stadinger - Stad's.

L to R: LK1, LK2, LK3. Llardo of Spain produced these 90mm (3-9/16-inch) plastic Knights. Value $20 each. Courtesy Paul Stadinger - Stad's

Jecsan plastic Western Woman. Value $15. Courtesy Paul Stadinger - Stad's.

L to R: RI1, RI2, RI3, RI4. Rubber Indians and Cowboy by Barcelona's Reamsa. The middle two are copies of Britains. Value $5 each. Courtesy *Plastic Warrior*.

Reamsa plastic Arab from its Lawrence of Arabia set. Value $25. Courtesy Paul Stadinger - Stad's.

Reamsa Knight, plastic. Value $15. Courtesy Paul Stadinger - Stad's.

England
Metal, Hollowcast
54mm standard (approx. 2-1/8")

✕ **Timpo** ✕

by K. Warren Mitchell

Timpo Toys was formed in the mid 1940s by Ally Gee and Solly Lander. The original products were wood and composition toys until 1946, when, following the war, metal was again available. Figures produced until 1950 were from all prewar molds purchased from Stoddart and Kew, plus composition figures. From 1950 on, Timpo developed its own figures and style. It tried flock coating on guards' hats and animals for awhile, with limited appeal.

Timpo's style of full bodies and animation, plus colorful painting, made for a generally "fun" figure.

Among the most collectible series are U.S. GIs, West Point Cadets, Wild West and Big Game Hunt. Their "Farm" series and Wild West would appear to be exact copies of the prewar larger German composition figures, reduced to 54mm, and done in metal. By 1960, the company was converting over to plastic figures, using the exact same poses as metal.

The name is usually found under the base. *Prices are given for soldiers in very good condition.*

L to R: Timpo metal, prewar; German composition.

L to R: Timpo metal, prewar; German composition.

U.S. ARMY AND NAVY

No.	Description	VG
9000	At ease	$12.00
9000A	As Negro	35.00
9001	Marching	12.00
9001A	As Negro	35.00
9002	Observer	14.00
9003	Mine Detector	14.00
9004	Crawling	12.00
9005	Officer with map	10.00
9006	Field Telephone	10.00
9007	Despatch Rider	30.00
9008	Walkie-Talkie	10.00
9009	Officer	12.00
9010	On Guard	14.00
9010A	As Negro	35.00

L to R: #9000, #9000A, #9001, #9001A.

#9002

L to R: #9003, #9004.

#9005

#9006

#9007 (detachable).

#9008

#9009

L to R: #9010, #9010A, #9011.

No.	Description	VG
9011	Firing Standing	12.00
9012	Mortar Unit (3 pieces)	25.00
9013	Charging	14.00
9014	Grenade Thrower	12.00
9015	Tommy Gunner	12.00
9016	Bazooka	10.00
9017	Machine Gunner	13.00
9018	Firing kneeling	10.00
9019	Firing lying	12.00
9020	Ceremonial marching	12.00
9021	Standard Bearer	18.00
9022	Ceremonial Officer	14.00
9023	Washing	12.00
9024	Stretcher Unit (3 pieces)	40.00
9025	Wounded walking	14.00
9026	Eating	10.00
9027	Sailor walking	12.00
9028	Sailor with Telescope	18.00

#9012
(3 piece).

#9013

No.	Description	VG
9029	Sailor on Guard	15.00
9030	Naval Officer	10.00
9032	Military Police	15.00
XT-1	Frogman with Knife	20.00

#9017

L to R: #9014, #9015, #9016.

L to R: #9018, #9019.

L to R: #9020, #9022, #9021.

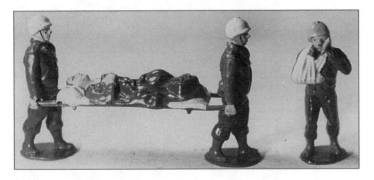

L to R: #9024 (3 pieces), #9025.

L to R: #9026, #9023.

L to R: #9029, #9028, #9027, #9030.

#9032

XT-1 Frogman.

BRITISH SOLDIERS

No.	Description	VG
1	Kneeling Firing	$10.00
2	Standing Firing	10.00
3	Lying Firing	10.00
4	On Rocks Firing	12.00
5	Crawling	10.00
6	Grenade Thrower	10.00
7	Officer Pointing	10.00
8	Charging, Running	10.00
9	Charging, Bending	10.00
10	Charging to Kill	12.00
XT-2	Rare Doctor from set #CU74	40.00

L to R: #1, #7, #9, #2.

XT-2 Doctor.

L to R: #4, #6, #8, #10.

WILD WEST

Note: All riders detachable from horses.

No.	Description	VG
WW2000	Mounted Cowboy (two-gun)	$15.00
WW2001	Mounted Cowboy (rifle on back)	16.00
WW2002	Buffalo Bill (on horse)	35.00
WW2003	Mounted Sheriff (with whip)	18.00
WW2004	Mounted Cowboy (with lasso)	15.00
WW2005	Mounted Cowboy (hands bound)	15.00
WW2006	Mounted Cowboy (fatigued)	15.00
WW2007	Mounted Cowboy (lassoing wild horse)	20.00
WW2008	Mounted Cowboy (surrendering)	15.00
WW2009	Mounted Cowboy (wounded)	18.00

Early box label.

1st Version Western Set. Circa 1946 using stoddart-made figures.

L to R: WW2000, WW2001.

WW2002

WW2003 (minus whip).

WW2004

L to R: WW2006, WW2005.

WW2009

WW2007

WW2008

WW2012

WW2010

WW2011

No.	Description	VG	No.	Description	VG
WW2010	Mounted Indian (with shield)	15.00	XT-3	Wild West Wagon with two Horses and Cowboy	85.00
WW2011	Mounted Cowboy (firing rifle)	16.00	2021	Indian large tom-tom	10.00
WW2012	Cowboy tied to tree	16.00	2022	Indian small tom-tom	10.00
WW2013	Mounted Indian with bow	15.00	2023	Indian Walking	10.00
WW2014	Mounted Indian with spear	15.00	2024	Indian with Rifle	10.00
WW2015	Standing Indian with bow	10.00	2025	Chief Standing	10.00
WW2016	Kneeling Indian with bow	10.00	2026	Chief Sitting	10.00
WW2017	Two sitting Cowboys with campfire (3 pieces)	20.00	2027	Sheriff Standing	10.00
WW2018	Indian crawling	10.00	2028	Timpo Tim	12.00
WW2019	Indian running	10.00	2029	Slim	12.00
WW2020	Canadian Mounted Police	15.00	2030	Bandit Right	10.00
			2031	Bandit Left	10.00
			2032	U.S. Mail	12.00
			2033	Squaw	12.00
			2034	Cowboy tied to Tree Trunk	20.00

WW2013

L to R: WW2015, WW2018.

WW2017 (3 pieces).

WW2019

XT-3

#2022

L to R: #2027, #2030.

#2033

#2100

L to R: #2101, #2102, #2103.

#2029

HOPALONG CASSIDY

No.	Description	VG
2100	Hopalong, standing	$30.00
2101	Hopalong, fighting	30.00
2102	Lucky, standing	25.00
2103	California, standing	25.00
2104	Hopalong, mounted	40.00
2105	Lucky, mounted	35.00
2106	California, mounted	35.00

WEST POINT CADETS

No.	Description	VG
7000	Drum Major	$12.00
7001	Fifer	10.00
7002	Side Drummer	10.00
7003	Cymbal	10.00
7004	Bugler	10.00
7005	Trumpet	10.00
7006	Trombone	10.00
7007	Tuba	10.00
7008	Bass Drummer	12.00
7009	Flag Bearer	17.00
7010	Officer marching with sword	10.00
7011	Present Arms	10.00
7012	Marching	10.00
7013	At Ease	10.00
7014	Firing Standing	10.00
7015	Firing Kneeling	10.00
7016	Mounted	20.00
7017	Officer Walking	10.00
7018	Officer Saluting	12.00
7019	Officer at Ease	12.00

Note: 7005 has 2 hands on trumpet, compared to 7004.

#2104
(wrong horse).

L to R: #7000, #7003, #7002, #7008.

L to R: #7004, #7006, #7010, #7011, #7012.

L to R: #7007, #7001.

#7009

L to R: #7013, #7017, #7014, #7015.

#7018

#7019

#3002

L to R: #3008, #3004.

L to R: #3018, #3019.

XT-4

GUARDS

No.	Description	VG
3000	Drum Major	$12.00
3001	Guard Fifer	10.00
3002	Drummer	10.00
3003	Cymbal	10.00
3004	Bearer with Flag	17.00
3005	Bugler	10.00
3006	Trombone	10.00
3007	Bass drummer with drum	12.00
3008	Officer	10.00
3009	Present Arms	9.00
3010	Marching	8.00
3011	Shooting	9.00
3012	Kneeling	9.00
3013	Lying	9.00
3014	Tuba	10.00
3015	R. H. G. Standing	10.00
3016	R. H. G. Officer	17.00
3017	R. H. G. Private	17.00
3018	Scot. Officer	15.00
3019	Scot. Marching	10.00
3020	Scot. Piper	15.00
XT-4	Guards Officer	25.00

Note: Headpieces came smooth or flocked.

KNIGHTS IN ARMOUR

No.	Description	VG
KN50	Knight Mounted with Sword	$15.00
KN51	Knight Mounted with Spear	15.00
KN52	Knight Standing Visor Open	10.00
KN53	Knight Standing Visor Shut	10.00
KN54	Knight Standing with Sword	10.00

Note: At times, these figures were given colored feathers (as plumes) that fit into airhole at top of helmet.

Ivanhoe Series

A series of seven detachable mounted knights. Each carried detachable lance and shield, visor moved, and colored brush hair plume. Each had colors of surcoat and shield to match horse cover color.

No.	Description	VG
KN55	Ivanhoe (all black)	$25.00
KN56	Sir de Bois-Guilbert (blue on white)	20.00
KN57	Sir Hugh de Bracy	20.00

L to R: KN50, KN51.

L to R: KN52, KN53, KN54.

No.	Description	VG
KN58	Front de Boeuf	20.00
KN59	Philip de Malvoisin	20.00
KN60	Ralph de Vipont (red on yellow)	20.00
KN61	Crusader (cross on shield)	20.00

King Arthur Series

Basically the same as Ivanhoe figures, in different color combinations; plus King Arthur and four knights on foot.

No.	Description	VG
KN70-77	Various mounted knights, each	$20.00
KN78	King Arthur, mounted	30.00
KN79	Sir Lancelot (all red) on foot	18.00
KN80	Sir Mordred (all black) on foot	18.00
KN81	Simon on foot	15.00
KN82	Lambert on foot	15.00
KN83	King Arthur on foot, crown, sword up	25.00

Quentin Durward Series

No.	Description	VG
HF500	Quentin Durward, mounted	$25.00
HF501	Phillip de Creville, mounted	25.00
HF502	Duke's guard, mounted	20.00
HF503	Duke's guard, standing with lance	12.00
HF504	Phillip de Creville on foot	17.00
HF505	Quentin Durward on foot	20.00
HF506	William de la Marck on foot	17.00
HF507	Gluckmeister on foot	20.00
HF508	Landsknecht with musket	18.00
HF509	Landsknecht with crossbow	18.00
HF510	Royal Guard, standing with lance	12.00

Note: All weapons were detachable, and either plastic or metal.

KN60

KN75

L to R: KN80, KN83.

L to R: KN81 (sword), KN8 (mace).

L to R: HF500, HF503, HF502.

HF505

L to R: HF506, HF508 (no weapon).

HF509

POLICE FORCE

No.	Description	VG
6150	Traffic Policeman	$10.00
6151	Standing Policeman	8.00
6152	Walking Policeman	8.00
6153	Police Inspector	8.00
6154	Mobile Policeman	30.00
6155	Mounted Policeman	22.00
6156	Police Woman	10.00

L to R: #6151, #6156, #6152.

#6153

#6155

RAILWAY FIGURES

No.	Description	VG
8000	Station Master	$12.00
8001	R.W. Guard	10.00
8002	R.W. Signalman	12.00
8003	R.W. Porter with barrow (2 pieces)	14.00
8004	R.W. Porter with luggage	11.00
8005	R.W. Porter with whistle	10.00
8006	Mother and Child	13.00
8007	Girl	10.00
8008	Boy	10.00
8009	Sailor	20.00
8010	Soldier	20.00
8011	Hiker	20.00

L to R: #8005, #8017, #8012, #8014, #8016.

#8010

L to R: XT-5 Beefeater (no weapon), footman with sword, outrider. (VG) $8.00 each.

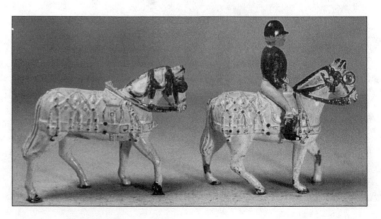

XT-5 Horses and rider (4 pair to set).

No.	Description	VG
8012	Commercial Traveler	10.00
8013	Business Man	10.00
8014	Mr. Brown	10.00
8015	Mrs. Green	10.00
8016	Mr. Smith	11.00
8017	Mrs. Smith	11.00

CIRCUS

No.	Description	VG
6000	Gypsy Organ Grinder with Bear	$55.00
6100	Clown Conductor	20.00

XT-5 Coronation Coach, 8 horses with 4 riders. (VG) $125.00.

#6000

No.	Description	VG
6101	Clown Flute	20.00
6102	Clown Accordion	20.00
6103	Clown Fiddle	20.00
6104	Circus Ringmaster	17.00
6105	Circus Horse	17.00
6106	Bare Back Rider	20.00

ZOO

No.	Description	VG
MZ4000	Elephant	$20.00
MZ4001	Baby Elephant	10.00
MZ4002	Camel	8.00
MZ4003	Giraffe	12.00
MZ4004	Hippopotamus	10.00
MZ4005	Rhinoceros	10.00
MZ4006	Lion	8.00
MZ4007	Lioness	8.00
MZ4008	Tiger	9.00
MZ4009	Monkey	7.00
MZ4010	Monkey on Tree	10.00

L to R: #6100, #6101, #6103.

MZ4001

MZ4002

MZ4003

MZ4000

MZ4004

L to R: MZ4008, MZ4020, MZ4010.

MZ4009

MZ4011

L to R: MZ4016, MZ4024, MZ4012.

MZ4027

MZ4028

MZ4029

MZ4050

MZ4051

MZ4052

No.	Description	VG	No.	Description	VG
MZ4011	Mountain Goat	8.00	MZ4025	Pelican	7.00
MZ4012	Stag	10.00	MZ4026	Eagle	7.00
MZ4013	Bear, Standing	10.00	MZ4027	Bison	15.00
MZ4014	Bear, Walking	10.00	MZ4028	Texas Longhorn	15.00
MZ4015	Baby Bear	6.00	MZ4029	Indian Water Buffalo	12.00
MZ4016	Kangaroo	6.00	MZ4050	Zoo Keeper	12.00
MZ4017	Sea Lion	5.00	MZ4051	Zoo Inspector	10.00
MZ4018	Tortoise	5.00	MZ4052	Zoo Sweepers	12.00
MZ4019	Crocodile	12.00			
MZ4020	Squirrel	9.00			

FARM ANIMALS AND FIGURES

No.	Description	VG
MZ4021	Zebra	7.00
MZ4022	Penguin	4.00
MZ4023	Stork	4.00
MZ4024	Ostrich	7.00

No.	Description	VG
MF1000	Cow, standing	$4.00
MF1001	Cow, mooing	5.00
MF1002	Cow, feeding	4.00
MF1003	Bull, standing	5.00
MF1004	Shire Horse, standing	5.00

MF1000

MF1001

MF1002

MF1003

MF1004

MF1005

MF1006

MF1007

MF1008

No.	Description	VG	No.	Description	VG
MF1005	Shire Horse, feeding	5.00	MF1030	Milkmaid, sitting	8.00
MF1006	Horse, standing	4.00	MF1031	Milkmaid, walking	8.00
MF1007	Shire colt	4.00	MF1032	Woman, haymaking	8.00
MF1008	Calf, standing	4.00	MF1033	Woman, feeding chicks	8.00
MF1009	Calf, turning head	4.00	MF1034	Scarecrow	10.00
MF1010	Sheep, standing	3.00	MF1035	Hurdle	4.00
MF1011	Sheep, feeding	3.00	MF1036	Trough	3.00
MF1012	Sheep, lying	3.00	MF1037	Bench	4.00
MF1013	Lambs	3.00	MF1038	Hedge and Bush	5.00
MF1014	Sheep Dog	4.00	MF1039	Tree	9.00
MF1015	Goat	4.00	MF1041	Bucket	2.00
MF1016	Pig, standing	3.00	MF1042	Churn	3.00
MF1017	Sow with Piglets	8.00	MF1043	Large Tree	11.00
MF1018	Piglets	3.00	MF1044	Small Tree	8.00
MF1019	Goose	3.00	MF1045	Gander, Wild	3.00
MF1020	Gander	3.00	MF1046	Donkey	4.00
MF1021	Cockerel	3.00	MF1047	Farmer leading Bull	20.00
MF1022	Chicken, standing	3.00	MF1048	Turkey Hen	3.00
MF1023	Chicken, feeding	3.00	MF1049	Turkey Cock	3.00
MF1024	Hen, brooding	3.00		Farmcart with horse	25.00
MF1025	Chicks, 2 on base	5.00		Watercart with Horse	35.00
MF1026	Farmer with Wheelbarrow	12.00		Logwagon with Horses	50.00
MF1027	Man Haymaker	8.00		Farm Roller with Horse and Farmer	40.00
MF1028	Drover	9.00		Farm Harrow with Horse and Farmer	40.00
MF1029	Shepherd	9.00			

MF1009

MF1010

MF1011

MF1012

MF1013

MF1014

MF1015

MF1016

MF1017

MF1018

MF1019

MF1020

MF1021

MF1022

MF1023

MF1024

MF1025

L to R: MF1026, MF1029, MF1034.

L to R: MF1032, MF1031, MF1033, MF1027.

L to R: MF1047, MF1028.

ARCTIC SET

No.	Description	VG
XT6	Sled pulled by 5 pair of dogs	$25.00
XT7	Man with whip	25.00
XT8	Man with slung rifle	25.00
XT9	Man firing rifle	25.00
XT10	Igloo	25.00
XT11	Polar Bear	10.00
XT12	Seal	10.00
XT13	Penguin	7.00
	Complete set, boxed, (VG)	225.00

L to R: XT7, XT6.

L to R: XT10, XT7, XT8, XT9.

BIG GAME HUNTING SET

No.	Description	VG
XT14	Elephant, trunk up	$35.00
XT15	Elephant, trunk down	30.00
XT16	Howdah	10.00
XT17	Maharajah	15.00
XT18	White hunter	20.00
XT19	Elephant boys	20.00
XT20	Native with spear	18.00
XT21	Tiger	15.00
XT22	Tiger, wounded by spear	20.00
XT23	Tantor the elephant and Tarzan, boxed (VG)	60.00
	Complete Set, 14 figures, boxed (VG)	295.00

L to R: XT11, XT12, XT13.

Riders, L to R: XT17 in XT16, XT19; Elephant: XT15.

Riders, L to R: XT17 in XT16, XT19; Elephant: XT14.

L to R: XT20, XT22.

XT23

✕ **Timpo Plastic** ✕

According to *Plastic Warrior's* "Timpo Solid Figures," Timpo's first plastic soldiers probably began about 1953, aside from earlier lances made for their metal medieval figures. The first designs for specific plastic production seem to date from about 1955, but possibly a few years later. Alas, the second phase employed chalk in the plastic to help paint to adhere, with the result as the years wore on that many pieces have become extremely brittle. Most of the plastic design was by Norman Tooth. Other sculptors included Roy Selwyn-Smith and (a few pieces) Peter Rogerson.

Timpo Foreign Legionnaires and Arabs. All but the mounted Arab at bottom right were made in 1957 in a plastic that becomes fragile with time (note the nearly broken-off rifle and sword at top left). The figure at bottom right, sold in the 1970s, is of a better grade of plastic, but isn't as well sculpted. Arabs on camels worth $20.00 mint, foot figures $9.00 in mint.

L to R: TA1, TA2, TA3, TA4, TA5, TA6. Timpo plastic swoppet Arabs. Value $10.00 each foot, $15.00 mounted. Photo by Gary J. Linden.

L to R: N1, N2, N3. Timpo 54mm soft plastic Napoleonic figures. Value $6.00 each in mint. Photo by Gary J. Linden.

L to R: C1, C2. Timpo 55mm soft plastic Cossacks. Value $10.00 each in mint. Photo by Gary J. Linden.

Timpo 7th Cavalry, foot. Value $2.50 each. Photo by Joseph F. Saine.

Timpo swoppet-style Civil War Gatling gun and crew. Value $18.00. Photo by Joseph F. Saine.

Timpo 7th Cavalry. Value $5.00 each. Photo by Joseph F. Saine.

Timpo Chariot. Value $75.00. Photo by Joseph F. Saine.

Timpo Mexican, mounted. Value $15.00. Photo by Paul Stadinger.

Timpo swoppet-style Civil War, mounted. Value $6.00 each. Photo by Joseph F. Saine.

Timpo solid Roman. Value $30.00. Photo by Paul Stadinger - Stad's.

Timpo foot Vikings, value $8.00 each. Timpo Siege Tower, value $40.00. Photo by Joseph F. Saine.

Timpo swoppet-style foot Knights of the Great Helm. Value $15.00 each. Photo by Joseph F. Saine.

Timpo swoppet-style mounted Romans. The standard bearer is worth $50.00; the rest $13.00 each. Photo by Joseph F. Saine.

Timpo swoppet-style foot Knights of the Great Helm. Value $15.00 each. Photo by Joseph F. Saine.

Timpo "Action Pack" of Civil War figures. Value $5.00 mint. Photo by Joseph F. Saine.

Timpo mounted Knights of the Great Helm, swoppet style. Value $25.00 each. Photo by Joseph F. Saine.

Timpo swoppet-style foot Romans. Value $8.00 each. Photo by Joseph F. Saine.

Timpo swoppet Eskimo kayak. Value $20.00. Photo by Paul Stadinger.

Timpo swoppet Apache. Value $8.00. Photo by Paul Stadinger—Stad's.

Timpo Cossack. Value $25.00. Photo by Paul Stadinger.

England
Aluminum, Solidcast
54mm standard (2-1/8")

✕ Wend-Al ✕

by K. Warren Mitchell

Formed in 1947. Dies were purchased by the owners from Quiralu of France. With initial help from experienced French labor, they started the production of aluminum toy soldiers. When the French casters and painters returned home, Wend-Al had difficulties maintaining the fast production needed to compete with plastic. It's reported that to keep costs down, some production was done at Lewes Prison, using prison labor. Wend-Al tried making the line more appealing by "flocking" some pieces, and even tried plastic production for awhile. Cost of material and competition from plastic led to the end of its catalogued line in 1956. Wendan Manufacturing Co., Ltd., the true name of the company, is said to still be in operation, doing some custom and contract work.

Identification is not easy. Original figures had stick-on labels under bases, which usually fell off in time. *Prices for a foot figure in very good condition range from $10-12 each. Mounted figures in similar condition range from $18-22 each.*

L to R: Cowboy with guitar, Cowboy tied to post.

Cowboys fighting.

L to R: Life Guard, Horse Guard. Photo by Will Beierwaltes.

Life Guard Band. Photo by Will Beierwaltes.

Big Game Hunter.

Salvation Army Band (in red jackets). Photo by Will Beierwaltes.

L to R: Life Guard Standard, Lancer, Scots Greys Drummer. Photo by Will Beierwaltes.

L to R: Drum Major, Boy Scouts. Photo by Will Beierwaltes.

France

France
Metal, Solidcast
55mm standard (approx. 2-1/4")

✕ Lucotte (Maison Lucotte) ✕

by Lenoir Josey

Founded in 1840, Maison Lucotte was originally a small Parisian manufacturer of high quality lead, tin and pewter ware. At the turn of the century, its retail shop, known as Au Plat d'Etain, was located in the same building as its factory at 39, rue des Sts. Peres, Paris. Apparently being motivated by the success of its next door neighbor, Maison E. Sandre, a maker and retailer of toy soldiers since 1866, Lucotte began production of very high quality solidcast 55mm infantry and 75mm cavalry in 1903-04.

The first Lucottes were First Empire or French Revolutionary figures at attention, marching and in action. Since Lucottes were manufactured by plugging and soldering a number of separate molded parts to a standard body, much variation in pose and uniform was possible. Apparently, all regiments of French Napoleonic troops were produced and in many different poses. The most common infantry pose was marching at the slope, though early figures are often at present arms, at ease, firing, assaulting or loading the musket. The most common cavalryman is on a walking horse, though standing horses were available in the early years and rare trotting horses are known. A galloping horse was added around 1913, when the firm was bought by M. Margat. All riders were removable from their horses, as were all saddles, except on the Margat walking horse of 1913.

In the early 1900s, the very popular "Napoleon and his Marshals" series was introduced. These could be purchased singly or in boxes of six, 12, 18 or 24. The figures were specially painted to a finer degree and were, consequently, more expensive. Foreign troops, such as British, Austrians and Germans, were also added very early as were mounted and foot artillery teams and train. A series of contemporary French infantry and cavalry was also added in the early years and greatly expanded in scope and popularity immediately before and during World War I to include all regiments of French and foreign World War I troops.

In the mid- to late 1920s, either just before or just after the sale of the company to Mignot, Lucottes were remodeled to a slightly fuller and more realistic figure, and a new fuller walking horse was created. The painting of Lucotte figures during its first year or so was slightly crude, but thereafter it became not only very fine but also historically accurate, due to the specially commissioned prints that the small factory followed meticulously (until after the sale to C.B.G. Mignot in 1928 when painting guides were used). Production during World War II is rare and much less finely executed. Post-World War II Lucottes are meticulously, but not as accurately, painted (usually in high gloss).

Lucottes were boxed in handsome red boxes with large, colorful Maison Lucotte labels and yellow tie cards. After Mignot's 1928 purchase, the new labels mention no firm, but do bear the LC trademark. Infantry was sold in sets of 12 (including one officer, flag and drum or cornet), 17 (with four more infantrymen plus a mounted officer), 18 (two more infantry minus the mounted officer) and 23 or 24 (with or without the mounted officer). Infantry bands of 12 or 18 figures were also produced, as were sets of the "Heads of Columns" consisting of sapeurs, drummers and fifers. Sometimes, very large sets of a regiment were produced and were packaged in four or more boxes of 18-24 figures each.

Cavalry could be bought in boxes of one, six or 12. The boxes of six were the most popular and consisted of a bugler and five troopers, though different configurations were prevalent in the early years. Post-World War II sets usually had an officer, flag, bugler and three to six troopers. Large boxes of cavalry are known, but are very rare, probably due to the weight of the solid-lead figures and their cost. Mounted bands were also made and are generally six or 12 figures, including a band leader.

Reproductions of Lucottes abound; though generally of good quality, the collector and novice must be on guard. They are not considered Lucottes and, although offered at Lucotte prices, are not considered to be of equal value. They can be recognized by:

- Usually being of lighter weight
- Having a speckled lead texture or grey paint on the underside of the base
- Having less rigid parts, due to a different lead mix

- Sometimes being slightly smaller scale, due to being recast
- Usually having a Lucotte emblem embossed on the base of the infantry figure.

Total repaints are less common, since a scuffed-up Lucotte is worth more than a repainted one. Unfortunately many Lucottes, due to age, are partially repainted. If the repainting is only the plume or sword, value is not damaged, as in the repainting of the body or face, which compromises the integrity of the figure. In excellent condition, Lucotte foot figures begin at $25 and cavalry at $50, and generally average around $50 and $100, respectively.

The easiest way to recognize a Lucotte is by finding its trademark of "LC" with a bee in the middle on a figure's base. However, most Lucottes were not stamped with the mark, so the next easiest method is to check the shoulder area of the figure to determine if the arm and head are "plugged" to the body. Only a few rare World War I Lucottes had arms molded to the body, while all post-World War II-manufactured Lucottes have the separately cast arms soldered to the body. These late soldered Lucottes can be further identified by their high gloss paint, whereas earlier Lucottes are usually more dull. The earliest Lucotte infantry had smaller heads and plumes than later figures, while the earliest cavalrymen (for a short time) sported Edwardian mustaches and beards and had horses with wire reins and green bases, vs. the more common moveable reins and beige bases.

For additional information on Lucottes, the reader should pursue the author's 1995 series of articles in the *Old Toy Soldier Newsletter,* Vol. 19, Nos. 1-3. Photos by Lenoir Josey and K. Warren Mitchell.

Elite Horse Gendarmes. L to R: Flagbearer, Bugler (to 1806), Kettle Drummer, Bugler (after 1806), Musician. Photo by Lenoir Josey.

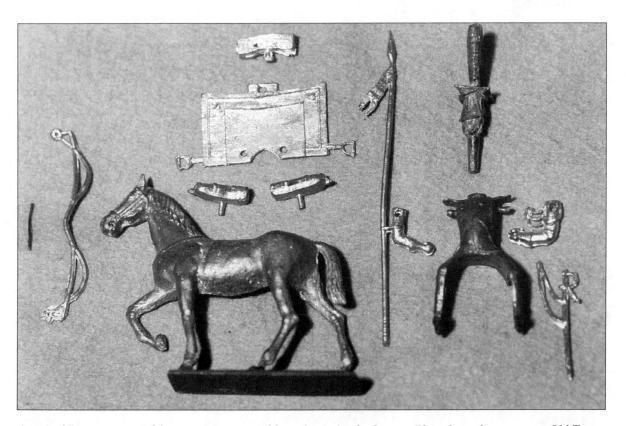

A typical Lucotte mounted figure prior to assembly and painting by factory. Photo by author, courtesy Old Toy Soldier Newsletter.

Note the right heel position. Photo by K. Warren Mitchell.

Logo under base on some figures. Also appeared raised on top of some bases. Photo by K. Warren Mitchell.

Lucotte horses. Note moveable reins. Photo by author, courtesy Old Toy Soldier Newsletter.

L to R: Marshal Murat, ADC to Marshal Ney, Marshal Ney, Napoleon with a Mameluk attendant, Marshal Poniatowski, Emperor Francis I of Austria, Tsar Alexander of Russia. Photo by Lenoir Josey.

General officer 1st version reins of twisted wire. Photo by K. Warren Mitchell.

L to R: English 7th Hussar Officer, English 7th Dragoon Guard, English Life Guard Officer, Austrian Horse Artillery, Silesian 2nd Hussars, Russian Cossack. Photo by Lenoir Josey.

Top, L to R: Grenadier of 1st Regt.; Grenadier of 1st, drummer; Grenadier of 1st, drum major; Grenadier of 1st, musician (1st version); Grenadier of 1st, musician (2nd version); Grenadier of 1st, sapeur with axe. Bottom, L to R: Grenadier of 1st, field uniform; Grenadier of 1st, officer; Dutch Grenadier de la Garde, 1905 musician; Dutch Grenadier de la Garde, 1912 fifer; Voltigeur - Chasseur de la Garde; Chasseur - Pied Drum Major. Photo by Lenoir Josey.

L to R: 1st Regt. Light Horse Lancer, 2nd Regt. Light Horse Bugler, 5th Regt. Light Horse Officer, 30th Regt. Lancer, 30th Regt. Lancer's Bugler, Lancer Gendarmes of Spain. Photo by Lenoir Josey.

Marine de la Garde. Photo by K. Warren Mitchell.

Gendarmes d'Ordonnance (green uniform, pink and silver undervest). Photo by K. Warren Mitchell.

L to R: Narrow head until 1905, wide head after 1905. Photo by K. Warren Mitchell.

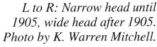

Imperial Grenadier Guards. Photo by K. Warren Mitchell.

Genie de la Garde (dark blue uniform, red plume). Photo by K. Warren Mitchell.

Regiment Latour d'Auvergne, Carabiniers (green uniform, red plume). Photo by K. Warren Mitchell.

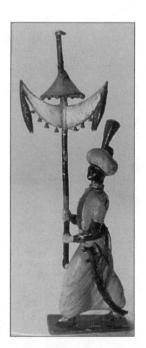

Bat. Neuchatel Band. Photo by K. Warren Mitchell.

Band of 1st Grenadiers of Imperial Guard (partial) (blue tunic, red vest, white plume). Photo by K. Warren Mitchell.

Bataillon Valaisan Grenadier Band (blue coat with yellow roping on sleeves, white vest, white over blue plume). Photo by K. Warren Mitchell.

Irish Legion Grenadiers (dark green uniform, trimmed in yellow, red plume). Photo by K. Warren Mitchell.

Foot Artillery of Imperial Guard (very dark blue uniform, red plume). Photo by K. Warren Mitchell.

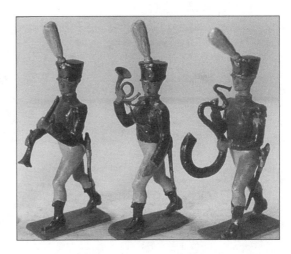

Bataillon Neuchatel Band (dark blue tunic, red vest, white plume). Photo by K. Warren Mitchell.

Heavy Cavalry of The Line. L to R: 1st Cuirassier Bugler, 1st Officer, Carabinier and Bugler (pre-1810 uniform), Bugler and Carabinier at attention (1810 uniform). Photo by Lenoir Josey.

Napoleon, winter coat of soft lead. Photo by K. Warren Mitchell.

Lucotte (Maison Lucotte)   ✠   283

Bataillon Neuchatel (Swiss) Fusiliers (red tunic, short blue pom on shako hat, drummer and fifer in blue jacket, red vest). Photo by K. Warren Mitchell.

World War I Mounted. L to R: French Dragoon, French Cuirassier, Italian Gen. Caderna, Polish Gen. Pilsoloski, German Uhlan Bugler, Japanese Officer. Photo by Lenoir Josey.

World War I Infantry. Top, L to R: British Infantry charging, British Officer wounded, Senagalese wounded, French Medic, French wounded (lying), French Zouave firing. Bottom, L to R: Japanese advancing, German surrendering, Russian, Serbian, Serbian bugler, French Sailor firing. Photo by Lenior Josey.

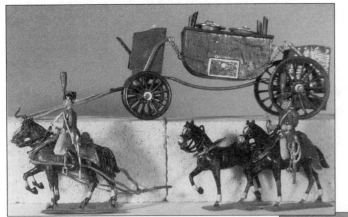

HORSE-DRAWN EQUIPMENT

The following items have been reissued by C.B.G. Mignot, using the original molds. Prices indicated are for reissued sets in "very good" condition.

		VG
816	4 horse field kitchen	$300.00
817	4 horse forge	300.00
818	4 horse Baron Wurst ambulance	300.00
827	4 horse pontoon section	300.00

#816. Photo by K. Warren Mitchell.

#817. Photo by K. Warren Mitchell.

#818. Photo courtesy Hansens.

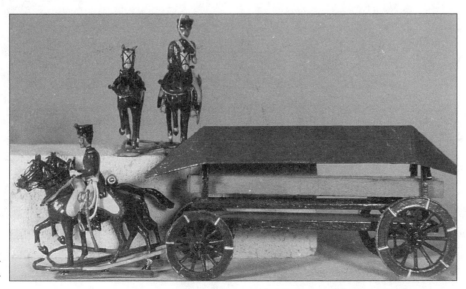

#827. Photo by K. Warren Mitchell.

France
Metal, Solidcast
55mm Standard
(Approx. 2-1/2" high)

⚔ C.B.G.—Mignot ⚔

by K. Warren Mitchell

C.B.G.—Mignot is the oldest toy soldier company still in operation. Known as "Mignot" to the English speaking world, it's known in France as "C.B.G." only or "Cebege."

On July 4, 1872, in Paris, the partners, Cuperly, Blondel and Gerbeau registered the trademark "C.B.G.," but the origins go back even further, to 1832, when Blondel & Son created its line of 60mm flat lead figures. The next 40 years saw a coupling of names through marriages of various partners' offspring until C.B.G. emerged. It was Gerbeau in 1875 who created the first 55mm fully round figure for the market. The association grew rapidly with Gerbeau as the driving force.

In 1897, Henri Mignot, a grandnephew of Cuperly, joined the company as technical advisor. During those years, C.B.G. ran a showroom/store, at which a customer could buy parts, have pieces repaired or look over the stock and have their own special sets prepared. Competitors, including Madame Lucotte, would order bulk stock to repackage under their own names to sell.

The turn of the century saw the elder Gerbeau pass on and his son M. Gerbeau and H. Mignot announced their new "association" in 1904. By 1912, H. Mignot ended the association and took full control of C.B.G. It's interesting to note that from 1900 to the beginning of World War I, C.B.G. was a diverse company, making many different products, including games, toy trains, religious articles and small hardware. We know the company primarily today for its Napoleonic figures, but, in 1903, a sampling of orders from various Paris shops show during a given period that 1,200 Farm sets were ordered, but only 27 sets of Napoleonic figures.

In 1928, C.B.G. bought controlling interest in Lucotte and seem to have marketed them side-by-side with its own line. Also marketed, but little is known about them, was a line of hollowcast figures in 55mm. These were introduced around World War I and were a profitable item until the beginning of World War II (See "French Misc." section).

Get out the magnifying glass for this one! It's Mignot's "War of the Worlds" diorama, which sold at Christie's New York auction in 1985 for $3300. Courtesy Christie's New York.

During the early 1930s, the firm introduced the solid aluminum figures under the name of "Migalu," followed by two more innovations in the late 1930s: Tiralu, a 60mm soldier that fired a gun and Arcalu, a 60mm figure that fired arrows. Surprisingly, in 1948, aluminum figures were its biggest sellers. It also started a line of plastic figures in 1955. In spite of ownership changes, several major wars and a bankruptcy, it continues to produce today.

Traditionally, always high priced compared to its competitors and even considered "connoisseur figures" by some, these figures have found a permanent home among collections, on the shelves with W. Britain, Heyde and other less expensive makers. In 1950, for the price of one set of Mignots, you could buy five or six sets of W. Britains.

Pricing

As in most toy soldiers, condition is the major factor in price. Mismatched sets, damaged, restored, repaired or repainted pieces reduce the prices shown in the following pages a great deal. For whatever reason, it seems you can still buy a nice prewar set at nearly the same price as a contemporary set.

Pricing of sets is difficult, due to the change in makeup of sets through the years. In 1955, C.B.G. changed the standard "Foot" set from 12 pieces to eight and four ("4 packs" have figures tied (later glued) to bottom and covered with plastic lid). "Mounted" sets changed at the same time from six pieces to five, plus singles mounted on wood blocks and packaged with similar plastic cover. During the same period (1955 on), personality figures were mounted on wood blocks and packaged with similar plastic cover.

With the variations in piece count and the fact that the majority of pieces that appear are seldom in "sets," boxed, we've chosen to show the "single" price in Very Good condition, in almost all cases. To determine the "set" price, *in a box,* just multiply the number of pieces X the price, plus 10% for the box.

Grading

Due to the pliability of the soft lead weapons, Mint is seldom seen, in or out of the box. Paint flaking off weapons is common, so we've chosen a grade of Very Good as a standard for price. Very Good means a few minor paint chips.

Identifying

Mignots are made in pieces and then assembled and painted. This gave Mignot the chance to offer a wide range of figures by simply plugging different heads in and changing the colors of paints, which is especially true in its Napoleonic range. All riders are detachable.

Although it made a variety of sizes, the following listing and photos are of its most popular size: 55mm for a foot figure (about 2-1/4" tall). Unlike English makers, C.B.G. did not generally put set numbers on its boxes, making it a bit confusing. The box label usually only tells you the size of the figure (55mm being their #214) and the number of pieces and subject matter, all hand-written. (i.e. 214/12 Imperial Guard). This system prevailed until around 1950. Following that, C.B.G. placed an additional actual item number on the outside bottom of the box tray or end of cardboard packs. The following listing relies on those item numbers, compiled by Donald Grant.

Identification is not always easy once the figures are outside the box, due to similarity of uniforms in First Empire period and 1900-14 and the changing standard of paint over a 100-year span.

Determining age can be roughly done by using the following rules of thumb:

- Green bases (called "Gerbeau green") were done until about 1900.
- No markings appear under base prior to World War II. Color tended to be grey to tan. After World War II, until 1954, the base originally had an oval blue and white sticker that read "Made in France" (on figures exported). Color runs from tan to medium brown.
- Postwar imprints under bases, such as C.B.G., Made in France, etc., sometimes appear together in the same boxed sets.
- Prewar paint was semi-flat, right up into the early 1950s.
- From 1955-1980, paint was high-gloss with fine detail, such as outlining pockets, etc.
- Contemporary figures are done in flat finish (called matte).

The author would like to thank Donald P. Grant for his research and formulating a workable numbering system; the late George B. Keester, one of the earliest pioneers in documenting C.B.G. production for the World War I period; Gus and Renay Hansen who, against the obstacles, continue to make Mignot available in North America and helped with photos and answers; Christian Blondieau, who opened a lot of eyes to the diversity of C.B.G.—Mignot with his book; and Lenoir Josey and Robert Avenell for some needed insights.

Thanks also to Harold and Rachel Sieroty for photos of their collection and the *Old Toy Soldier Newsletter* for permission to reprint some photos that had appeared in the Sieroty articles in the magazine. Additional photos courtesy of Guernsey's auction house, William Doyle Galleries, Christie's New York and the Jim and Ann Morris collection.

FOOT FIGURES (Single piece price)

		VG
01	Egyptians, 1000 B.C.	$15.00
02	Assyrians, 600 B.C., marching	15.00
03	Greeks, 400 B.C., marching	15.00

		VG
04	Gauls, 100 B.C., in combat	15.00
05	Romans, 100 B.C., marching	15.00
06	Franks, 6th-7th Cent.	15.00
873	Romans, 4-piece set	80.00
07	Crusaders, 11th-12th Cent., marching	16.00

#01

#02

#03

#04

Back row: These four pieces came as Set #873, shields overhead in defensive "tortoise" formation. Front row: #05.

#06

#07

#07

#08

#08

#09

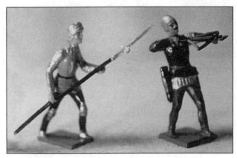

#10

#10

#09

#10

	VG			VG
14	Pikesmen Marching, Henry IV, 17th Cent. 15.00		18	Swiss Guards, Louis XIV, 1670 .... 14.00
15	Musketeers Marching, Louis XIII, 17th Cent. 15.00		19	French Guards, Louis XV, 1740 .... 14.00
16	French Guards, Louis XIV, 1670 .... 14.00		20	Touraine Regiment, Louis XV, 1740 .... 14.00
17	Champagne Regiment, Louis XIV, 1670 .... 14.00		21	Swiss Guards, Louis XV, 1740 .... 14.00
			21/A	French Guards, Louis XVI, 1789 .... 14.00

#11

#12

#13

#14

#15

#16. Dark blue coats trimmed in red, red breeches and stockings.

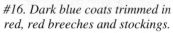

#16. Dark blue coats trimmed in red, red breeches and stockings.

#17. All white trimmed in gold.

#18. Red trimmed in blue, white breeches.

#19. Dark blue trimmed in red, white breeches.

#21. Red uniform trimmed in blue.

#21/A. Dark blue uniform trimmed in red and white.

#21/B

#21/C. Red jacket with blue front, white breeches.

#22

#22/A

#23

#24. Dark green jacket, caterpillar helmet.

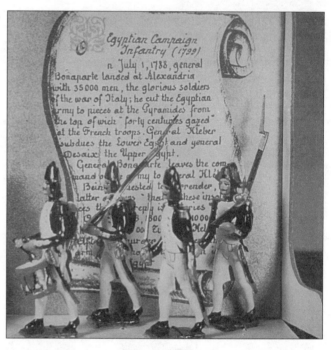

#25 in plastic-covered pack with biography card. 4-piece pack.

#26. Red edge to bottom of coat, red plume.

#27

L to R: #28, #28/A, #28/B, mix.

		VG
26	Grenadiers of the Guard marching, 1812	15.00
26/A	Grenadiers of the Guard standing firing, 1812	17.00
26/B	Grenadiers of the Guard assaulting, 1812	17.00
27	Grenadiers of the Guard at attention, 1812	17.00
28	Grenadiers of the Guard, Sappers and Drummers, 1812	16.00
28/A	Grenadiers of the Guard, Sappers, 1812	16.00
28/B	Grenadiers of the Guard, Drummers and Drum-Major, 1812	16.00
29	Fusiliers of the Military School of Saint-Cyr marching, 1812	16.00
29/A	Fusiliers of the Military School of Saint-Cyr firing, 1812	17.00
29/B	Fusiliers of the Military School of Saint-Cyr assaulting, 1812	17.00

		VG
30	Voltigeurs (Skirmishers) of the Guard marching at slope, 1812	15.00
30/A	Voltigeurs of the Guard assaulting, 1812	17.00
30/B	Voltigeurs of the Guard standing firing, 1812	17.00
31	Marines of the Guard marching, 1812	15.00
31/A	Voltigeurs of the 33rd Regiment of the Line marching, 1812	16.00
31/B	Flankers of the Guard marching, 1812	15.00
31/H	Marines of the Guard at attention, 1812	17.00
31/J	Voltigeurs of the 33rd Regiment of the Line at attention, 1812	18.00
32	Engineers of the Guard marching, 1812	15.00
32/H	Engineers of the Guard at attention, 1812	17.00
33	Dragoons of the Guard marching (on foot), 1812	15.00

#29

#30. Red over blue plume.

#31

#32

#33 Officer and ranks. Green coat, red plumes, rifle slung barrel down.

#33/A. Green coat, yellow over green plume.

#34. Dark blue uniform, yellow over green plume.

#35. Blue coat, red collar, red plume.

#36. Blue coat, yellow collar, yellow over green plume.

#36/A, White coat, blue panel in front, white over blue plume.

#37. White edge to bottom of coat, red plume.

#37/A. Dark blue uniform, red plume.

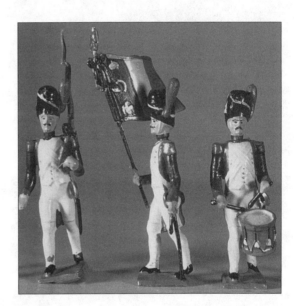

#38. Dark green coat, red plume.

#39. Dark green uniform trimmed in yellow, green over yellow plume.

#40 and #41. White uniform trimmed in red, red plume.

		VG			VG
40/A	Band of the 3rd Regiment of Grenadiers of the Guard, formerly Dutch Grenadiers, 1809	18.00	42	Band of the Grenadiers of the Guard, 1805	19.00
40/B	Drum Major and Drummers of the 3rd Regiment of Grenadiers, 1812	16.00	42/A	Band of the Imperial Guard of Strasbourg, 1805	19.00
41	Dutch Grenadiers at attention, 1812	18.00	43	Austrian Infantry marching, 1800	14.00
41/A	4th Swiss Regiment, 1812, marching	16.00	43/A	Austrian Infantry standing firing, 1800	15.00
41/B	Imperial Guard of Strasbourg, 1805	16.00	43/B	Austrian Infantry assaulting, 1800	15.00
41/C	1st Regiment of Isembourg, 1806	17.00	43/H	Austrian Infantry at attention, 1800	17.00
41/J	4th Swiss Regiment at attention, 1812	17.00	44	English Infantry marching, 1812	14.00
41/K	1st Regiment of Isembourg at attention, 1806	18.00	44/A	English Infantry standing firing, 1812	16.00
			44/B	English Infantry assaulting, 1812	16.00
			45	Russian Grenadiers marching, 1812	14.00

#41/B

#41/C. Medium blue uniform, red plume.

#41/A. Red coat with dark blue front panel, dark green over yellow plume.

#43, #43/A, #43/B. All white uniform, flag yellow.

#42. Dark blue coat with red panel on front. White plume between red and blue poms.

#44, #44/A, #44/B. Red jacket, medium blue trousers.

#45. Dark green jacket.

45/A	8th Bavarian Regiment marching, 1812	14.00
45/B	Russian Grenadiers standing firing, 1812	16.00
45/C	Russian Grenadiers assaulting, 1812	16.00
45/E	13th Prussian Regiment of the Line, 1806	14.00
45/H	Russian Grenadiers at attention, 1812	17.00
45/K	8th Bavarian Regiment at attention, 1812	17.00
46	Chasseurs on foot, 2nd Empire period, 1860	14.00
47	Infantry of the Line, 2nd Empire period, 1860	14.00
47/A	Colonial Infantry marching, 1880	15.00
47/B	2nd Regiment of the Foreign Legion in Mexico, 1863	16.00
47/M	Colonial Infantry assaulting with one foot off the ground, 1880	17.00
47/N	Colonial Infantry standing firing, 1880	17.00
47/P	Colonial Infantry kneeling firing, 1880	17.00
47/Q	Colonial Infantry lying firing, 1880	18.00
48	Confederates marching in kepis with slung rifles, 1863	15.00
48/A	Confederates marching, kepis, slope arms, 1863	16.00
48/B	Confederates marching, brim hats, slope arms, 1863	15.00

48/C	Confederates marching with brim hats, slung rifle, 1863	14.00
49	Confederates standing firing, in kepis, 1863	15.00
49/B	Confederates firing, brim hats, 1863	15.00
50	Confederates assaulting, kepis, 1863	16.00
50/B	Confederate Infantry assaulting, brim hats, 1863	15.00
51	Confederates kneeling firing, kepis, 1863	15.00
51/B	Confederates kneeling firing, brim hats, 1863	14.00
52	U.S. Army marching, kepi, 1863	15.00
53	U.S. Army standing firing, kepi, 1863	15.00
54	U.S. Army assaulting, kepi, 1863	15.00
55	U.S. Army kneeling firing, kepi, 1863	15.00
56	Confederate Labor Battalion, kepi, 1863	16.00
57	U.S. Army Labor Battalion, kepi, 1863	16.00
57/A	Confederate Artillery Crew, kepi, 1863	15.00
57/B	U.S. Army Artillery Crew, kepi, 1863	15.00
57/R	Confederate Artillery Crew, red kepi, 1863	15.00
57/S	Confederate Artillery Crew, brim hats, 1863	15.00
58	Infantry of the Line in tunic, marching, 1914	14.00

#45/A. Light blue jacket with yellow panel in front.

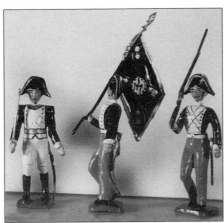

#45/E

#46. Dark blue tunic, grey trousers, green plume.

#48/C. Brim hat.

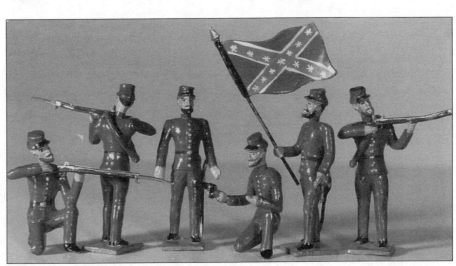

#49, #51. All grey uniform, kepi hat.

#50/B

#52

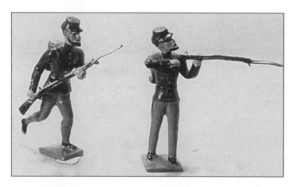

L to R: #54, #53.

#56

#57

#57/S

#58/A

#58/B

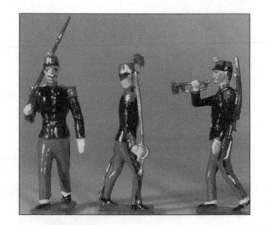

#59/B. Blue tunic, red trousers and kepi, green pom on kepi.

		VG				VG

58/A	Infantry of the Line in overcoat, marching, 1914	14.00
58/B	Infantry of the Line assaulting, 1914	16.00
58/C	Infantry of the Line standing firing, 1914	16.00
58/D	Infantry of the Line kneeling firing, 1914	16.00
58/E	Infantry of the Line lying firing, 1914	16.00
58/F	Infantry of the Line in overcoats running, one foot off ground, 1914	16.00
58/G	Motorcyclist, 1914	20.00
58/H	Machine Gunner and Machine Gun, 1914	17.00
58/J	Infantry of the Line, red kepi, 1914	16.00
58/X	Bicyclists riding, 1914	20.00
58/Y	Bicyclists standing next to bicycles, 1914	20.00
58/W	Wounded, 1914	17.00
59	Labor Battalion or Fatigue Party, red trousers, red kepi, 1914	16.00
59/B	Chasseurs on foot, in tunic, marching, 1914	14.00
59/M	Labor Battalion, blue trousers, kepis, 1916	16.00
59/N	Labor Battalion, steel helmets, 1916	17.00
60	Band of the Line, tunic, kepis, 1914	17.00
60/C	Band of the Line, overcoats, kepis, 1914	17.00
61	Zouaves, blue and red uniform, marching, 1914	16.00
61/A	Band of the Zouaves, blue and red uniform, 1914	18.00
61/B	Zouaves, blue and red uniform, assaulting, 1914	17.00

61/C	Zouaves, khaki, steel helmets, assaulting, 1915	17.00
61/D	Zouaves, blue and red uniform, standing firing, 1914	17.00
61/E	Zouaves, blue and red uniform, standing firing, 1914	17.00
61/F	Zouaves, blue and red uniform, lying firing, 1914	17.00
61/G	Zouaves, khaki uniform, steel helmets, standing firing, 1915	17.00
61/H	Zouaves, khaki uniform, steel helmets, kneeling firing, 1915	17.00
61/J	Zouaves, khaki uniform, steel helmets, lying firing, 1915	17.00
61/K	Zouaves, khaki uniform, steel helmets, marching, 1915	16.00
62	Turcos, blue uniforms, marching, 1914	16.00
62/A	Band of the Turcos, blue uniforms, 1914	18.00
62/B	Turcos, blue uniforms, standing firing, 1914	17.00
62/C	Turcos, blue uniforms, assaulting, 1914	17.00
62/D	Turcos, blue uniforms, kneeling firing, 1914	17.00
62/E	Turcos, blue uniforms, lying firing, 1914	17.00
62/F	Turcos, khaki uniforms, standing firing, 1915	16.00
62/G	Turcos, khaki uniform, assaulting, 1915	16.00
62/H	Turcos, khaki uniform, kneeling firing, 1915	16.00
62/J	Turcos, khaki uniforms, lying firing, 1915	16.00
62/K	Turcos, khaki uniform, marching, 1915	16.00

#60/C. Medium blue overcoats, red trousers.

#60

#61. Dark blue jacket, red trousers.

#61/A

#62/A. Light blue uniform.

		VG			**VG**
63	Cuirassiers on foot, 1914	16.00	64/G	Motorcyclists, blue, steel helmet, 1915	20.00
63/H	Cuirassiers on foot, horizon blue, 1915	17.00	64/H	Machine Gunner and Hotchkiss Machine Gun, 1915	17.00
64	Infantry of the Line, blue, marching, overcoat, 1915	14.00	64/J	Exercise Uniform, 1915	18.00
64/A	Infantry of the Line, blue, assaulting, 1915	15.00	64/K	Line Infantry, khaki uniform, steel helmet, 1915	14.00
64/B	Infantry of the Line, blue, standing firing, 1915	15.00	64/L	Band of Infantry of the Line, khaki uniform, steel helmets, 1915	17.00
64/C	Infantry of the Line, blue, lying firing, 1915	15.00	64/M	Band of the Line, blue, steel helmets, 1915	17.00
64/D	Infantry of the Line, blue, kneeling firing, 1915	15.00	64/N	Men throwing grenade, blue, steel helmet, 1915	18.00
64/E	Infantry of the Line, blue, at attention, rifle at present arms, 1915	17.00	64/P	Infantry of the Line, running one foot off ground, at slope, blue, 1915	15.00
64/F	Infantry of the Line, blue tunic, marching, 1915	14.00	64/Q	Line Infantry with slung rifles, blue, 1915	14.00

#62/C

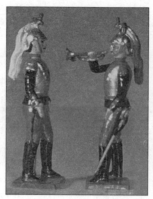

#63

#64

#64/F

#64/L. All khaki uniform.

#64/G

#64/P

#64/X

		VG
64/R	Line Infantry at attention, rifle at foot, blue, 1915	15.00
64/U	French Soldier, with wounded Prisoner of War	25.00
64/W	Wounded, blue, 1915	15.00
64/X	Bicyclists, blue, riding bicycle, 1915	20.00
64/Y	Bicyclists, blue, standing by bicycle, 1915	22.00
64/Z	Medical Unit, blue, 1915	18.00
65	Artillery Crew, blue, 1915	16.00
65/B	Artillery Crew, dark blue, 1914	16.00
66	Saint-Cyrians, 1900	15.00
67	Foreign Legion, khaki uniforms, white kepis, marching, 1914	15.00
67/A	Foreign Legion, khaki, white kepis, standing firing, 1914	16.00
67/B	Foreign Legion, khaki, white kepis, assaulting, 1914	16.00
67/C	Foreign Legion, khaki, white kepis, kneeling firing, 1914	16.00
67/D	Foreign Legion, khaki, white kepis, lying firing, 1914	16.00
67/E	Band of the Foreign Legion, khaki, white kepis, 1914	18.00
67/H	Foreign Legion Machine Gunner and Gun, khaki, white kepi, 1914	20.00

		VG
68	Guards of Paris, 1900	14.00
69	Band of the Guards of Paris, 1900	17.00
70	Alpine Chasseurs, white, marching with cane, 1914	16.00
70/A	Band of the Alpine Chasseurs, white uniforms, 1914	17.00
70/B	Alpine Chasseurs, white uniform, mule carrying mountain cannon barrel, plus pine tree, 1914	35.00
70/C	Alpine Chasseurs, white uniform, mule carrying mountain cannon trail, plus pine tree, 1914	35.00
70/D	Alpine Chasseurs, white uniform, mule carrying wheels of mountain cannon, plus pine tree, 1914	35.00
70/E	Alpine Chasseurs, white uniforms, skiers, plus pine tree, 1914	35.00
70/F	Alpine Chasseurs, white uniforms, mule carrying ammunition boxes for mountain cannon, handler and officer, 1914	35.00
70/H	Alpine Chasseurs, blue, marching, 1914-18	17.00
70/J	Alpine Chasseurs, blue, mule carrying mountain cannon barrel, 1914-18	35.00
70/K	Alpine Chasseurs, blue, mule carrying mountain cannon trail, 1914-18	35.00

#64/Z

#64/Z

#67

#68 (top row), #69 (bottom row). Dark blue jacket, dark grey trousers, red plume.

#70/E

70/L	Alpine Chasseurs, blue, mule carrying mountain cannon wheels, 1914-18	35.00
70/M	Alpine Chasseurs, blue, mule carrying ammunition boxes for mountain cannon, 1914-18	35.00
70/N	Alpine Chasseurs, blue, assaulting, 1914-18	18.00
70/P	Alpine Chasseurs, blue, standing firing, 1914-18	18.00
70/Q	Alpine Chasseurs, blue, kneeling firing, 1914-18	18.00
70/R	Alpine Chasseurs, blue, lying firing, 1914-18	18.00
70/S	Alpine Chasseurs, blue, artillerymen in action, 1914-18	16.00
70/Z	Alpine infantry skiers, dark blue tunic, red trousers, blue beret, 1900	18.00
71	Alpine Chasseurs, blue uniform, marching with cane, 1914	17.00
71/A	Band of the Alpine Chasseurs, blue uniform, 1914	19.00
71/B	Alpine Chasseurs, blue uniform, mule carrying barrel of mountain cannon, plus pine tree, 1914	35.00
71/C	Alpine Chasseurs, blue uniform, mule carrying mountain cannon trail, plus pine tree, 1914	35.00
71/D	Alpine Chasseurs, blue uniform, mule carrying wheels of mountain cannon, plus pine tree, 1914	35.00

71/E	Alpine Chasseurs, blue uniforms, skiers, plus pine tree, 1914	35.00
71/F	Alpine Chasseurs, blue uniform, mule carrying ammo boxes for mountain cannon, 1914	35.00
71/G	Alpine Artillerymen, dark blue uniform, red trim, 1914	16.00
71/N	Alpine Chasseurs, blue overcoat, mule carrying barrel of mountain cannon, plus pine tree, 1914	35.00
71/P	Alpine Chasseurs, blue overcoat, mule carrying mountain cannon trail, plus pine tree, 1914	35.00
71/Q	Alpine Chasseurs, blue overcoat, mule carrying wheels of mountain cannon, plus pine tree, 1914	35.00
71/R	Alpine Chasseurs, blue overcoat, mule carrying ammo boxes for mountain cannon, plus pine tree, 1914	35.00
71/T	Alpine Chasseurs, blue uniforms, assaulting, 1914	17.00
71/U	Alpine Chasseurs, blue uniforms, kneeling firing, 1914	17.00
71V	Alpine Chasseurs, blue uniforms, kneeling firing, 1914	17.00
71/W	Alpine Chasseurs, blue uniforms, lying firing, 1914	17.00
71/Z	Alpine Chasseurs, dark blue tunic, white trousers, 1900	17.00

#70/H

#70/Z

#71/A

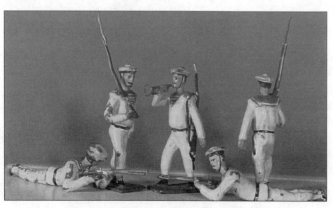

#72 and #72/D.

#73

		VG
72	Sailors, white uniforms, marching, 1914	15.00
72/A	Sailors, white uniforms, assaulting, 1914	17.00
72/B	Sailors, white uniforms, standing firing, 1914	17.00
72/C	Sailors, white uniforms, kneeling firing, 1914	17.00
72/D	Sailors, white uniforms, lying firing, 1914	17.00
72/M	Naval Band, white uniforms, 1914	18.00
72/N	Sailors, white uniforms, labor battalion, 1914	17.00
73	Sailors, blue uniforms, marching, 1914	15.00
73/A	Sailors, blue uniforms, assaulting, 1914	17.00
73/B	Sailors, blue uniforms, standing firing, 1914	17.00
73/C	Sailors, blue uniforms, kneeling firing, 1914	17.00
73/D	Sailors, blue uniforms, lying firing, 1914	17.00
73/M	Naval Band, blue uniforms, 1914	18.00
73/N	Sailors, blue uniforms, labor battalion, 1914	17.00
74	Marine Fusiliers, marching, 1914	15.00
74/A	Marine Fusiliers, assaulting, 1914	17.00
74/B	Marine Fusiliers, standing firing, 1914	17.00
74/C	Marine Fusiliers, kneeling firing, 1914	17.00
74/D	Marine Fusiliers, lying firing, 1914	17.00
75	Prussian Infantry, marching, khaki, spiked helmets, 1914	15.00
75/A	Prussian Infantry, assaulting, khaki, spiked helmet, 1914	17.00
75/B	Prussian Infantry, standing firing, khaki, spiked helmet, 1914	17.00
75/C	Prussian Infantry, kneeling firing, khaki, spiked helmet, 1914	17.00

		VG
75/D	Prussian Infantry, lying firing, khaki, spiked helmet, 1914	17.00
75/G	Prussian Motorcyclist, khaki, spiked helmet, 1914	20.00
75/H	Prussian Machine Gunner, khaki, spiked helmet, 1914	17.00
75/M	Prussian Infantry Band, khaki uniforms, spiked helmet, 1914	18.00
75/W	Prussian Infantry, wounded, khaki, spiked helmet, 1914	18.00
75/V	French Aviators, 1914-18	16.00
75/X	Prussian Bicyclist, khaki, spiked helmet, 1914	20.00
75Z	Prussian Prisoners of War with hands raised, 1914, one held and assisted by French soldier	20.00
76	Highlanders marching, 1900	16.00
76/A	Highlanders assaulting, 1900	18.00
76/B	Highlanders standing firing, 1900	17.00
76/K	Highlanders, khaki, steel helmets, 1914	18.00
77	West Point Cadets, winter uniforms, 20th century	14.00
78	West Point Cadets, summer uniforms, 20th century	14.00
79	Prussians, khaki, steel helmets, marching, 1914	14.00
79/A	Prussians, khaki, steel helmets, assaulting, 1914	16.00
79/B	Prussians, khaki, steel helmets, kneeling firing, 1914	16.00

#74

#75/Z

#76

#79

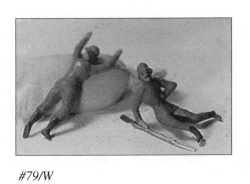

#79/W

#80/B

79/C	Prussians, khaki, steel helmets, kneeling firing, 1914	16.00
79/D	Prussians, khaki, steel helmets, lying firing, 1914	16.00
79/G	Prussians, khaki, steel helmets, motorcyclist, 1914	20.00
79/H	Prussians, khaki, steel helmets, machine gunner, 1914	18.00
79/M	Prussians, khaki, steel helmets, Band, 1914	18.00
79/W	Prussians, khaki, steel helmets, wounded, 1914	18.00
79/X	Prussians, khaki, steel helmets, bicyclist, 1914	18.00
80	Firemen marching, 20th century	14.00
80/B	Firemen in action positions, 20th century	17.00
81	Prussian Infantry, marching, field gray, steel helmets, 1914	14.00
81/A	Prussian Infantry, assaulting, field gray, steel helmets, 1914	15.00
81/B	Prussian Infantry, standing firing, field gray, steel helmets	15.00
81/C	Prussian Infantry, kneeling firing, field gray, steel helmets, 1914	15.00
81/D	Prussian Infantry, lying firing, field gray, steel helmets, 1914	15.00
81/G	Prussian Motorcyclist, field gray, steel helmets, 1914	20.00
81/H	Prussian Machine Gunner, field gray, steel helmet, 1914	17.00
81/M	Prussian Infantry Band, field gray, steel helmets, 1914	17.00
81/W	Prussian Infantry, wounded, field gray, steel helmets, 1914	18.00
81/X	Prussian Bicyclist, field gray, steel helmets, 1914	18.00
82	Prussian Infantry, marching, blue tunics, spiked helmets, 1914	15.00
82/A	Prussian Infantry, assaulting, blue tunics, spiked helmets, 1914	16.00
82/B	Prussian Infantry, standing firing, blue tunics, spiked helmets, 1914	16.00
82/C	Prussian Infantry, kneeling firing, blue tunics, spiked helmets, 1914	16.00
82/D	Prussian Infantry, lying firing, blue tunics, spiked helmets, 1914	16.00
82/G	Prussian Motorcyclist, blue tunics, spiked helmets, 1914	20.00
82/H	Prussian Machine Gunner, blue tunic, spiked helmets, 1914	17.00
82/M	Prussian Infantry Band, blue tunic, spiked helmets, 1914	17.00
82/W	Prussian Infantry, wounded, blue tunic, spiked helmets, 1914	18.00
82/X	Prussian Bicyclist, blue tunic, spiked helmets, 1914	19.00
83	Goumiers on foot marching, 1900	18.00
84	Touregs marching, 1900	18.00
84/A	Touregs standing firing, masked, 1900	18.00
85	Annamites marching, khaki, flat hats, 1914	18.00
86	Senegalese marching, blue, steel helmets, 1915	18.00
86/A	Senegalese assaulting, blue, steel helmets, 1915	18.00
86/B	Senegalese standing firing, blue, steel helmets, 1915	18.00
86/C	Senegalese kneeling firing, blue, steel helmets, 1915	18.00
86/D	Senegalese, lying firing, blue, steel helmets, 1915	18.00
86/P	Senegalese Tirailleurs, assaulting, blue tunic, red cap, 1900	18.00
86/Q	Senegalese Tirailleurs, firing, blue tunic, red fez, 1900	18.00
86/R	Senegalese Tirailleurs, kneeling firing, blue tunic, red fez, 1900	18.00
86/S	Senegalese Tirailleurs, lying firing, blue tunic, red fez, 1900	18.00
86/T	Senegalese Tirailleurs, marching, blue tunic, red fez, 1900	16.00
87	Africans firing, 1900	18.00
88	Sakalaves standing firing, 1900	18.00
89	Dahomeyans, 1900	18.00
90	Siamese Guards marching, 1900	17.00
91	Sudanese marching, 1900	17.00
91/A	Sudanese firing, 1900	17.00
92	Tonkinese firing, 1900	18.00
93	Hindus marching, khaki, 1914	16.00
93/A	Hindus assaulting, khaki, 1914	17.00

#83

#84/A

#88

#89

#91

			VG
93/B	Hindus standing firing, khaki, 1914		17.00
94	Boy Scouts, 1900		20.00
95	Americans, khaki, marching, montana hats, 1917		15.00
95/A	Americans, khaki, assaulting, montana hats, 1917		16.00
95/B	American Band, khaki, montana hats, 1917		18.00
95/C	Americans, khaki, standing firing, montana hats, 1917		16.00
95/D	Americans, khaki, kneeling firing, montana hats, 1917		16.00
95/E	Americans, khaki, lying firing, montana hats, 1917		16.00

			VG
95/H	American machine gunners, khaki, montana hats, 1917		17.00
95/X	American bicyclists, khaki, montana hats, 1917		20.00
95/Y	American bicyclists, khaki, montana hats, 1917		
95/Z	American stretcher bearers, stretcher and wounded man, 1918 (set)		50.00
96	Canadians, khaki, marching, 1914		16.00
96/A	Canadians, khaki, assaulting, 1914		17.00
96/B	Canadians, khaki, standing firing, 1914		17.00
96/C	Canadians, khaki, kneeling firing, 1914		17.00
96/D	Canadians, khaki, lying firing, 1914		17.00
97	Greek Infantry, khaki, marching, 1914		16.00

#92

#93

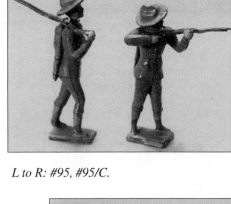

L to R: #95, #95/C.

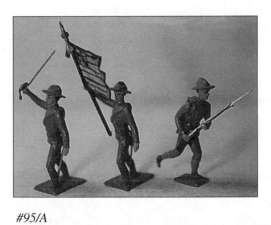

#95/A

#97

#98

#99

#102/A

#102/F

*102/P
(bayonet).*

97/A	Greek Infantry, khaki, assaulting, 1914	17.00
97/B	Greek Infantry, khaki, standing firing, 1914	17.00
97/C	Greek Infantry, khaki, kneeling firing, 1914	17.00
97/D	Greek Infantry, khaki, lying firing, 1914	17.00
97/N	Greeks, blue tunics, kepi with white plume, marching, 1900	15.00
97/P	Greeks, blue tunics, kepi with white plume, assaulting, 1900	16.00
97/Q	Greeks, blue tunics, kepi with white plume, standing firing, 1900	16.00
97/R	Greeks, blue tunics, kepi with white plume, kneeling firing, 1900	16.00
97/S	Greeks, blue tunics, kepi with white plume, lying firing, 1900	16.00
98	Japanese Infantry, marching, 1900	16.00
98/A	Japanese assaulting, 1900	17.00
98/B	Japanese standing firing, 1900	17.00
98/C	Japanese kneeling firing, 1900	17.00
98/D	Japanese lying firing, 1900	17.00
98/W	Japanese wounded, two positions, 1900	18.00
99	Chinese marching, 1900	16.00
99/A	Chinese assaulting, 1900	17.00
99/B	Chinese standing firing, 1900	17.00
100	Americans marching, khaki, helmet, 1917	13.00
100/A	Americans assaulting, khaki, helmet, 1917	15.00
100/B	Americans standing firing, khaki, helmet, 1917	15.00
100/C	Americans kneeling firing, khaki, helmet, 1917	15.00
100/D	Americans lying firing, khaki, helmet, 1917	15.00
100/X	American bicyclists, riding, khaki, steel helmets, 1918	17.00
100/Y	American bicyclists, standing by bikes, khaki, helmet, 1918	20.00
101	Prussian Chasseurs assaulting, 1914	15.00
101/B	Prussian Chasseurs standing firing, 1914	15.00
101/C	Prussian Chasseurs kneeling firing, 1914	15.00
101/D	Prussian Chasseurs lying firing, 1914	15.00
101/E	Prussian Chasseurs marching, 1914	14.00

102/A	Russian Infantry assaulting, overcoat, peakless cap, 1914	15.00
102/B	Russian Infantry standing firing, peakless cap, 1914	15.00
102/C	Russian Infantry kneeling firing, 1914	15.00
102/D	Russian Infantry lying firing, 1914	15.00
102/E	Russian Infantry marching, 1914	14.00
102/F	Russian Infantry assaulting, white cap, 1914	15.00
102/G	Russian Infantry standing firing, white cap, 1914	15.00
102/H	Russian Infantry kneeling firing, white cap, 1914	15.00
102/J	Russian Infantry lying firing, white cap, 1914	15.00
102/K	Russian Infantry marching, white cap, 1914	15.00
102/L	Russian Infantry assaulting, fur hat, overcoat, 1914	16.00
102/M	Russian Infantry standing firing, fur hat, overcoat, 1914	16.00
102/N	Russian Infantry kneeling firing, fur hat, overcoat, 1914	16.00
102/P	Russians, Pavlowski Regt., marching, 1900	16.00
102/Q	Russians, Grenadiers, 1900	14.00
102/R	Russians lying firing, overcoat, fur hat, 1914	16.00
102/S	Russians marching, overcoat, fur hat, 1914	16.00
102/T	Russians in tunics, marching, 1900	15.00
102/U	Russians marching, tunic, white cap	15.00
102/V	Russians marching, tunic, fur hat	15.00
103	Rumanian Infantry marching, 1914	15.00
103/A	Rumanian Infantry assaulting, 1914	15.00
103/B	Rumanian Infantry standing firing, 1914	16.00
103/C	Rumanian Infantry kneeling firing, 1914	16.00
103/D	Rumanian Infantry lying firing, 1914	16.00
103/P	Rumanian Infantry marching, 1900	14.00
103/Q	Rumanian Infantry assaulting, 1900	15.00
103/R	Rumanian Infantry standing firing, 1900	15.00
103/S	Rumanian Infantry kneeling firing, 1900	15.00
103/T	Rumanian Infantry lying firing, 1900	15.00
104	Serbian Infantry marching, 1914	16.00

 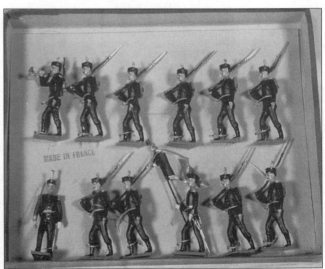

#103 Boxed set, prewar (bill-less cap with plume).

#106. Medium green, red pom on kepi.

#107. Light green, large bushy plume.

#108. Blue and white paper label used 1946-52, under base.

#109

#110. Khaki jacket.

#111/A, #111 (various colored jackets).

113	Israeli Infantry marching, winter uniforms, 1948	15.00
113/A	Israeli Infantry marching, summer uniforms, 1948	16.00
113/U	Israeli Guerrilla fighters in combat, 1948	17.00
114	Israeli Infantry in combat, summer uniforms, 1948	17.00
115	Head of Column, 1st Regt. Gren. of the Guard, 28 figures, 1812	15.00
116	Foreign Legion, uniform of 1906, marching	16.00
116/H	Foreign Legion machine gun unit, 1906 uniform, gun, operator, feeder, officer with binoculars (set)	50.00
116/A	Band of the Foreign Legion, uniform of 1906	18.00
117	Foreign Legion standing firing, 1906	17.00
118	Foreign Legion, uniform of 1906, assaulting	17.00
119	Battalion of Neufchatel, marching, 1808	16.00
120	Polish Grenadiers, Legion of the North, marching, 1806	16.00
121	Grenadiers of ClevesBerg, 1812	16.00
122	English Grenadiers, 1st Regiment, marching, 1813	16.00
122/A	English Grenadiers, 1st Regiment, standing firing, 1813	18.00
122/B	English Grenadiers, 1st Regiment, assaulting, 1813	18.00
123	German Infantry in the Austrian Army, marching, 1806	16.00
123/A	German Infantry in the Austrian Army, standing firing, 1806	17.00

123/B	German Infantry in the Austrian Army, assaulting, 1806	17.00
124	Royal Deux Ponts Regt., American War of Independence, 1778	16.00
125	English Grenadiers 33rd Regt., American War of Independence, 1776	16.00
126	New England Regiments, American War of Independence, 1776	16.00
127	New York and New Jersey Regiments, American War of Independence, 1776	16.00
128	Elite Gendarmes on foot, First Empire 1804	16.00
129	Regiment of La Tour d'Auvergne, First Empire, 1806	16.00
130	Valaison (Swiss) Battalion, First Empire, 1805	16.00
1900-291	Rumanian Chasseurs, 1900	14.00
1911-260	Gendarmes (Police), 1900	15.00
1911-261	Artillerymen on foot, 1900	15.00
1911-262	Engineers, 1900	14.00
1911-262/H	Engineers, 1900	14.00
1911-263	Supply Corps, 1900	15.00
1911-265	Transport Cavalry on foot, 1900	15.00
1911-265/H	Baggage Train, 1916	15.00
1911-270	English Infantry, red tunic, spiked helmet, 1900	15.00
1911-271	Belgian Infantry marching, 1900	14.00
1911-271A	Belgian Infantry assaulting, 1900	15.00
1911-271B	Belgian Infantry standing firing, 1900	15.00
1911-271C	Belgian Infantry kneeling firing, 1900	15.00
1911-271D	Belgian Infantry lying firing, 1900	15.00

#111/C

#113/A

#116

#127

#1911-260

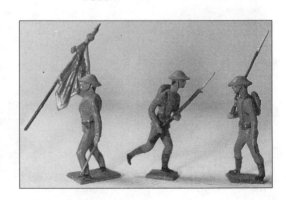

#1911-275/A, #1911-275.

1911-272	Belgian Infantry marching, 1914	14.00
1911-272/A	Belgian Infantry assaulting, 1914	15.00
1911-272/B	Belgian Infantry standing firing, 1914	15.00
1911-272/C	Belgian Infantry kneeling firing, 1914	15.00
1911-272/D	Belgian Infantry lying firing, 1914	15.00
1911-273	Buffalo Hunters marching, 1870	18.00
1911-273/A	Buffalo Hunters assaulting, 1870	18.00
1911-273/B	Buffalo Hunters standing firing, 1870	18.00
1911-273/C	Buffalo Hunters kneeling firing, 1870	18.00
1911-273/D	Buffalo Hunters lying firing, 1870	18.00
1911-274	Spanish Infantry in overcoats marching, 1900	14.00
1911-274/A	Spanish Infantry in overcoats assaulting, 1900	15.00
1911-274/B	Spanish Infantry in overcoats standing firing, 1900	15.00
1911-274/C	Spanish Infantry in overcoats kneeling firing, 1900	15.00
1911-274/D	Spanish Infantry in overcoats lying firing, 1900	15.00
1911-274/T	Spanish Infantry in tunics marching, 1900	14.00
1911-275	English Infantry, khaki uniform, marching, 1914	14.00
1911-275/A	English Infantry, khaki uniform, helmet, assaulting, 1914	15.00
1911-275/B	English Infantry, khaki uniform, helmet, standing firing, 1914	15.00

1911-275/C	English Infantry, khaki, helmet, kneeling firing, 1914	15.00
1911-275/D	English Infantry, khaki, helmet, lying firing, 1914	15.00
1911-275/G	English Infantry, khaki, helmet, motorcyclist, 1914	18.00
1911-275/H	English Infantry, khaki, helmet, machine gunner, 1914	16.00
1911-275/W	English Infantry, khaki, helmet, wounded, 1914	16.00
1911-275/X	English Infantry, khaki, helmet, bicyclist, 1914	16.00
1911-276	Boxers (Chinese Boxer Rebellion), 1900	17.00
1911-277	American Infantry, blue uniforms, kepis, marching, 1900	17.00
1911-278	American Infantry, blue uniforms, spiked helmets, marching, 1900	17.00
1911-278/A	American Infantry, blue uniforms, spiked helmets, assaulting, 1900	17.00
1911-278/B	American Infantry, blue uniforms, spiked helmets, standing firing, 1900	17.00
1916-257	Enemies, wounded, 1914	18.00
1916-258	Comrades (soldier carrying wounded on back), blue uniforms, kepis, 1914	35.00
1916-259	Portuguese Chasseurs marching, 1914	14.00
1916-259/A	Portuguese Chasseurs assaulting, 1914	15.00

#1911-275/B

#1911-276

#1916-257

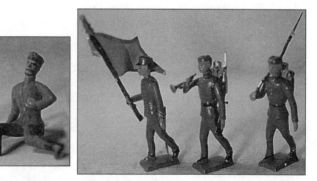

#1916-259. Brown tunic and cap.

#1952-31, #1952-32, #1952-33. Dark blue jacket trimmed in red, grey trousers.

#1952-34, #1952-35, #1952-36. Dark green jacket trimmed in orange, grey trousers.

1916-259/B	Portuguese Chasseurs standing firing, 1914	15.00
1916-259/C	Portuguese Chasseurs kneeling firing, 1914	15.00
1916-259/D	Portuguese Chasseurs lying firing, 1914	15.00
1929-249	Women of the Red Cross, 1914	14.00
1952-31	Prussian Grenadiers marching, 1st Empire Period	16.00
1952-32	Prussian Grenadiers firing, 1st Empire Period	16.00
1952-33	Prussian Grenadiers assaulting, 1st Empire Period	17.00
1952-34	Russian Infantry marching, 1st Empire Period	16.00
1952-35	Russian Infantry firing, 1st Empire Period	17.00
1952-36	Russian Infantry assaulting, 1st Empire Period	17.00
1952-49	Chasseurs on foot, green uniforms, 1st Empire Period	16.00
1952-205	Siamese Infantry marching, 1900	15.00
1952-205/B	Siamese Infantry standing firing, 1900	16.00
1952-205/C	Siamese Infantry kneeling firing, 1900	16.00
1952-206	Egyptian Infantry marching, 1900	15.00
1952-206/A	Egyptian Infantry assaulting, 1900	16.00
1952-206/B	Egyptian Infantry standing firing, 1900	16.00
1952-206/C	Egyptian Infantry kneeling firing, 1900	16.00
1952-206/D	Egyptian Infantry lying firing, 1900	16.00
1952-207	Austrian Infantry marching, 1900	14.00
1952-207/A	Austrian Infantry assaulting, 1900	15.00
1952-207/B	Austrian Infantry standing firing, 1900	15.00

1952-207/C	Austrian Infantry kneeling firing, 1900	15.00
1952-207/D	Austrian Infantry lying firing, 1900	15.00
1952-207/P	Austrian Infantry marching, 1914	14.00
1952-207/Q	Austrian Infantry assaulting, 1914	15.00
1952-207/R	Austrian Infantry standing firing, 1914	15.00
1952-207/S	Austrian Infantry kneeling firing, 1914	15.00
1952-207/T	Austrian Infantry lying firing, 1914	15.00
1952-209	Portuguese Infantry, 1914	14.00
1952-210	English Grenadiers, 1900	14.00
1952-211	English Colonial Infantry marching, 1880	16.00
1952-211/A	English Colonial Infantry assaulting, 1880	17.00
1952-211/B	English Colonial Infantry standing firing, 1880	17.00
1952-211/C	English Colonial Infantry kneeling firing, 1880	17.00
1952-211/D	English Colonial Infantry lying firing, 1880	17.00
1952-220	Monacans, blue uniforms, 20th Century	15.00
1952-221	Monacans, white uniforms, 20th Century	15.00
1952-227	Polytechnicans, 1914	14.00
1952-234	Marine Infantry in overcoats marching, 1914	14.00
1952-234/A	Marine Infantry in overcoats assaulting, 1914	15.00
1952-234/B	Marine Infantry in overcoats standing firing, 1914	15.00
1952-234/C	Marine Infantry in overcoats kneeling firing, 1914	15.00

#1952-207/Q. Medium green uniform.

#1952-209. Medium blue uniform.

#1952-210

#1952-211/A. Red tunic.

L to R: #1952-211/A, #211/B, #211/C.

L to R: #1952-220, #1952-221.

#1952-234

#1952-239. Various color shirts.

		VG
1952-234/D	Marine Infantry in overcoats lying firing, 1914	15.00
1952-234/F	Marine Infantry in overcoats running, 1914	15.00
1952-234/G	Marine Infantry in overcoats standing firing, 1915	15.00
1952-234/H	Marine Infantry in overcoats kneeling firing, 1915	15.00
1952-234/J	Marine Infantry in overcoats lying firing, 1915	15.00
1952-234/K	Marine Infantry in overcoats marching, 1915	14.00
1952-234/L	Marine Infantry in overcoats assaulting, 1915	15.00
1952-234/T	Marine Infantry in tunics marching, 1914	14.00
1952-239	Moroccans marching, 1914	16.00
1952-239/A	Moroccans assaulting, 1914	17.00
1952-239/B	Moroccans standing firing, 1914	17.00
1952-240	North American Indians on foot, 1870	18.00

#1952-241

1952-241	Malgaches marching, 1900	16.00
1952-241/A	Malgaches assaulting, 1900	17.00
1952-241/B	Malgaches standing firing, 1900	17.00
1952-248	Chasseurs on foot in overcoats marching, 1914	14.00

		VG
1952-248/A	Chasseurs in overcoats assaulting, 1914	15.00
1952-248/B	Chasseurs in overcoats standing firing, 1914	15.00
1952-248/C	Chasseurs in overcoats kneeling firing, 1914	15.00
1952-248/D	Chasseurs in overcoats lying firing, 1914	15.00
1952-248/F	Chasseurs in overcoats running, 1914	15.00
1952-248/G	Chasseurs in overcoats standing firing, 1915	15.00
1952-248/H	Chasseurs in overcoats kneeling firing, 1915	15.00
1952-248/J	Chasseurs in overcoats lying firing, 1915	15.00
1952-248/K	Chasseurs in overcoats marching, blue, steel helmets, 1915	14.00
1952-248/L	Chasseurs in overcoats assaulting, blue, steel helmets, 1915	15.00
1952-248/T	Chasseurs in tunic marching, 1914	14.00

CAVALRY (Price per piece)

Note: Napoleonic cavalry (starting with #211) had several characteristics. Officer would almost always be on rearing white horse, trumpeter on walking white horse, flagbearer on rearing dark horse. Trumpeter would usually wear opposite colors of rest of regt. (i.e., green jacket with pink trim for troopers; pink jacket with green trim for trumpeter).

200	Gaul Cavalry at the trot, 100 B.C.	$22.00
200/A	Roman Cavalry, 100 B.C.	22.00
200/B	Greek Cavalry, 400 B.C.	22.00
201	Hun Cavalry, 5th Century	22.00
201/A	Frank Cavalry, 5th Century	22.00
202	Mounted Crusaders at the trot, 11/12th Century	22.00
203	Mounted Knights of the Middle Ages at the trot, 13th Century	22.00
204	Mounted Knights attacking, 13th Century	23.00

#200

#200/A

#200/B

#201

#201/A

#202

#203

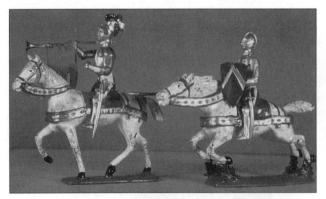

L to R: #203, #204.

#204

#205

#205

#206

		VG
205	Cavalry of Henry IV at the trot, 1589-1610	22.00
206	Musketeers of Louis XIII at the trot, 1610-1643	22.00
207	Guards of Richelieu, 1610-1643	22.00
208	Cavalry of Louis XIV, Balthazar Regiment at the trot, red, blue or white 1670	21.00
209	Cavalry of Louis XV, Anjou Regiment, 1740	21.00
210	Dragoons of Louis XV, 1740	22.00
211	Grenadiers of the Guard, mounted, 1809	24.00
211/A	Dromedary Camel Regiment, Egyptian Campaign, 1799	27.00
212	Dragoons of the Guard, 1809	24.00
213	Guards of Honor, 1813	24.00
214	Cuirassiers, 1809	24.00
215	Carabiniers, 1812	24.00
216	Chasseurs of the Guard, mounted, 1809	24.00
217	Artillerymen, mounted, 1809	24.00
218	Chasseurs of the Line, mounted, 1809	24.00
219	Light Horse Lancers, 1st Regiment, 1812	24.00
220	Light Horse Lancers, 2nd Regiment, 1812	24.00
221	Light Horse Lancers, 5th Regiment, 1812	24.00

		VG
222	Elite Gendarmes, 1810	24.00
223	Mamelukes, 1810	24.00
224	Hussars, 1st Regiment, 1808	24.00
225	Hussars, 2nd Regiment, 1808	24.00
226	Hussars, 3rd Regiment, 1808	24.00
227	Hussars, 4th Regiment, 1808	24.00

#208

#209

#209

#210

#211 Trumpeter. Medium blue jacket, red over blue plume.

#212. Dark green jacket, red plume.

#213. Blue jacket, red trousers, red over blue plume. (Trumpeter should be on a white horse.)

#214 Bugler. Yellow jacket trimmed in blue, red plume.

#215. Left: Gold chest armour, white sleeves, red plume; Right: Trumpeter. Gold chest armour, medium blue sleeves, red plume.

#216. Dark green jacket trimmed in yellow, red over green plume, white breeches.

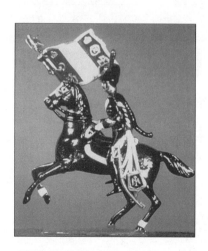

#217. Dark blue, trimmed in red, red plume.

#218. Dark green uniform, trimmed in red. (Bugler's horse incorrect.)

Left: #220. Dark green uniform, orange chest panel; Right: #219. Dark green uniform, red chest panel.

VG			VG
228	Hussars, 5th Regiment, 1808 .... 24.00	230	Lancers of the Vistula, 1808 .... 24.00
228/A	Imperial Guard of Strasbourg, mounted, 1805 . 24.00	231	Dutch Lancers, 1812 .... 24.00
229	Polish Lancers, 1812 .... 24.00	231/A	Prussian Hussars, 1813 .... 24.00
229/A	Lancers of Berg, 1809 .... 24.00	231/B	Austrian Hussars, 4th Regiment, 1813 .... 24.00

#221. Dark green uniform, light blue chest panel.

#222. Dark blue coat, red vest.

#223. Dark green vest and shirt. Rider on far right is later version with yellow sleeves.

Left: #224. Sky blue uniform, black over yellow plume; Right: #225. Brown uniform, blue over black plume.

Left: #226. Grey uniform, red over grey plume; Right: #227. Royal blue uniform, red plume.

#228. Sky blue uniform, white trim on pelisse (hanging jacket), black over yellow plume.

#229. Blue sleeves, red chest panel, white plumes. (Flagbearer should be on rearing horse.)

#230. Dark blue uniform with yellow chest panel, blue over black plume.

#231. Red uniform, with dark blue chest panel.

#231/B. Dark green jacket trimmed in yellow, red breeches, green over yellow plume.

#232 General of Division.

#233

#233. All grey uniform, yellow cap.

#234. Dark blue jacket, light blue breeches.

#235. Gold armour.

		VG				VG
236	Cossacks, red tunics, at the attack, 1900	24.00		241	Goumiers trotting, 1914	24.00
236/T	Cossacks, red tunics, at trot, 1900	24.00		241/A	Goumiers on dromedary camels, 1914	30.00
237	Prussian Uhlans in black uniforms, 1900	24.00		241/G	Goumiers attacking, 1914	26.00
237/K	Prussian Uhlans in khaki uniforms, 1914	26.00		242	Guards of Paris, 1900	22.00
238	Prussian Hussars, black uniforms, 1900	24.00		243	Saint Cyrians, 1900	22.00
238/K	Prussian Hussars, khaki uniforms, 1914	26.00		244	Hussars, 1914	22.00
239	African Chasseurs, 1900	24.00		244/H	Hussars, blue kepis, tunics, 1915	22.00
240	Spahis, 1900	24.00		245	Dragoons in winter cloaks, 1914	24.00

#236

#236/T

#237

#237/K

#238

#238 Officer.

#239

#239

#240

#241

		VG			VG
245/A	Cuirassiers, 1914	22.00	248	USA Cavalry, olive drab uniforms, montana hats, at trot 1918	24.00
245/B	Dragoons in tunics, 1914	22.00	248/A	USA Cavalry, steel helmets, at trot, 1918	24.00
245/C	Dragoons in blue, steel helmets, 1915	22.00	248/B	USA Cavalry, montana hats, at gallop, 1918	24.00
245/D	Cuirassiers in blue, 1915	22.00	248/C	USA Cavalry, steel helmets, at gallop, 1918	24.00
246	English Life Guards, full dress, red tunic, 1900	22.00	248/H	USA Cavalry, montana hats, at halt, 1918	24.00
246/K	English Life Guards, khaki, 1916	24.00	249	English 1st Life Guards, 1815	24.00
247	English Horse Guards or "Blues", full dress, 1900	22.00	250	Rumanian Hussars, 1900	22.00
			251	Austrian Dragoons, 1914	22.00

#242 Bugler.

#243. Light blue jacket.

#245 Bugler.

#245/A

#245/B Bugler.

L to R: #246, #247.

#248

#1911-323/K Officer.

		VG
252	Austrian Lancers, 1914	22.00
253	Hindu Cavalry, khaki, 1914	24.00
254	Kettle Drummers, 1st Empire, C.B.G./Mignot version, 1st Empire	27.00
255	Spanish Hussars, 1808	24.00
256	Hussars, 9th Regiment, "Red Hussars", 1812	24.00
257	Hussars, 11th Regiment, 1812	24.00
258	Scouts of the Young Guard, 1813	24.00
259	5th Belgian Light Dragoons (Waterloo), 1815	25.00
260	Bengal Lancers, Army of India, 1900	25.00
261	Volunteer Hussars of Death (French Revolution), 1793	24.00
262	7th Hussars (Green Hussars), 1st Empire, 1805-1813	24.00
263	Hussars-Lancers of Lauzun (American War of Independence), 1778-1783 264 Bavarian Uhlans, 1808	26.00
264	Bavarian Uhlans, 1808	26.00
265	Dragoons of Kleber (Egyptian Campaign), 1799	26.00
266	Foreign Legion in blue and white uniforms on dromedaries, 1906	30.00
1911-322/A	English Dragoons, full dress uniform, 1900	22.00
1911-322/K	English Dragoons, khaki uniforms, 1916	23.00
1911-323/A	English Hussars, full dress uniform, 1900	22.00
1911-323/K	English Hussars, khaki uniforms, 1916	23.00
1911-324	English Colonial Cavalry, 1900	24.00
1911-324/K	English Colonial Cavalry, khaki	24.00
1911-325/A	Italian Dragoons, 1900	22.00
1911-325/B	Italian Lancers, 1900	22.00
1911-325/C	Italian Lancers, 1900	22.00
1911-326	Spanish Cavalry, 1900	22.00
1911-328	Japanese Cavalry, 1900	23.00
1911-329	Boer Cavalry, 1900	24.00
1911-335	Cavalry of the Transport Corps, 1900	22.00
1911-336	Gendarmes or Policemen, 1900	23.00
1916-332	Belgian Guides, 1900	22.00
1916-333	Belgian Lancers, 1900	22.00
1929-341	Agent on horseback at repose, 1929	22.00
1929-342	English Cavalry, khaki, 1929	22.00
1929-350	General Staff, 1914 uniforms, 1914	24.00
1929-351	General Staff, blue uniforms, 1915	24.00
1933-337	Chinese Cavalry, 1933	24.00
1933-338	Greek Cavalry, 1933	22.00
1933-339	Swiss Cavalry, 1933	22.00
1952-57	Cavalry of Louis XIV, red uniforms	22.00
1952-58	Cavalry of Louis XIV, white uniforms	22.00
1952-301	Russian Dragoons, 1900	22.00
1952-302	Prussian Dragoons, 1900	22.00
1952-302/K	Prussian Dragoons, khaki, 1916	22.00
1952-303/A	Cossacks in blue at trot, 1900	22.00
1952-303/B	Cossacks in blue at gallop, 1900	22.00
1952-306	Chasseurs a cheval, 1914	22.00
1952-306/H	Chasseurs a cheval, blue, 1914	22.00
1952-308	Mounted Artillerymen, dark blue, kepis, 1914	22.00
1952-308/H	Mounted Artillerymen, light blue, 1915	22.00

#1911-325/A Officer.

#1911-329

#1952-306 Officer.

#1952-317/K

Display Set #5 of flats, boxed.

		VG
1952-315	Indians (North American), 1870	24.00
1952-316	Buffalo Hunters (North American), 1870	24.00
1952-317	Prussian Cuirassiers, 1900	22.00
1952-317/K	Prussian Cuirassiers, khaki, spiked helmets, 1916	23.00

HISTORIC PERSONAGES ON FOOT

		EXC
100	Jeanne d'Arc (415)	$35.00
101	Louis XV (433)	35.00
102	Louis XVI (434)	35.00
103	Napoleon ler, redingote (443)	35.00
104	Napoleon ler, Grand tenue	35.00
105	Louis XI (416)	30.00
106	Henri III (426)	30.00

French Army (1914) display in box. Sold for $3,200.00 in 1995 through William Doyle Galleries.

		EXC			EXC
107	Henri IV (428)	30.00	401	Nebuchadnezzor, 600 B.C.	35.00
108	St. Louis (Louis IX) (409)	35.00	402	Cleopatra, 1st Century B.C.	35.00
109	Marechal Joffre (452)	35.00	403	Saint Denis, martyr, 3rd Century A.D.	35.00
110	Marechal Lyautey (452)	35.00	404	Saladin, 12th Century A.D.	35.00
111	President Poincare (448)	35.00	405	Richard the Lion Hearted	35.00
112	Dames de le Cour de Henri III	30.00	406	Simon de Montfort	40.00
113	Dames de Moyen Age	30.00	407	Raymond de Toulouse	35.00
114	Pape (Pope) (441?)	30.00	408	Blanche de Castille	30.00
115	Mme. de Maintenon (432)	30.00	409	Saint-Louis (Louis IX)	30.00
116	Louis XIV (429)	30.00	410	Duguesclin	35.00
117	George Washington (440)	35.00	411	Duguesclin, standard	40.00
KQ	King and Queen (450 and 451?)	65.00	412	Etienne Marcel	30.00
400	Ramses II, Pharaoh, 1300 B.C.	35.00	413	John the Fearless	30.00

#101

#102

#103

#105

#106

#107

#108

#109

#401

#402

#405

#422

#423

#435

#439

#446

#447

#450

	EXC
414	Christopher Columbus, standard 35.00
415	Joan of Arc 35.00
416	Louis XI 30.00
417	Charles le Temeraire 30.00
418	Tristan l'Hermite 30.00
419	Bayard 35.00
420	Anne de Bretagne 35.00
421	Diane de Poitiers 30.00
422	Catherine de Medicis 30.00
423	Reine Margot 30.00
424	Francois Ier 30.00
425	Marie Stuart 30.00
426	Henri III 30.00
427	Charles I of England 35.00
428	Henri IV 30.00
429	Louis XIV 30.00
430	Marie-Therese 35.00
431	Madame de Montespan 30.00
432	Madame de Maintenon 30.00
433	Louis XV 30.00
434	Louis XVI 35.00
435	Marie Antoinette 35.00
436	Marie Antoinette at Trianon 35.00
437	Louis XVII, Dauphin 30.00
438	Princess de Lamballe 30.00
439	LaFayette 35.00
440	George Washington 40.00
441	Pope Pius VII 30.00
442	Napoleon Ier 35.00
443	Napoleon Ier, en redingote 35.00
444	Marie-Louis, Empress 30.00
445	Josephine, Empress 35.00
446	President Lincoln 35.00
447	Queen Victoria 35.00
448	President Poincare 30.00
449	Marshal Joffre 30.00
450	King George V of England 35.00
451	Queen Mary of England 35.00
452	Lyautey, Resident General of Morocco 30.00
453	General Petain 30.00

HISTORIC FIGURES ON HORSEBACK

		EXC
150	Bonaparte (622 or 623)	$50.00
151	Charlemagne (603)	50.00
152	Joan of Arc (609)	50.00
153	Richelieu (616)	45.00
154	Louis XIV (619)	45.00
155	Napoleon I (624)	50.00
156	Caesar (601)	50.00
157	Vercingetorix (600)	50.00
158	St. Louis (608)	45.00
159	Louis XI (610)	45.00

#152

#153

#155

#158

#159

#160

#161

#165

#168

#169

#604

#607

#611. Mounted in typical plastic pack of the 1955-1980 period. Background is a biographical card about her, in French and English.

#625

LARGE FLAG SERIES
(figures mounted on wood blocks)

		VG
900	House of the King 1565	$60.00
901	Swiss Regiment 1585	60.00
902	Regiment of the King 1589	60.00
903	Picardie 1680	60.00
904	Brittany 1680	60.00
905	Saintonge 1680	60.00
906	Royal Galley 1680	60.00
907	Louis XIV flag 1680	60.00
908	Royal Artillery 1690	60.00
909	Dauphine Regiment 1747	60.00
910	87th of Brie 1748	60.00

		VG
911	24th of the Queen 1749	60.00
912	Royale Marine Guards 1740	60.00
913	Royal Standard 1740	60.00
914	Saxe 1780	60.00
915	Salis-Samade 1782	60.00
916	Side of the Ocean 1680	60.00
917	Dillon 1786	60.00
918	Royal Roussillon 1680	60.00
919	Admiral of France 1680	60.00
920	Sainte-Opportune Batallion 1789	60.00
921	Saint-Jacques Hospital Ship Batallion 1789	60.00

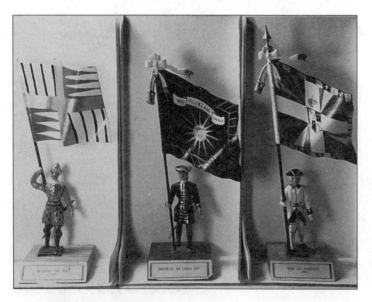

L to R: #900, #907, #933.

#908

#931

#935

#941

L to R: #944, #943.

		VG
922	Oratoire Batallion 1789	60.00
923	Saint-Louis in Isle Batallion 1789	60.00
924	Carmes-Dechausses 1789	60.00
925	Saint-Germain l'Auxerrois Batallion 1789	60.00
926	3rd Regiment of Voltigeurs of the Line 1809	60.00
927	Grenadiers of the Guard 1812	60.00
928	Chasseurs on foot 1812	60.00
929	Marine Guards 1812	60.00
930	French Guards (Louis XVI) 1780	60.00
931	Royal Corse 1755	60.00
932	Bourgogne Regiment 1750	60.00
933	Dauphin Regiment 1750	60.00
934	Royal Normandie 1750	60.00
935	Grenadiers of France 1756	60.00
936	Blancs-Manteaux Batallion 1789	60.00
937	Champs-Elysees Batallion 1789	60.00
938	Saint-Severin Batallion 1789	60.00
939	Saint-Marcel Batallion 1789	60.00
940	Popincourt Batallion 1789	60.00
941	Genadiers of the Guard on horse 1812	60.00
942	Chasseurs of the Guard on horse 1812	60.00

		VG
943	3rd Voltigeur of the Young Guard 1812	60.00
944	13th Voltigeurs 1813	60.00
945	5th Tirailleurs grenadiers of the young guard 1813	60.00

VEHICLES

		EXC
800	Chariot of Ramses II with Escort	
	Chariot	$200.00
	Escort, each	20.00
802	Chariot of Nero	200.00
1513	French covered truck with driver, 1916	120.00
1520/C	French staff car, 3 figures	150.00
1521/C	Prussian staff car, 3 figures	160.00
1522/C	U.S. staff car, in montana hats, 3 figures	150.00
3002	American Civil War cannon, comes with ammo wagon	200.00
	3002/C: Confederate; 3002/U: Union (same for both armies, except uniform)	
3003	American Civil War ambulance	175.00
	3003/C: Confederate; 3003/U: Union (same for both armies, except uniform color)	

#800

#802

#829 *"Review at Longchamp."*
Value $250.00 Excellent.

"Napoleon's Farewell at Fountain Blue." $400.00 in Excellent.

#1513

#1520/C

#3002/U

#3002/U
Ammo wagon.

#3002/C Ammo wagon.

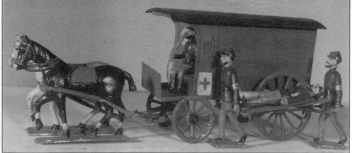

#3003

POMPIERS (Fire Service) (1900-1914)

		EXC
1300	Mobile Boiler with 1 sitting fireman	$115.00
1301	Horse-drawn ladder with 1 sitting fireman	135.00
1302	Hand Pump with 2 firemen	55.00
1303	Reeling Machine with 2 firemen	55.00
1304	Fire Officer	14.00
1305	Fireman with fire hose	15.00
1306	Fireman with pick	15.00
1307	Fireman with hatchet	15.00
1308	Fireman with rope	15.00
1309	Fireman with bucket	15.00
1310	Fire officer with map	15.00
1311	Running fireman with ladder	22.00
1312	Fireman with shovel	15.00
1313	Fireman with trumpet	15.00
1314	Sitting fireman	14.00
1315	Walking fireman	14.00
1316	Running fireman	14.00
1317	Cycling fireman	22.00
1318	Fireman with victim in arms	24.00
1319	Fireman with flag	15.00

Four firemen holding jump net. Value $50.00 Excellent.

Courtesy W. Doyle Gallery.

#1310

		EXC
1320	Sitting fireman with whip	15.00
1321	Running fireman (as with 1302 and 1303)	15.00
1322	Ladder automobile with 1 sitting fireman	125.00
1323	Horse-drawn Boiler with 1 sitting fireman with whip	130.00
1324	Call Box	6.00
1325	Policeman	14.00
1326	2 Firemen with stretcher and victim	42.00
1327	Command-car of Dion-Bouton with 2 firemen, 1910	95.00

MISCELLANEOUS CIVILIANS

Average $15.00 each in VG.

From Set #846 Modern Sports (c. 1920).

#577/2 A.L.V.F. Unit - Railway Gun Diorama. (Exc. boxed) $2,000.00.

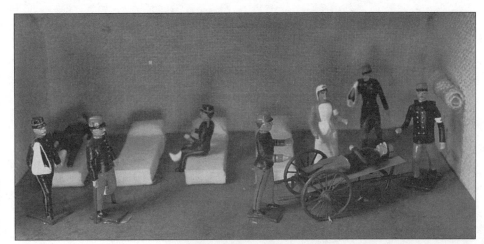

#584 Field Hospital Diorama, 1914.

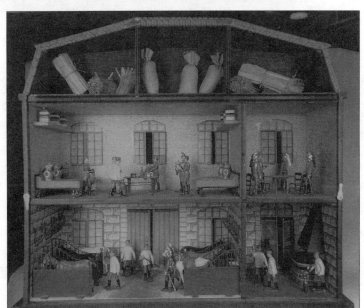

#375 "Cavalry Barracks" 3-tier diorama. (Exc.) $750.00. Photo by Gerard McFerren.

Above and right: #545 "Aviation" large version (with 2 planes). All mounted on one long base. Pilots, mechanics, officers, dog and doghouse, trees, hangar, ports, and civilians looking over fence. (Exc.) $1,000.00.

France
Aluminum, Solidcast
54-60mm standard
Plastic

✕ Miscellaneous ✕ French Aluminum & Plastic

by K. Warren Mitchell

There were three major makers of aluminum toy soldiers in France; Mignalu (C.B.G.-Mignot), Frenchal and Quiralu (Quiralu was owned by M. Quirin). They appeared on the market in the mid-1930s and reached their highest popularity at the end of the 1940s, then gave way to plastic, due to price.

As a rule, none are marked in such a way as to be easily identifiable. Many exported ones had paper stickers under the bases, which fell off long ago. Hence, we group all makes together here and identify those we can.

Price averages in Very Good: Mounted $18, Foot $12, Civilian $8, Animals $5.

Mignalu set shown in normal manner of packaging, tied in standing position. Photo courtesy Guernsey's.

Mignalu "General," detachable.

Unknown. Photo by Will Beierwaltes.

Unknown. Photo by K. Warren Mitchell.

Unknown. Photo by John O'Neill.

Unknown. Photo by Joe Saine.

Quiralu set in box. Photo by K. Warren Mitchell.

Unknown. Photo courtesy Jim and Ann Morris.

Unknown. Photo by K. Warren Mitchell.

Unknown. Photo by K. Warren Mitchell.

Unknown. Photo by K. Warren Mitchell.

Mignalu. Photo by K. Warren Mitchell.

Unknown. Photo by K. Warren Mitchell.

A plastic Aztec given away by a French gum company. Value $4.00. Courtesy Paul Stadinger - Stad's.

L to R: FR42, FR43. These are by Frenchal and a little larger than Britains. Aluminum. Photo by Harold Haseley.

L to R: FR44, FR45. These are by Frenchal, and a little larger than Britains. Aluminum. Photo by Harold Haseley.

Unknown. Photo by K. Warren Mitchell.

Nicely done French plastic coffee premiums. L to R: "Light Foot" and "Big Fisherman" by Café Lesal and "Robinson Crusoe" by Café Martin. Photo courtesy Plastic Warrior.

⚔ Miscellaneous ⚔ French Hollowcast Metal

by K. Warren Mitchell

Like myself, many collectors get frustrated at finding a really interesting figure, but discover no markings to tell us the maker. All of the following are marked "France" and/ or "Depose," and deserve attention; but a lack of documentation, in the way of old catalogs, leaves these a mystery. Price is in the "eye of the beholder," generally ranging from $10-$15 for foot figures and $15-$20 for mounted.

#1. Possibly Mignot.

L to R: #2 (in blue), #3. 54mm.

L to R: #4, #5, #6, #7. Probably Mignot hollowcast 54mm.

#8. Unmarked.

L to R: #9, #10, #11, #12. Possibly Mignot 54mm.

L to R: #13, #14. Unknown 54mm.

L to R: #15, #16, #17. Unmarked 60-65mm.

#18. Unknown 54mm, but marked "G.M." DEPOSE. Right heel is similar to Lucotte. Photo courtesy Jim and Ann Morris.

#19. Unmarked 54mm. Right heel is up like Lucotte.

#20. Solidcast 56mm. Photo courtesy Jim and Ann Morris.

#21. Unmarked 54mm.

#22. Moveable arm, 75mm.

#23. 75mm.

L to R: #24, #25 (latter may be U.S.-made, William Feix). 75mm.

#26. 75mm.

#27. 55mm.

#28. 75mm, marked G.M. Photo by K. Warren Mitchell.

#29. 65mm.

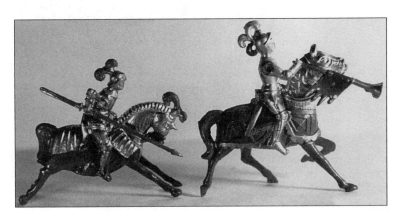

L to R: #30, 70mm; #31, 75mm.

#32. 54mm.

#33. 54mm.

#34. 54mm, 2-piece.

#35. 54mm (almost exactly like J. Hill Co.).

#36. 75mm.

#37. 60mm.
Photo by
Joseph F. Saine.

L to R: #38, #39. 75mm.

L to R: #40, #40A, #40B. 60mm. Photo by Joseph F. Saine.

#41. 60mm. Photo by Joseph F. Saine.

#42. 60mm. Photo by Joseph F. Saine.

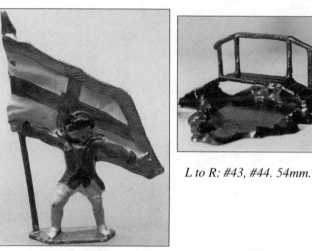

L to R: #43, #44. 54mm.

#45. 50mm.

#46. 54mm.

#47. 70mm.

#48. 65mm.

#49. 54mm.

L to R: #50 and #51, 54mm; #52 and #53, 65mm.

L to R: #54, #55. 70mm.

L to R: #56, #57, #58, #59. 70mm.

L to R: #64, #65, #66, #67. 54mm.

L to R: #60, #61, #62, #63. 65mm.

L to R: #70, #71, #72, #73. 65mm.

L to R: #68, #69. 70mm.

#74. 65mm.

L to R: #75, #76, #77, #78. 65mm.

#79. 65mm.

L to R: #80, #81. 65mm.

L to R: #82, #83, #84, #85. 65mm.

#89

#90. 54mm.

L to R: #87, #86. 65mm.

#88. 54mm.

L to R: #91, 70mm; #92, 65mm; #93 and #94, 70mm.

#95. 54mm.

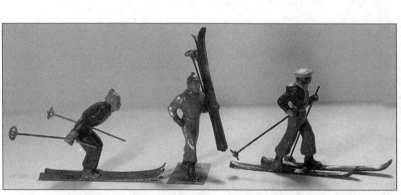

L to R: #96, #97, #98. 70mm.

L to R: #99, #100, #101, #102. 54mm.

#103.
54mm.

#104. 54mm.

#105. 75mm.

#106. 75mm.

30mm.

France
Plastic
60, 40, 20mm

⚔ **Starlux** ⚔

by Tom Figiel

Like many European manufacturers, Starlux began by producing figures in composition. After World War II, it switched to injection-molded plastic. Its first attempts are very crude in both sculpting and painting. By the late 1950s-early 1960s, vast improvements were made and delightful lines of Knights, Napoleonics, Cowboys, Indians, Pirates, Romans, Gauls, Modern Soldiers, French historical themes and Animals were produced. Many were made in the three scales listed above. Two different paint styles were manufactured: "Luxe," which is the best and "Choc," which is very simple.

In the late 1980s, much of its production was discontinued and many of their lines are now offered only in "Choc." Prices in Luxe (60mm) generally run $6 for foot and $12 for mounted. Prices in Choc 60mm pieces generally reach $2 for foot and $3 mounted. All the figures shown here are 60mm (about 2-1/2" high). Starlux's own numbers are shown where possible. Unless noted, photos are by Joseph F. Saine. (*Plastic Warrior* magazine has recently determined that Starlux began plastic production under Pierre Beffara, who bought the firm in 1945.)

L to R: CW1, CW2.

L to R: CW3, CW4.

L to R: CW5, CW6, CW7, CW8.

L to R: CW9, CW10, CW11, CW12.

L to R: CW13, CW14.

L to R: CW15, CW16.

L to R: CW17, CW18, CW19, CW20.

L to R: CW21, CW22, CW23, CW24.

Starlux Hitler (discontinued). Value $20.00. Photo by Paul Stadinger - Stad's.

L to R: SP1, SP2, SP3. Starlux Pirates, value $8.00 each. Photo by Paul Stadinger - Stad's.

L to R: SC1, SC2. Early Starlux. Value $10.00 each. Courtesy Paul Stadinger - Stad's.

L to R: #4105, #4104, #7001, #7002.

L to R: #6007-B, #6007-A, #6066, 6008.

L to R: #6009, #6058, #6010, #6050.

L to R: #6012, #6011, FH2023 (Dugesclin), #6052.

L to R: #6014, #6030, #6013, #6029.

L to R: #6016, #6017, #6015, #6018.

L to R: #6019, #6067, #6034, #6021.

L to R: #6023, #6022, #6024, #6032.

L to R: #6024 (Ivanhoe), #6118.

L to R: #6026, #6027, #6025, #6028.

L to R: #6035, #6002, #6001.

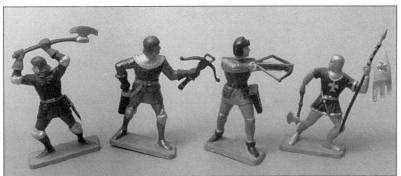

L to R: #6036, #6039, #6005, #6049.

L to R: #6045, #6051, #6048, #6031.

L to R: #6047, #6046, #6043, #6033.

L to R: #6055, #6056, #6006, #6057.

L to R: #6061-A, #6061-B, #6004-B, #6004-A.

L to R: #6062, #6063, #6004, #6037 (Ivanhoe).

L to R: #6101, #6201.

L to R: #6103, #6105.

L to R: #6106, #6102.

L to R: #6107, #6108.

L to R: #6110, #6109.

L to R: #6117, #6120.

L to R: #6113, #6104.

L to R: #7004, #7011, #7012.

L to R: #7008, #7003, #7005, #7009.

*L to R:
FH41032,
FH41031,
#7027, #7029.*

*L to R:
#7031, #7032,
#7023, #7024.*

L to R: #7022, #7028, #7030, #7025.

L to R: #7102, #7105.

L to R: #7104, #7101.

L to R: #7106, #7103.

L to R: #7123, #7122.

L to R: #7126, #7121.

L to R: #41017, #7001, #41016, #41013.

France
Metal, Solidcast, Hollowcast
60mm (approx. 2-1/2")

⚔ Gustave Vertunni ⚔ (1884-1953)

by Will Beierwaltes

Though they are most eagerly sought by toy soldier collectors, the toy soldiers of Gustave Vertunni are really not so much toys as collectors miniatures. His work was a vast assortment of historical figures and their supporting cast of armies produced as individual pieces to a high artistic standard.

Vertunni was an Italian, the "temperamental master," who preceded his famous line of single portrait figures with two lesser-known attempts at producing (Mignot-style) standard toy soldiers, first in France before the First World War, and then a more elaborate figure range in Belgium after the war. He returned to France in 1935 and began the line of figures for which he has become famous. His range was particularly popular with the French, whose history was the core theme of his work. His figures were not imported out of France until he was discovered by the Americans and British during their occupation of Paris after World War II. His associations with American and British collectors led to a small line of American historical personalities and an expansion of the number of British subjects, all in the same characteristic style.

Vertunni was originally a wood carver, and various collectors have suggested that his originals from which the molds were taken were all carved in wood. This resulted in the typical rounded and relaxed static poses that characterize them all. While he did the research and carved the masters, his (second) wife, with a group of four to six hired "girls" did the painting in a very consistent style and beautiful eggshell patina. It was this unusual standard of quality, along with the marketing of single pieces rather than armies, which makes the production of Vertunni the real forerunner of the connoisseur figure and the "military miniature" of today.

The end of his career seems to be a matter of some speculation. Various authors have suggested he immigrated to either Britain or the United States in the last years of his production, but it is more likely that he traveled to those locations after the war, due to his new popularity in the new export opportunities not previously realized. The French collecting community, who know his work the best, suggest he remained in Paris until his death in 1953. His wife (the painter) continued production from his molds for some time after his death. Though it is not clear when production actually ceased, it most likely ended in the mid 1950s.

The work of Vertunni is characterized as a series of robust 60 mm portrait figures covering a broad spectrum of European historical subjects and personalities from antiquity to the middle ages on to the 1940s. It primarily represented individuals from the French courts (royal and imperial), but included a variety of European and English historical personages; the representations were drawn from a number of historical sources. In each "epoch," he included a sampling of representative common soldiers, including medieval men-at-arms and French 18th century and a particularly broad selection of Napoleonic soldiers. Because of the similarity of uniforms, unlike the personalities, various regiments could be made from common molds, greatly expanding the production of this era. His catalog also included some (but few) mounted figures, including a mounted knight and a variety of Napoleonic cavalry. Most standing figures are solid-cast lead, but the broader-based figures with flowing robes, thrones or dresses and the horses are hollowcast. The French collector Crahet has documented over 500 original molds, many of which might produce more than one catalog entry. Despite the voluminous possible catalog, the figures actually available in the United States were more limited, probably as only a function of what was immediately available. The accompanying listing is taken from the different postwar mail-order catalogs of Corr's and the House of Miniatures in the early 1950s and probably is a reasonable (though not complete) representation of the pieces readily available to U.S. collectors.

Identification of individual pieces can be a real problem, as no illustrated catalog is known and figures are rarely (but sometimes) labeled. Because of the variety of figures, value is difficult. Standard foot figures and uncomplicated castings of personalities in Good to Excellent condition usually range from $25 to $30, while more collectible famous personalities may fetch up to $40. Large complex pieces (such as seated on a throne) may bring as much as $60, and a mounted figure (with horse) in excellent shape could bring as much as $75.

Partial U.S. distributor's catalog of the figures of Gustave Vertunni (numbers are drawn from the U.S. commercial catalogs and probably do not represent Vertunni's own cataloging):

1. Julius Caesar
2. Charlemagne
3. Marie Therese
4. Marie Leczinska
5. Isabeau de Baviere
6. Louis IX
7. Charles VI
8. Duchess Chateauroux
9. Henry VIII of England
9. Henri I
10. Phillipe Auguste
11. Charles VIII
12. Francois I
13. Francois II
14. Henri II
15. Marie de Medici
15. Philippe August
16. Louis XIII
16. Isabelle ed Hainaut
17. Louis XIV
18. Louis XV
19. Napoleon (sacre)
19. Louis IX (St. Louis)
20. Marie Louise
21. Henry VII of England
22. Anne Boleyn
22. Duc de Choiseul
22. Chev. Francais of Jean le Bon
23. Arbaletrier of Joan of Arc
24. Footman of Joan of Arc
25. Soldats d' Aventure, Francis I
26. Swordsman of Francis I
23. Anne of Cleves
24. Catherine Parr
25. Queen Elizabeth I
25. Marie Antoinette
26. Mary Stewart
27. Catherine de Medici
27. Charles IV
27. French Guard, Louis XIV
28. Colonial Infantry, Louis XIV
28. Charles IX
29. Henri III
30. Henri IV
31. Cardinal Richelieu
32. Maurice of Saxony
33. Louis XVI
29. Chasseur Fischer, Louis XVI
30. Guard Artillery, Louis XVI
31. Chasseur Officer, Louis XV
32. Queens Dragoons, Louis XV

33. Royal Dragoon, Louis XV
33. Charles V
34. Scotch Guard, Louis XV (gardes Ecossaises)
34. Marie Antoinette
35. General Buonaparte
35. Jean Sans Peur
35. Eugene de Beauharnais
36. Napoleon (redingote)
36. Arquebusier, Henry III
37. Arquebusier, Henry IV
38. Dante
37. Louis Bonaparte
38. Marshal Ney
38. Charles VI
39. Isabel de Bavaria
39. King George VI of England, ceremonial robes
40. Queen Elizabeth, ceremonial robes
41. Liutgarde, Charlemagne's wife
41. Louis d'Orleans
42. Louis d'Orleans (alternate)
42. Charles VII
43. Marie d'Anjou
42. Louis VI Le Gros
43. Philip IV Le Bel
44. Louis X
45. Charles IV
46. Jeanne de France
47. Charles V
48. Jeanne de Bourbon, wife of Charles V
49. Charles VII
50. Charlotte de Savoie, wife of Louis XI
51. Philip Le Bon, Duke of Burgundy
52. Jeanne d'Albert, mother of Henry IV
53. Elisabeth d'Autriche, wife of Charles IX
53. Margaret of Scotland (d'Ecosse)
54. Comte de St. Mailgrim
55. Duc de Luynes
56. General Lasalle
57. General Duroc, as Grand Chamberlain
57. Philippe le Bon
58. Baron Dubois, perf. police
58. Charles VIII
59. Cuirassiers (Nap)
60. Dragoons (Nap)
61. Gendarmes d'Elite (Nap)
61. Marie e'Angleterre
62. Gardes Ecossaises, Louis XV
57. Philippe le Bon
58. Charles VIII
61. Mary of England
63. Francis I (Francois)
69. Henry II
70. Catherine de Medicis
71. Antoine de Bourbon
75. Francis II (Francois)
76. Marie Stewart
78. Charles IX
79. Elizabeth of Austria
82. Henry III
83. Louise de Lorraine
87. Henry IV
88. Marguerite de Valois
89. Marie de Medicis

Court ladies and Louis XIV. L to R (starting with second from left): #83, #125, #99.

90. Gabrielle d'Estrees
99. Louis XIV
100. Marie Therese
101. Madame de Maintenon
109. Grande Madamoiselle (Melle)
114. Louis XV
115. Marie Lesczinska

#114

#115

117. Dutchess de Chateauroux
122. Duc de Choiseul
123. Louis XVI
125. Marie Antoinette
125. Countess d'Artois
129. Bailli de Suffren
131. De Beaumarchais
215. Philippe II of Spain
216. Henry VII of England

218. Henry VIII of England
220. Anne Boleyn of England
222. Ann Cleves of England
224. Catherine Parr
? General George Washington
141. General Lafayette
? Jeanne Hachette
141. General Hoche
? Dante
? King George VI (Coronation Robes) 1937
? Queen Elizabeth (Coronation Robes) 1937

Medieval figures w/Jeanne Hatchette.

VERTUNNI'S ARMIES OF THE FIRST EMPIRE ETAT MAJOR

148. Napoleon (Great Coat)
146. General Bonaparte
149. Napoleon (Coronation Robes)
150. Josephine (Coronation Robes)

#148

Napoleon, L to R: Egypt, Court (#149), Field (#146).

L to R (starting with second from left): #140, #141, #36, #37.

L to R: #150, #149.

Etat Major. Third from left: #153; Fourth from left: #163; Second from right: #56.

151. Josephine de Beauharnais
152. Marie-Louise
153. Louis Bonaparte
155. Murat, Roi de Naples
163. Marshal Ney
164. Marshal Suchet
166. Marshal Grouchy
167. Marshal Brune
168. Marshal Lannes
169. Marshal Saint Cyr
170. Marshal McDonald
173. Marshal Berthier

174. Marshal Lefebvre
181. General Cabronne
183. General Castella
184. General Bertrand
186. Marshal Nansouty
187. General Daumesnil
197. Commandant Kirman
198. General Russe
205. Duroc, Grand Chamberlain
Colonel Lasueur

IMPERIAL GUARD

	Dragoon Officer (dsmtd)
V9	Grenadier
V10	Foot Chasseurs
V11	Foot Artillery
V17	Sapeur, Grenadier Garde
V20	Officer, Mounted Chasseurs of the Garde
V21	Officer, Imperial Guard Artillery

GRAND ARMY

| D | Officer, Gendarmes d'Elite |
| E | Officer, Grenadiers |

V12	Officer, Mounted Chasseurs (dsmtd)
V13	Train d'Equipage
V14	Vive l'Empereur
V15	Trumpeter, 20th Rgt., Mt Chasseurs (dsmtd)
V16	Drum Major, Grenadier Band, Garde de Paris
V18	Sapeur, Grenadiers, Garde d'Paris
V19	Hussar, 10th Rgt., Compagnie Elite

ALLIES, NAPOLEONIC

| F | English Horse Guard (dsmtd) |

Napoleon's Troops.

Napoleonic Marshals and Troops. Third from left: V19; Fourth from left: V16; Second from right: #60.

Germany and Austria

✕ **Elastolin Plastic** ✕

by Joseph F. Saine and Tom Fiegal

Hausser Elastolin first produced plastic figures in 1947. The most popular, without a doubt, are the Prince Valiant/ Normans series. These figures, along with the working siege machines and castles, are the high point of what many plastic collectors consider to be the finest-painted and sculpted toy figures ever produced.

Along with the Normans, Elastolin also made Cowboys, Indians, Vikings, Huns, Romans, Space Creatures, African Natives, Landsnechts, Revolutionary War, Civil War, 20th Century Soldiers, and a wide variety of Farm and Zoo animals. They also made a full line of accessories, such as forts, wagons, zoo cages and campfires.

70mm was the standard size and 40mm an attempt to make the figures more affordable. In 1960, a 70mm foot figure cost $1 and mounted $2. The largest castle sold at $50, quite pricey for toys. Elastolin also made a cheaper soft plastic range to compete with the lower-priced Britains and Timpo figures so popular at the time. The firm ceased production in 1983.

The value of an Elastolin figure is determined by its age and condition. Broken figures have little value. There are basically three different color styles. Identifying the painting will given you a better idea of the value.

Version I 1955-1963

Base: Silver/pearl colored for Romans/Indians
Plastic: Ivory-colored, very brittle
Paint: Looks like candlewax applied as a wash
Siege equipment molded in white plastic and fully painted

Version II 1964-1967

Base: Pale green
Plastic: White
Paint: Fully painted flesh, garments used to create shading

Version III

Base: Bright green, though it is possible to have any base
Plastic: Pink
Paint: Fully painted except the flesh, which was left unpainted
Shading drybrushed

Preiser of Germany now produces almost the entire Elastolin line. They are done in Version II. Most Preiser figures have a redesigned base. The base is still marked "Elastolin" but no longer has the characteristic raised circle.

Prices are for third version. Add 50% for second version. Add 100% for first version.

Many thanks go to Jeff Anusbigian and Rick Berry for opening their homes to have their collections photographed.

(All photos by Joseph F. Saine)

		MINT
6800	Totem Pole	$20.00
6801	Chief with Spear	20.00
6802	Chief with Spear and Shield	20.00
6805	Indian Boy with Urn	20.00
6808	Chief with Spear and Peace Pipe	20.00
6818	Medicine Man	20.00
6824	Stalking with Tomahawk and Shield	20.00
6827	Running with Spear and Shield	20.00
6828	Crawling with Tomahawk	20.00
6829	Chief Shooting Bow Standing	20.00
6830	Chief Kneeling Shooting Bow	20.00
6832	Squaw Kneeling with Bowl	20.00

L to R: #6818, #6805, #6829.

		MINT
6833	Squaw with Papoose	20.00
6834	Firing Rifle Behind Rock	20.00
6835	Brave Sitting with Spear	20.00
6836	Brave with Tom Tom	20.00
6837	Chief Sitting with Peace Pipe	20.00

L to R: #6837, #6838, #6839.

6838	Chief Sitting with Spear and Shield	20.00
6839	Chief Sitting with Rifle and Shield	20.00
6840	Chief Standing Firing	20.00
6842	Brave Lying with Rifle	20.00

INDIANS
Mounted

L to R: #6844, #6845.

6844	W/Tomahawk and Shield at Chest	$10.00
6845	W/Shield on Back Firing	10.00
6846	Throwing Lasso	10.00

L to R: #6846, #6848.

L to R: #6847, #6853.

		MINT
6847	Crouching Shooting Bow	10.00
6848	Shooting Bow Forward	10.00
6850	Shooting Bow Left	10.00
6851	Firing Rifle Left	10.00

L to R: #6851, #6850.

6852	W/War Club	10.00
6853	Throwing Spear	10.00
6854	Chief with Spear	10.00

Foot

6867	Aiming Tomahawk	10.00
6868	Shooting Bow (working)	10.00
6869	Throwing Spear	10.00
6880	Shooting Bow (shot)	10.00
6881	War Dance with Tomahawk	10.00
6882	Kneeling with Knife Throwing Tomahawk	10.00
6883	Firing Revolver with Knife	10.00
6884	Throwing Axe with Shield	10.00
6885	War Dance with Shield and Tomahawk	10.00
6887	Throwing Spear with Shield Chief	10.00
6888	With Scalp Overhead	10.00
6890	Brave Throwing Spear with Shield	10.00
6892	Chief with Knife and Tomahawk	10.00
6894	Brave with Rifle Hand on Brow	10.00

COWBOYS
Foot

6901	Scout with Rifle Across Waist	$10.00
6902	Indian Scout Hand Raised	10.00
6905	Firing Pistol From Hip	10.00
6906	Bandit with Money Bag Fleeing	10.00
6907	With Hands Raised	10.00
6908	Bandit Firing Pistols	10.00

		MINT
6910	Trapper Firing Pistol	10.00
6911	Clubbing with Rifle	10.00
6913	On One Knee Firing Pistols	10.00
6915	Kneeling Firing Rifle (no hat)	10.00
6916	Kneeling Firing Rifle (hat)	10.00
6917	Standing Firing	10.00
6921	Arms Open with Rifle	10.00
6958	Cowboy Tied to Tree	10.00
6966	Pioneer Standing Firing	10.00
6967	Pioneer with Knife and Musket	10.00
6969	Pioneer with Pistol	10.00
6970	Cowboy in Buckskins with 2 Guns	10.00
6976	Cowboy Running with Rifle	10.00
6978	Cowboy Throwing Lasso	10.00

L to R: #6978, #6976, #6980.

6980	Pioneer with Musket Port Arms	10.00
6982	Pioneer Stalking with Musket	10.00
6985	Sheriff with Drawn Pistol	10.00

Mounted

6990	Full Gallop with Rifle	20.00
6992	Firing Pistol, Running	20.00
6994	At Halt Scouting	20.00
6996	Running Firing Rifle	20.00
6998	Galloping Tossing Lasso	20.00

L to R: #6996, #6992.

L to R: #6998, #6990.

		MINT
6999	At Halt Firing Pistol	20.00
7001	Full Gallop Bandit with Pistol	20.00
7000	Running Firing to Left	20.00

7th CAVALRY

7020	Kneeling Firing	$10.00

L to R: #7020, #7024, #7022.

7022	Officer Running with Pistol	10.00
7024	Firing Pistol with Standard	10.00
7030	Mounted Officer with Pistol	20.00
7032	At Halt with Standard	20.00

#7032

REVOLUTIONARY WAR COLONIALS

7080	George Washington Mounted	$16.00
7083	George Washington on Foot	10.00
7091	Marching	8.00
7092	Drummer	8.00
7093	Fifer	8.00
7094	Flagbearer	10.00
7096	Spirit of '76 Fifer	10.00
7097	Drummer Boy	10.00
7098	Spirit of '76 Drummer	10.00

#7030

L to R: #7080, #7083, #7091, #7092, #7093.

L to R: #7502, #7500, #7510, #7516, #7515.

L to R: #7506, #7512, #7504, #7508.

#7514

L to R: #7534, #7532, #7533, #7531.

L to R: #7538, #7540, #7539, #7535.

L to R: #7542, #7541.

JUNGLE FIGURES

		MINT
7500	Native Running with Spear and Shield	$10.00
7502	Native Throwing Spear	10.00
7504	Native Throwing Spear with Shield	10.00
7506	Native Kneeling with Bow	10.00
7508	Native Standing with Bow	10.00
7510	Native with Parcel on Head	10.00
7512	Native on Back with Knife and Shield	10.00
7514	Natives Carrying Game on Pole	20.00
7515	Hunter with Rifle on Shoulder	12.00
7516	Hunter Standing Firing	12.00

KARL MAY FIGURES

7521	Old Shatterhand (in buckskins)	$10.00
7529	Winnetou	10.00
7531	Old Shatterhand	10.00
7532	Sam Hawkins	10.00
7533	Will Parker	10.00
7534	Dick Stone	10.00
7535	Rattler	10.00
7537	Kle Khi-Petra	10.00
7538	Intscha-Tschuna	10.00
7539	Winnetou (in buckskins)	10.00

		MINT
7540	Nscho-Tschi	10.00
7541	Old Shatterhand with Knife	10.00
7542	Meta-Akva with Knife	10.00
7550	Old Shatterhead Mounted	20.00
7551	Winnetou Mounted	20.00

WESTERN

7703	Covered Wagon with Family	$75.00
7712	Stage Coach (including 2 riders and drivers) with 2 Horse Hitch	75.00
7714	Stage Coach (including 2 riders and drivers) with 4 Horse Hitch	100.00

ROMANS

8401	Marching with Spear	$12.00
8402	Walking with Sword	8.00
8403	With Eagle Standard	8.00
8404	With Straight Horn	8.00
8405	With Curved Horn	8.00
8406	With Drum	8.00
8407	With Standard	8.00
8410	Officer Issuing Orders	8.00
8412	Commander	8.00
8420	Running with Sword	8.00

L to R: #7550, #7551.

#7703

#7712

L to R: #8407, #8410.

L to R: #8412, #8420.

L to R: #8421, #8422.

L to R: #8423, #8424.

#8425

#8450

#8453

#8457

#8459

#8750

#8752

#8754

#8756

		MINT
8421	Throwing Spear at Walk	8.00
8422	Throwing Spear at Halt	8.00
8423	With Sword at Down Thrust	8.00
8424	With Sword at Up Thrust	8.00
8425	Defending with Sword	8.00
8430	Running with Bow	8.00
8431	Firing Bow	8.00
8435	Aiming Sling	8.00
8436	Loosing Sling	8.00
8450	Galloping with Sword, Mounted	16.00
8453	Running with Standard, Mounted	16.00
8457	Galloping with Spear, Mounted	16.00
8459	Charging with Sword, Mounted	6.00

VIKINGS

8500	Drawing Sword	$10.00
8501	With Spear	10.00
8502	Throwing Spear	10.00
8503	Swinging Battleaxe	10.00
8504	Fighting with Sword	10.00
8505	With Shield and Battleaxe	10.00

ARCHERS

8642	Drawing Arrow From Quiver	$15.00
8643	Notching Arrow	15.00
8644	Loosed Arrow Upward	15.00
8646	Arrow Shooting	25.00
8647	Shooting Down	15.00

MOUNTED HUNS

8750	Kettle Drummer	$35.00

		MINT
8752	With Axe and Standard	30.00
8754	With Horn and Sword	30.00
8756	Drawing Arrow	30.00
8757	With Spear	30.00
8760	Pulling Arrow	30.00
8761	With Sword and Shield	30.00

NORMANS

8801	Prince Valiant	$15.00
8802	Sir Gawain	15.00
8803	Prince Valiant Fighting	15.00
8804	Prince Arne	15.00
8810	Aleta (Courtmaiden)	15.00
8830	Running with Spear	12.00
8831	With Spear Overhead	12.00
8832	Climbing Assault Ladder	15.00
8833	With Sword at Side	12.00
8835	Catapult Lever	12.00
8836	Dropping Rock	12.00
8837	Swinging Sword Sidearm	12.00
8838	Swinging Sword Down	12.00
8839	Blacksmith	12.00
8854	With Axe and Round Shield	22.00
8855	Charging with Lance	22.00
8857	With Spear Overhead	22.00
8866	At Gallop with Lance	22.00
8867	At Gallop with Lance and Cape	22.00
8868	At Gallop with Lance Cape and Triangle Shield	22.00
8880	Rearing Horse with Mace	25.00

#8757

#8760

#8761

L to R: #8801, #8802, #8803, #8804.

L to R: #8810, #8830, #8831, #8833.

#8832

L to R: #8835, #8836, with #9892 (catapult).

L to R: #8837, #8838, #8839.

L to R: #8866, #8897.

L to R: #8867, #8855.

L to R: #8868, #8857.

L to R: #8880, #8882.

		MINT
8882	Rearing Horse Throwing Spear	25.00
8882	Rearing Horse with Sword	25.00
8886	Rearing Horse with Lance	25.00

KNIGHTS

8931	Attacking with Sword	$8.00
8932	With Shield and Mace	8.00
8934	Sword Pointing Down	8.00
8935	With Lance at Waist	8.00
8936	With Lance Pointed Down	8.00
8937	Standing with Lance	8.00
8938	Walking with Lance	8.00
8939	Thrusting Sword Up	8.00

		MINT
8940	Slashing with Sword	8.00
8965	Mounted with Lance Up	14.00
8966	Mounted Attacking with Lance	14.00

LANDSKNECHTS

9001	With Shouldered Lance	$15.00
9003	Marching with Standard	15.00
9004	Fifer	15.00
9005	Drummer	15.00
9021	Loading Musket	15.00
9022	Aiming Musket	15.00
9025	Running with Standard	15.00
9026	Running with Lance	15.00

L to R: #8931, #8932, #8934.

L to R: #8935, #8936, #8937.

L to R: #8938, #8939, #8940.

L to R: #8965, #8966.

L to R: #9001, #9003.

L to R: #9004, #9005, #9021, #9022.

L to R: #9026, #9025, #9028.

L to R: #9029, #9030, #9031.

L to R: #9040, #9041, #9042.

L to R: #9043, #9044, #9045.

L to R: #9110, #9112, #9120.

L to R: #9122, #9124, #9126.

L to R, all #9136: British, American Militia, Washington's Militia, unknown, Prussian Infantry.

L to R: #9141, #9142, #9143, #9144.

		MINT				MINT
9028	Standing with Lance	15.00	9155	Fifer		No Price Found
9029	Thrusting Pike Up	15.00	9156	Flagbearer		No Price Found
9030	Thrusting Pike	15.00	9160	Officer with Sword		No Price Found
9031	Thrusting Pike Down	15.00	9161	Loading Musket		No Price Found
9040	Officer	15.00	9162	Advancing		No Price Found
9041	Standing with Ramrod	15.00	9163	Running with Rifle		No Price Found
9042	With Ramrod	15.00	9164	Kneeling Firing		No Price Found
9043	With Ramrod	15.00	9165	Standing Firing		No Price Found
9044	Fusilier	15.00	9169	Maid with Pitcher		No Price Found
9045	Rolling Barrel	15.00				

TURKS

		MINT
9110	With Sword and Pistol	$15.00
9112	Standing Firing	15.00
9120	With Lance	15.00
9122	With Square Shield and Sword	15.00
9124	With Round Shield and Sword	15.00
9126	Firing Bow	15.00

PRUSSIAN INFANTRY

9150	Mounted	No Price Found
9151	Officer on Foot	No Price Found
9153	Marching	No Price Found
9154	Drummer	No Price Found

UNION

9170	Officer Sword Drawn	$10.00
9171	Marching	12.00
9172	Drummer Boy	10.00
9174	Flagbearer	12.00
9175	Officer Mounted	20.00
9176	Prone Firing	10.00
9177	Kneeling Loading	10.00
9178	Standing Firing	10.00

CONFEDERATES

9180	Officer Sword Drawn	$10.00
9181	Marching	12.00
9182	Drummer Boy	10.00
9184	Flagbearer	12.00
9185	Officer Mounted	20.00
9186	Prone Firing	10.00

L to R: #9170, #9171, #9172, #9174.

L to R: #9176, #9177, #9178, #9175.

L to R: #9180, #9181, #9182, #9184.

L to R: #9186, #9187, #9188, #9185.

		MINT				MINT
9187	Kneeling Loading	10.00	4915	Cactus		15.00
9188	Standing Firing	10.00	4930	Rock Formation		15.00

TREES

					ORDNANCE	
4900	Double Pine	$10.00	9800	Howitzer		$35.00
4901	Large Pine	10.00	9802	Foot Mortar		35.00
4905	Birch	10.00	9803	Cannon Balls		5.00
4906	Oak	10.00	9804	Bombarde		100.00
4907	Poplar	10.00	9808	Culverin		50.00
4910	Palm Trees	20.00	9810	Heavy Culverin		50.00

L to R: #4901, #4900, #4905.

L to R: #4910, #4915, #4907.

#9800

#9802

#9804

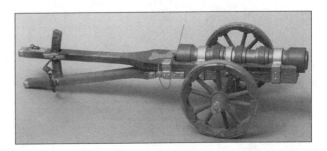

#9808

		MINT
9812	Skorpion Cannon	35.00
9880	Lance Catapult	50.00
9881	Arrow Catapult	35.00
9883	Camp Fence	10.00
9885	Siege Tower	85.00
9887	Scaling Ladder	15.00
9888	Small Catapult	25.00
9890	Medium Catapult	25.00
9892	Large Catapult	60.00
9894	Battering Ram	100.00
9896	Movable Shield	15.00
9898	Movable Shield	15.00

#9864. Roman Chariot. No price found.

#9880

#9885

#9890

#9896

#9898

#9892

TRAIN

		MINT
7731	Locomotive	$150.00
7736	Passenger Car	50.00
7738	Flat	25.00

#7731

#7736

#7738

✕ "Flats; Zinnsoldaten" ✕

by Will Beierwaltes

What today is often referred to as the "FLAT," is really the original tin soldiers, or Zinn Soldaten. This refers to a broad spectrum of two-dimensional military and civilian figures cast in pure tin. The standard (or Neurenberg) scale of figures is 30mm (1-3/16") from base to head top, but flats come in any variety of sizes, from minute to very large, especially those from before the scale standardization of 1924. They are generally paper thin and cast on one or both sides in relief.

Historically, flat figures can be traced as far back as the 13th and 14th centuries, to its roots in Germany. As early as the mid 1500s, Zinn Soldaten came under the control of the Pewterers, and the first major commercial production began by Hilpert in the mid 1700s. The most famous, and clearly the most prolific, manufacturer was Heinrichson, who began with the dawn of the European Industrial revolution in the 1830s, and produced from thousands of molds. This also heralded the beginning of the true "toy soldier" (available to common children), and also the flat as a toy.

The flat is historically a German toy, and popular in Austria, Switzerland and Scandinavia, though the French (Mignot and Segom) have produced flats in more limited quantities. They have never caught on well in England or North America, so their availability is often quite limited in the United States.

Flats are cast from slate molds, in which the cavity is actually engraved. Because of their two-dimensional nature, extensive detail and complex images can be translated into a toy. Painting was often done as cottage industry, child labor or even prison labor, and the early flats were sold by weight, rather than in the fancy set presentation boxes one thinks of with fully round figures. A figure is often the product of the work of an artist, an engraver who transforms the art into the mold, and the editor who commissions the piece and markets it. Commonly, molds may pass between manufacturers, making identification even more difficult. The best identification key is often the base of the figure, as the shape of the base, or artist or trade marks on its underside provide a key as to who the manufacturer may be. Some examples from the more famous makers are provided.

The older "toy" figures are often smaller than 30mm, and are more stylized than truly anatomical in their sculpting. The painting is often simple or stylized, employing the thin alcohol-based paints rather than the opaque heavy paints of the mid-1900s. Several grades of paint were often available for different markets. Since the 1930s, the flat has taken on a new life, much like the dissociation of the fully round toy soldier and the (assemble and paint yourself) military miniature. Most flats are now highly detailed and beautiful miniatures offered unpainted or painted to a high artistic standard. Value is a tough call, as today's unpainted figures may cost from $1 to $10 each, depending on the complexity, while older toys, fully painted and of historical significance, may cost only a fraction of that. The most interesting are complex sets of a variety of poses, especially with an original box. The best suggestion is to determine what something is worth to you, follow your instincts, and go from there. In any purchase of flats, keep in mind that there is practically no commercial market for these toys compared to the fully round figures in the United States.

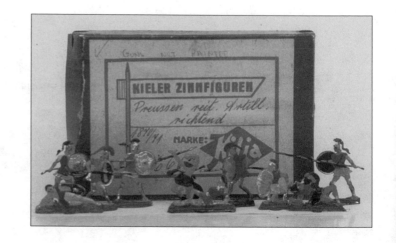

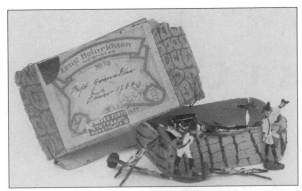

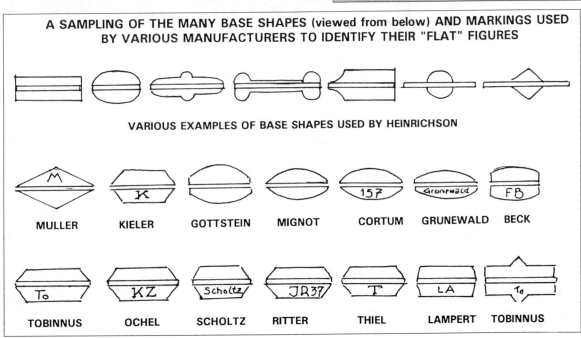

A SAMPLING OF THE MANY BASE SHAPES (viewed from below) AND MARKINGS USED BY VARIOUS MANUFACTURERS TO IDENTIFY THEIR "FLAT" FIGURES

VARIOUS EXAMPLES OF BASE SHAPES USED BY HEINRICHSON

MULLER   KIELER   GOTTSTEIN   MIGNOT   CORTUM   GRUNEWALD   BECK

TOBINNUS   OCHEL   SCHOLTZ   RITTER   THIEL   LAMPERT   TOBINNUS

✕ German Composition ✕

by Jack Matthews

General Description: Method of Manufacture

Composition soldiers and other figures have been manufactured in Germany and other Western European countries since the turn of the century. The method of making such figures derived from materials used in European doll manufacturing since 1850. Pfeiffer of Vienna perfected the soldier technique around 1898. Pfeiffer figures are usually found without a base.

The process is quite simple. A multi-part, accurately machined brass mold is prepared and a cereal-like mixture of wood flour, kaolin and animal glue is hand-pressed into both halves. These ingredients, particularly the fine wood flour, were very cheap and readily available. A skeleton is inserted of thin wire having been bent to the proper shape by hand. The molds are then joined, air-dryed and then heated for a time, to cure the figures. After cooling, the figures were removed from the mold and, while still slightly flexible, trimmed by hand and hand-painted. There is disagreement among experts as to whether undercoating or fillings were routinely used, since the paint usually bonded with the "tacky" surface of the figures. While factory painters were used, most of the figures were painted at home by "kitchen labor" on a piece-work basis, according to strict painting instructions and standards laid down by the manufacturer.

Despite their paper-mâché appearance, composition figures are surprisingly tough and resistant to damage. The paint, while subject to some chipping through play and a certain amount of age fading, usually holds up quite well after 50 to 75 years. Mint or near mint figures made more than 75 years ago can still be found. However, if subjected to undue moisture, major damage (large cracks, rusting and overall deterioration of the composition material) will occur. Often, in these circumstances, the bases will warp. Needless to say, such damage substantially detracts from the value and appearance of the figure. Deterioration in value of such a damaged composition piece is no different than it would be for comparable damage to a Britains or other metal toy soldier.

Elastolin and Lineol

While many companies produced composition figures in France, Belgium, Italy, Denmark, Germany, Czechslovakia and Austria from 1905-1960, only two achieved prominence in the field: O&M Hausser (Elastolin), founded in 1904 in Ludwigsberg in Southern Germany, and Lineol, founded by Oskar Wiederholz in 1905 in Brandenburg/Havel. These firms were major competitors, had the bulk of the composition soldier market and the worldwide sales and marketing networks. For more than 50 years, they produced a vast array of the highest quality soldiers and associated military tinplate toys and trenchworks. Both companies also manufactured a wide range of "civilian" figures, animals, barnyard scenes, castles, forts, zoo scenes, railway sets and Christmas scenes. Both firms were among the major exporters of Christmas creche scenes throughout the world, particularly to the United States. Lineol also produced a limited line of children's cooking and tea sets and wooden toys, while Hausser produced a much larger line of wooden and other toys, such as scooters, pull toys, boxed games and table tennis. Contrary to popular belief, these non-military items constituted the majority of the pieces made. For example, in the 31-page Hausser catalog of 1939-40, at the height of nationalistic fervor, 20 pages are devoted to "civilian" pieces.

Elastolin

During the early years of the company's existence, numerous sizes of figures up to and more than 20cm were made. However, few company records were maintained. From 1912-1928, the most popular figures were 10.5cm in heights (approximately 4-1/2"). Few catalogs of this era were published, the most important being the Catalog F of 1920, which had several editions thereafter. These catalogs listed several hundred figures and sets. There were usually not more than two standard sizes in the Elastolin line at any one time, in the 5cm, 6.5cm and 10.5cm sizes, with the emphasis on the latter.

From the earliest production known, the basic figures were made without heads. The head would be made separately in appropriate national headdress and inserted before painting. This meant that thousands of varieties of figures were possible. The basic body, for almost all figures, was a German one. A marching British figure at slope would have a German torso with German equipment, e.g., bread bag, canteen, hand grenade, etc. The distinguishing features were the head and the way the figure was painted. This company advertised, as did Lineol, that it could manufacture any nation's soldiers, including flags, at no additional cost. Large sale boards with dozens of tinplate flags of different nations were maintained for marketing purposes. Most of the early figures, of any nation, have the dis-

Composition figures, mainly Elastolin. Courtesy Christie's New York.

tinctive twirling mustaches of the day. Hausser made marvelous boxed scenes of Eskimo hunts, Buffalo Bill's Wild West Show and Tiger Hunting Safaris, complete with large mounted elephants and gunbearers, as well as massive circus sets. Few sets, if any, remain intact; although often accumulaions of similar figures are attempted to be sold as complete sets. Many of these were actually the creation of Pfeiffer. Their distinctive, baseless 10.5cm figures are now quite rare. Pfeiffer "personality" figures range in price from $200 to $600 each, depending on condition. Its marvelous Indian elephant scenes, for example, are equally expensive.

The 5cm, 5.5cm, 6cm and 6.5cm sizes remain the least popular of Elastolin figures, although tens of thousands of these smaller figures were sold in the United States painted as WWI doughboys. They are very common, notwithstanding their age and are not highly sought-after by collectors. 10.5cm figures, while not the most popular size, continue to be an excellent collectible, particularly among European collectors, many of whom tend to shy away from Nazi-era political figures. Again, the common "doughboy" type variety in this size are quite common and not particularly desirable.

During the 1930s, around the time the company moved from Ludwigsburg to its new headquarters at Neustadt bei Coburg near the center of the German doll and toy industry,

it acquired the assets of some competitors, including Durolin of Czechslovakia. The move coincided with the rise of National Socialism and Hitler. Hausser then emphasized the production of the figures of the German Army and the Nazi era. They are best known for these figures today. During this period, the standard size became 7.5cm (3-1/4"). It is these figures that are the most highly prized by modern collectors. Advances by the Elastolin technical department resulted in the manufacture of hundreds of different and difficult poses. These include figures firing caps, battery-operated electric fires and searchlights, etc.

The years from 1932-1942 can be rightly called the "golden age" of composition figures and related toys, since it was during this period particularly that the marvelous tinplate vehicles, cannon and horse-drawn items made by Hausser, Lineol and Tipp & Co., of Nuremburg, were produced. Hundreds of different figures of all the services were made: Army, Navy, Luftwaffe, Panzer Corps, Flak Corps and all of the various "political" divisions including SA, SS Labor Corps and Hitler Youth. For collecting purposes, figures of this era may be roughly divided into several categories and subcategories. (a) general army figures consisting of slope, action, leisure, medical, Panzer mounted, artillery, band and communications; (b) navy; (c) luftwaffe; (d) political; (e) civilian; (f) cowboys and Indians; and (g) other, including

18th century Frederician Prussians and Knights. Prior to World War II most of these categories, although not all, were made up in the uniforms of numerous foreign countries, the most prominent being France, Italy, Britain, United States, Belgium, Denmark and Switzerland. In terms of rarity (a term often abused), Navy, Luftwaffe, Frederician Prussians and certain political figures are the most difficult to obtain. Immediately after the war, many "political" toys bearing the outlawed swastika were destroyed; today, such figures are still confiscated by German authorities.

In a class by themselves are the Elastolin "personality" figures. These are figures of identifiable personages, such as Hitler, Mussolini, Hindenburg and other national heroes. Prior to the 1930s, only a few personality figures were manufactured, in 6cm size, including Hindenburg, Von Seekt, George Washington, Frederick the Great and his generals Von Siethen and Seydlitz. Hindenburg, Kaiser Wilhelm II and his Kaiserin were made in the 10.5cm size. In the 1930s, such figures became very popular and more than 20 poses in 7.5cm scale were manufactured, including Generals Von Ludendorf, Von Blomberg, Field Marshall Von Mackensen, President Hindenburg, Admiral Raeder, several versions of Hitler and Goring, party figures Von Schirach (Hitler Youth), Hess and Ernst Roehm (first head of the SA). Foreign dignitaries were included, such as Franco of Spain (two versions, one with porcelain head), Mussolini and General Guisan of Switzerland.

In 1936, Elastolin began producing personality figures with hand-painted porcelain heads made by the Hartwig firm of Thuringia. About 10 different porcelain-head figures were sold, mostly to adults as "mantle" pieces. These have increased considerably in value in the last few years. Lineol made no figures of this type. Porcelain head personalities are the most difficult Elastolin figures to obtain in good condition, and this situation reflects their market price. While comparatively few composition fakes, repaints and restorations abound, fakes of personalities, due to their high prices, should be watched for.

While accurate records are not available, owner and employee recollections indicate that figure production in the late 1920s-early 1930s was about one-half million per year, but rose to around 3 million by the end of war-time production. The percentage of those figures that were exported is unavailable. Apart from the early years, there are numerous prewar Elastolin catalogs available. Each spans a two-year period. The last war-time catalog is 1939-1940. Reproductions are easily obtainable, at modest cost, from some dealers. Original postwar catalogs, published on an annual basis, may still be found at modest cost.

Hausser figure production ceased in early 1943, as best can be determined. As materials such as paint and good composition materials became more difficult to obtain, the

Elastolin, top to bottom: S.A. drummers, British infantry, German marching machine gunners. Courtesy Christie's East.

quality of the famous figures commenced a slow, but steady, deterioration. Paints varied according to availability. These late war or "Kreigs produktion" figures are usually less full bodied than mid-late 1930s figures and are often found in one or two colors only, usually all brown or brown and blue-grey. They may corrode more easily. A beginning Elastolin collector should quickly learn to make these quality, time period and size distinctions, since most general toy soldier dealers are not knowledgeable on the subject and tend to rate all Elastolin figures roughly the same.

Postwar Elastolin

The reconstructed postwar Hausser company continued production of composition figures until the early 1960s. In 1946-47, the American Military Government Control Commission of the occupying forces authorized new production, consistent, of course, with the new strict laws banning any item relating to the Nazi era and its symbols. Thus for 20 postwar years, Hausser produced a composition range of Swiss, British, West German and U.S. soldiers, cowboys and Indians, knights and American Revolutionary War figures, together with a very limited range of modified vehicles and cannon painted in khaki, forts, castles and western stockades. No trenchworks were made after World War II. Most of the postwar soldier figures were made from prewar molds with different heads. And it is reported that much of the remaining prewar stock of unpainted and even painted figures was utilized when postwar production began. This was achieved by simply removing the old German head, inserting the new non-German head and painting it in the proper uniform colors. The same was true of the limited number of postwar vehicles and cannons marketed. These sell at well less than one-half the price of similar prewar items.

The postwar cowboys and Indians are a significant improvement over their prewar brethren and, in the opinion of many experts, represent the best animation and molding done by the company. While such figures are now becoming more difficult to obtain in excellent condition, until four or five years ago they were perhaps the most common of Elastolin figures and priced accordingly. Postwar soldiers include a range of more than 30 Swiss figures and a lesser number of similar poses representing British and U.S. occupation and West German troops. Again, the usual Elastolin practice of having one basic "German" body with different heads was followed. Special postwar figures clearly identifiable and made to represent a specific, accurate country or unit included Scots, British Manchester Regiment and British Guards. They were made in both mounted and marching poses. These figures, together with West Point cadets, are the most difficult to obtain of all postwar figures and are priced higher than a Swiss (the most common), U.S. or British figure.

Hausser gradually moved to its current and extremely attractive range of all plastic figures in the late 1950s. A number of transition figures can be obtained, particularly Swiss with plastic insert heads and composition bodies.

These have no special additional value. The all-plastic range included an entirely new and broader line of magnificent figures, including many more Cowboys and Indians, Knights, Romans, Huns, Turks, Ottomans, Landsknechts, Tartars, Vikings, Normans, Gauls, American Revolutionary and Civil War troops of both sides and a vast assortment of medieval cannon, siege weapons, castles, stagecoaches, chariots, wagons and domestic animals (including several personality figures). Many of these figures are now being marketed by the Preiser company following the closing of the Hausser factory in the early 1980s. Earlier Elastolin 7.5cm and 4cm plastic figures and accessories, particularly when found in a box, have at least doubled in value.

Lineol

Lineol's production commenced in Brandenburg in 1905. Early soldiers were in a very large 14cm scale or larger and have a very old toy "heavy" appearance. Old Lineol figures have the trade name embossed on the rectangular base or on the figure itself, it if does not have a base. Like Hausser, Lineol tinplate pieces have the firm's name embossed on the tires, barrels of cannon, etc. Lineol's boxes, like Hausser's, were generally covered by a glazed red paper and often had a colored picture sticker on the top such as a tank climbing an embankment, boys marching in paper hats or the traditional Lineol trademark of three walking geese. Early Lineol sets featured huge parade groupings, some with more than 100 figures.

Unlike Britains, very few Lineol or Hausser boxed soldier sets or boxed tinplate or horse-drawn toys are found today. When they are discovered, the boxes are usually in poor condition. Presence of a box however adds a premium to the value of the contents. Like Hausser, Lineol made figures in a number of sizes. Its larger, most popular size in the first 25 years of its existence was 8cm to 9.5cm in height, somewhat smaller than Elastolin 10.5cm. The range included, as did Hausser's, a few large horse-drawn units. Both companies' items of this type often appear in U.S. or British Army style. Evidently, Lineol did not export heavily to the United States in these early years, since few 9cm figures turn up in this country; when they do, they are usually in poor condition and of the common U.S. uniform variety. Later Lineol figures were also standardized at 7.5cm during the 1930s. Except for its excellent horses and animals, Lineol's earlier 9.5cm figures are not, in the opinion of most experts, as attractive as the large 10.5cm Elastolin figures. Conversely, Lineol's 7.5cm figures, which came into vogue as did Hausser's in the 1930s, are generally considered overall to be superior in molding, painting, animation and creativity to those of Elastolin. Thus, most Lineol 7.5cm figures are priced somewhat higher.

The very large (125 or so pages) Lineol 1932 Export Catalog illustrates the large range of figures manufactured prior to that date and is superior in detail to Elastolin Catalog F, previously described. This catalog was printed in four languages and copies are available with a 20-page English wholesale price list!. The large variety of mounted and medieval figures are of particular interest. Like Hausser, Lineol produced catalogs every other year but not as many. Only about eight to 10 Lineol catalogs are known to exist and rarely turn up in good original condition. Reproductions of some are available, such as the two excellent Lineol Export Catalogs No. 10 of 1937-1938 with text in French/Italian and the other in English/German. Two small catalogs of the postwar East German company "Lineol Plastik Dresden" exist. The quality, layout and descriptions of the Hausser and Lineol catalogs are comparable.

Apart from foreign troops, which were seldom illustrated, a set of post-1930 catalogs allows a collector to ascertain more than 80% of the "German" production line of both companies. During the late-1920s to early 1930s, the most common scale and one greatly exported to the United States in common "doughboy" marching groups and associated horse-drawn units, was 6.5cm in height. As in the case of Elastolin, this intermediate size did not prove particularly popular, and they are not highly sought after, although antique and general toy dealers often fail to make any distinction, thus substantially overpricing these common figures. 6.5cm U.S.-Lineol figures in good condition are worth but a few dollars to a regular collector, since they have little trade value and are easily obtainable. By the end of the 1930s Lineol had produced more than 600 different "German" figures in the 7.5cm scale.

In 1938, the company introduced a line of marvelously molded and detailed 4cm figures designed for play on a limited surface. Thus far, they have been discovered painted in German, Danish and Italian uniforms. Several dozen different 4cm soldiers were produced, including tiny piles of ammunition, flags and Navy and Luftwaffe figures. They are highly sought-after, but still not too difficult to obtain. They are rarely cracked or chipped, probably due to their size and lack of hard outdoor usage; thus, they often are found in very good condition. Only four die-cast vehicles and a cannon were made in this scale and are considered quite rare. Elastolin only produced a few 4cm figures.

Since the companies were quite competitive, it is not surprising that their lines coincided to a considerable degree. While Lineol did not make the variety of uniforms of German troops and political figures as did Hausser, the number of different poses manufactured during this period was about the same. Lineol's figures, with some exceptions, are clearly superior in all respects and tend to be somewhat hardier. Most of its action figures such as the working gas generator piece, metal pontoon boat, radio troops, motorcycles and its knights and cowboys and Indians cannot be matched by Elastolin. Prices are thus about 20% to 50% higher. For example, while a common Elastolin marching bandsman can be obtained for from $25-$35, a corresponding Lineol piece would be in the $30-$60 range. Foot figures are $15 and $25 respectively, in mint condition.

Lineol's "political" figures also have a clear edge over Elastolin's in quality and, particularly, robustness. Elastolin's political range, while considerably greater (many different uniform variations on the same figure) tend to be somewhat puny in comparison. Generally, Elastolin SS, SA, Hitler Youth and similar figures tend to be grossly overpriced, perhaps due to the general overall interest in military memorabilia of this era.

Lineol produced more than 30 7.5cm personality figures during the 1930s, few of which were exported,

Lineol figures. Photo by Ed Poole.

Lineol, top to bottom: French World War II troops, American infantry, American flagbearer and German troops. Courtesy Christie's New York.

including several different poses and uniforms of Hitler and Goring. Like Hausser, several foreign dignitaries were included. Lineol's rarest figures are those of Emperior Haile Selassie of Ethiopia, Kings Edward VIII and George VI of England, Albert and Leopold of Belgium and General Guisan of Switzerland. The very tall King Christian X of Denmark made in precise scale, was also produced, but is comparatively more available, as are the foot and mounted Lineol figures of Mussolini. All Lineol personality figures in good condition are now the highest priced of composition figures, usually selling in the $200-$500-plus range.

Perhaps the most interesting of all Lineol figures are those referred to as "special" figures made to specifically match the foreign soldiers they were intended to represent and not utilizing the cost- and time-saving device of using the standard German body. Most of these figures are shown on p. 23 of the Lineol No. 10 Export Catalog entitled "Assortment of Special English Figures" and p. 25, illustrating similar Italian and Abyssinian troops for the Italian Abyssinian War. Apart from personality figures, these are the most difficult Lineol items to obtain. They include a beautifully-sculpted Coldstream Guards

Drum Major in State Ceremonial dress, Highlanders, Mounted Life and House Guards, Italian Fascist, Alpine and Bersaglieri troops and the aforementioned Abyssinian war contingent. Unfortunately, paint utilized on the white-uniformed Abyssinian troops and Italian native Askaris tends to flake very badly, thus detracting from the value of such figures. Special figures also included Canadian Mounties, accurate British Line troops, Danish Guards, American Revolutionary War figures and Frederician Prussians. The last two were described only in the 1920s Lineol Export Catalog and are seldom seen.

The last known prewar Lineol catalog of 1939-40 illustrated about two dozen new figures that are perhaps the best ever produced. A series of nine artillery figures are outstanding. This "set" including men fusing shells, two-man AA machine gun teams, seated 2cm integrated composition-metal AA gunner and a map group with a monocled general and staff officer, are unique to their perfection among composition figures. Four tinplate vehicles, mortars and cannon are included in this final company offering. All of these pieces were among the last exported to the United States and are the rarest of Lineol action figures.

Postwar Lineol

The Lineol factory in Brandenburg/Havel was not destroyed during the war. In 1949, the company was nationalized and moved to Dresden, East Germany. A small late-1950s catalog describes the company as "VEB, Lineol-Plastik Dresden" and illustrates a limited line of new but excellent Indian figures and domestic and wild animals, including mounted camels and elephants. These figures are still difficult to obtain in Germany and are expensive. A number of postwar Lineol military figures of the German Democratic Republic were also produced. The bases on most (except for band figures) have been changed from the standard rectangular shape to elongated oval (marching) or circular bases (standing). About 15 military figures are known but no "action" poses seem to have been produced. A few flag bearers had linen-type East German cloth flags. These military figures are squat, crude and somewhat poorly painted.

Related Tinplate Items

Both Hausser and Lineol (along with Tipp & Co.) produced a wide range of military vehicles, cannon and horse-drawn pieces that modern experts have long since believed to be some of the finest examples of tinplate toys ever made. Most had numerous working parts such as headlights, turn indicators, cap-firing AA guns, searchlights and, of course, complete working key-windup motors. The range of vehicles of all three companies included cannons of all sizes, flak and searchlight trucks, ambulances, several staff-car versions (Kubelwagons) large lorries, communications vehicles and armored cars and half-tracks (prime movers). Horse-drawn pieces included several towing cannon, mortars, AA carts, field kitchens and bakeries, covered wagons and ambulances. Most could be ordered with two, four and sometimes six horses. All of these pieces were meticulously modeled after actual items in use by the German Army. So much so that, according to the Hausser family, all new vehicles produced in the 1930s had to receive official clearance, and the company had to submit copies of the drawings and photos and an actual working model of the new toy before production could be commenced.

Tipp & Co. produced a broad range of similar pieces, but did not make horse-drawn pieces. However, unlike Lineol and Hausser, Tipp produced several excellent airplanes, including items that dropped cap-firing bombs and dirigibles which today command very high auction prices when complete and in fine condition. Tipp tinplate toys generally sell at much lower prices than do those of Hausser and are generally more common. All Lineol, Elastolin and Tipp tinplate items have risen considerably in the last few years and are becoming increasingly hard to find.

The Value and Pricing of Composition Figures

It is impossible to prepare a price list of Elastolin and Lineol figures, since literally thousands were produced over the 60-70 year history of these companies. Apart from the English language partial list of German military Elastolin figures contained in Reggie Polaine's 1979 book *The War Toys*, no published complete list of Lineol or Elastolin production has ever been compiled, and it would probably be impossible to do because of the numerous foreign variations of basic German figures that were never cataloged. Uncataloged figures are constantly turning up and will continue to do so.

It is possible, however, to approximate the ranges of prices for the composition figures that are generally available to the average collector. The ranges given herein will be based on a general knowledge of prices realized for a number of categories of such figures at the major German auction houses over the last several years and of the price lists of composition figures which have appeared in the same time period. Prices in many of these categories, i.e., band, foot and action pieces, have risen, but remain reasonably stable. The price ranges take into account the popularity of certain groups, i.e, some (eg: SA/SS) are much harder to sell than others. Prices realized at the occasional auctions of composition figures by the major U.S. and British auction houses are of little use since the ranges are so extreme. This situation can perhaps be ascribed to auction fever occurring at such times and the unusually high reserve prices often placed on such pieces by unknowledgeable sources. On a critical note, it is observed that the description and grading of composition condition by the major non-German auction houses continues to, with few exceptions, be optimistic. This may be ascribed to wishful thinking, but more likely on overall lack of expertise in the area.

As is the case with other subject areas of toy soldier collecting, condition cannot be overemphasized. While very minor cracking and fading of compositions can often be expected, major cracks, paint loss and chips significantly detract from an item's value, notwithstanding its apparent rarity. Tinplate vehicles and cannon and horse-drawn items bear similar caution. Horse-drawn pieces are often found with the tinplate parts in fine shape, but with the horse teams in a bad state of deterioration (with the seller making no distinction in price). Such items should be ignored by the beginning collector since he/she will simply have to replace this inferior piece later on.

This listing does not attempt to value the figures produced by the approximately 20 competitors of Lineol and Elastolin such as Durso (Belgium), Durolin, F.F., Schusso, Leyla, N.F. Italy, Armee, Trico (Japan), etc. The quality of the production of these companies varies greatly, but generally the figures are clearly inferior to those of the big two.

The following table of price ranges for types and sizes of Elastolin and Lineol figures assumes Grade II (average, no paint loss, occasional minor cracking at extremities) figures without major corroding, paint fading or any missing or broken parts. It covers figures generally available from collectors, dealers and auction houses and does not include unusual figures or hard-to-obtain personality and special foreign troops. Nor does it attempt to catalog individual prices for the few hundred or so tinplate, horse-drawn and trenchwork/fortification pieces manufactured by Lineol, Elastolin and Tipp & Co. While average prices for certain of these pieces, e.g. the Lineol '88 cannon and staff car continue to be reasonably stable, prices for other major tinplate military toys have increased across the board, based, it is assumed, on their increasing rarity.

Finally, as is often stated, but often disregarded, a seller of Lineol and Elastolin items in quantity cannot nearly expect to receive a price based on "retail" prices for individual pieces, if it is desired to sell all at one time for personal convenience nor can a dealer pay "retail" prices when buying such items for resale.

New Cavendish Books has published two excellent and recommended volumes on Elastolin and Lineol. Since the last edition, prices of the rarer Elastolin and Lineol figures have risen dramatically, particularly in the "Personality" series. Prices for the more common 7.5cm marching, band and action army figures have remained relatively stable, perhaps rising 10% to 20%.

LINEOL
(All Lineol photos by K. Warren Mitchell)

9 cm, marching U.S.	$15.00
9 cm, marching foreign	25.00
9 cm, mounted U.S.	30.00
9 cm, mounted foreign	45.00
6.5 cm, marching	6.00
6.5cm mounted	15.00
6.5cm action	6.00-8.00
4cm single	20.00-45.00
4cm mounted	25.00-50.00

7.5cm (1930-42)

Luftwaffe, marching	$30.00-$40.00
Luftwaffe, artillery	40.00-50.00
Luftwaffe, band	75.00
Luftwaffe, flagbearers	75.00-100.00
Navy, marching	60.00
Navy, officer	60.00
Navy, flagbearer	75.00
Knights, foot	50.00
Knights, mounted	100.00-400.00
Cowboys/Indians, foot	30.00
Cowboys/Indians, mounted	90.00
Frederick the Great, foot	100.00

Army

Marching	$12.00-$20.00
Mounted	30.00-60.00
Flagbearers	50.00-100.00
Band, marching	25.00-35.00
Band, standing	100.00-200.00
Action/Artillery/communications/ hospital/leisure	20.00-50.00

Political

Hitler Youth	$75.00
Hitler Youth, brown shirt	60.00
Hitler Youth, band/flag	90.00-200.00
Hitler Youth, leisure	75.00
Indians/Cowboys, foot/action	60.00
Cowboys/Indians, mounted	100.00
Knights, foot	60.00
Knights, mounted	200.00-400.00
SA/SS marching	30.00-60.00
SA/SS band	50.00-90.00
SA/SS mounted	75.00-150.00
SA/SS flagbearers	75.00-125.00
SA/SS leisure/communications	75.00-125.00

Lineol.

Lineol.

Lineol.

Lineols. Value (VG) $15.00 each.

Lineol.

Lineol.

Lineol.
Value (VG)
$25.00.

Lineol. Value (VG) $65.00.

Lineol.

Lineol. Value (VG) $65.00.

Lineols. Value (VG) $35.00 each.

Lineol. Value (VG) $40.00.

Lineol. Value (VG) $22.00

Rare Lineols. Value (VG) $80.00 each.

PREWAR ELASTOLIN
(All Elastolin photos by K. Warren Mitchell)

10.5cm (1905-1930)

Pfeiffer-Foreign Troops at slope	$50.00
Slope U.S./British Khaki	25.00
Mounted U.S./British Khaki	45.00
Bandsmen/Flagbearers	40.00-50.00
Leisure	20.00
Action	20.00
Scots	30.00
Guards	30.00
Foreign Slope	25.00
Foreign Action/Leisure	25.00
Foreign Mounted	30.00-50.00
Pfeiffer Personalities	200.00-600.00

5.5, 6.0cm (1905-1930)

All Slope/leisure/action	$9.00
All Mounted	15.00

7.5cm (1930-1943)

Infantry-average-slope/officers march	$30.00
Army, communications	35.00
Army, action	20.00-40.00
Army, hospital	20.00-40.00
Army, leisure	20.00-40.00
Army, mounted	50.00-80.00
Army, artillery	40.00-60.00
Army, pioneers	30.00-50.00
Army, flagbearers	40.00
Navy, slope	60.00
Navy, officer	70.00
Navy, band (white)	100.00-250.00
Luftwaffe/Flak, slope	60.00
Luftwaffe/Flak, artillery	50.00-80.00
Luftwaffe/Flak, band	100.00
Luftwaffe/Flak, flagbearer	100.00

Political

SA/SS, marching	$20.00-25.00
SA/SS, band	30.00
SA/SS, mounted	40.00-70.00
SA/SS, flagbearers	75.00

Small-size Elastolins like these often appear to the uninitiated to be valuable because they look (and are) so old. But they are common and not much sought after. Value for the above (VG) $8.00 each.

Elastolin. Value (VG) $30.00 each.

Small Elastolin U.S. troop. Value (VG) $15.00.

Elastolin. Value (VG) $30.00 each.

Elastolin Colonials once sold in U.S. five and tens.

Elastolin U.S. and British troops. Value (VG) $16.00 each.

Elastolin Colonials once sold in U.S. five and tens.

Elastolins cleaning up. Value (VG) $22.00 each.

Elastolin Ethiopians. Value (VG) $25.00 each.

Elastolin French infantry of the line. Value (VG) $15.00 each.

Elastolin U.S. band. Value (VG) $17.00 each.

Elastolin U.S. raft set. Value (VG) $75.00.

Elastolins once sold in U.S. five and tens.

Elastolin Highlanders once sold in U.S. five and tens.

Elastolin. Value (VG) $15.00 each.

Elastolin.

SA/SS, leisure/communications 25.00-40.00
RAD (Labor Corps), slope 75.00
RAD (Labor Corps), band 100.00
RAD (Labor Corps), pioneer 75.00

POSTWAR ELASTOLIN
7.5 cm

West Point Cadets $50.00
Rev. War, foot 30.00
Rev. War, flagbearer 60.00
Rev. War, George Washington, mounted 60.00
Swiss/U.S./British/German
        Action/leisure/hospital/slope 20.00
Swiss /U.S./British/German mounted 35.00
Swiss Band 25.00
Knights, foot 25.00
Knights, mounted 45.00
Cowboys, foot 15.00-20.00
Indians, foot 15.00-20.00
Cowboys, mounted 25.00-40.00
Indians, mounted 25.00-40.00
Scots, marching 40.00
Scots, band 55.00
Guards, marching 60.00
Guards, band 75.00
Coldstream Guards, mounted 100.00
Manchester Guards, foot 75.00
Manchester Guards, mounted 125.00

A large Elastolin next to a 3-1/4"-high American toy soldier. Value of the Elastolin (VG) $40.00.

Elastolin troop drying himself. Value (VG) $22.00.

Elastolin.

Elastolin.

Elastolin.

R to L: unknown, #0/6606, #0/6607, #0/6608 (last two). Elastolin railway figures, 1930s, 5 cm (2") and 7-1/2 cm (2-15/16") high. Value (VG) $15.00 each.

L to R: #0/6610, #0/6623, unknown, #0/6634, unknown. Elastolin railway figures, 1930s, 5 cm (2") and 7-1/2 cm (2-15/16") high. Value (VG) $15.00 each.

⚔ German Composition ⚔ Civilian Figures

by James Theobald

German composition soldiers have long been popular among collectors. Until recently, however, modern collectors have not strongly focused on civilian figures, including zoo and farm figures and scene accessories.

Composition figures were manufactured from the late 1890s until the early 1960s. The materials and production method were used by doll makers in the latter half of the 18th century. Brass molds were hand-filled with a mixture of wood flour, fine white clay and glue. While the mixture was soft, a wire or wood armature was embedded into the mold. The mold pieces were then joined and dried. The figure was removed while warm and flexible, trimmed and painted. The result was an inexpensive, relatively durable toy figure of impressive detail.

Tipple-Topple, a branch of the Pfeiffer doll company of Vienna, Austria, was the first commercial producer of composition soldiers, about 1898. Composition figures were subsequently produced by many companies across the European continent, but the two most prominent manufacturers were Elastolin and Lineol. Elastolin was founded in 1904 by brothers Otto and Max Hausser in Ludwigsberg, Germany and Lineol in 1905 by Oskar Wiederholz in Brandenburg/Havel, Germany. Elastolin and Lineol introduced civilian production lines about 1914. They were major competitors in both German and export markets.

In the 1930s, corresponding with the rise of Hitler, Elastolin relocated to Neustadt bei Coburg, nearer the German doll and toy manufacturing hub of the era. During the period, heavy emphasis was placed on military soldier production. The company ceased production in 1943 due to the ravages of World War II, but resumed limited production of civilian and foreign soldier figures in 1946 under cooperative agreement with postwar occupational forces. In the 1950s, Elastolin began producing plastic figures, which completely replaced composition production by the early 1960s. Elastolin produced high-quality, detailed civilian and soldier figures.

Lineol figures were generally more accurate and detailed than Elastolin figures. Lineol took over Tipple-Topple in the 1920s. Production continued throughout World War II, but the company was nationalized in 1949 and relocated to Dresden, East Germany. Very limited production of plastic figures was continued in East Germany, but they were not available to Western markets.

This section of the book focuses primarily on Elastolin (E) and Lineol (L) figures. The two prices listed for each figure approximate current collector value of figures in good condition (minor leg crack, paint chip acceptable) and in near mint condition (bright paint, no cracks or chips). As with virtually all toy collectible categories, price is significantly influenced by rarity, condition and demand.

Because Elastolin and Lineol manufacturing records were destroyed during World War II, early production documentation does not exist. Without such records, it is impossible to know precisely how many or what figures were produced. Sales catalogues and price lists published during production are today invaluable records, although sometimes inaccurate, of company production. Of those manufactured, there is no way to estimate how many figures survived the destruction of the war and the elements of time. It is, nonetheless, obvious to any collector of composition toys that figures in excellent condition are now quite rare. German composition civilian figures are

James Theobald, a native of Bloomington, Illinois, is a Lieutenant Colonel in the U.S. Air Force, currently stationed at the Pentagon in Washington DC. He lived in Germany for six years with his wife, Marge, and children, Jon and Katy. While there, he assembled an extensive German composition civilian figure collection. A dedicated, if eclectic, private collector of toy figures, cast iron cars, electric trains, political memorabilia, Viennese bronzes, and other interesting artifacts, Jim aspires to be an educator and antique dealer after retirement from military duty.

frequently of greater rarity than soldiers from the same production periods. Although causes are speculative, it is believed soldier production was much greater than animal production in the war and prewar years. Animal figures were often larger than soldiers and were designed with more fragile parts, i.e., ears, antlers/horns, legs and tails. The result was more frequent cracks and breaks than their soldier counterparts. Also, soldiers of the German Reich era were preserved as "mementos" of World War II, but animals did not have the same socio-political association and were, therefore, seldom preserved. Regardless of the actual reasons, many civilian figures are quite difficult to locate in today's collector market.

Condition of any comparison toy, civilian or soldier, will greatly affect the value of the figure. Mint or Near-Mint specimens of composition figures are highly prized and difficult to locate. Humidity and temperature changes caused more damage to figures than children playing with them. Storage in uninsulated attics or damp basements in Europe and the United States have made Mint examples quite rare. Pieces often cracked and warped when subjected to moisture, as the interior wire armature rusted and expanded. Expansion and contraction in extreme temperatures would also cause the rigid figures to crack apart. In the modern market, minor damage, such as a small crack in a leg or a paint chip, reduces the value of a figure, unless it is exceedingly rare or uncatalogued. Major damage, such as missing or badly deteriorated sections,

repaint or reconstruction of a figure or broken and bent legs that affect the upright standing position of a figure, of course, render all but the very rare figure virtually valueless.

During recent decades, civilian figures have lagged behind toy soldiers in popularity and interest among collectors. This was not only true for German composition figures, but for toy figure collecting in general, including W.B. Britains, Barclay, Grey Iron and other manufacturers of both civilian and soldier lines; however, in very recent years, civilian figures have gained significant recognition and appreciation. Although not as popular as toy soldier collecting (yet), there are compelling new reasons for preserving animal toys that will likely increase the popularity of civilian figure collecting in the future. As German toy soldiers were keepsakes of a past period in history following the end of World War II, animal and farm toys have become a part of preserving the fading heritage of rural life styles, threatened animal species and a rich natural environment.

In the United States and Germany, composition animals are now prized additions to many toy collections. Despite the fact that extensive collections of figures are rarely available for sale in the modern collector's market, individual civilian figures continue to surface at antique shops, flea markets and auctions. Persistence and patience reward new and advanced collectors with the find of German composition civilian figures.

(All photos by James Theobald)

	GD	NM		GD	NM
1E Farm display (house/barn/fence)	220.00	340.00	8L Circus Orangutan (young) with ball	16.00	25.00
1E House Only	110.00	190.00	9L Circus Monkey with mirror	35.00	60.00
2E Farm display (house/barn/fence)	70.00	110.00	10L Circus Tiger Club with ball	15.00	28.00
3L Circus display			11L Indian Elephant	180.00	240.00
(performance ring/stands/step)	160.00	270.00	12L Elephant Calf	70.00	110.00
4L Circus tiger performing	18.00	35.00	13E Raging African Bull Elephant	245.00	325.00
5L Animal Keeper	22.00	35.00	14L Indian Elephant	180.00	240.00
6L Circus Animal Wagon			15L Elephant Calf	55.00	80.00
(with no animal)	90.00	140.00	16L Raging African Bull Elephant	320.00	425.00
6L Circus Animal Wagon (with animal)	115.00	180.00	17L Snake	35.00	55.00
7L Circus Bear Cub with milk bottle	35.00	60.00	18L Crocodile	20.00	35.00

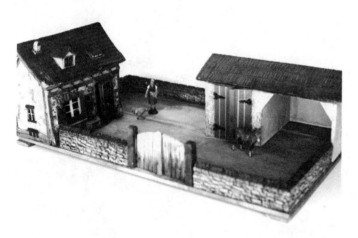

#1E Farm Display.

#2E Farm Display.

#3L Circus Display.

#4L Circus Tiger Performing.

#5L Animal Keeper, #6L Circus Animal Wagon.

L to R: #5L Animal Keeper, #6L Circus Animal Wagon (with Animal).

L to R: #7L Circus Bear Cub w/milk bottle, #8L Circus Orangutan (young) with ball, #9L Circus Monkey w/mirror, 10L Circus Tiger Cub w/ball.

Top, L to R: #11L Indian Elephant, #12L Elephant Calf, #13E Raging African Bull Elephant; Bottom, L to R: #14L Indian Elephant, #15L Elephant Calf, #16L Raging African Bull Elephant.

L to R: #11L Indian Elephant, #14L Indian Elephant.

L to R: #12L Elephant Calf, #13E Raging African Bull Elephant, #15L Elephant Calf.

#16L Raging African Bull Elephant.

L to R: #17L Snake, #19L Tortoise, #20L Tortoise, #18L Crocodile.

Top, L to R: #17L Snake, #18L Crocodile, #19L Tortoise, #20L Tortoise; Middle, L to R: #21E Llama (young), #22E Llama, #23L Guinea Pig, #24L Zebra, #25E Zebra Colt, #26E Zebra; Bottom, L to R: #27L Cobra Snake, #28L Anteater, #29L Sable Antelope, #30L Orynx (gembok), #31L Kudu.

L to R: #23L Guinea Pig, #27L Cobra Snake, #33L Porcupine, #32L Armadillo.

L to R: #24L Zebra, #25E Zebra Colt, #26E Zebra.

L to R: #30L Orynx (gembok), #31L Kudu, #29L Sable Antelope.

Top, L to R: #32L Armadillo, #33L Porcupine, #34L Beaver, #35E Badger, #36E Badger, #37L Wild Boar; Middle, L to R: #38L Yak, #39L Gnu, #40L Water Buffalo, #41L Kangaroo; Bottom, L to R: #42E Caribou, #43L Hyena eating meat, #44L Bison, #45L Bison.

L to R: #37L Wild Boar, #34L Beaver, #28L Anteater.

L to R: #40L Water Buffalo, #38L Yak, #39L Gnu.

L to R: #41L Kangaroo, #56L Tapir.

	GD	NM
19L Tortoise	20.00	35.00
20L Tortoise	16.00	25.00
21E Llama (young)	18.00	30.00
22E Llama	28.00	45.00
23L Guinea Pig	14.00	20.00
24L Zebra	40.00	65.00
25E Zebra Colt	28.00	45.00
26E Zebra	40.00	65.00
27L Cobra Snake	40.00	65.00
28L Anteater	24.00	40.00
29L Sable Antelope	45.00	75.00
30L Orynx (gembok)	60.00	110.00
31L Kudu	65.00	110.00
32L Armadillo	14.00	20.00
33L Porcupine	14.00	20.00
34L Beaver	14.00	20.00
35E Badger	8.00	12.00
36E Badger	8.00	12.00
37L Wild Boar	24.00	40.00
38L Yak	70.00	130.00
39L Gnu	40.00	65.00
40L Water Buffalo	70.00	130.00
41L Kangaroo	20.00	35.00
42E Caribou	40.00	65.00
43L Hyena eating meat	18.00	30.00
44L Bison	80.00	140.00
45L Bison	65.00	110.00
46E Squirrel on branch	12.00	18.00
47L Squirrel on branch	12.00	18.00
48E Wolf	12.00	18.00
49E Wolf	10.00	16.00
50E Fox	14.00	20.00
51L Marten on branch	12.00	18.00
52L Wolf running	10.00	16.00
53L Hippopotamus	95.00	155.00
54L Hippopotamus (young)	20.00	35.00
55L Hippopotamus	40.00	65.00
56L Tapir	24.00	40.00
57E Ibex	18.00	30.00
58L Moose	75.00	120.00
59E Moose	55.00	95.00
60L Chamois	28.00	45.00
61L Rhinoceros	80.00	135.00
62L Bactrian Camel (young)	24.00	40.00
63E Bactrian Camel	35.00	55.00
64L Bactrian Camel	35.00	55.00
65L Dromedary Camel	35.00	55.00
66L Dromedary Camel	45.00	75.00
67L Dromedary Camel (young)	24.00	40.00
68L Bactrian Camel	45.00	75.00
69L Giraffe (young)	40.00	60.00
70E Giraffe	95.00	155.00
71L Giraffe	110.00	180.00
72E Ostrich	15.00	22.00
73E Peacock	16.00	25.00
74L Peacock	14.00	20.00
75L Marabou Stork	12.00	18.00
76L Pelican	10.00	16.00
77L Penguin	14.00	20.00
78L Emperor Penguin	18.00	30.00
79E Emperor Penguin	14.00	20.00
80L Auk Penguin	16.00	25.00

	GD	NM
81E Ostrich	18.00	30.00
82L Ostrich	16.00	25.00
83E Eagle	24.00	40.00
84E Emu	18.00	30.00
85L Eagle	24.00	40.00
86L Swan	12.00	18.00
87E Vulture with lamb	14.00	20.00
88L Elk bellowing	40.00	65.00
89L Deer	16.00	25.00
90E Polar Bear	20.00	35.00
91L Brown Bear Cub sitting	18.00	30.00
92E Brown bear	18.00	30.00
93E Brown Bear standing	28.00	45.00
94E Deer Stag	18.00	30.00
95L Deer	40.00	60.00
96L Deer Stag	45.00	70.00
97L Deer grazing	40.00	60.00
98E Deer Fawn grazing	24.00	40.00
99E Deer	35.00	55.00
100L Elephant Seal	45.00	70.00
101E Sea Lion	20.00	35.00
102E Panther	16.00	25.00
103E Leopard	16.00	25.00
104L Seal	14.00	20.00
105L Gorilla	40.00	65.00
106L Mandrill Baboon	40.00	60.00
107L Monkey	6.00	10.00
108L Monkey	15.00	22.00
109L Monkey grooming	18.00	30.00
110E Orangutan on branch	40.00	60.00
111E Tiger	18.00	30.00
112E Tiger	18.00	30.00
113L Tiger Cub	12.00	18.00
114L Tiger Cub	12.00	18.00
115E Tiger	18.00	30.00
116L Lioness	18.00	30.00
117L Lion Cub standing	12.00	18.00
118L Lion Cub lying	12.00	18.00
119L Lion Cub	12.00	18.00
120L Lion	16.00	24.00
121L Lion	14.00	20.00
122E Lion	16.00	25.00
123L Lion	28.00	45.00
124L Lion	28.00	45.00
125E Tree (pine)	16.00	25.00
126E Crow	12.00	18.00
127E Tree (aspen)	65.00	90.00
128E Collie Dog	12.00	18.00
129L Saint Bernard Pup	12.00	18.00
130E Dog	10.00	16.00
131E Pup	10.00	16.00
132E German Shepherd Dog	15.00	22.00
133E Rooster	12.00	18.00
134L Hen	8.00	12.00
135E Hen	8.00	12.00
136E Hen on nest	14.00	20.00
137E Chick	5.00	8.00
138L Woman feeding birds	24.00	40.00
139L Goose	8.00	12.00
140E Goose	10.00	16.00
141E Goose	10.00	16.00
142E Goose	10.00	16.00

L to R: #45L Bison, #44L Bison.

Top, L to R: #46E Squirrel on branch, #47L Squirrel on branch, #48E Wolf, #49E Wolf, #50E Fox, #51L Marten on branch, #52L Wolf running; Middle, L to R: #53L Hippopotamus, #54L Hippopotamus (young), #55L Hippopotamus, #56L Tapir, #57E Ibex; Bottom, L to R: #58L Moose, #59E Moose, #60L Chamois, #61L Rhinoceros.

L to R: #53L Hippopotamus, #61L Rhinoceros.

L to R: #57E Ibex, #88L Elk bellowing, #60L Chamois.

L to R: #58L Moose, #59L Moose.

Top, L to R: #62L Bactrian Camel (young), #63E Bactrian Camel, #64L Bactrian Camel, #65L Dromedary Camel; Bottom, L to R: #66L Dromedary Camel, #67L Dromedary Camel (young), #68L Bactrian Camel, #69L Giraffe (young), #70E Giraffe, #71L Giraffe.

L to R: #67L Dromedary Camel (young), #66L Dromedary Camel, #62L Bactrian Camel (young), #68L Bactrian Camel.

L to R: #69L Giraffe (young), #70E Giraffe, #71L Giraffe.

Top, L to R: #72E Ostrich, #73E Peacock, #74L Peacock, #75L Marabou Stork, #76L Pelican, #77L Penguin, #78L Emperor Penguin, #79E Emperor Penguin, #80L Auk Penguin; Bottom, L to R: #81E Ostrich, #82L Ostrich, #83E Eagle, #84E Emu, #85L Eagle, #86L Swan, #87E Vulture with lamb.

L to R: #73E Peacock, #85L Eagle, #84E Emu, #72E Ostrich.

L to R: #80L Auk Penguin, #79E Emperor Penguin, #77L Penguin, #78L Emperor Penguin.

Top, L to R: #88L Elk bellowing, #89E Deer, #90E Polar Bear, #91L Brown Bear Cub sitting, #92E Brown Bear, #93E Brown Bear standing; Bottom, L to R: #94E Deer Stag, #95L Deer, #96L Deer Stag, #97L Deer grazing, #98E Deer Fawn grazing, #99E Deer.

L to R: #90E Polar Bear, #91L Brown Bear Cub sitting, #93E Brown Bear standing, #92E Brown Bear.

L to R: #95L Deer, #96L Stag, #97L Deer grazing.

Top, L to R: #100L Elephant Seal, #101E Sea Lion, #102E Panther, #103E Leopard; Bottom, L to R: #104L Seal, #105L Gorilla, #106L Mandrill Baboon, #107L Monkey, #108L Monkey, #109L Monkey grooming, #110E Orangutan on branch.

L to R: #104L Seal, #100L Elephant Seal, #101E Sea Lion.

L to R: #109L Monkey grooming, #107L Monkey, #105L Gorilla, #106L Mandrill Baboon.

Top, L to R: #111E Tiger, #112E Tiger, #113L Tiger Cub, #114L Tiger Cub, #115E Tiger; Middle, L to R: #116L Lioness, #117L Lion Cub standing, #118L Lion Cub lying, #119L Lion Cub, #120L Lion, #121L Lion; Bottom, L to R: #122E Lion, #123L Lion, #124L Lion.

L to R: #124L Lion, #116L Lioness, #118L Lion Cub lying, #117L Lion Cub standing, #119L Lion Cub, #123L Lion.

Top, L to R: #125E Tree (pine), #126E Crow, #127E Tree (aspen); Bottom, L to R: #128E Collie Dog, #129L Saint Bernard Pup, #130E Dog, #131E Pup, #132E German Shepherd Dog.

L to R: #125E Tree (pine), #126E Crow, #127E Tree (aspen), #189E Rabbit running.

Top, L to R: #133E Rooster, #134L Hen, #135E Hen, #136E Hen on nest, #137E Chick, #138L Woman feeding birds, #139L Goose, #140E Goose, #141E Goose, #142E Goose; Middle, L to R: #143E Ram, #144E Sheep, #145L Goat, #146E Goat Kid, #147L Goat Kid playing, #148E Goat, #149E Duck, #150L Duck; Bottom, L to R: #151L Sheep, #152L Sheep lying, #153L Lamb lying, #154L Lamb, #155L Sheep lying, #156L Shepherd, #157L Sheep grazing, #158L Ram.

L to R: #145L Goat, #147L Goat Kid playing, #148E Goat.

L to R: #150L Duck, #138L Woman feeding birds, #135L Hen, #137E Chick, #139L Goose, #187L Turkey.

	GD	NM		GD	NM
143E Ram	8.00	14.00	205E Horse	18.00	28.00
144E Sheep	8.00	14.00	206E Horse	18.00	28.00
145L Goat	18.00	28.00	207L Colt	15.00	22.00
146E Goat Kid	10.00	16.00	208L Indian Elephant with Rider	220.00	320.00
147L Goat Kid playing	10.00	16.00	209L Dromedary Camel with Rider	175.00	260.00
148E Goat	18.00	28.00	210E Alligator (large scale)	17.00	26.00
149E Duck	10.00	16.00	211E Turtle (large scale)	15.00	22.00
150L Duck	8.00	12.00	212E Chimpanzee (large scale)	10.00	16.00
151L Sheep	16.00	24.00	213E Anteater (large scale)	20.00	35.00
152L Sheep lying	15.00	22.00	214E Wild Boar (large scale)	15.00	22.00
153L Lamb lying	15.00	22.00	215L Baboon (large scale)	18.00	30.00
154L Lamb	15.00	22.00	216L Badger (large scale)	10.00	16.00
155L Sheep lying	15.00	22.00	217E Polar Bear (large scale)	18.00	30.00
156L Shepherd	28.00	45.00	218L Polar Bear Cub		
157L Sheep grazing	15.00	22.00	standing (large scale)	10.00	16.00
158L Ram	18.00	28.00	219L Polar Bear Cub (large scale)	10.00	16.00
159L Cow lying	24.00	40.00	220L Brown Bear (large scale)	12.00	18.00
160L Calf	16.00	25.00	221E Elephant (large scale)	28.00	45.00
161E Calf lying	15.00	22.00	222E Zebra (large scale)	18.00	30.00
162L Calf feeding	20.00	34.00	223E Gnu (large scale)	20.00	35.00
163E Calf lying	12.00	18.00	224E Llama (large scale)	18.00	30.00
164L Cow mooing	28.00	45.00	225E Elephant (miniature scale)	28.00	45.00
165E Bull	40.00	60.00	226E Alligator (miniature scale)	22.00	30.00
166L Calf	16.00	25.00	227E Brown Bear (miniature scale)	18.00	26.00
167L Cow lying	24.00	40.00	228E Polar Bear (miniature scale)	18.00	26.00
168E Cow lying	20.00	35.00	229E Bactrian Camel (miniature scale)	22.00	34.00
169L Woman milking	24.00	40.00	230L Horse on wheels	45.00	80.00
170E Calf	15.00	22.00	231E Wood Fence section	8.00	12.00
171E Cow	28.00	45.00	232E Wood Fence section with gate	20.00	30.00
172E Cow	24.00	40.00	233E Wood Fence section	8.00	12.00
173L Cow grazing	28.00	45.00	234E Zoon Fence section with gate	12.00	18.00
174L Cow mooing	28.00	45.00	235E Donkey (early plastic)	8.00	14.00
175L Cow	28.00	45.00	236E Calf (early plastic)	8.00	14.00
176L Cow	28.00	45.00	237E Cow lying (early plastic)	8.00	14.00
177L Pig	18.00	30.00	238E Cow (early plastic)	10.00	16.00
178E Pig	15.00	22.00	239E Cow mooing (early plastic)	10.00	16.00
179E Pig running	18.00	28.00	240E Cow grazing (early plastic)	10.00	16.00
180E Piglet	8.00	12.00	241E Bull (early plastic)	14.00	22.00
181E Piglet	6.00	10.00			
182E Piglet sitting	8.00	12.00			
183E Pig	10.00	16.00			
184L Donkey	18.00	30.00			
185E Donkey	12.00	18.00			
186L Donkey in halter	20.00	35.00			
187L Turkey	12.00	18.00			
188E Turkey	14.00	20.00			
189E Rabbit running	8.00	12.00			
190E Rabbit running	10.00	16.00			
191L Pony	20.00	35.00			
192L Work Horse	40.00	60.00			
193L Work Horse grazing	40.00	60.00			
194E Work Horse	40.00	60.00			
195E Work Horse Colt	20.00	34.00			
196E Horse	18.00	28.00			
197L Horse trotting	18.00	28.00			
198L Horse trotting	18.00	28.00			
199L Horse	20.00	35.00			
200E Horse grazing	15.00	22.00			
201E Horse grazing	18.00	28.00			
202L Horse grazing	18.00	28.00			
203L Horse running	20.00	35.00			
204E Horse	20.00	32.00			

These animals are all early plastic. Top, L to R: #235E Donkey, #236E Calf, #237E Cow lying, #238E Cow; Bottom, L to R: #239E Cow mooing, #240E Cow grazing, #241E Bull.

L to R: #153L Lamb lying, #156L Shepherd, #157L Sheep grazing, #158L Ram.

Top row, L to R: #159L Cow lying, #160L Calf, #161E Calf lying, #162L Calf feeding, #163E Calf lying; Second Row, L to R: #164L Cow mooing, #165E Bull, #166L Calf, #167L Cow lying; Third Row, L to R: #168E Cow lying, #169L Woman milking, #170E Calf, #171E Cow, #172E Cow; Bottom Row, L to R: #173L Cow grazing, #174L Cow mooing, #175L Cow, #176L Cow.

L to R: #165E Bull, #170E Calf, #171E Cow.

L to R: #166L Calf, #167L Cow lying, #164L Cow mooing.

L to R: #174L Cow, #169L Woman milking, #175L Cow, #162L Calf feeding.

Top, L to R: #177L Pig, #178E Pig, #179E Pig running, #180E Piglet, #181E Piglet, #182E Piglet sitting, #183E Pig; Middle, L to R: #184L Donkey, #185E Donkey, #186L Donkey in halter, #187L Turkey, #188E Turkey, #189E Rabbit running, #190E Rabbit running; Bottom, L to R: #191L Pony, #192L Work Horse, #193L Work Horse grazing, #194E Work Horse, #195E Work Horse Colt.

L to R: #179E Pig running, #180E Piglet, #178E Pig.

L to R: #191L Pony, #186L Donkey with halter, #184L Donkey.

L to R: #192L Work Horse, #194E Work Horse, #193L Work Horse feeding.

L to R: #196E Horse, #207L Colt, #199L Horse.

Top, L to R: #196E Horse, #197L Horse trotting, #198L Horse trotting, #199L Horse; Middle, L to R: #200E Horse grazing, #201E Horse grazing, #202L Horse grazing, #203L Horse running; Bottom, L to R: #204E Horse, #205E Horse, #206E Horse, #207L Colt.

#208L Indian Elephant with Rider.

#209L Dromedary Camel with Rider.

These animals are all large scale. Top, L to R: #201E Alligator, #211E Turtle, #212E Chimpanzee, #213E Anteater, #214E Wild Boar; Middle, L to R: #215L Baboon, #216L Badger, #217E Polar Bear, #218L Polar Bear Cub standing, #219L Polar Bear Cub, #220L Brown Bear; Bottom, L to R: #221E Elephant, #222E Zebra, #223E Gnu, #224E Llama.

These animals are all miniature scale. L to R: #225E Elephant, #226E Alligator, #227E Brown Bear, #228E Polar Bear, #229E Bactrian Camel.

Displaying size comparison of miniature to full scale.

#230L Horse on wheels.

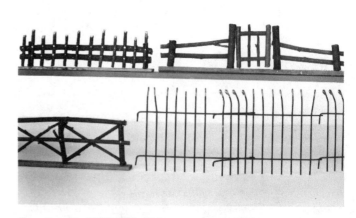

Top, L to R: #231E Wood fence section, #232E Wood fence section with gate; Bottom, L to R: #233E Wood fence section, #234E Zoo fence section with gate.

Germany
Metal, Solidcast
48mm Standard
(approx. 1-3/4")

⚔ Heyde ⚔

by Steve Balkin

George Heyde established his toy soldier company in Dresden, Germany, in 1872. The then recently concluded Franco-Prussian War of 1870-71 provided ample subject matter for his early production. Heyde's toy models soon gained favor overseas in England and the United States. These new markets provided new subject matter for Heyde's production, and creating figures for the consumption of those markets greatly increased both business and Heyde's reputation.

The years from the turn of the century to the outbreak of World War I proved to be the golden age for Heyde. The company truly reflected the spirit of exploration as well as the armed conflicts of the latter half of the 19th century. The United States offered such subjects as the Wild West, which was rich in its imagery of buffalo hunts, Indian villages and army maneuvers, as well as the adventures of a young nation in the Pacific. The colonial empires of Europe generated headlines that Heyde transformed into dioramas depicting incidents in the Sudan, India, China and South Africa, as well as Polar explorations and the birth of aviation.

The ancient world was not neglected by Heyde. The armies of Alexander and Darius were vividly brought to life, as was Caesar's "Triumph of Germanicus." The Fall of Troy is a magnificent display, which includes the wooden horse, as well as Achilles' chariot dragging the unfortunate Hector around the walls of the city. The legend of Siegfried was another favorite topic, as were medieval knights in their shining armor. Crusaders with their Saracen opponents also created colorful displays.

Until the outbreak of World War I, Heyde was the leading exporter of toy soldiers in the world. A wide variety of themes and poses was one reason; but in addition the company could appeal to the children of any country by a simple change of heads and paint to represent that nation's army. Today, this leads, of course, to the problem of set numbers. A set #515 in the United States will look different from a set #515 found in France or Spain. The makeup will be the same but with different hats/heads and uniform colors.

The end of World War I was finalized by the signing of the Treaty of Versailles. It is believed that one article of the

Heyde 42-piece French Infantry, Cavalry and Artillery Display. Courtesy Christie's New York.

treaty prohibited the production of "war toys" or specifically, toy soldiers, for export. This opened the door for W. Britains to fill the void in the world market and a number of small companies in the United States to pirate Heyde's style and designs. Heyde struggled back by placing more emphasis on civilian figures, while the composition figure makers seemed to avoid the problem by concentrating on British and American figures. Heyde continued to produce up to World War II, but on a much smaller scale. The fire-bombing of Dresden destroyed all but the front of its complex. From there, a few employees continued to make figures into the late 1940s, before closing under pressure from the East Germans.

The identification of Heyde and other German manufacturers has always been a difficult task for collectors. First, the mold makers supplied similar molds to the various toy soldier companies. Second, smaller companies were often absorbed by larger companies which would continue to use the acquired molds under the new company's banner.

An interesting note: During World War I, when all metals were considered to be critical war materials, German children were encouraged to donate their metal toys to support the war effort. Ironically, because of the wholesale melting of these toys, to this day, old Heyde figures are more readily found in the Americas and Great Britain than they are in Germany.

The following figures shown are of standard Size "2" (48mm) unless otherwise noted.

(Photos by author and K. Warren Mitchell unless otherwise noted)

Advancing WWI British infantry.

Heyde Roman Chariot, 4-horse. Value $125.00 in very good condition.

Heyde Roman foot figures. Average price per each in very good condition $16.00.

Heyde foot Indians.

Heyde mounted North American Indians.

Heyde Cowboys.

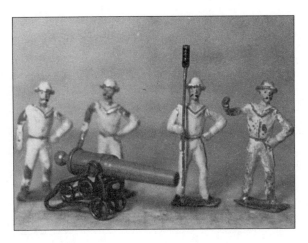

Heyde Sailors.

L to R: French, Bulgarian, Russian Czarists. (VG) $15.00 each.

Size "0" Arab on camel. (VG) $65.00.

L to R: Size "0" (115mm) U.S. Cavalry, Size 2 (65mm).

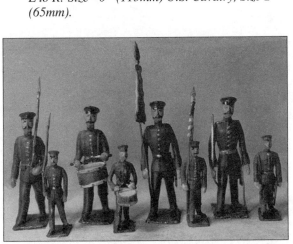

Comparison U.S. Infantry Size "0" (75mm) and Size 2 (48mm). Courtesy Jim and Ann Morris.

Size "0" British colonial troops (1890) and infamous Highlanders in "miniskirts." (VG) $40.00 each.

Size "0" British colonial troops attacking. (VG) $35.00 each.

Size 2 Arab on horse. (VG) $20.00.

Undersize Arab mosque made of wood and papier-mâché, and standard Size 2 Arab for size comparison. (VG) $100.00.

U.S. Marine.

British Signal Unit Set (still tied to card). Tapping the key blinked the light. Group (EXC) $200.00.

L to R: Prussians (2), Germans (2), Japanese.

L to R: English cavalry, German cavalry. (VG) $16.00 each.

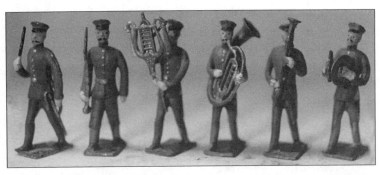

U.S. Band, WWI. (VG) $16.00 each.

Left: Boer, (VG) $15.00; Middle: Doctors attending wounded - no base - all connected, (VG) $55.00; Right: Pilot.

Turkish Lancer in sun helmet. (VG) $20.00.

Scots Grey band. (VG) $20.00 each.

U.S. "Doughboys" in campaign hats. (VG) $12.00 each.

U.S. Artillery. Set (VG) $100.00.

Greeks. (VG) $15.00 each.

U.S. Ammo Limber. Set (VG) $100.00.

L to R: Prussian Hussar, Dragoon. (VG) $16.00 each.

English Signal Unit stringing wire. (VG) $15.00 each.

L to R: Arab on camel, Chinese (?) soldier.

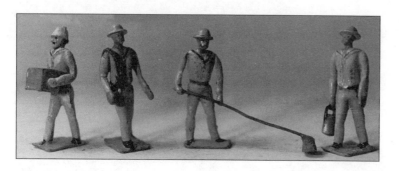

U.S. Sailors.

Street Worker. (VG) $14.00.

U.S. Sailors in action. (VG) $15.00 each.

English Guards band (partial). (VG) $15.00 each.

West Point band 12-piece set. (VG) $190.00. Photo courtesy Doyle Galleries.

Knights

Heyde mounted and foot knights.

Values (VG) $22.00 each.

Value (VG) $22.00 each.

Values (VG), L to R: $50.00 (2 on 1 base); $16.00; $16.00.

Values (VG) $16.00 each.

Value (VG) $22.00.

*Value (VG)
$15.00.*

Value (VG) mounted $24.00, foot $14.00 each.

American Revolution - English dragoons (Set #827). (VG) $22.00 each.

Size 2 Indian hanging under horse. Scarce. (VG) $40.00.

American Revolution - Washington's life guards (Set #827). (VG) $22.00 each.

U.S. Cavalry Bugler (Indian Wars). (VG) $22.00.

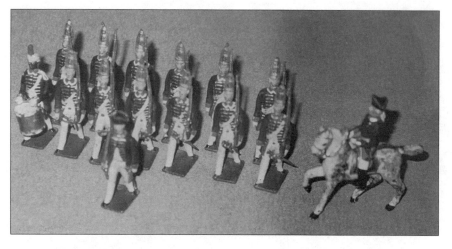

L to R: Potsdam Grenadiers, (VG) $16.00 each; Frederick the Great, (VG) $35.00. Photo by Steve Balkin.

Greeks attacking (Set #1366). (VG) $16.00.

Crusaders. Photo courtesy Guernsey's.

American Revolution Continental Regulars. (VG) $16.00 each.

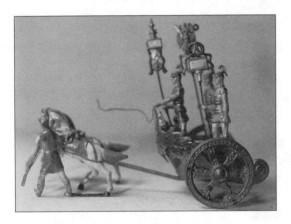

Size "0" American Indians. (VG) $60.00. Photo by Steve Balkin.

2-horse Roman chariot. (VG) $120.00.

3-horse Roman chariot. (VG) $110.00.

Radiomen from airport set. All 1 piece. (VG) $85.00.

Boy Scouts cooking, all on 1 base (Set #1450). (VG) $65.00.

French in North America. (VG) $16.00 each.

Western corral scene, composition shack

Indians attacking wagon - Cavalry to the rescue.

Various African Hunt and Native Scenes

#1283 Elephant Hunt (partial).

Natives. (VG) $16.00.

White hunter seated on young dead elephant. Rare. (VG) $75.00.

#1285 Tiger Hunt (partial).

Buffalo hunt.

Jockey on racehorse. (VG) $27.00.

Well. (VG) $20.00.

Cowboys leaving corral.

Boy Scouts (Set #1443). (VG) $18.00 each.

Romans. Value (VG), L to R: unknown, $20.00, $45.00, $35.00.

L to R: Boy Scouts, (VG) $18.00 each; Royal footman.

Romans.

English Police. (VG) $13.00.

Various polar expedition figures, representing 3 countries. Norwegians wore white, Italians wore brown and Americans wore dark blue. (VG) $20.00-$35.00 each. Sets #1375-77.

U.S. policemen with moveable arms. Scarce. (VG) $25.00.

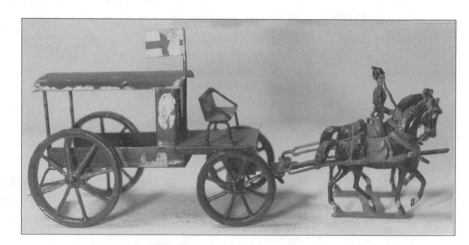

Ambulance. (VG) $100.00.

Chinaman Getting Hair Braided (from Boxer Rebellion street scene). (VG) $100.00.

L to R: Market stall, table with fish and basket made of composition (sign gone off pole), (VG) $50.00; Little girl sitting on chair, (VG) $20.00; Gentleman, (VG) $13.00.

Zoo scene showing rare animal cages, ticket booth, monkeys hanging on lampposts.

Caravan. Note camels carrying sections of artillery gun.

Turks, set still in box. Photo courtesy Guernsey's.

Heyde Italian Invasion of Abyssinia, circa 1935-36. Italian infantry attacking Ethiopians, including Emperor Haile Selassie and his Royal Bodyguard. Selassie, umbrella and boy are aluminum. Auctioned for $600.00 in December 1989. Photo courtesy Phillips New York.

Heyde had some of the most magnificent sets of all. This is The Sack of Troy, which sold at auction for $1045.00 in March 1982 at Christie's New York. Photo courtesy Christie's New York.

Heyde Set #364 U.S. Infantry Band, 12th Regiment.

Heyde Prussian Band. Photo courtesy Christie's New York.

Heyde U.S. Army New York Regiment. Photo courtesy Christie's New York.

⚔ Leyla ⚔

Not much seems to be known about this German company, except that its composition figures were produced both before and after World War II. Its name is found under the bases of most of its pieces.

L to R: LI1, LI2, LI3. Leyla. Value (VG) $12.00 each. Photo by K. Warren Mitchell.

Leyla Bunny School. Value $150.00 for the group. Photo by Joseph F. Saine.

LI8. Leyla. Value (VG) $20.00. Photo by K. Warren Mitchell.

L to R: LI4, LI5, LI6, LI7. Leyla. Value (VG) $12.00 each. Photo by K. Warren Mitchell.

L to R: LC4, LC5, LC6. Leyla. Value (VG) $12.00 each. Photo by K. Warren Mitchell.

L to R: LC2, LC3. Leyla. Value (VG) $20.00 each. Photo by K. Warren Mitchell.

L to R: LI10, LC1. Leyla. Value (VG) $20.00 each. Photo by K. Warren Mitchell.

LI9. Leyla. Value (VG) $20.00.

⚔ Miscellaneous German ⚔ and Austrian Composition

Austria's Tipple Topple produced the Indian chief (value $20.00) and the duplex Cowboy throwing Indian (value $175.00). Photo by Joseph F. Saine.

Germany's Arnold produced this tinplate jeep with composition GIs. Value $100.00. (Also came with MPs). Photo by Joseph F. Saine.

✕ Miscellaneous ✕ German Plastic

Merten Centaurs, value $25.00 each. Merten, of Berlin, is more properly known as Berliner-Miniatur-Plastiken. It seems to have gone into business about 1940, owned by Walter Merten. Courtesy Paul Stadinger - Stad's.

Dom "plastic" (actually a rubbery material) 70mm Tarzan, value $10.00. It also came in soft plastic, unpainted, according to Andreas Dittmann in his Domplastic zine for Plastic Warrior. *According to Dittmann, Dom-Plastik began by offering plastic toys in "surprise-bags" that came with candy. Courtesy Paul Stadinger - Stad's.*

A plastic version by Marolin of a figure originally made in composition. Courtesy Plastic Warrior.

This plastic samurai came in a "kinder-egg," a kind of surprise package. Value $15.00. Courtesy Paul Stadinger - Stad's.

Winterhilfswerk: Very early German plastic produced and sold during WWII as propaganda figures for the Winterhilfswerk, the social welfare organization of the Nazi party. 45mm, unpainted. No price found. Information and photo courtesy Plastic Warrior.

Manurba of Germany produced these swoppet-type Indians, 54mm, value $4.00 each. Courtesy Paul Stadinger - Stad's.

L to R: UN354, UN355, UN356. Plastic ancient Olympic athletes that were given away with a German margarine. Maker unknown. Value $10.00 each. Courtesy Paul Stadinger - Stad's.

Austria/Germany
Composition, solid
12cm (4-3/4") standard

✕ Pfeiffer of Vienna ✕ (1898-1904)

by K. Warren Mitchell

In 1898 Pfeiffer, a well-known dollmaker, perfected the first composition toy soldier to be sold widely in the Western world. It was a logical evolution--its dolls' heads, hands and feet were made from composition--and it doubled its potential market by adding little boys to its list of customers.

The figures were sturdy, solid and well painted. Like dolls, they have no bases, but stand firmly on their own. Examples shown are uniformed in U.S. "Federal" dress of the late 1880s, with proper spiked helmets and the khaki uniform worn by Teddy Roosevelt's Rough Riders of the Spanish-American War. Also shown is a red-jacket version, probably English.

Pfeiffer was purchased, or at least the toy soldier operation was purchased, by O.M. Hausser, another dollmaker, in 1904. Hausser then concentrated on toy soldiers, under the brand name "Elastolin." Average price for foot figures in Very Good condition would be $30 and mounted at $50.

L to R: U.S. Federal Dress of 1890; Federal Dress rifle slung; Officer, khaki, in "Rough Rider" hat.

Federal Dress at slope.

British infantry of the line. Red jacket, white spike helmet.

Poland

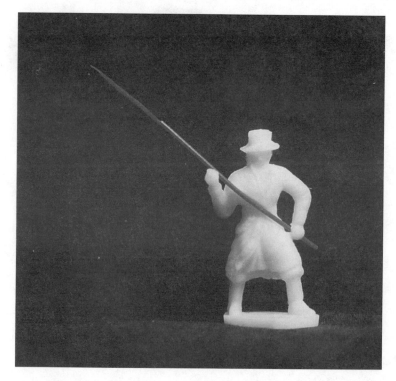

This extraordinary piece is in plastic, and is a winged hussar. Its Polish maker is unknown, and no price was found. Courtesy Plastic Warrior.

A circa 1790s Polish revolutionary. It was made from excess plastic from toilet seat and wash basin production. Maker was Polish, but is otherwise unknown. Value $4.00. Courtesy Paul Stadinger - Stad's.

Belgium

Durso

by Joseph F. Saine

The Durso Company began in 1935 and was located at 87 Rue Saint-Gilles, Liege, Belgium. It has been said that Durso was a product of the dissolution of the Incamim Company, also known for its interesting composition figures. Durso models have mound-shaped, irregular oval bases clearly marked on the underside "DURSO MADE IN BELGIUM."

Translated catalogs indicate a varied and interesting range. Besides Belgian military troops, the armies of the world were represented by the U.S., Russians, English, French, Germans and the Scottish. Other lines included Farm, Zoo, Wild Animals, a circus grouping, cowboys and Indians (both action and campfire), Canadian Mounties (complete with bandits), Vikings, Gauls, Mongols, Knights, Hunters (with natives from the Congo), a hunting party from India and the Tarzan of the Jungle group, as well.

Durso paid homage to the play-value of the hero and sprinkled its ranges liberally with character figures. Here is a partial list of examples: King George, Churchill, Prince Albert, Eisenhower, Stalin, King Clovis, Attila the Hun, Napoleon, Tarzan, Jane, Boy & Cheeta, Buffalo Bill, Davey Crockett and Charlie Chaplin.

In any given Durso catalog, the amount of single figures to choose from numbered more than 500 pieces. It is important to note that all figures were available singly, not in sets, though they can be collected by series groupings. Difficult to find, satisfying to collect, they seem to crop up at toy soldier shows in small lots and through private collections.

Durso 1/17 King Clovis with Crown, value $50.00. (2nd Series, Hommes D'Armes, catalog #1.) Photo by Joseph F. Saine.

Durso Atilla the Hun, value $75.00. Courtesy Brian Carrick.

Durso Charlemagne, value $75.00. Photo by Joseph F. Saine.

Durso, L to R: 1/12 Celt (throwing javelin), 1/11 Mongol (attacking w/ spear), value $20.00 each. (1st Series Hommes D'Armes.) Photo by Joseph F. Saine.

Durso, L to R: 1/6 Gaul w/horn & ax, Knight firing flaming arrow, value $20.00 each. (1st Series Hommes D'Armes.) Photo by Joseph F. Saine.

L to R: DV1, DV2, DV3. Durso Vikings, value $20.00 each. (1st Series Hommes D'Armes.) Photo by Joseph F. Saine.

Durso, L to R: 1/1 Gaul, 1/5 French, value $20.00 each. (1st Series Hommes D'Armes.) Photo by Joseph F. Saine.

Durso catapult, value with 3 figures $100.00. Photo by Joseph F. Saine.

Durso Viking Ship, value with 6 Normans $400.00. Photo by Joseph F. Saine.

Durso Tarzan on tree, value $150.00. (Tarzan Series, catalog #9011.) Photo by Joseph F. Saine.

Tarzan on Elephant, value $200.00. (Tarzan Series, catalog #9010.) Photo by Joseph F. Saine.

Durso, L to R: Eisenhower, Stalin, Marshal Zhukov. Photo by K. Warren Mitchell.

L to R: DH1, DH2, DH3. Durso Congo series. Hunters, value $25.00 each. Photo by Joseph F. Saine.

L to R: DN1, DN2, DN3. Durso Congo series. Natives, value $25.00 each. Photo by Joseph F. Saine.

L to R: DK1, DK2, DK3. Durso Knights, value $20.00 each. (2nd Series Hommes D'Armes.) Photo by Joseph F. Saine.

L to R: DHU1, DHU2, DHU3. Durso Huns, value $20.00 each. (1st Series Hommes D'Armes.) Photo by Joseph F. Saine.

L to R: DI1, DI2, DC1. Durso Cowboys & Indians series, value single figures $20.00, duplex $75.00. Photo by Joseph F. Saine.

DC2. Durso Cowboy on Bucking Bronco, value $130.00. Photo by Joseph F. Saine.

L to R: DI3, DC3. Photo by K. Warren Mitchell.

L to R: DC4, DC5, DC6. Durso Cowboys, value $20 each. Photo by K. Warren Mitchell.

Belgium
Metal-Solidcast
60mm
(Approx. 2-1/2")

✕ MIM ✕

by K. Warren Mitchell

Although properly considered as "military miniatures," MIMs were sold in the U.S. through toy-soldier outlets, as were Vertunnis and Courtenays, and found a place in many collections, displayed next to Mignots.

They were produced by Emmanuel Steinback from 1935-48, and came in two standards--MIM and NIMIM (NIMIM being the simpler one-piece casting, with a little less detail). Both are extremely well done by today's standards, and command a dedicated following by those collectors who have been exposed to them.

Subject matter can encompass the range of history, from ancients to World War II, but the most in-demand would be the Napoleonics of the First Empire. Toward the end, as it ran into financial trouble, MIM tried to counter this by producing composition figures, such as a stagecoach set, etc., under the name INCAMIM. But it wasn't enough. The composition stock and molds were then bought by Durso around 1948.

Identification is fairly easy--rectangular base and most carry number and name of figure under the base. Riders detach from horses. Prices range from $50 for very good condition foot figures to $85 for mounted figures in like condition.

Thanks to E. Gerard McFerren for photos and help in identifying; and photos from Peter Greenhill.

MOUNTED

Photo No.		MIM No.
1	1st Empire Grenadier A Cheval	337-158
2	1st Empire Cav, Lourde Cuirassier	96-158
3	1st Empire Cav, Lourde Carabinier	94-158
4	1st Empire Garde Imp Grenadier	139-158
5	1st Empire Garde Imp Gardes D'Honneur	147-159
6	1st Empire Garde Imp 2nd Rgt Chevau-Legers Lancers-Rouges	145-159
7	1st Empire Cav Legere Hussards	108-159
8	1st Empire Cav Dragoon Flagbearer	—
9	1st Empire Cav Legere Hussards	90-159
10	1st Empire Garde Imp Artillerie A Cheval	166-159

FOOT SOLDIERS

11	1st Empire Garde Imp 3rd Rgt Grenadiers Officer	106
12	1st Empire Garde Imp 3rd Rgt Grenadiers	107
13	1st Empire Legion Piedmontaine	359
14	1st Empire Garde Imp Fusiliers Grenadiers Officer	111
15	1st Empire Rear Detail of #12 (107)	107
16	1st Empire Inf Legere Carabiniers	192
17	1st Empire Garde Imp. 1st Rgt Grenadiers	101
18	1st Empire Imp Legere Chasseurs	189
19	1st Empire Garde Imp Tirailleur Grenadier	116

#1

#2

#3

#4

#6

#8

#9

#10

#11

#12

#13

#15

#16

#19

#26

#28

#35

#36

#37

#38

#39

#43

#47

Persian King. Photo by Peter Greenhill.

Ancients - Egyptians.

Ancients - Romans.

Typical underside of base.

Assyrians. Photo by Peter Greenhill.

Italy

✕ Atlantic ✕

Atlantic, located in Rome, seems to have started about 1972, according to Garratt's *The World Encyclopedia of Model Soldiers*. According to a reader's letter in the publication *The Worlds of Plastic Figures*, all of Atlantic's pieces in 20mm are exactly the same as those in 60mm, even to small weapons sprues. No longer in business. Prices given are for the larger, 60mm figures.

Atlantic Greek Life figures, value $2.00 each. Courtesy Paul Stadinger - Stad's.

Atlantic's Hitler. Produced as a 20-piece set, Hitler and the S.S., the entire group sells for $50.00. Courtesy Plastic Warrior.

Part of the Hitler-S.S. set. Courtesy Plastic Warrior.

The Volkswagen from the Hitler-S.S. set. Hitler could stand in its back. Courtesy Plastic Warrior.

Atlantic produced these Russian revolutionaries with Lenin as part of the set. Courtesy Plastic Warrior.

L to R: AE1, AE2, AE3, AE4. Atlantic Egyptians, value $2.00 each. Courtesy Paul Stadinger - Stad's.

Atlantic's Mussolini and his Blackshirts. Mussolini, top right, is worth $20.00, his cohorts $8.00 each. Courtesy Paul Stadinger - Stad's.

Atlantic Sailors, value $1.00 each. Courtesy Paul Stadinger - Stad's.

Atlantic Germans, value $1.50 each. Courtesy Paul Stadinger - Stad's.

Atlantic U.S. Infantry, value $1.00 each. Courtesy Paul Stadinger - Stad's.

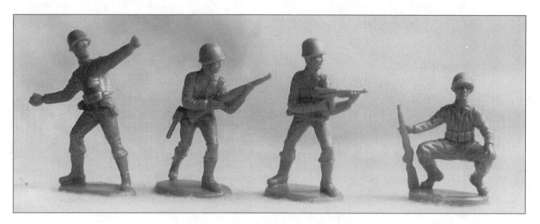

Atlantic U.S. Infantry, value $1.00 each. Courtesy Paul Stadinger - Stad's.

Atlantic Russians, value $2.00 each. Courtesy Paul Stadinger - Stad's.

Atlantic Germans, value $1.50 each. Courtesy Paul Stadinger - Stad's.

Atlantic Air Force figures, value $1.00 each. Courtesy Paul Stadinger - Stad's.

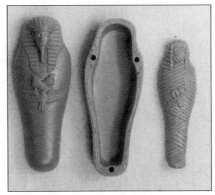

*Atlantic Mummy, value $2.00.
Courtesy Paul Stadinger - Stad's.*

*Atlantic Germans,
value $1.50 each.
Courtesy Paul
Stadinger - Stad's.*

*L to R: ATL190, ATL191,
ATL192, ATL193.
Part of Atlantic's 9-piece
(plus machine gun)
WWII Indian Army set,
value $2.00 each. Courtesy
Paul Stadinger - Stad's.*

Atlantic Japanese, value $2.00 each. Courtesy Paul Stadinger - Stad's.

✕ Italian Composition ✕ and Plastic

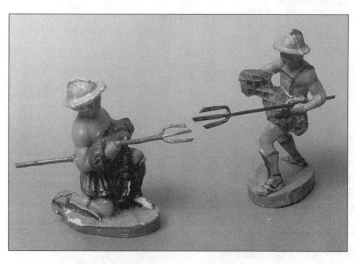

Italian Composition: Chialu gladiators. Value $15.00-20.00 each. Photo by Joseph F. Saine.

Italian Composition: Value (VG) $10.00 each. Photo by K. Warren Mitchell.

Italian Composition: Chialu Indians. Value foot $15.00-20.00 each, mounted $20.00-35.00 each. Photo by Joseph F. Saine.

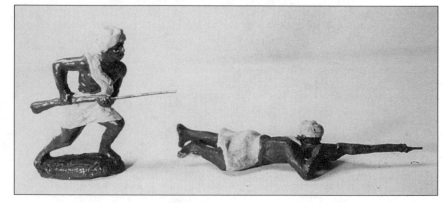

Italian Composition: Natives. Value $15.00 each. Photo by Joseph F. Saine.

Italian Composition: Value (VG) $10.00 each. Photo by K. Warren Mitchell.

*Italian Composition:
Chialu Cowboys & Indians.
Value foot $15.00-20.00 each,
mounted $20.00-35.00 each,
wounded $20.00-30.00 each.
Photo by Joseph F. Saine.*

*Italian Composition: Figur Brevett, Papal Guards, Italian Army. Value $8.00-12.00 each.
Photo by Joseph F. Saine.*

Italian Composition: Chialu. Value (VG) totem pole $30.00, fighting $35.00. Photo by K. Warren Mitchell.

Italian Plastic: Figurens. Value $12.00-15.00 each. Photo by Joseph F. Saine.

Denmark

Denmark
Aluminum, Solidcast
70mm standard (app. 2-3/4")

⚔ **Krolyn** ⚔

by Joseph F. Saine

The year 1945 is witness to the fall of the Nazi regime, as well as the surrender of all patents of German origin. Scuttled Messerschmitts provide postwar Denmark with an abundance of salvageable aluminum. This, coupled with a nation's need for new playthings, gave birth to the sturdy aluminum Krolyn figures. The first produced by G. Krohn-Rasmussen were blatant copies of Elastolin and Lineol figures. In 1950, Krohn-Rasmussen took a partner, Knud Lyngsaa, and registered the name Krolyn. Production continued until 1958.

After the 1950 partnership was formed, Krolyn introduced original pieces, as well as modified Elastolin and Lineol poses. Note the knights on Elastolin Indian ponies as examples. The line was to include the western theme, Vikings, Robin Hood, etc. Krolyn can be identified by the name Krolyn on the base, as well as the Rode-Orm (meaning Red Snake) emblazoned on the base bottoms. The range is small, but very compatible with similar-sized figures by composition makers. *Prices noted are for mint condition examples.*

Many thanks to Bertel Bruun for his previous research into the Krolyn line.

(Photos by Joseph F. Saine)

Hamlet by Krolyn. Value $35.00-50.00.

Krolyn mounted Indians. Value $15.00-25.00 each. Copied from Lineol Indians.

Krolyn, L to R: Lone Ranger, 7th Cavalry, Texas Ranger, Buster Jones. Value $12.00 each. Krolyn also made a mounted Tom Mix.

Krolyn, L to R: Robin Hood, Friar Tuck. Value $15.00-25.00 each.

Krolyn Robin Hood series, L to R: Allan a' Dale, Little John. Value $15.00-25.00 each.

L to R: Knight,
Richard the Lion-Hearted,
Knight. Value $30.00-45.00
each. (Note: Copies of
Elastolin's Indian horses.)

Krolyn Vikings from
the Red Snake series.
Value $20.00-35.00 each.

Krolyn Vikings from the Red Snake
series. Value $20.00-35.00 each.

Krolyn

FIGURER

Alle figurer er fremstillet i brudsikkert letmetal

Cowboys

1201 - a - b   1202 - a   1203 - a - b   1204 - a   1205 - a

1206 - b   1207 - a   1208 - a - b   1209 - a - b   1210 - a - b

1211 - a - b   1212 - a - b   1213 - a   1214 - a

Indianere

1251   1252   1253   1254a - b - c   1255a - c

1256   1257   1258   1259a - c

1260   1261a - b - c   1262   1263

A Krolyn catalog. (1214-a is Tom Mix.)

1264a - b

1270

Robin Hood-serien

1001

1002

1003

1004

1005

1006 - a - s

1007

1008 - a

1009

A Krolyn catalog.

South Africa

South Africa
Metal
54mm (approx. 2-1/4")
30mm (approx. 1-1/4")
40 mm (approx. 1-3/4")

✕ Swedish ✕ African Engineers (SAE)

by Lou Sandbote and Vadis Godbey

"Union of S. Africa" and "S. Africa" stamped on the bottom of the base of solid-cast figures usually indicates a product of Swedish African Engineers, a company whose box art used the initials SAE. Much maligned for careless castings and pitiful paint jobs, the design of most of this work sprang from the genius of Holger Eriksson's earlier work for Comet/Authenticast. A 1950 fire destroyed Comet's Authenticast factory in County Galway, Ireland, causing the factory's production manager, Curt Wennberg, and his new partner, Frederick Winkler, to form a new business with Wennberg's in-law, Sixten Crafoord, beginning in the early 1950s, in the then-Union of South Africa. The venture had a rocky start, but, by May 1958, the company was turning out 4,000 figures a day, mostly shipped to the United States and Germany, with only 1% sold locally.

The basis of this new business was master figures, molds and machinery that Wennberg salvaged after the fire in Ireland. In the beginning, these old Authenticast rubber-disk centrifugal molds churned out 54mm castings identical to castings previously produced by Authenticast, even down to the name "EIRE" and the initials of the model designer incised on the base and without any indications that they were produced by SAE in South Africa. The master designer of them all was Holger Eriksson, (1899-1988), a Swedish engineer. His run-together initials "HE" are found on many SAE 54mm figures. Also found are the initials "FR" and "LN" for Frank Rogers and Lennart Norke (1913-1981), a Comet employee and a Swedish architect.

As time went on, Holger Eriksson made modifications to many of his older figures. Some of the figures were changed to make casting easier or to create new figures. In some cases, the cruciform base with the initials "HE" and "EIRE" was removed and a rectangular base with "Union of S. Africa" or "S. Africa" incised on the bottom and

"HE" incised on the top was added. In some of the Milicast sets, figures with both type bases can be found. Eriksson also created many new 54mm figures with this new rectangular-type base, as well as hundreds of master figures in the 30mm scale. SAE's production of the same figures usually compare unfavorably, both with respect to casting and painting, with its Authenticast counterpart in 54mm scale. But it is not always easy to properly identify the manufacturer of a figure that is incised with "EIRE" on the base. While some Authenticast figures have a paper label marked "EIRE" on the base and SAE figures are more likely to be simply one-piece castings, probably the most telling clue is the painting of the eyes. In most cases, Authenticast figures have small eyes and painted eyebrows while SAE figures have larger eyes with no eyebrows. Toward the end, a new master modeler, name unknown, created some new master figures for SAE. Near the end of production, many superbly cast and painted figures were produced.

SAE 54mm figures were distributed in the United States by Military Cast of Valley Stream, N.Y., under the "Milicast Historical Models" label. Military Cast is believed to have been owned by a man named Bechtel, and it appears to have been the main, if not only, importer of SAE military figures into the United States during the production years. (O'Brien: "Bechtel" was probably Irving Bechky, a schoolteacher who seems to have been SAE's sole U.S. distributor. He also had a shop on Hillside Avenue in Queens, N.Y.) A company called ALABRI, Inc., of New York imported SAE 40mm railroad figures.

While Eriksson's magnificently designed horses highlight the 54mm production, his work on the 30mm figures' extraordinary animation blazes through even the careless paint jobs of the poorly trained Bantu native women and the ill-cast figures. Bent-at-the-waist, turned-in-the-saddle, hatchet-raised-overhead, hooves-kickingup-dirt action of these tiny figures delight collectors almost four decades after their production. Eriksson, apparently disgusted by the execution of his models, turned to private commissions from 1957 until his death, selling castings directly to interested collectors and public and regimental museums.

SAE's 30mm production figures, used in early war-gaming, have found their way into museum dioramas, especially the Confederama exhibit in Chattanooga, Tenn., where hundreds of boxes of 30mm U.S. Civil War SAE figures found a permanent home in the United States.

The SAE collector must learn to take with a grain of salt the fact that his Indians are painted with metallic bronze paint, that the same sets are sometimes painted in flats and sometimes in gloss, or that a color is completely wrong. A favorite foible is found in 30mm set #1501 "U.S. Infantry 1777 Smallwood Regiment" in which one of the marching musicians sports a tiny plastic saxophone, a musical instrument invented in Paris in 1846! But the movement, the action all shines through: A World War II Army corpsman kneels and gently pats his German Shepherd. An American Indian's shoulder arches back, gathering the powerful momentum for a spear throw. A U.S. Civil War general turns on his walking horse to glance behind. A bored sentry cocks a hip out to shift his weight. A guards officer charges forward with drawn sword, head turned to urge on his troops. All these and dozens more encapsulated attitudes are captured in the tiny, 30mm scale figures of the SAE production.

Non-Comet-related figures were also produced by SAE over the years, most notable being sculptures by Mitford Barbeton in 54mm personality figures of the history of South Africa, designed for local consumption as premiums distributed by Caltex Gasoline stations.

Packaging

Single-mounted 54mm figures were sold in a small red box (4-1/2" by 4") as shown in Picture 11. The base of the figure was wedged into a slot in a pasteboard insert with a printed barracks scene and the name of the figure written on the front at the bottom. The cover would fold so that the figure could be displayed in its box. Standard boxing for both sets of six 55mm mounted figures and large sets of 30mm figures was a flimsy red-orange large pasteboard box (6-1/4" by 12") with "S.A. Sculptured Models" printed on the top. Inside was placed a slotted, pasteboard platform into which bases of the figures were wedged. Packing was poor. Six horsemen were crammed, head to head, into the red box and shipped from South Africa to the United States. Sets that survived unbent and unchipped

were rare. The large 30mm sets of approximately 12 to 20 pieces that used the four-digit set numbering system survived a little better. The lighter weight of the smaller figures kept them in place. The smaller pieces are also quite bendable and survive rough treatment much better.

It appears that painted 54mm foot figures were shipped to Military Cast in bulk and assembled into six-figure sets by them. The standard box (3-3/4" by 12") is tan with "Milicast Historical Models" in red on the top. The six figures are secure inside within a slotted insert. A set was usually made up of six identical figures and was most often given the same set number as the SAE number of the figures. When the six figures were not identical, the set number was usually the same as the SAE number on one of the figures in the set.

Smaller 30mm sets of six standing/three riders of horses, etc., utilized green coverless boxes (3" by 9") allowing instant viewing and saving production costs. These "green box sets," which number in the hundreds, use numbering of three digits or less, causing confusion with the 54mm three-digit and four-digit numbering system.

A definitive SAE catalog is not known and it is possible that one never existed for the U.S. market. However, Military Cast produced extensive lists of painted and unpainted 54mm castings that could be purchased as singles or as sets of six painted figures. These lists included more than 500 foot figures and 100 mounted figures. Several pages of both small and large 30mm sets are also included.

Valuation

SAE figures, except mint-boxed sets examples, are quite affordable still, with 54mm foot figures averaging $5-$8 in good and up to $15 in mint condition at national shows. More rare two-piece 54mm horse and rider figures average $30. Loose 30mm foot figures average $1-$2, and typical 30mm single-unit casting horse and rider average $3-$5 loose. Boxed/mint sets command somewhat higher prices: 6 mounted 54mm boxed $100; large set 30mm "red box" sets $40-$70; 30mm small green 3 horsemen or 6 foot $15-$25.

(Contributing information is acknowledged from Steve Sommers, *Old Toy Soldier* and Chris Bartlett. Sharing an enthusiasm for ID and exchange of information about Holger Eriksson's sculptures, the Holder Eriksson Collector's Society publishes a twice-annual, color illustrated newsletter: HECS, c/o Lou Sandbote, 5307 E. Mockingbird, Ste. 802, Dallas, TX 75206-5109.)

SAE 30mm Large Sets (Red Box 6.25" by 12")

No.	Description	No. Figures
900	U.N. Infantry Action	
1043	Civil War 20th Tennessee	
1049	Civil War 1st Virginia Cavalry	
1051	Civil War Confederate Cavalry Marching	9 cavalry on walking horses, flagbearer
1052	Civil War Union Cavalry Charging	7 galloping (all different castings), flagbearer, bugler
1053	Union Army Marching	17 marching, 2 flag bearers with Stars and Stripes officer, all in kepis
1061	Civil War Confederate Camp Set	18 camp-makers with general turned in saddle, rest foot action figures and washer woman with bucket
1064	Civil War Charleston Zouaves	
1070	Civil War Bordan's Sharpshooters	
1071	Civil War Duryea's Zouaves	
1072	Civil War Moagher's Zouaves (NY 69th)	
1115	U.S. Army, 1945-60, Combat Engineers	
1116	U.S. Army, 1945-60, Infantry Inspection	
1117	U.S. Army, 1945-60, Hospital and Gun Crew	
1118	U.S. Army, 1945-60, Mortar and AA Crew	
1119	U.S. Army, 1945-60, Motorcycle Group	
1120	U.S. Army, 1945-60, Dispatch Group	
1213	British Grenadiers Action	
1214	British Grenadiers Firing	
1227	Black Watch 1815	17 foot: officer, flagbearer, 15 marching at slope
1247	British African Forces, 1942	
1260	Canada Governor General Guard	
1261	Canada Infantry Action, 1945	
1272	Scot Infantry, 1900-1940	
1284	South African Scots & Air, 1960	
1286	South African Army and Navy, 1960	
1400	30 Years War Inf. & Cav., 1630	
1401	30 Years War Action, 1630	
1408	Prussian Infantry Action	
1409	Prussian Infantry & Cavalry	
1409	Prussian Cavalry 1815	13 pc: 5 horse, officer and 7 foot
1452	German Afrika Korps, 1942 Action	
1501	U.S. Inf 1777 Smallwood Regiment	17 marching, officer, flagbearer, fifer, drummer, saxophone player [!?], 5 at slope, 5 advancing
1522	French Foreign Legion Action	
1550	French Inf., 1778 Regt. Bayonne	
1551	French Inf., 1778 Regt. Deux Ponts	
1552	French Inf., 1778 Regt. Soiesonais	
1560	French Cav., 1878 Regt. Bourgogne	
1561	French Cav., 1778 Regt. Gayenne	
1562	French Cav., 1778 Regt. LaSarre	
1674	Moroccan Forces, 1945	
1690	Belgian Inf. Parade, 1960	
1804	Russian Infantry, 1904 Action	
2015	Papal Procession, Cardinals of the Vatican	Pope in tiara, cardinals, bishops, monks, nuns and choir boys (17 total)

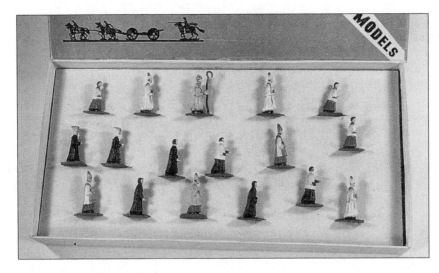

30mm Set 2015 Cardinals of the Vatican—a rare set complete, but individual figures commonly found. Value $100.00, though individual pieces only $2.00 to $5.00. Photo by Lou Sandbote.

No.	Description	No. Figures
2071	Italian Bersaglieri Action, 1942	
2079	Italian African Forces, 1942	
2123	Yugoslav Infantry Parade, 1960	
2144	Greek Inf. Action, 1960	
2123	Italian Infantry Action, 1940	
2137	Jordanian Infantry, 1960	
2217	Swedish Infantry, 1960	
2800	Canadian Royal Mounted Lancers, 1960	
3205	India Viceroy's Bodyguard	
4800	Japanese Infantry 1904	17 foot: officer with sword over head, flagbearer standing, 3 kneeling firing, 6 standing firing, 4 advancing, 2 bayoneting
4801	Japanese Infantry, 1904 Action	
5100	Greek Evzones, 1880-1960 Action	
5307	Dutch Infantry, 1940	
5351	Swiss Infantry, 1945	
5603	Austrian First Grenadiers	
5604	Austrian Second Grenadiers	
5605	Austrian First Infantry	
5606	Austrian Ninth Infantry	
6414	French F/A Gun Team 1815	3 riders, 3 riderless horses, limber and gun

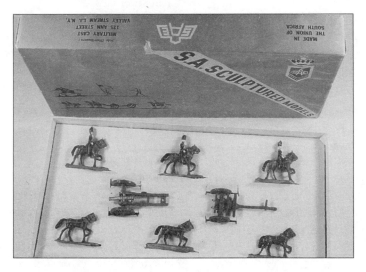

30mm Set 6414 French Field Artillery, 1815, in original "red box." Value $50.00. Photo by Lou Sandbote.

No.	Description	No. Figures
6437	U.S. Civil War Confederate Gun Limber Horses 1863	6 (plus gun/limber)
6438	U.S. Civil War Confederate Horse-Drawn Caisson, limber, 6 horses	6 identical galloping riders plus gun limber
6439	Confederate Ambulance	1 horseman, 5 riderless, 2-pc ambulance w/turning wheels, card stock "canvas cover"
6440	U.S. Civil War Confederate Pontoon Team 1863	2 Postilions, 4 riderless horses, delicate wagon for heavy cast flat-bottom boat, plus bridge roadway pieces
6444	U.S. Civil War Union Ammunition Limber	3 Postilions, 3 horses, limber, 10 pounder Parrot gun
6465	Ambulance British, 1900	4-wheel articulated wagon, 6-horse team (3 mtd.), paper "ambulance hood" cut-out
6466	British Gun Team, 1900	3 riders in khaki/pith helmet, 3 horses, limber & gun
6467	RE and Ammo Wagons, 1900	limbered wagon pulled by 4 horses, + covered 2-wheel cart, 2 horses
6470	British Pontoon Team, 1900	similar 6440 above
6497	Krupp Howitzer	
6502	German Caisson, 1914	3 spike-helmeted WWI horsemen, plus 3 horses walking with limber, separate ammo wagon

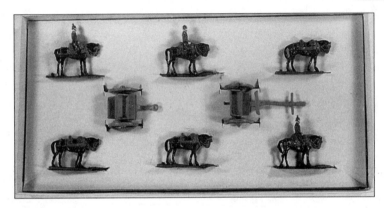

30mm Set 6502 German Horse-Drawn Caisson, 1914. Value $50.00. Photo by Lou Sandbote.

SAE 30mm Small Boxes Sets (Green Box 3" by 9")

No.	Description	Notes

FOOT FIGURES

No.	Description	Notes
1/1	New York Regt., 1776	marching
1/2	Smallwood's Regt., 1776	marching
1/3	Pennsylvania Regt., 1776	marching
1/4	2nd Maryland Regt., 1777	marching
1/8BA	Continental Band Musicians, 1777	
1/11a	American Rifleman, 1777	action
1/12	Continental Artillery, 1777	
2/a	Confederate Infantry, 1863	action
2au	Confederate Ambulance Unit	
2bm	Confederate Band, 1863	
2/f	Confederate Infantry, 1863	firing
2gcr	Confederate Gun Crew	
2/m	Confederate Infantry, 1863	marching
4/a	Union Infantry, 1863	action
4au	Union Ambulance Unit	
4bm	Union Band	marching
4/f	Union Infantry, 1863	firing
4gcr	Union Gun Crew	
4/m	Union Infantry, 1863	marching

30mm figures from sets, L to R: 6/au U.S. Infantry, 1954 Ambulance Unit; ? signal/search light; 6/m U.S. Infantry Marching, 1954; 11/m U.S. Marines Marching, 1954; 10/sf U.S. Military Police, 1954 standing with flag. Note Eriksson's "long-stride" signature design in flag bearers. Photo by Lou Sandbote.

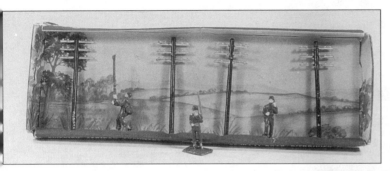

30mm 6TF U.S. Army Telephone Unit with plastic telephone poles, in basic "green box" set. Value $20.00.

SAE 11/mf? U.S. Marines. Photo by Roger Hocking.

No.	Description	Notes
6/a	U.S. Infantry, 1954	with Tommy gun
6AA	U.S. Anti-aircraft Gun Crew	
6/au	U.S. Infantry, 1954	Ambulance Unit
6/b	U.S. Infantry, 1954	with bazooka
6CAV	U.S. Engineers, 1958	
6/ch	U.S. Infantry, 1954	charging
6E	U.S. Engineers, 1958	action
6F	U.S. Infantry Firing	
6/ft	U.S. Infantry, 1954	with flamethrower
6/gcr	U.S. Gun Crew, 1954	
6/m	U.S. Infantry, 1954	marching
6MC	U.S. Dispatch Riders	
6/mg	U.S. Infantry, 1954	with machine gun
6PA	U.S. Paratroopers	
6PC	U.S. Infantry, Gas Masks, 1958	action
6/s	U.S. Infantry, 1954	standing
6TF	U.S. Telephone Unit	
6TF	U.S. Tank Crew & Mine Detector Unit	
6TV	U.S. Television Combat Unit	
10/sf	U.S. Military Police, 1954	standing with flag
11/mf	U.S. Marines, 1954	standing with flag

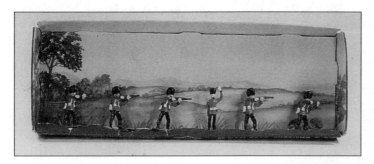

*16f 30mm British Guards firing, 1900.
Value $15.00. Photo by Lou Sandbote.*

*30mm 20/s Moroccan Infantry standing,
1954 (with French officer). Value $15 in
common green box, showing slotted, fold-over
tab to secure 6 figures. Photo by Lou Sandbote.*

No.	Description	Notes
12	American Indians	fighting
14A	Russian Infantry, 1957	action
14MG	Russian Machine Gunners, 1957	
15AIR	British Royal Air Force, 1957	
15AU	British Ambulance Unit, 1957	
15B	British Infantry with Bazooka, 1957	
15CR	British Artillery Gun Crew, 1957	
15F	British Infantry Firing, 1957	
15FT	British Infantry, flame thrower, 1957	
15M	British Fusiliers, 1957	marching
15MC	British Infantry on Motorbikes, 1957	
15MG	British Machine Gun Set, 1957	
15TD	British Middle East Action, 1957	
15TF	British Telephone Unit, 1957	
16/a	British Guards, 1900	action
16CH	British Charging, 1915	
16/f	British Guards, 1900	firing
16M	British Guards, 1957	marching
16SP	British Guards Present Arms, 1957	
17/a	Scottish Regts., 1914	action
17/s	Scottish Regts., 1914	standing
18CH	British Colonial Infantry	action
19/s	German Infantry, 1939	
20/s	Morocco Infantry, 1954	standing
21ACH	Italian Askaris, 1939	charging
21B	Italian Infantry/Bazooka, 1957	
21CH	Italian Bersaglieri, 1957	charging
21F	Italian Alpini, 1957	firing
21FT	Italian Infantry/Flame Thrower, 1957	
21GCR	Italian Gun Crew, 1957	
21M	Italian Infantry Marching, 1957	
21MC	Italian Infantry/Motorbikes, 1957	
21MG	Italian Machine Gunners, 1957	

No.	Description	Notes
22A	Australian Infantry, 1957	action
22AU	Australian Ambulance Unit	
22F	Australian Infantry, 1957	firing
22GCR	Australian Gun Crew	
22MC	Australian Infantry/Motorbikes	
22MG	Australian Machine Gunners	
22S	Australian Infantry, 1957	standing with flag
22/s	Australian Infantry, 1939	standing
23/s	Musketeers, 1630	standing
24/s	Mexican Spy Company, 1847	standing
25/ch	French with Cap	charging
25TA	French Turcos in Action, 1870	
25ZUA	French Zouaves in Action, 1870	
26/ch	Prussian Infantry	charging
27A	Canadian Infantry	action
27AU	Canadian Ambulance Unit	
27F	Canadian Infantry	firing
27GCR	Canadian Gun Crew	
27MC	Canadian Infantry/Motorbikes	
27MG	Canadian Machine Gunners	
28/a	British Infantry, 1954	action
29	Belgian Infantry on Cycles, 1914	
29/gcr	Gun Crew, 1777	
29M	Belgian Infantry, 1957	marching
30	Virginian Riflemen, 1775	charging
31M	Yugoslav Infantry, 1957	marching
32A	Albanian Infantry, 1957	action
32B	Bulgarian Infantry, 1957	action
35	Japanese Marines, 1957	standing with flag
36	Chinese Infantry, 1957	charging
38M	Brazilian Infantry, 1957	marching
39M	Argentine Infantry, 1957	marching
40	Austrian Infantry, 1914	charging
41	American Settlers	fighting

MOUNTED FIGURES

No.	Description	Notes
42CM	Belgian Chasseurs, 1957	marching
46/C	Jordaanian (sic) Infantry	charging
46CA	Jordanian Camel Corps, 1957	3 on camels
46CH	Jordanian Infantry Charging, 1957	
47CH	Turkish Infantry, 1957	charging
50/ch	Captain Green's Troop, 1777	charging
51CH	Confederate Cavalry Charging, 1863	
51/m	Confederate Cavalry, 1863	marching
51/ms	Confederate Cavalry, 1863	with Standard
53CH	Union Cavalry Charging, 1863	
53/m	Union Cavalry, 1863	marching
53/ms	Union Cavalry, 1863	with Standard
54HS	U.S. First Dragoons, 1845	
54I	Infantry, 1854	
55m	U.S. Cavalry, 1880	marching
55/ms	U.S. Cavalry, 1880	with Standard

No.	Description	Notes
56	U.S. Dragoons, 1800	
57/m	U.S. Cavalry, 1914	marching
57/ms	U.S. Cavalry, 1914	with Standard
58	U.S. Philadelphia Cavalry, First Troop, 1912	
59	Cowboys	fighting
59wh	Cowboys	with wild horses
60M	Russian Cossacks, 1815	
61	American Indians	fighting
61/b	American Indians	hunting bison
61/CH	American Indian Chiefs	
61/wh	American Indians	with mustangs
64	Austrian Dragoons, 1914	with Standard
64	Austrian Dragoons, 1914	
65	Danish Hussars, 1914	
66	French Spahis, 1914	
67	French Cuirassiers, 1914	
68	German Cuirassiers, 1914	
69	British Royal Lifeguards, 1954	
70	British Royal Horse Guards, 1954	
71	Royal Canadian Mounted Police, 1954	
72	Royal Swedish Dragoons, 1700	charging
72A	Swedish Artillery Gun Crew, 1700	
72I	Swedish Infantry, 1700	
73	Indian Cavalry, 1914	
73C	Indian Camel Corps	
73IA	Indian Irregular Infantry	action
74	Royal British Dragoons, 1805	
75	Knights mounted at the charge	
75S	Knights mounted with banner	
76	Roman Cavalry Marching	
78S	Swedish Hussars, 1957	
79M	Swedish Horseguards, 1957	
80C	Arabs Mounted, 1957	charging
80CA	Arabs on Camels, 1957	
82	South African Navy, 1957	
83	South Africa Pres. Kruger Regt., 1957	action
84	South Africa Natal Carabiniers, 1957	charging
85	South Africa Duke of Edinburgh Rifles, 1957	marching
86	South Africa Transvaal Scots, 1957	action
87	South Africa Queens Own Cape Town Highlanders	standing with flag
88	Boer Cavalry, 1900	
90	Swiss Infantry/Bazooka, 1957	
90CH	Swiss Infantry, 1957	charging
90M	Swiss Infantry, 1957	marching
105	Danish Inf on cycles, 1914	3 on bicycles
105G	Danish Guards	
108A	Greek Evzones, 1957	action
109A	Greek Infantry, 1957	action
110A	Egyptian Infantry, 1957	action
110C	Egyptian Camel Corps, 1957	
115A	Israel Infantry, 1957	action
120	Rhodesian Infantry, 1957	action

No.	Description	Notes
121	Nigerian Infantry, 1957	action
122	Ghana Gold Coast Regt., 1957	
123	Mauritius Infantry, 1957	action
124A	New Zealand Infantry, 1957	action
124B	New Zealand Infantry/Bazooka, 1957	
124M	New Zealand Infantry, 1957	marching
124MG	New Zealand Machine Gunners, 1957	
125	British Askaris	charging
126A	Pakistan Infantry, 1957	action
126M	Pakistan Infantry, 1957	marching
128M	Finnish Infantry, 1957	marching
150	Washington, Staff, 1776	
151	Sweden King Charles XII, 1700	with Staff
152	Frederic the Great	
153	Hannibal and Carthaginian Cavalry	
154	Colleoni and Condottieri	
155	Napoleon/Staff Officers, 1815	
160A	Swedish Infantry, 1957	action
160GM	Swedish Guards, 1957	marching
160M	Swedish Infantry, 1957	marching
181CH	Mexican Cavalry Charging, 1845	
183M	Mexican Infantry Marching, 1957	
200	Tenth Hussars, 1815	charging
201	93rd Regt., Argyle & Suth., 1815	Highlanders
202	42nd Regt., Royal Highlanders, 1815	
203A	Cold Stream Guards, action, 1815	
204	Second Lifeguards, 1815	charging
205	Infantry of Line, 1815	kneeling
206	Corps of Sappers/Miners, 1815	
207A	First Footguards (Grenadiers), 1815	
250A	Dutch Infantry, 1957	action
250M	Dutch Infantry, 1957	marching
250MG	Dutch Machine Gunners, 1957	
401CH	French Cuirassiers, 1815	charging
402CH	French Chasseurs a Cheval, 1815	charging
403CH	French Old Guards Charging, 1815	
404CH	French Young Guard, 1815	charging
405CH	French Infantry of Line, 1815	charging
406A	Russian Infantry, 1815	action
406/CH	Russian Infantry Action, 1914	

54mm Soldiers of the World
(separate horse/rider in single box)

No.	Description
C/1355	Officer 1st Lifeguards, 1945
C/2360	Swedish Officer Charles XII
R/C 1357	Officer Royal Horse Guards, 1945
??	Colonial Jodhpur Lancer
??	Trooper, 2nd Bombay Lancers

Left: C1355 - Officer 1st Life Guards, 1945; Middle: C1359 - Trumpeter 1st Life Guards, 1945; Right: C1357 - Officer Horse Guards, 1945. All 54mm. Photo by Vadis Godbey.

54mm C/1355 Officer 1st Life Guards, 1945 (left) and C/1357 Officer Royal Horse Guards, 1945 (right) flank box for one of these figures. 30mm figures from sets (l to r) 16m Guards Parade, 1914; 16/a British Guards, action, 1900; 69 Life Guards; and two from 16m Guards Parade, 1914. Value 54mm $40.00 boxed each. Photo by Lou Sandbote.

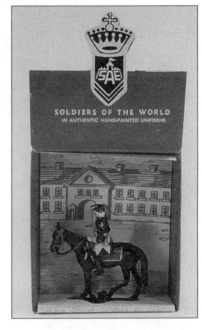

C/2360 Swedish Officer Charles XII, shown boxed in Soldiers of the World fold-up-face box. 54mm horseman is separate casting from horse. Value $30.00. Photo by Lou Sandbote.

From Milicast Set 30 - British Footguards on Parade, 1956. Photo by Vadis Godbey.

Left: From Milicast Set 48 - British infantry in Asia marching, 1942; Middle: From Milicast Set 41 - Scots marching, steel helmets, 1918; Right: From Milicast Set 26B - British infantry marching, 1914. Photo by Vadis Godbey.

Left: From Milicast Set 105 - Italy Alpini marching, 1940; Second: From Milicast Set 106 - Italy Alpini advancing, 1940; Third: From Milicast Set 110 - Italy Bersaglieri marching, 1942; Right: From Milicast Set 107 - Italy Bersaglieri parade, 1942. Photo by Vadis Godbey.

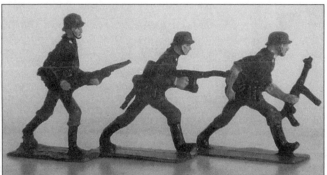

All figures in this and the next photo are from the same Milicast set, 54mm, # unknown. Left: SAE #193 - German Non-com charging with grenade, WW2; Middle: SAE #192a - German soldier throwing grenade, with rifle, WW2; Right: SAE #192 - German soldier throwing grenade, WW2. Photo by Vadis Godbey.

All figures in this and the preceding photo are from the same Milicast set, 54mm, # unknown. Left: SAE #194d - German soldier advancing with rifle, WW2; Middle: SAE # unknown - German soldier advancing with machine pistol, WW2; Right: SAE # unknown - German soldier striding with machine pistol, WW2. Photo by Vadis Godbey.

Left: From Milicast Set 235 - Chinese Nationalist marching, caps, 1956; Right: From Milicast Set 236 - Chinese Nationalist marching, peak hats, 1950. Photo by Vadis Godbey.

Left: From Milicast Set 302 - Austrian infantry on parade, 1914; Second: From Milicast Set 181 - Germany Mountain Troops marching, 1945; Third: From Milicast Set 180 - Germany Mountain Troops on parade, 1945; Right: From Milicast Set 204 - Bavarian line infantry on parade, 1910. Photo by Vadis Godbey.

Left: From Milicast Set 1500 - Swiss infantry on parade, 1945; Middle: From Milicast Set 2085 - German African Corps in action, 1942; From Milicast Set 1575 - Albanian infantry on parade, 1914. All 54mm. Photo by Vadis Godbey.

Left: From Milicast Set 1653 - Russian Guards advancing, 1945; Right: From Milicast Set 173 - Russian Line Infantry marching, 1905. All 54mm. Photo by Vadis Godbey.

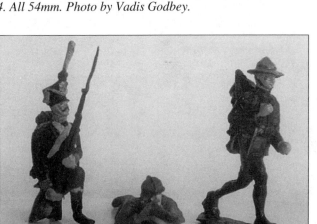

Left: From Milicast Set N14A - France Napoleonic, Tirailleur, kneeling defense; Middle: From Milicast Set 146 - French infantry prone firing, 1916; Right: From Milicast Set 68 - United States infantry marching, 1914. Photo by Vadis Godbey.

C1171, 54mm. Confederate Staff Officer, 1861. Photo by Vadis Godbey.

Left: C1781 - Trooper Polish Legion Lancers; Middle: C1760 - Napoleon Bonaparte; Right: SAE # unknown - Royal Canadian Mounted Police. All 54mm. Photo by Vadis Godbey.

From six-figure SAE Set C2351 - Officer and trooper of Charles XII 1700 on galloping white horses, 54mm. Left two figures: C2351 - Trooper 1700; Right: C2350 - Officer of Charles XII 1700. Photo by Vadis Godbey.

From six-figure SAE Set C2351 - Officer and troopers of Charles XII 1700 on standing black horses, 54mm. Left two figures: C2351 - Trooper 1700; Right: C2350 - Officer of Charles XII 1700. Photo by Vadis Godbey.

Left: C3321 - Trooper 1st Skinner's Horse; Right: C3305 - Trooper 15th Bengal Lancers. Both 54mm. Photo by Vadis Godbey.

All figures in these next three photos are from two similar sets, 54mm, # unknown. Left: SAE #SG3 - German infantry standing firing, WW1 spiked helmet, 1915; Middle: SAE #SG4 - German infantry kneeling firing, WW1 spiked helmet, 1915; Right: SAE #SG5 - German infantry standing loading, WW1 Broderick cap, 1914. Photo by Vadis Godbey.

Left: SAE #SG2a - German officer prone, WW1 spiked helmet, 1915; Middle: SAE #SG3 - German infantry standing firing, WW1 spiked helmet, 1915; Right: SAE #SG 2 - German infantry prone firing, WW1 spiked helmet, 1915. All 54mm. Photo by Vadis Godbey.

SAE #29 - British Machine Gun and Prone Crew, 1944, 54mm. Photo by Vadis Godbey.

Left: SAE #SG9a - German officer charging, WW1 spiked helmet, 1915; Middle: SAE #SG9 - German infantry charging, WW1 spiked helmet, 1915; Right: SAE #SG11 - German infantry advancing, WW1 spiked helmet, 1915. All 54mm. Photo by Vadis Godbey.

54mm 3-piece Set 188 - German Machine Gun and Prone Crew, 1945. Marked "UNION OF S. AFRICA" and "HE" on bottom side of figure. Value $30.00. Photo by Lou Sandbote.

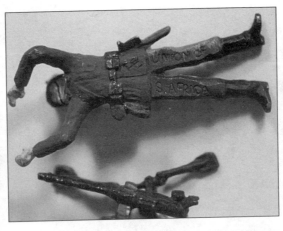

54mm Belt Feeder from Set 188 - German Machine Gun & Prone Crew, 1945. Notice "HE" inscribed on figure's tunic, followed by "Union of S. Africa" written along legs. Photo by Lou Sandbote.

SAE #200, 54mm. German trench mortar with crew, loader kneeling. Photo by Vadis Godbey.

54mm French Foreign Legionnaire from SAE, possibly as a special order by Irving Bechky, SAE's sole U.S. distributor. I (R.O'B.) bought the two pieces at Bechky's shop sometime between 6/63 and 12/66.

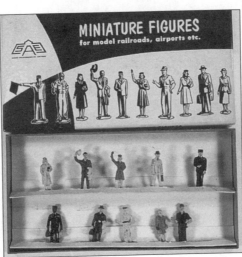

Boxed 40mm "Miniature Figures for model railroads, airports, etc." Value $60.00. Photo by Lou Sandbote.

54mm figures, SAE number unknown. L to R: French Infantryman, Italian Bersaglieri officer with drawn pistol. Photo by Vadis Godbey.

30mm Boers and Zulus. Photo by Lou Sandbote.

SAE's two sizes. Photo by K. Warren Mitchell.

30mm action U.S. Army figures. Photo by Lou Sandbote.

30mm K-9 Medical Unit marked "Union of S. Africa." Photo by Lou Sandbote.

L to R: 30mm RCMP, American Revolution, British Guards Officer, Napoleonic, illustrating four of the dozens of differing poses in Eriksson's tiny horse sculptures. Photo by Lou Sandbote.

54mm Confederate Cavalry Charging (left) and Napoleonic at halt (right). Note differing styles for base and paper export tag. Both riders separate castings. Neither have "HE" marking, though Confederate obvious HE design. Hoof in tuft of grass is common design-for-balance trait of Eriksson pieces. Values: $35.00, $20.00. Photo by Lou Sandbote.

40mm Miniature Figures Labor set. Value $60.00. Photo by Lou Sandbote.

54mm Russian Cossacks, lancer off horse to show characteristic reins incorporated into casting of horse/saddle. Characteristic is that riders fit snugly into saddle. Photo by Lou Sandbote.

54mm typical "former Authenticast" castings produced by SAE with only variation consisting of SAE rectangular base versus cruciform Authenticast bases. Photo by Lou Sandbote.

54mm Italian Garibaldi's Red Shirts advancing, bases marked "S. AFRICA" and "HE" in front of "Eriksson Models by S.A.E." Unusual, single-figure box in "opening book" format. Photo by Lou Sandbote.

54mm Russian Cossacks.
Photo by Lou Sandbote.

Caltex gas station promotional 54mm figures of South Africa historical personalities Piet Retief and Maria de la Quellerie, given away in small, snug boxes—the origin of the description of eight differing figures as "spark plug figures." Common in South Africa, but rare in the United States. Value $20.00 each USA. Photo by Lou Sandbote.

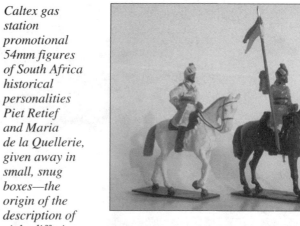

Left: India Cavalry Officer - SAE # unknown; Right: India Cavalry Lancer - SAE # unknown. Both 54 mm. Photo by Vadis Godbey.

Left: French Cuirassier Officer - SAE # unknown; Middle: 2nd Life Guards Trooper, 1815 - SAE # unknown; Right: 2nd Life Guards Officer, 1815 - SAE # unknown. All 54mm. Photo by Vadis Godbey.

Three British Rifle Regiment figures. SAE #s unknown, 54mm. Photo by Vadis Godbey.

Four Russian soldiers from a six-figure Milicast set, charging in summer uniform. Milicast set # unknown and SAE #s unknown, 54mm. Photo by Vadis Godbey.

Two French Infantrymen and one Musician. SAE numbers unknown, 54mm. Photo by Vadis Godbey.

Three Italian Bersaglieri Musicians. SAE #s unknown. 54mm. Photo by Vadis Godbey.

Japan

⚔ Toy Soldiers ⚔
Made in Japan

by Bill Beierwaltes

First, it should be explained that essentially all toy soldiers made in Japan were for an export market, especially after World War II, when cheap copies of popular goods were produced under the Marshall Plan in the revitalization of the Japanese economy. Japanese kids didn't play with toy soldiers in 1949. A large volume of eclectic figures can be found in various media from plaster to celluloid. Most of these are only novelties rather than an effort to produce a line of toy soldiers. For these reasons, much (but not all) Japanese production found in the United States is postwar. A number of examples are shown below, but probably have more value to collectors of "Occupied Japan" ephemera or of celluloid toys than to a soldier collector. However, there are several notable and collectable exceptions which come to us from Japan, among them a variety of Japanese copies of American Dimestore (Barclay) soldiers, with one box labeled "BESTMADE" American Soldier set. While nothing is known about this line, it is contemporary with the dimestore figures they copy. Better known to most collectors are four companies exporting Japanese figures, including TRICO, A.H.I., Sonsco and, of course Minikin. Some of these have loyal collector support and can be of considerable interest.

Top, L to R: JA1, JA2, JA3, JA4, JA5; Bottom, L to R: JA6, JA7, JA8, JA9, JA10. These Japanese-made composition figures, about 2-3/4" high, were sold in the United States prior to World War II. Value in mint about $10.00 apiece. Courtesy Gene Coffman.

JA10A (belongs with the JA1-JA10 grouping). Photo by Will Beierwaltes.

JA10B (belongs with JA1-JA10). Courtesy Bud Wagner. Photo by Military Artists Guild.

L to R: JA11, JA12, JA13, JA14, JA15. A boxed set of ceramic soldiers made in Japan and sold in the U.S. prior to World War II. Average $18 in mint. All but the machine gunner were shown in a 1938 N. Shure catalog. Courtesy Robert D. Worthen.

Top, L to R: JA16, JA17, JA18, JA19, JA20, JA21, JA22; Bottom, L to R: JA23, JA24, JA25, JA26, JA27, JA23. Japanese "Barclays." Most were nearly exact copies, even to the early Barclay "eye," but the sailor flagbearer appears to be a conversion of B49. These were sold circa 1939, and average $35.00 in mint.

Another shot of the Japanese "Barclays" showing the ensign in blue, and the copies of B18 and B12. Photo by Ed Poole.

L to R: JA28, JA28a. Value for Japanese "Barclays" is about $35.00 in mint. Photo by Ed Poole.

Top, L to R: JA31, JA32, JA33; Bottom, L to R: JA34, JA35, JA29, JA30. All of these figures are hollow lead. JA31 and JA32 appear to be by the same company. JA33 is unusual in that the bowstring is wire. JA34 is marked "Made in Occupied Japan." JA35 appears to be by the same company, as does a holdup man and Indian with knife (JA60, JA99), all three of them crude copies of Manoils. JA29 and JA30 are Japanese "Barclays" in blue. Value for JA34 and JA35 about $18.00 in mint. For JA32-35 $28.00 in mint.

L to R: JA36, JA37, JA38. These ceramic soldiers are 2-1/2" high. These may have been made in occupied Japan, as they go with JA104, which was sold with that label. Photo by Bob Hornung.

L to R: JA45, JA46, JA47. Hollow lead copies of Elastolin soldiers. Value about $10.00 in mint. Photo by Ron Eccles.

Top, L to R: JA39, JA40; Bottom, L to R: JA41, JA42, JA43, JA44. 54mm figures, some of them obviously copies of Barclays. JA44 is plastic. (See photo of boxed set, which contains some of these figures.) All are marked "Japan." Photo by Ed Poole.

L to R: JA48, JA11(?). Ceramic figures, 6" high. Photo by Ron Cadieux.

Standing, L to R: JA49, JA50, JA51, JA12?, JA52; Lying in front: JA53. More ceramic figures. Photo by Ron Cadieux.

JA60

Back, L to R: JA54, JA55, JA56, JA57; Front, L to R: JA58, JA59. Composition soldiers with cardboard trench. Photo by Ron Cadieux.

L to R: JA61, JA62, JA63, JA64, JA65, JA66, JA67. Courtesy Don Pielin.

L to R: JA68, JA69, JA70, JA71, JA72, JA73, JA74, JA75. Note the copies of Barclay figures. Courtesy Don Pielin.

L to R: JA76, JA77, JA78, JA79, JA80, JA81, JA82, JA83, JA84. Courtesy Don Pielin.

L to R: JA85, JA21. Collector Ed Poole sent this photo showing that even the Japanese copies of Barclays had variations. The previously unknown figure at left has JAPAN written on his back. The other, more common figure has JAPAN on its base.

The box top (above) and the types (below) found in this 9-piece set in an approximately 54mm height. The figures are (l to r) AJ85, JA86, JA87, JA88, JA89. A 1939 Butler Bros. catalog shows some of these pieces in a boxed set that included out-of-scale copies of Barclay's 3-1/4" soldiers JA19, JA22, and what seems to be an as yet unidentified Barclay copy. These pieces are all hollowcast lead, and the two figures in gas masks are carrying a stretcher. Photo by Don Pielin. Courtesy Pielin and Old Toy Soldier.

L to R: JA91, JA92, JA93, JA94, JA95, JA91, JA96. 54mm "Lead Perfection Toys," pre-WWII. No Price Found. Photo by Ed Poole.

JA90. This looks much like JA89, but there are differences, including height, as this is dimestore size (nearly 4" high). Possibly another figure from "Bestmaid" to be sold with the Barclay copies. Photo by Ed Poole.

L to R: JA97, JA98. These are both lead and dimestore size. Photo by Ron Steiner.

JA101. This hollow lead cowboy on bucking bronco is dimestore size. No price found. 4" high to top of hat. Photo by Robert Worthen.

JA99. Dimestore-size Indian with hatchet, hollow lead and obviously based on a Manoil. Photo by Harold Haseley.

L to R: JA102, JA12A. Ceramic figures, with JA102 3-3/4" high. These appear to be the soldiers shown in a 1938 N. Shure catalog. Photo by Mike Simes. Courtesy Jerry Combs.

JA103. Hollow lead. Value $8.00 mint. Courtesy Hank Anton.

**Note: JA105-JA114
are in the Sonsco section.**

JA104. The paper tag on the flagstaff says "Made in Occupied Japan." Ceramic. No price found. Photo by Jerry Combs.

JA115. Hollow lead, approx. 3-1/4" high. No price found (tail missing). Courtesy Charlie Breslow.

L to R: JA25 (blue), JA116 (ceramic). No prices found. Courtesy Charlie Breslow.

L to R: JA117, JA117, JA118. The back of JA117 shown to illustrate the rising sun on his back. The 3" high JA118 is by K.I. of Japan. It has been sold attached to a base marked "Rogers Ranger Ft. William Henry, N.Y." Both figures are hollowcast lead. No prices found. Courtesy Charlie Breslow.

JA119. Ceramic Mountie, 3-3/4" high. No price found. Courtesy Bud Wagner. Photo by Military Artists Guild.

JA120. Composition knights, 2-3/4" high. No price found. Courtesy Bud Wagner. Photo by Military Artists Guild.

L to R: JA121, JA122, JA123, JA124, JA125, JA126. Metal, 2-1/8" high, arms move. No price found. Courtesy Bud Wagner. Photo by Military Artists Guild.

JA127. Dimestore size, composition. No price found. Courtesy Bud Wagner. Photo by Military Artists Guild.

JA128. This is similar to All-Nu's AN35, and the same size. It is marked "Japan," with a logo that resembles a double-humped camel. There also seems to be another American version. Photo by Roy Bonjour.

JA129. 4-1/2" high, this mounted Indian is hollowcast. The lasso is wire. No price found. Photo by Phil Savino.

L to R: JA130, JA131. Solidcast Indians about 3-1/2" high. The weapons are soldered on and the Indians are soldered to their bases. Phil Savino, who took this photo, is sure they weren't sold as souvenirs. No prices found. Photo by Phil Savino.

JA132. A bisque copy of the Barclay postman. Unmarked, but it appears to be from Japan. JA133 and JA134 seem to be from the same firm. Courtesy Bob Emmons.

JA133. Photo by Phil Savino.

JA134. Photo by Phil Savino.

JA135. Ceramic pilot, 3" high. No price found. Photo by Bill Holt.

L to R: JA136, JA137. Hollowcast, marked only *"Japan,"* but probably post-WWII. Value each $5.00 in mint. The cowboy is a bit over 2-3/4" high. Monochromatic, as if sold as souvenirs.

Plastic copies of 7cm plastic Elastolins. Photo by Will Beierwaltes.

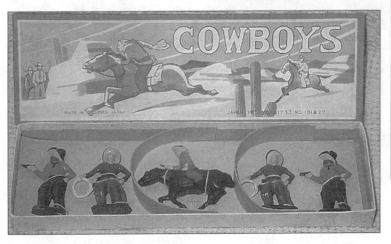

These are rubber, in 7cm range, and copies of Lineols. No price found. Photo by Will Beierwaltes.

Except for the mounted figure these are metal copies of Beton cowboys, made in occupied Japan. The same firm produced a boxed set of metal Indians, one of the three types being a copy of Beton's BT21. Value of each set, mint in the box, about $50.00. Photo by Don Patman.

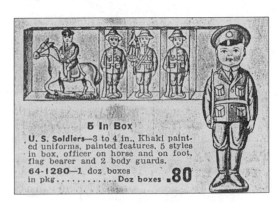

Lead football players, approx. 60mm high. No prices found. Courtesy K. Warren Mitchell.

What seem to be bisque soldiers, 3 to 4 inches high, as shown in the September 1934 Butler Bros. catalog. No prices found. These are probably Japanese-made. Also shown in the November/December 1936 Butler Bros. catalog.

⚔ A.H.I. (Japan) ⚔

by Will Beierwaltes

A Japanese import of 30mm (solid) metal figures covering a variety of historical subjects available in the late 1950s and early 1960s, they are often mistaken for the Holger Ericksson-sculpted SAE figures, from which A.H.I. often, but not always, pirated its castings. The A.H.I. figures are painted in a more simplified toy-like style, and they are unmarked (whereas the SAE bases were always marked in the castings base). John Garratt had suggested they produced 30mm figures also in plastic, but this is unlikely. A.H.I. marketed its figures in larger sets, often included adversaries (as illustrated), and they have a certain charm in their simplicity. The small scale is not widely collected, and expected values would be around $1 per foot and $2 to $3 per mounted figure. Complete sets with an original box would increase the value of the figures it contained by as much as 50%.

American Revolution battle by AHI (Japan) with British, colonials and a mounted George Washington.

✕ **Minikin (Japan)** ✕

by Will Beierwaltes

"Occupied Japan" is a term synonymous with the generally cheap export goods from the U.S.-controlled postwar economy of Japan. It was from this venue that a surprisingly good (though often variable quality) production of toy soldiers named "Minikin" arose. Minikins or Minikin (interchangeable) was the name given to a line of figures imported exclusively by International Models, Inc. of New York City, by Lou Barnett. G.I.s returning from Europe after the war brought back some of the fine miniature soldiers from France and England (Vertunni, Carman, Stadden, etc.), which largely replaced the toy soldier in popularity until the mid 1980s. It seems that Minikin was aimed at providing figures that would be of high enough quality to fit in with Vertunni and Courtenay figures, but priced like Britains. While they did not always manage to live up to their expectations, the line has some of the most unusual and beautiful mass-produced single figures available.

While all of the figures came boxed, most were in nondescript grey cardboard with the name of the set rubber-stamped on the lid. However, the large "sets" of figures had bigger boxes with illustrated labels. These were often printed in two or three colors. Sets with labeled boxes will be noted on the list, and these, when found in their original boxes, are more collectible, increasing the overall value by 20% to 30%. Minikins figures were made for export and probably never sold in Japan. Most of the early postwar Japanese production seems to have been sold to distributors who packaged or identified them as they saw fit. While Minikin is an exception in its consistency of production, the name and the unusual comprehensive cataloging can be attributed to Barnett.

The initial group of figures available from Minikin was introduced in 1948 or 1949, and covered catalog entries H-1 through H-30. These include obvious copies of Britains 16th century knights, Courtenay foot knights and Heyde's ancient Greeks. The figures may be labeled "made in Occupied Japan," "Made in Japan," "Japan," and "IMP Japan" (for International Model Products). The figures labeled "Occupied" are the earliest production and most collectible as the soldier collector must compete with aficionados of Occupied Japan ephemera. Within the catalog were a series of French Colonial figures, a set of Highlanders, and the first of a series of Samurai warriors.

The catalog was expanded in 1952 to include Minikin's largest and most unique set, H-31--Historic Hannibals Elephant Invasion, further additions to the series of Samurai, and a delicate series of American Revolution figures. None of these series, except for the five highlanders, were sold as sets, and all the figures were packaged individually. Finally, also in 1952, two small non-military offerings, the "Biblical" nativity and "barnyard" series, were offered. Also a less remarkable "X-series" consisting of three American figures, was introduced. The entire line seems to have been imported only until 1958, though residual stock may have been sold well into the 1960s in some stores. The figures introduced in the later series do not carry the "Occupied Japan" label, which was not required after 1952. Sales seem to have been localized to the East Coast, though available by mail from Bob Bard and other catalog outlets.

The figures of Minikin were all hand-painted, though some more precisely than others. Particularly notable was the Highland series and the Samurai. Interestingly, some of the pieces seem to have been painted using a spray technique (especially larger mounted pieces) with the detailing added by hand. While all the figures came fully painted (except H18), certain of the figures were also available completely in a metallic finish of gilt, brass, bronze or silver. These were identified in the catalog with the suffix "A." Additionally, three pieces of the catalog are completely different, including a large-scale Samurai helmet, a brass cannon and a 4-1/2" brass-finished armored knight. Most all the other figures were in 54mm to 58mm scale, except for the Heyde copies, which were appropriately smaller.

Because Minikin is the only well-cataloged metal figure of Japanese origin, the name is often used mistakenly to describe all figures imported from Japan (especially Sonsco). The catalog listing provided below includes the entire documented production of Minikin. Only a set of HO train figures and a standing 50mm woman in fur-collared coat, both which have been attributed to Minikin but not documented, have been omitted. The reader is directed to the author's series of articles in the "Old Toy Soldier Newsletter," Vol. 5 and 6, for additional information on Minikin.

The Minikin Catalog

H1	14-15th Century Knights (set of 1 mtd and 4 foot)	$34.00
H2	As H1, but 2 mtd, 4 foot	44.00
H3	As H1, but 4 mtd, 4 foot (H1-H3 set boxes are illustrated with castle and knights)	64.00
	Single mounted knight	10.00

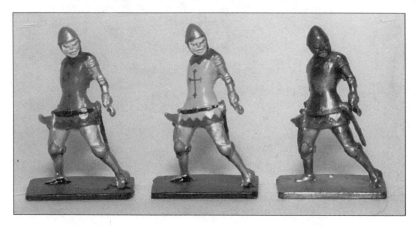

H1-3.

L to R: H4, H4, H4A.

L to R: H7, H6.

H4	Norman Knight (after Courtenay, in red, green, yellow or blue tunics)	24.00
H4A	As H4 in metallic finish	20.00
H5	Henry the 4th, mounted	45.00
H5A	As H5 in metallic finish	35.00
H6	Napoleon, mounted as in crossing the Alps	45.00
H6A	As H6 in metallic finish	40.00
H7	British Dragoon mtd, 1850	36.00
H8	British Coldstream Guard, 1742	18.00

THE FRENCH COLONIAL SERIES (H9-H15)

H9	French Artillery, 1892	$18.00
H10	French Ski Scout Trooper, (blue) 1936	32.00
H11	French, Algerian Tirailleur 1936	25.00
H12	French Chasseur, 1917	28.00
H13	French fortress (Maginot) gunner, 1939	20.00
H14	French Senegalian Tirailleur, 1914	24.00
H15	French Indochinese Soldier, 1925	20.00
H16	The Spirit of 1776 (3 figure set with box decorated in music of Yankee Doodle)	50.00
H17	American Indian mounted	35.00

H5

H8

H14

L to R: H9, H10, H11, H13, H15, H12.

H16

H17

H18	Anne, Duc de Montmorency, Constable of France (4.5" tall in brass, plastic sword) 50.00	H19A	As H19, metallic finish 38.00
H19	Miamotono Yoritomo, mounted Samurai 45.00	H20	Samurai warrior on foot, with removable weapon (pink or teal tunic) 35.00
		H21	Japanese Samurai War Helmet (large scale) 30.00

L to R: H18, from H1-3.

L to R: H19A, H19.

L to R: H20, H32.

L to R: H21, H18, H4.

H22

H23

H24

H22	8 Pound field Piece (6" long and all in brass)	45.00
H23	Roman Crusaders, 1203, set of 2 mtd and 4 foot (40mm figures after Heyde, hollow bases, shields have crosses. An unusual variation has man carrying torch)	48.00
H24	Tamerlane (1336-1405)	28.00

THE HIGHLAND SERIES
(AFTER PILKINGTON JACKSON) (H25-30)

H25	Officer, 74th Regiment, 1846	$32.00
H26	Piper, the Black Watch, 1815	32.00
H27	Drummer, 74th Highlanders, 1914	30.00
H28	Field Officer, Kings Own Scottish Borders, 1686	28.00

L to R:
H29, H26,
H27, H28, H25.

H29	Sgt. Major, Gordon Highlanders, 1914 .... 30.00	H32	Benkei, the fighting monk, 1180 .... 25.00
H30	Scotsman Boxed Set (all 5 figures; H25-30, blue box with historical insert) 160.00	H33	Kato Kiyomn Asa, 1560 .... 23.00
H31	Historic Hannibal's Elephant Invasion (9 pcs inc. 7 men as in H23 but with octagon shields decorated with dots, elephant and howdah with color box) 240.00	H34	Kinoshita Tokichiro, 1560 .... 23.00

H32   Benkei, the fighting monk, 1180 .... 25.00
H33   Kato Kiyomn Asa, 1560 .... 23.00
H34   Kinoshita Tokichiro, 1560 .... 23.00
H35   no catalog entry .... —
H36   Anayama Kosuko, 1600 .... 23.00
H37   no catalog entry .... —
H38   no catalog entry .... —

H31

H31

L to R: H34, H33, H36, H45, H46.

H42

L to R: H39, H44, H40, H43, H41, H42.

THE AMERICAN REVOLUTION SERIES
(H39-H44)

H39	British 40th Rgt., 1776	$20.00
H40	Green Mountain Ranger, 1775	20.00
H41	Green Mountain Ranger, private, 1775	20.00
H42	Pennsylvania Rgt., 1777	20.00
H43	Haslet's Delaware Rgt., 1776	22.00
H44	Gunner, Captain John Lamb's NY Artillery	25.00
H45	Warrior of the Kinoshita Tribe, 1560	25.00
H46	Archer of the Nitano Shiro Tribe	30.00

THE BIBLICAL SERIES

B1	The Nativity Set (12 pcs; including Holy family and farm animals)	$50.00
B2	The Three Wise Men	38.00

THE BARNYARD (F) SERIES

F1	Barnyard (including horse, cow, donkey, 2 sheep, rooster, 2 chickens, 3 doves; also sold singly)	$50.00

THE AMERICAN (X) SERIES

X1	West Point Kaydet [sic] 1802	$12.00
X1A	West Point Kaydet, 1952	12.00
X2	US Horse Marine, Boxer Rebellion, 1900	15.00

L to R: X1A, X1, X2.

B1

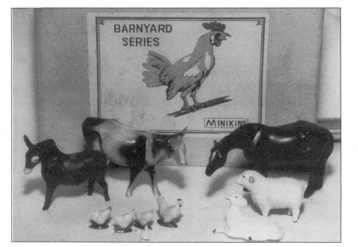

F1

X1A with boxes.

⚔ Sonsco (Japan) ⚔

by Will Beierwaltes

Sonsco produced what appears to be a varied range of 54mm metal hollowcast figures that were largely plagiarized from popular English toy soldiers in the postwar era, including Johillco, Britains and Charbens. Some even have a movable arm, and the figures were packaged as "sets" in traditional-shaped long flat toy soldier boxes with outrageous color lithographed box lids.

The most famous of its figures are the metal standing knight with halberd copied from Johillco in silver or black, which must surely be in every antique store in America. Also a copy of a Johillco mounted armored knight in silver is often found, and both are embossed JAPAN in the mold. As no catalogs are known, a number of similar hollowcast figures marked JAPAN are illustrated, but we can only say that these are "attributed to Sonsco," until we get some better documentation or find additional sets in original boxes.

However, it is possible that the figures were also sold in bulk, as dimestore counter packs. Some of the modifications, such as the fixed arm U.S. Army band in white helmets or French sailors based on Britains' U.S. Army GI are interesting adaptations; despite their simplified paint, they fit in nicely with a Britains collection. Value for these figures is around $4 to $5 per figure. The mounted knight in good condition would be $8, and the undersized U.S. Cavalry around $6. A complete boxed set (five to six figures) with a colorful cover could be valued at $35, and the charming circus figures somewhat more valuable at $6-12, depending on how large or complex they are.

Metal copies of Britains and Charbens Circus figures. No prices found. Photo by Will Beierwaltes.

Copy of Britains cannon, 54mm. No price found. Photo by Will Beierwaltes.

Photo by Will Beierwaltes.

Soldiers in a box marked "Made in Occupied Japan." Toy soldier collectors might pay $25.00 for the set. Fanciers of "Made in Occupied Japan" items would pay considerably more, $75.00-100.00.

L to R: JA105, JA106, JA107, JA108, JA109. Metal copies of Britains post-WWII U.S. infantry. 54mm. Photo by Will Beierwaltes.

Copies of Britains French Sailors, 54mm high, lead alloy. No price found. Photo by Will Beierwaltes.

L to R: JA110, JA111, JA112, JA113, JA114. Metal copies of Britains post-WWII U.S. infantry. 54mm. Photo by Will Beierwaltes.

✕ TRICO (Japan) ✕

by Will Beierwaltes

TRICO is the one major Japanese import with roots prior to the World War II. It produced a wide line of composition figures in the style of German figures of Elastolin. In fact, many of their pieces were copies of Elastolin, with a translation which gives them a pleasing, simplified toy-like quality not present in the craftsmanship of the German works. The dominant themes were U.S. doughboys in olive drab and cowboys and Indians in bright and festive colors. A variety of scales approximating the 6.5cm and 7cm figures of German composition to large 10cm figures were produced, in both marching and action poses. The bases are characteristically a thick oval with an elongated diamond with the name TRICO pressed into the bottom.

Additionally, TRICO made a small series of 7cm train-station figures, which were loosely copied from the Johillco metal figures produced for Lionel in the 1930s. In the train motif, it also produced an extensive line of village houses and buildings, undersized for the figures, in a hollow composition material with cellophane windows (often red cellophane) so that they could be effectively illuminated from within. Generally two sizes included a small 2.5" by 3" house or office, and a larger 4" by 9" building, such as a train station or a military hospital (presumably for train sets or for beneath a Christmas tree). The TRICO figures, especially the military ones, are plentiful today and are surprisingly collectible, considering that they are mostly copies of more established toys of higher quality.

A general guide for values of TRICO items in good condition (no broken appendages, etc.):

6.5cm to 7cm foot doughboy	$8.00
6.5cm to 7 cm mounted doughboy	15.00
6.5cm cowboy	12.00
6.5cm mounted cowboy	22.00
6.5cm Indian	12.00
6.5cm mounted Indian	22.00
9cm foot doughboy	10.00
9cm mounted doughboy	18.00
10cm foot doughboy	12.00
7cm train station figure	15.00
Small house/building	10.00
Large station	25.00
Large military hospital	30.00

Trico soldier, 4-1/8" range. Photo by Jerry Combs.

Trico composition U.S. Soldiers, 15cm. These were advertised in 1934. Photo by Will Beierwaltes.

Trico composition cowboys and Indians. The foot figures are about 4-1/4" high. Photo by Jerry Combs.

These Trico composition figures (6cm) are copies of Elastolins. Photo by Will Beierwaltes.

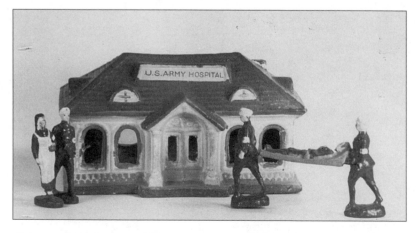

Trico medical figures (all Trico are composition) in front of a ceramic "Hospital," also made in Japan. Photo by Ed Poole.

These soldiers, all marked "Trico," were bought by Larry G. Alkire at a Kresge's five and ten about 1939 or 1940. In the early 1930s Langfelder, Homma & Hayward, importers at 915 Broadway in New York City, advertised composition figures "From our Nagoya factory." Several figures marked "Trico" have been found that match some of the pieces in the ads. In addition to the Tricos shown in this section, other pieces shown in the ads included figures that were either sailors or marines. The foot soldiers in this photo are about 4-1/8" high. Photo by Larry G. Alkire.

Tricos, the one at left in red jacket and white pants, and possibly a marine. Value about $30.00 each in mint. Courtesy Jerry Combs. Photo by Mike Sims.

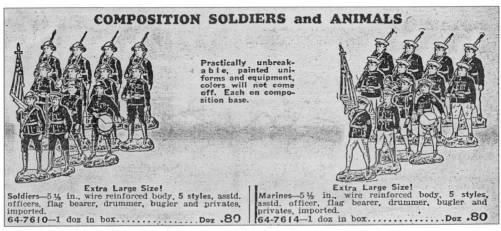

COMPOSITION SOLDIERS and ANIMALS

Practically unbreakable, painted uniforms and equipment, colors will not come off. Each on composition base.

Extra Large Size!
Soldiers—5½ in., wire reinforced body, 5 styles, asstd. officers, flag bearer, drummer, bugler and privates, imported.
64-7610—1 doz in box..............Doz .80

Extra Large Size!
Marines—5½ in., wire reinforced body, 5 styles, asstd. officer, flag bearer, drummer, bugler and privates, imported.
64-7614—1 doz in box..............Doz .80

From a September 1934 Butler Bros. catalog. These are almost certainly Tricos, as the marines echo those in a January 1933 Playthings ad by Langfelder, Homma & Hayward, who seem to have been Trico's importers.

Mexico

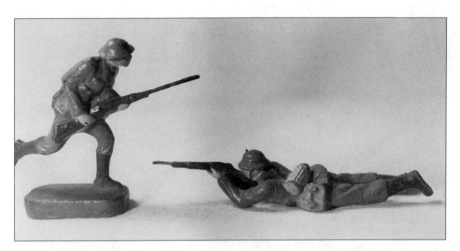

Prewar fascist influence on these.
Value (VG) $25.00 each.
Photo by K. Warren Mitchell.

Value (VG) $25.00.
Photo by K. Warren Mitchell.

Mexico's Garcia
Plastics produced
these plastic figures.
The painted ones sell
for $2.00 each, the
unpainted $1.00 each.
Courtesy Paul
Stadinger - Stad's.

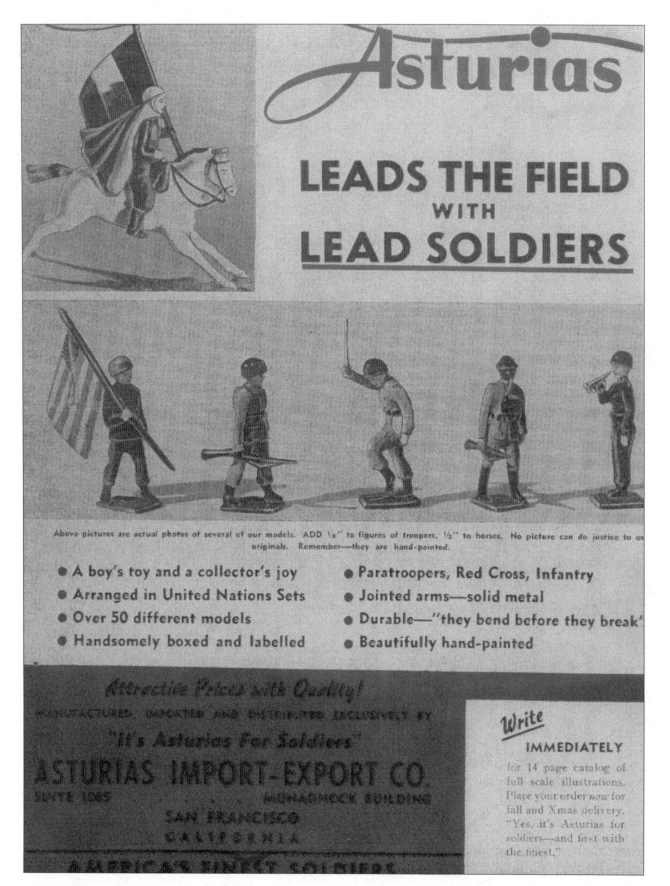

A July 1946 toy trade magazine ad. Was this a Mexican firm? Garratt, in his Encyclopaedia, has a vague mention of what seems to be a Mexican company of that name. The figures were lead, and 2" high. Apparently, nothing else is known. Courtesy Jack Matthews.

Seems like a dream ... NEW!

THE SENSATIONAL AND MOST COMPLETE LINE OF HAND PAINTED DIFFERENT NATIONS METAL SOLDIERS AND FIGURES

BY SKINFILL

WINNER OF FIRST PRIZE AT MEXICO CITY'S COMMERCIAL AND INDUSTRIES FAIR, 1946

U. S. Army Cavalry and Soldiers—French Soldiers and Cavalry—Cow Boys—North American Indians—Persian Soldiers Mounted—Medical Service—Arabs—Dutch Farms—and many others. All full shaped.

Beautiful box sets to retail at attractive prices. 100 boxes to shipping case. Shipping weight approx. 100 lbs. F. O. B. Laredo, Texas. Write for complete details to SOLE DISTRIBUTOR IN THE UNITED STATES:

JACK SHAPIRO
208 North Wells Street
CHICAGO 6, ILL.

This August 1947 Toys & Novelties ad suggests these metal soldiers by Skinfill were made in Mexico. Some but not all appear to be copies of Johillcos. Nothing more is known at present. Courtesy Jack Matthews.

Spain

This 60mm plastic figure of Buck from TV's "High Chaparral" was produced by Spain's Comansi. Value $7.00. Photo courtesy Paul Stadinger - Stad's.

L to R: JES61, JES40, JES41. Barcelona's Jecsan produced these 54mm plastic figures. Value, L to R: $12.00; $15.00; $15.00. Courtesy Paul Stadinger - Stad's.

Reamsa plastic Lawrence of Arabia. Value $25.00. Courtesy Paul Stadinger - Stad's.

Comansi of Spain produced this 60-70 mm (approx. 2-1/2") plastic cowboy. Value $2.00. Courtesy Paul Stadinger - Stad's.

L to R: LC1, LC2, LC3. Llardo of Spain produced these striking plastic, hand-painted 100mm (approx. 4-1/4") cowboys. Value $15.00 each. Courtesy Paul Stadinger - Stad's.

L to R: LK1, LK2, LK3. Llardo of Spain produced these 90mm (3-9/16") plastic knights. Value $20.00 each. Courtesy Paul Stadinger - Stad's.

Reamsa Knight, plastic. Value $15.00. Courtesy Paul Stadinger - Stad's.

Jecsan plastic Western Woman. Value $15.00. Courtesy Paul Stadinger - Stad's.

Reamsa plastic Arab from its Lawrence of Arabia set. Value $25.00. Courtesy Paul Stadinger - Stad's.

L to R: RI1, RI2, RI3, RI4. Rubber Indians and Cowboy by Barcelona's Reamsa. The middle two are copies of Britains. Value $5.00 each. Courtesy Plastic Warrior.

Argentina

That's right. The cover says 12 countries, and this is the 13th. Lagniappe. These photos were sent to me by collector Don Pielin, just two months before publication. Happily, Krause Publications agreed to wedge the information in.

Garratt states that Argentina seems to be the one country in Latin America that takes much interest in toy soldiers. Most or all of the pieces shown here seem to have been made by EG, which, according to the often-unreliable Garratt, set up shop in 1955. Apparently, they are all of solid metal.

All photos are by Pielin.

Pielin paid $15.00-20.00 for these farm folk, and $35.00 for the mounted gaucho.

A closeup of the dancers shown in the group photo.

Pielin paid $15.00 each for the farm folk, and $20.00-30.00 for the railroad figures.

A gaucho drinking yerba matte through a silver straw. No price mentioned on it. The bird is worth $5.00.

An EG box label.

An EG Toys box end.

These large animals are worth $10.00-12.00 and the small $5.00.

This set is worth $35.00. The rope goes through a hole in the horse's mouth.

Argentine accessories, L to R: Dog house, side of beef barbecuing, fire, grate set on bricks with sausages cooking, tea kettle on charcoal burner, basket, large trough, sunflower.

Argentine accessories, L to R: Well with pail, wire gate, picket gate, farm gate.

These animals are worth $10.00-12.00 each.

Appendix A: Contributors

Following are the names and addresses of people who contributed to this book. They are agreeable to hearing from readers new to this hobby who might like to get in touch with them regarding their areas of interest. It's suggested that, when writing, you include an SASE (self-addressed, stamped envelope).

K. Warren Mitchell: Dealer in old metal toy soldiers (W. Britains, Mignot, U.S. dimestore, etc.). Regular lists. P.O. Box 1123, Pataskala, OH 43062, (614) 927-1661.

Joseph Saine: Toy Soldiers, all types, collect and sell. Box 50506, Toledo, OH 43605, (419) 691-0008.

Stad's (Paul Stadinger): Sells plastic soldiers of all nations. 815 N. 12th St., Allentown, PA 18102, (610) 770-1140, Fax (610) 770-1740.

Steve Balkin: Dealer in toy soldiers of all types. Burlington Toys, 1082 Madison Ave., New York, NY 10028.

Gus Hansen: Sells Mignot, Britains, etc. 4645 Lilac Ave., Glenview, IL 60025.

John D. (Jack) Matthews: German composition and tinplate, WWII paper, etc. 13 Bufflehead Dr., Kiawah Island, SC 29455.

William Doyle Galleries: Toy soldier auctions. 175 E. 87th St., New York, NY 10128, (212) 427-2730, Fax (212) 369-0892.

Guernsey's: Toy soldier auctions. 108 East 73rd St., New York, NY 10021, (212) 794-2280 Fax (212) 744-3638.

The Toy Soldier (Jim Hillestad): New and old toy soldiers for sale, also museum (by appointment only). Paradise Falls, RR1, Box 379, Cresco, PA 18326, (717) 629-7227.

West Falls Toy Company: Solid castings from original Johillco, etc., molds. Send SASE for list. P.O. Box 3, West Falls, NY 14170.

Tim Oei: Buys, sells, trades, restores. Oei Enterprises, 241 Rowayton Ave., Rowayton, CT 06853-1227, (203) 866-2470.

Bob Hornung: Courtenay, also produces his own line of knights. 32 E. Charlotte, Cincinnati, OH 45215.

Ray Haradin: Original boxed Britains of the highest quality, other makes. Call 800-349-8009 for detailed catalog. Or write 1039 Lakemont Dr., Pittsburgh, PA 15243-1817.

James L. Theobald: German composition figures, etc. P.O. Box 701, Bloomington, IL 61702-0701.

William Beierwaltes: Collector of old toy soldiers of all types. 535 Barrington, Grosse Point, MI 48230.

E. Gerald McFerren: Collector of M.I.M. & C.B.G./Mignot. 499 Larkspur Ln., Chambersburg, PA 17201.

Lenoir Josey: Collector Lucotte, Courtenay, Ping, Warren figures. 504 Waugh Dr., Houston, TX 77019.

Don Grant: Collector of C.B.G./Mignot and Lucotte. P.O. Box 5, San Luis Obispo, CA 93406.

Peter Greenhill: Dealer of Courtenay, from original molds. 5 Westbourne Park Rd., Bournemouth, Dorset, BH4 8HG England.

Jeff Anusbigian: Collector European painted plastic figures. 21182 Wheaton Ln., Novi, MI 48375.

Tom Figiel: Collector of plastic Elastolin & Starlux figures. 14876 Chesterfield, Warren, MI 48089.

Rick Berry: Collector any American Civil War figures. 1719 Roszelle, Royal Oak, MI 48067.

Jim Morris: Toy soldiers of all types. 1100 Cherry St., Vicksburg, MS.

London Bridge Collector's Toys (Ron Ruddell): Dealers in Britains, etc., also Britains replacement parts, Bussler, etc. 1325 Chestnut St., Emmaus, PA 18049.

Vadis Godbey & Lou Sandbote: See Periodicals: Holger Eriksson.

Arnold Rolak: Britains dealer and collector. Texas Toy Soldier Society, 14121 Cashel Forest Dr., Houston, TX 77069, (713) 537-8518, Fax (713) 537-9901.

Harvey K. Rainess: Dealer in soldiers, vehicles, etc., U.S. & foreign. Rustic Ridge, N13, 289 Mount Hope Ave., Dover, NJ 07801, (201) 366-4677

Bill Nutting: Collector (only) early foreign & American soldiers, etc. P.O. Box 6725, Wheeling, WV 26003.

Appendix B: Periodicals

Note: For foreign, first class, air-mail rates, etc., please, query the publications.

Old Toy Soldier: Bimonthly, soldiers of all nations, $25 for six issues (in U.S.), 209 N. Lombard, Oak Park, IL 60302-2503.

Toy Soldier Review: Published irregularly, soldiers of all nations, $12 for four issues (in U.S.), Vintage Castings, 127-74th St., North Bergen, NJ 07047.

The Worlds of Plastic Figures: Bimonthly, plastic soldiers of all nations, $25 for six issues (in U.S.), Stad's, 815 N. 12th St., Allentown, PA 18102.

Plastic Warrior: Foreign plastic, $35 U.S. for six issues, 65 Walton Ct., Woking, Surrey GU21 5EE, England.

Plastic Figure & Playset Collector: Bimonthly, mostly U.S. Marx, $21 for six issues (in U.S.), Specialty Publishing Company, P.O. Box 1355, La Crosse, WI 54602-1355.

Toy Soldier & Model Figure: Bimonthly, new and old foreign soldiers, $29 for six issues (in U.S.), 3150 State Line Rd., North Bend, OH 45052.

Holger Eriksson Collector Society: Newsletter on the subject, $15 annual dues, c/o Lou Sandbote, 5307 E. Mockingbird, Ste. 802, Dallas, TX 75206-5109.

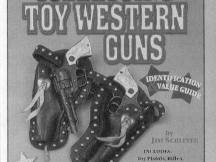